The Metaxas Myth

1. Ioannis Metaxas 1871 - 1941
Officer - Politician, Dictator 1936 - 1941

The Metaxas Myth

Dictatorship and Propaganda in Greece

Marina Petrakis

I.B. TAURIS

LONDON · NEW YORK

Revised paperback edition published in 2011 by I.B.Tauris & Co Ltd
6 Salem Road, London W2 4BU
175 Fifth Avenue, New York NY 10010
www.ibtauris.com

Distributed in the United States and Canada Exclusively by Palgrave Macmillan
175 Fifth Avenue, New York NY 10010

ISBN: 978 1 84885 781 0

A full CIP record for this book is available from the British Library
A full CIP record for this book is available from the Library of Congress
Library of Congress catalog card: available

Printed and bound in the UK by CPI Antony Rowe, Chippenham and Eastbourne
From camera-ready copy edited and supplied by the author

Contents

List of Illustrations

Acknowledgements

In the preparation of this work I had the assistance of many individuals and institutions. In particular I would like to acknowledge the help of the following: the staff, especially the Director Mr. Kois, at the Benaki Library who made available all the archival material of Metaxas' personal library; the staff at the State Archives in Athens; The Ministry of Foreign Affairs Archives; The Library at Vouli (Greek Parliament); The National Library; the ELIA (The Greek Literary and Historical Archives), for their help and the illustrations they supplied to me, many of which are reproduced in this book; Professor Thanos Veremis for his help and suggestions; ERT (*Elliniki Radiofonia Tileorasi*-Greek Radio and Television), especially Mrs. Arsenis who is in charge of the Film and Historical Archives; the Teniothiki Tis Ellados (Greek Film Institute) and Mr. Adamopoulos; The Theatrical Museum; The Library of the Theatrical Museum; Professor Alkis Rigos; The British Public Records Office; the staff of King's College Library; the London School of Economics Library; the British Library and the University of Kent Library. I am grateful to film Directors Mr. Fotis Labrinos, and Mr. Lakis Papastathis of Cinetic Co. who provided me with archival film material (*Panorama tou Aiona – Meres Tis Tetartis Augoustou*), which would be otherwise unavailable. I would also like to thank Mr. Ioannis Siaskas; Mr. Panagiotis Kiskilas; and Mr. Dimitrios Farmakis, who furnished me with useful information for the period examined. I owe a special word of thanks to my son-in-law George Ledakis for helping me with the preparation of the manuscript (CRC)

I am indebted to my supervisor, Professor David Welch, for his help, support and understanding, and for his being there whenever I needed his advice and guidance. I am especially grateful to him since I continued to receive his encouragement and valuable assistance in all stages of the preparation of this work.

My deepest debt, however, is to my husband Yiannis for, without his support and understanding, this book would not have been written.

Abbreviations used in the text

AMN	*Antidiktatoriko Metopo Neon* (Anti-dictatorial Youth Front)
ASE	*Anotaton Symvoulion Ekpedefseos* (Higher Board of Education)
ATE	*Agrotiki Trapeza Ellados* (Agrarian Bank of Greece)
BBC	British Broadcasting Corporation
DAS	*Diefthinsis Anotaton Scholon* (Administration of Higher Institutions)
DAE	*Diefthinsis Anotatis Ekpedefsis* (Higher Education Office)
DNB	The German News Office
DRYN	*Diefthinsis Radiofonias Ipourgeiou Naftikon* (Broadcasting Administration of the Admiralty)
DTA	*Diefthinsis Tagmaton Asfalias* (Work Battalions Administration)
ELIAMEP	The Hellenic Foundation for Defence and Foreign Policy
ELIA	*Elliniko Logotechniko ke Istoriko Archeio* (Hellenic Literary and Historical Archives)
ERT	*Elliniki Radiofonia Tileorasis* (Greek Radio and Television Service)
EON	*Ethnikos Organismos Neoleas* (National Youth Organisation)
FEK	*Fillo Efimeridos Kiverniseos* (Official Greek Gazette)
FO	Foreign Office
IKA	*Idrima Kinonikon Asfaliseon* (Foundation of Social Insurance)
KKE	*Kommunistiko Komma Ellados* (Greek Communist Party)
LUCE	*L'Unione Cinematografa Educativa* (Union of Educational Films)
NSDAP	*Nationalsocialistische Deutsche Arbeiterpartei* (National Socialist German Workers Party- the Nazi Party)
OSK	*Organismos Skolikon Vivlion* (Organisation of School Texts)
PNF	*Partio Nationale Fascista* (National Fascist Party)
RRG	*Reichsrundfunkgeselschaft* (Reich Radio Company)
SA	*Sturmabteilungen* (Storm Troopers)
SD	*Sicherheitsdienst der SS* (Secret Police Reports)
TTT	*Tachidromeio - Tilegrafeio - Tilefoneio* (Post - Telegrams-Telephones)
YTT	*Yfipourgeio Typou ke Tourismou* (Sub-Ministry of Press and Tourism)
YPE	*Ypiresia Radiofonikon Ekpobon* (Broadcasting Service)
VE	*Volksempfanger* (People's Receiver)

Introduction

'Propaganda by itself cannot win any struggle for allegiances
- hence the need in many instances to back it up with force or
coercion, which can range from the passing of mild punitive
legislation to the imprisonment or extermination of opponents.
The more extreme measures are especially characteristic of authorities
-authoritarians- which are insecure about whether their messages will
command, at best, general approval or, at least, popular acquiescence.'[1]

This book is based on the doctoral thesis which I wrote for the University
of Kent in 2000 and concerns the study of propaganda in Greece during
the Metaxas dictatorship in the years 1936-1940.[2]

    E Tetarti Augoustou (The 'Fourth of August') regime (as Metaxas'
dictatorship was known after its 'birth' date) was an authoritarian regime
which owed its existence to King George II and worked towards creating
a 'New State' based on lost supreme values and ideas. The realisation of
this goal necessitated the adoption of many fascist and Nazi features
like a centralised state, the creation of a powerful youth movement, the
suppression of political life, austere censorship and complete control of the
means of mass communication. Above all it necessitated the mobilisation
of a powerful propaganda machine able to proceed with the manipulation
of the Greek masses and disseminate to them the themes and ideology
fostered by the regime, hoping at the same time to obtain their support.

    This work attempts to provide a full account of the 'Fourth of
August' regime's political indoctrination and propaganda; to determine
the purposes behind it; to identify the themes and the techniques used for
their dissemination and to assess its success or failure exploring at the same

time the similarities of the propagated themes and the means employed for their dissemination between Metaxas' regime and other states with similar political schemes, notably the Third Reich and Fascist Italy.

It is important to establish a historiographical framework in which to place this case study, in order to elucidate the significance of this book within the field of research.

Until recently, few scholarly works have been written about Ioannis Metaxas and his dictatorship.[3] This is not surprising given the fact that Metaxas' regime is considered a hostile period by the average contemporary Greek and Metaxas himself a controversial and unpopular figure.[4] Another reason for this 'historical vacuum' could be the fact that the events which followed Metaxas' dictatorship (the Greco-Italian War, the German invasion, and the destructive civil war that followed) overshadowed the previous political and historical events and provided historians with ample material for scholarly work.

The most recent study on Metaxas' personality is the *Popular Autocracy in Greece 1936-41. A Political Biography of General Ioannis Metaxas* by P. J. Vatikiotis. Based on Greek sources, especially on Metaxas' diary and other personal documentation, Vatikiotis' work provides, however, little information on Metaxas' propaganda. Nevertheless it is a highly insightful book and succeeds at being fair to the most controversial and least liked figure in modern Greek history, shedding light on his life, his beliefs, his military and political achievements. The main body of the previous historiographical discussion concerning Metaxas' dictatorship concentrates on the nature of the regime, its structure, its ideology, its foreign policy and the oncoming war. Eleni Machera in her study on Metaxas' youth, *E Neolea Tis 4es Augoustou - Fotografes*[5] has identified a number of propagandistic elements (mainly symbols and photographs) associated with the National Organisation of Youth and has made an attempt to analyse their propagandistic contents.

Although propaganda under totalitarian states, especially German National Socialism and the Soviet Union under Stalin, has been the subject of many case studies and has provided valuable information regarding the political and social structure of those societies,[6] no significant historical research and discussion on the 'Fourth of August' regime propaganda has so far been undertaken. Any reference to the subject has been incorporated into the wider study of the 'Fourth of August' regime, and only as a means of stressing its totalitarian nature.

As the word propaganda[7] (which in itself carries many negative connotations for the majority of people) and its assumptions have become the subject of extensive studies, it is necessary to make an attempt to analyse its concept, briefly putting it in its historical and political context.

Although the art of political persuasion has been practised since the dawn of civilisation, it is only during the twentieth century that political propaganda has become a universal phenomenon with pejorative associations. The emergence of mass society and the rapid developments and expansion in the media of mass communication like the press, posters, radio and the cinema, created great possibilities for the effective application of propaganda. The mass audiences, through mass education, improvements in transport, and other technical developments, became easy targets for indoctrination and propaganda. Political propaganda was effectively introduced as a weapon during World War I (1914-1918) by all the powers involved, with the British setting the standard in modern 'scientific' propaganda[8]. The Great War did not only leave a defeated and humiliated Germany but also promoted the conviction that this defeat had been facilitated by the manipulation of public opinion.[9]

Since then the subject of political propaganda as a powerful weapon for influencing the masses has been extensively examined by many scholars and has given rise to different assumptions and interpretations of the term propaganda.

For many people propaganda is synonymous with something that is negative and evil, as they believe it consists only of lies which are disseminated throughout a powerless mass audience. However, according to David Welch in his study of propaganda in the Third Reich, 'In any body politic, propaganda is not, as often supposed, a malignant growth, but an essential part of the whole political process,'[10] a part which does not necessarily lie but as Philip Taylor has argued 'rarely tells the whole truth.'[11] Propaganda had always been at the service of political leaders in most states (not merely authoritarian ones) long before the word was associated with the Nazis and their propaganda 'genius' Goebbels, and it remained as powerful, if not more so, when Nazism and Fascism had been defeated. During the Cold War, which followed the end of the World War II a massive propaganda campaign was launched by the Americans and the Soviet both trying to portray a fearful image of the other as the 'enemy.' Every available means of mass communication was used to exploit and maintain the fear of each others' destructive intentions.[12]

In discussing propaganda as a powerful weapon (*Munitions of the Mind*), Philip Taylor observed that 'propaganda has always been an additional instrument in the arsenal of power, a psychological instrument, and it is its relation to power which has always attracted suspicion.'[13]

Metaxas, having established his 'Fourth of August' regime on the pretext of ending the prolonged political crisis[14] and saving the nation from the oncoming communist danger, suspended parliament and abolished all civil rights. Among the extraordinary powers he acquired was the total control of all the means of mass communication through the establishment of the *Yfipourgeion Typou ke Tourismou*, *YTT* (sub-Ministry of Press and Tourism), which was in fact a Ministry of Propaganda and Indoctrination. Its principal agent became the under-secretary Theologos Nicoloudis who controlled and directed the entire propaganda structure, in order to disseminate the themes epitomised by the regime and strengthen Metaxas' position. Metaxas' regime, through a complicated organisational network which involved the establishment of a powerful *Epitropi Logokrisias* (Censorship Committee) and the enactment of a large number of Emergency Laws backed up by a powerful police force *(Asfaleia)*, ascertained that all the means of mass communication; press, film, radio even theatre, were used as instruments of propaganda purposes

The establishment of a Ministry named Press and Tourism, soon after Metaxas came to power,[15] underlines the significance of the press as a vehicle for disseminating its ideology, while a number of 'measures' which included government directives, the formation of a Press Registry and benefits for members of the press, ensured the 'smooth' running of this form of mass communication. The formation and function of *EON Ethnikos Organismos Neoleas*, (National Youth Organisation) Metaxas' 'Golden Children' which represented his most systematic effort to built the popular base he lacked, ensured the assimilation of the regime's ideology and its most successful propagation. The unification of Greek youth under a well controlled organisation which left ample room for exploitation and manipulation guaranteed the dissemination of the themes associated with the regime. Central to those themes was that of the Metaxas Myth and the concept of charismatic leadership. The propaganda machine, through a number of devices and tactics adopted successfully by most contemporary authoritarian regimes, projected the image of Metaxas as an 'ideal type' of charismatic authority. Within this charismatic leadership process Metaxas acquired the title of the 'Saviour of the Nation', the 'First Peasant', the 'First Worker' the 'First Athlete' and the Chief of All Greeks.

Film, along with every other means of artistic expression, was incorporated into the sub-Ministry of Press and Tourism, which supervised every stage of production, distribution and screening. However, when discussing the films of Metaxas' regime it is essential to point out that, although the 'Fourth of August' leadership controlled and directed every artistic expression, it only encouraged the production of newsreels and not feature films as in other totalitarian states. This work helps to explain this preference and demonstrates how advantageous a propaganda medium for the 'Fourth of August' regime the newsreels were, in contrast to feature film, and how rich a source they can be as a historical document. Apart from the charismatic leadership concept which was central to film, as in every other medium of mass communication, themes like Metaxas' ideal relationship with the monarchy, the strengthening of values such as solidarity, love for one's country, family and religion were propagated through the use of film.

Theatre was also completely subordinated to the regime's policy and the theatrical plays were used to disseminate the themes linked with Metaxas' vision for a New State, the *Anagennisis Tis Ellados* ('regeneration of Greece') and the creation of the *Tritos Ellinikos Politismos* ('Third Greek Civilisation') which was meant to exceed in perfection the two previous civilisations (Classical and Byzantine) while radio, Metaxas' very own propagandistic instrument, became an excellent example of how the regime's ideological aims and political propaganda could be carefully combined with entertainment.

The evidence suggests that the 'Fourth of August' propaganda was effective in disseminating t.he themes and ideology associated with and fostered by the regime. However, the effective projection of Metaxas' image did not necessarily imply an equally successful reception by the masses. Despite the effort put in by Metaxas' propaganda to portray a picture of national euphoria, consent and acceptance of the regime's policies and beliefs, its impact on the majority of the Greek people seems to have been far less positive than the regime would have liked.

The research draws on many different sources for substantiation, which have been analysed from a historical perspective. The material used for the study of the organisation and objectives of 'Fourth of August' regime propaganda was found in archival material in the Archeio Ioannou Metaxa, Genika Archeia Tou Kratous (Metaxas' Private Papers at the Greek State Archives) in Athens, which contains state and private papers **selectively**[16] collected. Valuable information was also drawn from Metaxas' private library, which he bequeathed to *EON* at the Benaki Library. This library, apart from Metaxas' rich private collection of books, also contains a plethora of 'Fourth of August' and *EON* publications, photographs and Metaxas' personal items. There is also a large selection of people's tokens of love, such as poems, photographs and letters sent to Metaxas. Another historical document which has been a rich source is Metaxas' personal diary (*Ioannis Metaxas, To Prosopiko tou Imerologio)*[17] which he kept for more than forty years and throughout his dictatorship, along with his speeches which he delivered in great number and which were carefully selected by his officials. Most of the material concerning the *Ethnikos Organismos Neoleas, EON* (National Youth Organisation) was found in the State Archives in Metaxas' Private Papers, in Metaxas' own library, and in the author's collection. Additional information regarding the cinema, theatre, and radio propaganda was obtained from contemporary government Gazettes, contemporary newspapers and periodicals as well as from leaflets, posters and photographs. The study of films as propaganda material (newsreels and documentaries) presented me with many problems, as film viewing in Greece is still a very difficult procedure and it requires considerable time and effort. The film archives at *ERT-Elliniki Radiofonia-Tileorasi* (Greek Radio and Television) contain a number of newsreels but most of those are mainly scattered shots and lack information concerning their production and screening. The newsreels used in this work for the study of the Metaxas regime's cinema propaganda have been obtained from the *Teniothiki Tis Ellados* and the film directors Fotis Labrinos and Lakis Papastathis, based on archival material supplied by *ERT*.

The analysis and the evaluation of the impact of the 'Fourth of August' regime, as with most authoritarian regimes, has proved a difficult task due to strict censorship, the lack of public opinion surveys, and the very limited number of sources of reliable evidence that have survived. Most of the information supplied for assessing the success or failure of Metaxas' propaganda has been obtained from foreign despatches and the confidential reports of the British and American Legations and their Foreign Offices, as well as from foreign newspapers.

The 'Fourth of August' regime's propaganda aimed to create the conditions which would ensure that the dictator remained in power, and convince the people of the 'inspiring mission' of General Ioannis Metaxas. However, in this intrinsically linked process, apart from the techniques employed by the regime, it was the attitudes, the values and the prevailing opinions and prejudices of the Greek people which determined its success.

Chapter One

METAXAS' REGIME AND THE PRESS

Organisation and Structure

On the eve of Metaxas' dictatorship the Greek parliamentary system was once again experiencing political instabilities and there was continuous failure to secure a strong democratic government.[1] The political parties, divided by strong past antagonisms, were engaged in a constant war of securing political patronage, while the powerless voters depended on the politicians to intercede on their behalf with the corrupt state machinery.

The most important vehicle used by Greek politicians to promote their party interests, a practice which required close contact with the electorate on a permanent basis, was the press. Newspapers at the time were the most popular means of disseminating information, and since they expressed strong political convictions they had a powerful appeal to the readers, whose political views they influenced.[2] Newspapers had thus established themselves not only as disseminators of political ideologies, values and misconceptions, but also as 'shapers' of public opinion.[3] In this respect they exercised a tremendous influence on the Greek political scene and were extensively used for propaganda purposes. This great impact, often expressed through scandal-mongering and polemical savagery, is best reflected in the poetic motto of the time: *H Ipourgima mou dineis H efimerida vgazo* (Either you give me a Public Office or I issue a newspaper).[4] The statistical table below provides a vivid illustration of the number of daily and periodical publications in Athens alone, just before Metaxas' seizure of power in August 1936:

Daily and periodical press of Athens 1935 (Per period of issue)

Issuing period	Newspapers	Periodicals
Daily	33	42
Twice a week	2	-
Three times	-	4
Weekly	14	60
Twice a month	-	14
Monthly	-	-
Year	-	-
Issued only once	-	9
Various	-	6
Total	**49**	**139**

Daily and periodical press of Athens during 1935 (Per content)

Description of content	Newspapers	Periodicals
Political	43	41
Commercial & Economic	-	13
Tourism Hygienic & Sports	1	8
Art	-	6
Literature	1	34
Philosophic	-	1
Religious	1	3
Scientific	1	4
Technical	-	5
Agriculture	-	6
Informative	-	5
Satirical	1	2
Youth Press	1	5
Professional	-	3
Various	-	3
Total	**49** [5]	**139**

It can be noted from the above table that thirty-three newspapers and foty-two periodicals (most of a political nature) were issued daily. Thus the Government that controlled the press controlled and directed public opinion and ensured the dissemination of its structure and policies.[6]

Metaxas, who was aware that 'the Greek cannot live without his newspaper,'[7] upon his rise to power and the suspension of all constitutional rights, ensured that the press, along with all other means of mass communication, should come under his complete control.

On the evening of 4 August 1936 police called on the press and printing rooms and suspended the publications of the following day, while confidential instructions were delivered to the papers outlining their mission and specific functions.[8] According to these regulations the press was prohibited from printing any criticism of the regime and its work. Instead, all publications were expected to praise the new Government and emphasise its achievements. Anything that could imply an imposed censorship, including blank spaces, was strictly forbidden. Printing material regarding the government's financial policies, evaluation of currency and public debt was not to be published, while any reference to political parties or their leaders was not permitted. The same applied to material that referred to union activities and those of other organisations, unless these activities enjoyed the approval of the regime. Any reference to the rise of prices, cost of living, illicit profits, crime or even to natural disasters was deleted. All publications had to be thoroughly examined and legalised by the censor before their circulation.[9] Emergency Law 23, which was enacted on 19 August 1936, regulated newspapers' format, production and distribution.[10] On 27 August 1936 with the Emergency Law 45 the *Yfipourgeio Typou ke Tourismou YTT* (sub-Ministry of Press and Tourism) was established and Theologos Nicoloudis, an old politician and publisher of the newspaper *'Politeia'* (The State Polity) but above all a close friend of Metaxas, became its effective under-secretary.[11] However, despite the elaborate name, the *YTT* was in fact a Ministry of Propaganda and Indoctrination as Article 1(a) of Emergency Law 45, *Peri Systaseos Yfipourgeiou Typou ke Tourismou* (About Establishing the sub-Ministry of Press and Tourism) vividly illustrated:

> 'The sub-Ministry of Press and Tourism regulates and governs all issues concerning the indoctrination of public opinion through the Greek and Foreign daily and periodical press, through the control of all congresses, exhibitions, the theatre, cinema, and gramophone records, as well as any kind of cultural demonstrations. All these expressions including radio broadcasts, should be in accordance with the values and traditions of the nation'[12].

To underline the importance of the above legislative measures and ascertain their effective application by the bodies concerned, trying at the same time to suppress any opposition, Metaxas, along with Nicoloudis, set out to deal personally with the members of the press. On 13 September 1936 the dictator summoned the press representatives to Athens and delivered a speech, which reflected his awareness of the power of the press as an instrument of propaganda, and his determination to fully control and exploit it. He likened the press to an electricity plant, which turned the electricity into light, heat and other forms of energy.[13] In the same manner, Metaxas claimed, the press transformed public opinion into an effective aid to the government's policy:

> 'Gentlemen, the press is a business enterprise which exploits a great power that is diffused all over Greek society and is called public opinion. You should know that the State is determined to fully control this power. You realize therefore, that the first sacrifice, which the press will have to make is to become a partner and collaborator of the State in order to manipulate public opinion. All the newspapers will be linked by one characteristic: their complete identification with the State and the projection of its goals under the guidance of the State.'[14]

In order to convince the members of the press of his genuine support, Metaxas presented himself as a fellow journalist[15] much in the same manner Goebbels had done in March 1933.[16] In his speech delivered to the press in Thessaloniki on 25 October 1936, Metaxas declared that as a journalist he was aware of all the problems and difficulties of journalism as well as of its important mission. Yet, he claimed, more than a journalist he was a politician, and as such it was in his interest to shape, rather than express public opinion:

> 'It is of great importance for one who governs a country to have the press as his assistant: because, although we cannot shape public opinion as it forms itself through the needs and goals of society, we can express public opinion, and this can only take place through the press. You realise therefore, what a powerful instrument the press is when it is at the disposal of National Government and supports its program.'[17]

The significance of the press as an effective instrument of propaganda is reflected in the numerous legislative measures that the *YTT* took to ensure complete control and manipulation of public opinion. According to the Ministry's publications, fourteen new Emergency Laws and Royal Decrees were issued during the four years of Metaxas' dictatorship.[18] Among those the Royal Decree of 28 February 1937 specified the departments and the services of the newly established *YTT* as well as the distribution of personnel. Article 2 of the Decree stated that the department of the Greek Press was divided into the following Offices.

a) *Tmima Parakolouthiseos Esoterikou Typou* (Surveillance of the Greek Press Office)
b) *Grafeion Laikis Diafotiseos* (Public Indoctrination Office)
c) *Grafeion Nomothesias tou Esoterikou Typou* (Greek Press Legislation Office)
d) *Grafeion Epopteias tou Esoterikou Typou* (Control of the Greek Press Office)

The Public Indoctrination Office was responsible for the following functions:
a) The effective dissemination of values and ideas that served the national traditions and objectives.
b) The distribution for publication of all official directives
c) The issue of a *Minieon Deltion Typou* (Monthly Press Review)[19] and the publication of any other printed material that could elevate the national moral and propagate the ideology of the State.
d) The formation and maintenance of a library containing everything that concerned the Government and the press.[20]

With the above Royal Decree all Greek and foreign newspapers (the latter were also subjected to similar regulations) as well as any other form of publication, became the propaganda instruments of Metaxas' regime. It was, however, Emergency Law 1092, *Peri Typou* (About Press) passed on 22 February 1938, which was the most rigid and put the press under complete state control. This Press Law introduced stricter regulations on news coverage and imposed heavy penalties for editorials unauthorised by the regime.[21] The press was obliged to publish all the material distributed daily by the *YTT* marked 'compulsory', including large amounts of foreign news coming mainly from German sources.[22] German news was, at least at the beginning of Metaxas' regime, frequently published in the Greek daily press all over Greece as part of a well-orchestrated German propaganda campaign. According to confidential reports from Waterlow to Eden,[23] undisguised German propaganda appeared regularly in local newspapers. It was alleged that the editors of those newspapers were receiving 2000 drachmas for each article from German sources.[24] Severe censorship was also exercised on foreign correspondence and on all speeches, the content of which was restricted and in accordance with the values instituted by the 'Fourth of August' dictatorship.[25]

Morning and afternoon news bulletins were issued and distributed to every public sector all over the country. Similarly, weekly, monthly and yearly publications containing the regime's achievements, speeches and proclamations, as well as foreign correspondence that praised the government, ensured that the whole population was 'properly' enlightened.[26] Furthermore, the Public Indoctrination Office issued a plethora of publications with detailed reports on the achievements of the government, guidelines for people's moral elevation, and accounts, which exposed the State's 'enemies.'

Among these publications were thirty three books with titles like; *Nea Zoe* (New Life), *O Koumounismos is tin Ellada* (Communism in Greece), *To Neon Kratos* (The New State), *O Ioannis Metaxas Pros Tous Ergatas* (Ioannis Metaxas to the Workers), *Oi Neoi Nomoi Peri Typou* (The New Press Laws), *To Neon Kratos Ke o Rolos Tis EON* (The New State and EON), *Logoi tou Archigou Pros tous Agrotes* (The Chief's speeches to the Peasants), *Tessera Chronia Diakiverniseos Ioannou Metaxas* (Four Years of Metaxas' Government). All these publications and a large number of a similar nature adorned all public libraries and offices. To ensure that its propaganda reached both foreigners and Greeks who lived abroad, the Foreign Press Office issued a monthly news bulletin in four languages; English, French, German and Italian. Similarly, one hundred and ninety six weekly publications of an extremely propagandistic nature were issued in French (*Bulletin Hebdomadaire de Documentation*) until 1940.[27]

In Metaxas view there was no such thing as 'freedom of expression' and 'absolute objectivity' and the press should operate within the government's ideology and policy. Thus it should undergo vital changes and adjust its style of reporting to meet the needs of a new state; the 'Fourth of August State. 'We need a press which will become a companion to Greek society and a great assistant to the National State,'[28] Metaxas warned journalists in October 1936, and all the state machinery was orientated towards this objective. Poet Seferis, who at the time worked in the newly established *YTT*, commented on the role of the regime's press officials:

> 'They distributed the speeches of the dignitaries or their friends to the press and specified the place and time of their publication: They supplied instructions for the various boring and uninteresting commentaries or main articles that were written overnight: 'Why issue our own newspaper when we own them all?' they thought. On the other-hand their deepest fear was that the issuing of a newspaper could take the form of a plebiscite and naturally they did not wish to do that.'[29]

The truth is that Metaxas had no difficulties in controlling the press. Most of the newspapers' proprietors and editors-in-chiefs (even the ones which had in the past criticised Metaxas) willingly served the interests of the regime from the very first day.[30] Only the leading communist newspaper *Rizospastis* (Radical) which, in the morning of 4 August 1936, published an article on the oncoming dictatorship was banned immediately and its chief editor Panagiotis Kornaros was imprisoned. The newspaper continued to be published underground, without posing, however, a real threat to the regime. Among the other newspapers only the *Eleftheri Gnomi* (Free Opinion) suspended its publication on 21 January 1937 after the prosecution of its editor Kokinakis who had published an article, which was believed by the regime to imply opposition. All the rest became instruments of propaganda, reporting enthusiastically and extolling the virtues of the dictatorship.[31]

After all, business was booming as with Emergency Law 23/36 of 19 August 1936 Metaxas granted a number of benefits to both proprietors and editors to ensure their full co-operation and unreserved support.[32] Article 3 of this Law allowed the increase of the price of newspapers from one to two drachmas, while Article 5 granted exemption from taxation for imported printing paper. With the same legislation, provision was made for press personnel's wages to rise by 25%, while Sunday was granted as a holiday. Additionally, collective agreements between the newspaper owners and the staff were drawn up.[33] The long neglected provincial press[34] engaged so far in short publications concerning local news, acquired new status and significance with the regular publication of the material distributed by the government, and the benefits granted by the dictatorship. To ensure its full control and ascertain the enthusiastic support of the provincial press, the regime established the *Grafeio Eparcheiakou Typou* (Provincial Press Office) in January 1937, which undertook 'the surveillance of all provincial papers and the settlement of all the problems raised by them. A circular sent to each editor demanded that two copies of each publication be sent to the Provincial Press Office. They were thoroughly examined by specially commissioned staff who selected the material that needed attention and forwarded the same to the appropriate offices.[35] One of the main tasks of the 'specially commissioned personnel' was the selection and publication in the *Minieon Deltion Typou* of all the accounts extolling the regime. The following article published in the provincial paper *Korinthiaki Echo* (Corinthian Echo) provides an account of how the press in the provinces viewed the regime:

> 'The provincial press, which comes into close contact with the hard working people, had for long been forgotten. Today things have changed: the State, in its determination to elevate and upgrade the Greek press, has also turned its attention to the provincial press.'[36]

Furthermore, because most of the editorial material was distributed by the press officials with detailed directives ascertaining even its length and format, the work of journalists and editors became much easier. Any printing material coming from other sources was thoroughly examined and approved by the censor. In this respect the press was reduced from a powerful independent informative force to a mere propaganda tool. The chief editors and journalists became in reality civil servants, while the publisher and proprietor acted, according to the Press Law, as managers whose main responsibility was the newspapers' compliance with the press regulations. Additionally, the Emergency Law 1093 of 22 February 1938 and the Royal Decree of 9 May 1938 introduced a *Mitroon Typou* (Press Registry) so that everyone involved in the press was obliged to register.[37] This registration, which in fact granted potential journalists an entry into the profession, presupposed conformity to certain requirements and rules set by the *YTT*.

However, it was not only the Greek press, which willingly extolled the new regime. Many newspapers in Europe and elsewhere praised the dictatorship and underlined its important mission, especially its contribution to defying communism. Besides, severe censorship made sure that the foreign correspondence was favourable to the dictatorship and as such often received front-page publication.[38] Most of the foreign articles which praised the Metaxas regime came from states with similar governments and reflected not only their feeling towards the Greek political system but also their own regimes' values and ideologies. The following extract from the German newspaper *'E Efimeris tou Laou Tis Kolonias* (The Newspaper of the People of Koln) published in *Estia* on 20 October 1936 provides an idea of how part of the foreign press pictured Metaxas:

> 'What Metaxas is really after is basically the same thing that has been successfully accomplished in countries like Italy and Turkey, but mostly in the Third Reich. Metaxas' main goal and desire is to elevate the morale of the Greek people, help them regain their dignity, and reinstate their glorious past.'[39]

Similarly, the following article from the German newspaper *Efimeris tou Hrimatistiriou* (The Paper of the Stock Exchange) published also in *Estia* on 6 November 1936, praised Metaxas and the establishment of the *YTT*.

> 'Upon his seizure of power Metaxas realized that the successful governing of his country depended on the restriction of the freedom that the press had so far enjoyed. This freedom had exceeded all limits and had become anarchy. For this reason communist papers were banned and the *YTT* was established under the guidance of Theologos Nicoloudis who transformed the press from a private enterprise to a vital national factor.'[40]

2. "Fourth of August" Emblem

It can be noted that the above foreign articles, a sample of the large number published by the Press Office, came from small and insignificant foreign papers and reflected the government's effort to convey a broad approval and consensus. Eleni Vlachou, the daughter of the proprietor and publisher of the conservative contemporary newspaper *Kathimerini*, commented many years later on the political 'happenings' during Metaxas' regime:

> 'Browsing through *Kathimerini* of the time I detect the signs of a bad illness much better than I would have done then. I look at the congratulatory telegrams and favourable articles translated from insignificant foreign newspapers; I see the inaugurations, the festivities in the Stadium, the youth in their uniforms and the continuous manifestations at a time when the clouds of war were closing over Europe.'[41]

One thus realizes that articles like these published in the newspapers were intended to boost the image of the regime and convey a feeling of wide approval while lacking any sign of good journalism.

The *'Fourth of August'* Publications

All these regulations and measures taken by the *YTT* ensured the 'smooth' operation of the press and convinced the government of its unreserved support. At the same time the newspapers continued their publications 'happily,' and enjoyed the benefits granted by the regime: a fact noted by Nicoloudis who observed during an interview with journalists: 'I myself am a journalist and I know that you cannot silence the press. If a press manager who has the people on his side disagrees with the Government he shuts down his newspaper to show his protest. Well so far there has been no one who has done so.'[42]

Indeed, the only press opposition expressed, besides *Rizospastis*, was through the underground publication of very few non-communist papers. From those the first clandestine newspaper published by the ex-Minister Agelopoulos (a known royalist) was the *Paligenesia* (Regeneration) which, in the first issue of 5 August 1937, accused the King of violating the Constitution. Five more issues were published attacking Metaxas' dictatorship and his undemocratic policies before Agelopoulos was arrested and exiled.[43] The underground organisation *Philiki Heteria* (Society of Friends) was established in November 1937 and circulated three clandestine newspapers: the *Eleftheria* (Freedom) for six issues, *Syntagma* (Constitution) for five issues and *Dimokratis* (Democrat) one issue. The organisation also produced the *Kyrix* (Herald) of which one issue was printed only to be confiscated before publication.[44] Another newspaper the *Floga* (Flame) was published in 1937 by the *AMN-Antidiktatoriko Metopo Neon* (Anti-dictatorial Youth Front), and continued its publications until September 1938.[45] However, none of these underground press organisations and newspapers inflicted any real damage on the regime while the daily press 'fed' the public with 'banal' government accounts, advertisements and social events.

To ensure that the reader was not merely receiving information supplied by the government through the 'independent' daily press, but that he also became an active participant in the regime's policies and objectives, a number of government publications, which reflected and conveyed the new 'spirit' came to fill the vacuum of a 'national' press. The most significant one was *To Neon Kratos* (The New State) a political, social, philosophical, historical and artistic monthly review published between September 1937 (to mark one year of Metaxas' advent to power) and March 1941. The publisher and Chief Editor was Aristos Kabanis, a scholar and a journalist, but above all a strong advocate of the Metaxas regime. The tasks and values epitomised by this publication were:

> 1. 'The interpretation and explanation of the values and ideology which necessitated the last year's political and social change: the establishment of the 'Fourth of August' State.
> 2. The defence of the values, which had for long been condemned by the materialists of our century, especially national ideals, as epitomised by Ioannis Metaxas.
> 3. The total suppression and elimination of any idea that would endanger the nation's existence, and the revival of our old traditions and values, which ensure our national continuity.[46]

In the first panegyric issue of this publication Nicoloudis published an article with the title 'To Neon Kratos' (The New State) in which he underlined the policies, values and achievements of the new 'Fourth of August' State. In the same article he stressed the important mission of the new periodical, which was to serve and at the same time to demonstrate the will of the government to enforce its values. The periodical published articles written by many distinguished people of letters as well as experts on financial and social matters.[47] Another publication claiming to be an 'Instrument of International Thought and Hellenic Regeneration' was the political, scientific and artistic monthly review *Nea Politiki* (New Policy) published in 1937 by Professor Ioannis Tournakis.[48] This publication contributed greatly to the dissemination of the themes of the 'Fourth of August' regime, especially the concept of the 'regeneration of Greece' and the 'Third Greek Civilisation.'[49]

Other 'semi-official' publications of Metaxas' dictatorship, which were of less significance, included *Oi Neoi Dromoi* (The New Roads), *Ergasia* (Work) *Pitharcheia* (Discipline) *E Nea Epochi* (The New Era), *Nea Dynamis* (New Power) as well as many more, all of which bore titles that expressed the new spirit of the government. Hence the beginning of Metaxas' regime was marked by a plethora of new publications, especially periodicals, most of which became propaganda instruments. In 1937 there were 152 periodicals published in Athens, Piraeus and the suburbs, out of which more than thirty-five were new issues.[50]

EON, Ethnikos Organismos Neoleas (National Youth Organisation) and Press propaganda

'When I established the 'Fourth of August' State, it was You, The National Youth that I mostly had in mind.'[51]

Metaxas, unlike other authoritarian leaders, lacked a strong political base to support his dictatorship.[52] His small political party the *Eleftherophroness* (Free Opinion Party), founded by him in November 1922, was intended to provide an alternative choice to the two big parties, the Liberals and the Populists, and according to its manifesto of 13 October 1922 promised to 'replace the methods of the condemned past.'[53] Unfortunately the party never gained a substantial number of voters and was dissolved as soon as Metaxas came to power.[54] Metaxas' supporters and his propaganda machine presented a number of reasons for this political vacuum, which proved to be a 'blessing' for the Greek nation. According to Kallonas, who wrote Metaxas' biography in 1938, Metaxas 'failed' as a party leader because 'he disliked petty politics' and his integrity and honesty could not allow him to flatter and deceive the Greek masses.'[55] Similarly, Vasilios Papadakis in his book *E Chtesini ke E Avriani Ellas* (Greece of Yesterday and Tomorrow) claimed that the reasons behind Metaxas' failure to form a successful party could be attributed to three factors: first, Metaxas' inability to adopt the tactics and the 'unwritten' laws of the Greek parties; second, because unlike Venizelos, Metaxas was very hard on his friends, and third, 'possibly because divine providence had destined him for nobler and better things.'[56] Furthermore, Metaxas, despite the fact that he dominated the Greek political and military scene for more than thirty years, never gained wide public acceptance. In consequence Metaxas had to look elsewhere for a popular base which would be easily exploited and would support his regime. Thus, the moulding of the new generation, which would become faithful followers and disseminators of its values and ideologies became the regime's supreme objective.

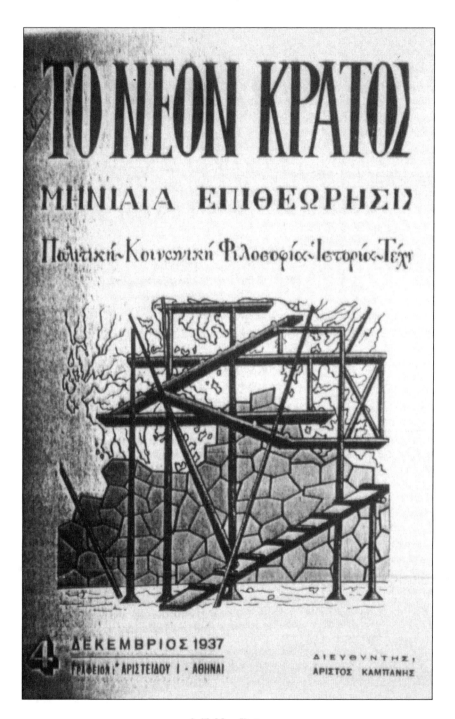

3. *To Neon Kratos*

On 7 November 1936 the *EON, Ethnikos Organismos Neoleas*
modelled on after the fascist youth organisation in Italy and the Nazi youth
in Germany,[57] was established under Emergency Law 334.[58] Alexandros
Kanellopoulos became the leader of the Organisation,[59] and the most
devoted and successful advocate of the regime's ideology and propaganda
policies. According to the Phalangite song dedicated to him by *EON* he was
to lead Greek youth to triumph and to roads of immortality and glory:

> You will arrive to a new Olympia, And the prophecy will
> come true. Listen, Youth calls you, With a brotherly voice,
> Waiting and longing, To walk triumphantly with You,
> You who will lead them, To a 'Regenerating Greece.'[60]

The Organisation, which grew to include almost the entire young population,[61]
represented the most systematic and successful effort of Metaxas to build a
force devoted to him and to the principles of the New State. The dictator's
expectations, dreams and major aspirations for the future of the nation and
the 'promotion' of supreme ideals like those of king, nation, religion and
family, were epitomised in the 'well being' and the successful operation of
EON.[62] This movement became the embodiment of the new national spirit
and the future 'regeneration of Greece.'[63] Naturally, as in most countries with
authoritarian governments, Greek national youth became the primary target
for political indoctrination and manipulation.[64] In fact, it has been argued
that the indoctrination of *EON* 'constituted the only large scale systematic
undertaking of this sort during Metaxas' four-year rule.'[65] The purpose of
this political propaganda was, according to the leader of *EON* Alexandros
Kanellopoulos, 'to project and practice the values and ideologies of the
regime in a successful and effective manner.'[66] Metaxas ascertained, through
a number of regulations and laws, that *EON*, whose members formed
a valuable and malleable material, was not left unguided. He warned the
officials of the Ministry of Education on 29 November 1938:

> 'You must realise that *EON*, which I created, is a State Institution
> which embodies my greatest hopes for the future. Recently, we tried
> to incorporate the Organisation into schools, so that they supplement
> each other. Gentlemen, I am determined to make this work and any
> opposition on the subject will be ruthlessly crushed.'[67]

By 1939 every other youth organisation had been abolished[68] and membership
of school children in *EON* had become almost compulsory. In his speech to
EON officials in January 1939 Metaxas made it clear that all Greek youth

should join the Organisation: 'Membership of *EON* is not compulsory, yet, he stated, you must ascertain that the Organisation includes the whole of the Greek youth.'[69] At the same time the instructions given by *EON* officials urged its members to 'pursue the expansion of the movement using every means available, because within the vital duties of each member is their obligation to enrol new members. The propagandists claimed that special effort should be given 'to enlist Skapaneis, who, because of their young age, could be easily moulded and manipulated to form the base of the New State.'[70]

The compulsory nature of *EON* membership was ensured through various tactics and strategies. For instance, school children were obliged to attend the *EON* meetings on Wednesdays and Sundays, which by order of the regime were established as days belonging to the National Organisation of Youth.[71] If they were absent from those meetings for a total of twenty days they were expelled from school. Additionally, *EON* subscription often became the 'passport' for securing a job, especially in the Public Sector. Circular 36 sent by Metaxas to all Ministries in October 1939, extolled the important mission of *EON* and requested that in cases where two or more candidates had applied for the same position, priority should be given to *EON* members.[72] The unification of Greek youth under a well-controlled organisation ensured the effective and rapid dissemination of the government's policy.

From the very outset of his dictatorship Metaxas claimed that one of the vital targets of his regime was 'The national education and indoctrination of Greek youth; the elevation of their spirit and character in order to enable the young boys to become conscientious Greek citizens and the young women conscientious Greek mothers.'[73] Through devices like the Chief's speeches, anthems,[74] paid uniforms, grand parades, effective slogans, holiday camps, film and theatrical plays all of which played on their emotions rather than their intellect, *EON*, Metaxas' 'Golden Youth' (*Ta Chrysa mou Pedia*) and his 'consolation' (*E Parigoria mou*)[75] became the 'most precious thing' the dictator possessed. When addressing them on 26 May 1940 he stated: 'The success of *EON* constitutes the success of my political life; even more, its success ensures a successful future for our Nation.'[76]

According to the Regulations of *EON* Internal Services (*Organismos Esoterikis Ypiresias EON*) the most important office of the Organisation was the Third Office. This office, simply known as the Propaganda Office, was entrusted with the national, political, and ethical indoctrination of the people, especially youth.[77] Department A, known as *Tmima Ethnikis ke Ithikis Agogis* (Section of National and Moral Education) was responsible for the national and moral education of the young through lectures and speeches, as well as for the establishment and inspection of training schools that would educate and train the propaganda officers. Section B, *Tmima*

Politikis Diapedagogiseo (Political Indoctrination Section) was responsible for the supervision and organisation of everything that concerned the propagation of the ideologies and values of the regime. This included the effective political propaganda, the radio transmission, the surveillance of the Greek and foreign press, and the selection of articles and publications concerning the life of *EON*. [78] The *EON Grafeion Typou* (Press Office) as the above section was also known, became a vital instrument of propaganda and indoctrination of the young and contributed greatly in disseminating the themes associated with the 'Fourth of August' regime. Among its responsibilities was the publication in the daily and periodical press of articles written by *EON* members, which extolled the Organisation's activities and the regime's policies, supporting these by relevant photographs. [79]

One of the most significant tasks of the Press Office was the publication and distribution of press material including 'suitable' books and periodicals, which would have a 'beneficial influence' on the hearts and minds of the young members. [80] Such a publication was *E Neolea* (Youth), a weekly magazine which became the most significant instrument of the 'Fourth of August' regime propaganda as far as youth was concerned. Introduced as 'A Medium of Spiritual, Religious, Social and Political Indoctrination' the magazine was first published in January 1938 and after a year its circulation had risen to 70,000. [81] Its contents were 'a general selection' of moral lectures, references to the glorious past and lessons in Greek history, as well as children's games, extracts from the Gospels, announcements of the Organisation's activities, and most importantly, political messages dominated by the Chief's speeches and slogans. According to Kanellopoulos, *E Neolea* constituted the 'most significant medium of education, indoctrination and propaganda; the great link between the *EON* members and its officials, and the best disseminator of the Organisation's slogans and campaigns.' [82] The press published articles stressing the importance of the magazine and its 'great contribution to the national enlightenment and moral education of youth,' [83] while the *EON* officials underlined the need for the wide circulation of the magazine 'which constituted not just a news bulletin but a vital medium of ideological struggle.' [84] In addition to *E Neolea, EON* publications included a plethora of small booklets which propagated the well-defined tasks and aims of the 'Fourth of August' State. These issues, which were designed to exploit and manipulate the young generation by instilling in them the regime's political outlook, bore titles that emphasised the themes fostered by the dictatorship and reflected the effort put in by its propaganda to create a new politically and nationally conscious Greek generation. Some of these publications were: *To Ethnos* (The Nation), *O Vasilefs* (The King), *Ecogeneia* (Family), *Kinovouleftismos ke Kommatismos*

4. Metaxas speaking at the *EON* Conference
January 1939

(Parliamentarism and Partisanship), *To Katantima tou Boselvikismou* (The Misery of Bolshevism), *Ethniki Kyriarhia ke Ethiki Anexartisia* (National Supremacy and Moral Independance), *Peri Technmis* (About Art) *O Archigos ke E EON* (The Chief and EON) *Phalangite ke Skapaneis to Nou Sas* (Phalangites and Pioneers Be Aware).[85] Great care was taken by the Organisation's propagandists to distribute these publications to every young *EON* officer and ensure their intensive study 'not for the sake of educating and making them any wiser, but to enable them to disseminate and satisfactorily propagate the ideology contained in these booklets to the very young members of *EON* who might have questions. In case there were no questions asked by the children the officers should provoke these and give the appropriate answers.'[86] Furthermore, authors and people of letters were mobilised to write books which would appeal to the young members of the Organisation and disseminate efficiently the ideology of the 'Fourth of August' regime.[87] With all these publications the regime's propaganda ensured that *EON* possessed a powerful 'armour' of propagandistic material which would enable the organisation to become the vehicle disseminating Metaxas' ideology.

Also with the aim of creating a broad political base the regime established the *Tagmata Ergasias* (Work Battalions), a paramilitary organisation that came under the command of the Governor of Athens Constantinos Kotzias. The Work Battalions resembled the Nazi model of the SA (*Sturmabteilungen*)[88] and constituted, 'a force ostensibly to utilise the unemployed in the execution of public works, but actually a praetorian guard under the control of the two strongest men in the 'Fourth of August' regime administration, Constantinos Kotzias and Constantinos Maniadakis.'[89] When Metaxas addressed the Work Battalions in December 1937 he urged them 'to work without shame and embarrassment with their hands and shovels; because manual work is the basis for every civilisation,'[90] while in 1938 he asked for their help 'to fight the nation's materialistic and moral obstacles.'[91] However, despite the great mission entrusted to them they must not have fulfilled Metaxas' initial ambitions as in November 1939, by the Dictator's orders, they were incorporated into *EON*. They formed a separate division named the *DTA* (*Diefthinsis Tagmaton Asfaleias*) within the *EON* Administration (*EON-DTA*) and were bound by the same regulations.[92]

With the establishment of *EON* and the Work Battalions, Metaxas' dictatorship proceeded with the 'enlightenment' of the Greek nation. Having accomplished the complete control of the daily and periodical newspapers and with the circulation of new 'government-inspired' publications, the regime had succeeded in making the press, at least in the beginning,[93] the main tool of its propaganda.

5. *EON* Phalangites

The Press and the making of a charismatic leadership

> 'A Prime Minister ought to master the psychology of the masses
> in order to succeed in his decisions; and Ioannis Metaxas had a
> special knowledge of the psychology and mentality of the Greek
> people.'[94]

The complete control of all the means of mass communication enabled the
Metaxas regime to plan and execute the massive 'flow' of its propaganda:
a propaganda which, in order to be effective, required that the leadership
style be associated with certain projected themes, such as a charismatic
personality, an appealing ideology or the identification with the beliefs and
expectations of the masses. By 4 August 1936 when Metaxas' dictatorship
was established in Greece, the leadership cult had already sprung up and
spread throughout Europe.

The concept of a charismatic leader had been successfully employed
by the totalitarian regimes, especially by Fascist Italy and the Third Reich, as
part of their propaganda in order to conquer the masses by projecting the
image of an 'ideal type' of charismatic authority. This authority, according
to Max Weber's much discussed model of a charismatic leadership, rested
on the 'heroism or exemplary character' of the leader, on the qualities
by which he was considered extraordinary and treated as endowed with
supernatural, superhuman or at least specifically exceptional powers.[95]

Yet, Metaxas lacked Hitler's magnetism as well as Mussolini's
pompous appearance.[96] On the other hand, his military and political
career coincided with those of the great charismatic personalities,
King Constantine and Premier Eleftherios Venizelos, who had enjoyed
tremendous affection from the masses and the support of a strong party
mechanism.[97] As previously stated, although Metaxas had been an active
officer and politician for many years and had broad cultural tastes, he
had never gained widespread popularity.[98] Furthermore, his inflexibility
and inability to communicate with the masses, aggravated by his imposed
dictatorship, as well as his unimpressive physical appearance, did not
contribute to his personal charisma. Short, overweight, always wearing his
spectacles,[99] with the looks of a civil servant or a retired primary school
teacher, rather than the striking appearance of a national leader, and
much older than the other politicians of the time, Metaxas represented a
negative model of the charismatic leader.[100] Indeed, he was conscious of his
unattractive style and lack of personal charisma, a fact that disturbed him
all his life: 'tonight tea with the English .We were all there. Yet I received
little attention. I do not speak English and I am too short,'[101] he wrote with
bitterness in his diary.

6. The *Chief* Ioannis Metaxas, The *Leader* Alexandros Kanellopoulos,
EON member

Given the lack of the attractive elements that were needed for the successful projection of the leadership cult and its reception by the masses (a dual and intrinsically linked process), his propaganda had to project a successful image of Ioannis Metaxas, based on his existing qualities. Thus his negative physical characteristics, which seemed to pose a threat to the image building process, were instead praised and emphasised as functional necessities and 'safety barriers' against past political 'factionalism and arrogance.'[102] The image of a simple man, an ideal humble servant of the state, an ordinary 'father and grandfather,` the good-natured *Barba Yiannis* (Uncle Yiannis), who would embrace all sections of community, and above all a man of duty and ethical values, rather than a demagogue of striking appearance, was therefore invented and conveyed to the masses through the press propaganda. To reinforce this image, Nicoloudis wrote in the regime's publication *Ellnikon Mellon* (Greek Future) :

'The people become frenzied with enthusiasm when they see him: yet, this leader has none of the attractive characteristics of a demagogue or a charmer of the masses. His looks are simple; his speech unsophisticated and 'square', and only his eyes attract attention. It is in those eyes alone that one can detect a deep faith in the values and ideas of the nation.'[103]

Similarly, accounts of Metaxas' humble, yet striking appearance, saw the light in numerous publications, while extracts like the following gave an illustrative description of the charismatic leader:

'His appearance suggests a person with little concern about his looks. It is true that he cares little for his aesthetic image. In vain one will search in him for signs of elegance and grace. Yet, his whole appearance radiates a feeling of sincerity and suggests a rich sentimental personality. His large hat, his stiff collar and his round spectacles together with his walking stick with the silver top create an image of a very peculiar character. All these are habits, which enforce in the minds of the masses a historical figure with the charm of the eccentric. When he laughs or rests he gives the impression that he is a simple-minded family man whose business is booming.'[104]

The above passage suggests that the propaganda machine operated a carefully planned scheme to ensure the projection of a leader who defied the 'superficial' image of the 'charmers' of the masses and relied on people's genuine support for his remaining in power.

In the process of establishing a charismatic leadership cult a number of new devices and symbols were introduced and transformed in such a way as to form an intrinsic link with past values and noble ideas, which the new regime epitomised and promoted. Thus, the emblem of the 'Fourth of August' State, the Greek flag with the burning torch and the number 4 in the middle, (Still 2) and the two Cretan Axes (adorning the *EON* flag) would harmoniously coexist with the Royal Crown and the National flag, while the raising of the right hand would revive the model of the ancient Greek salute.[105] Furthermore, appropriate slogans, which were, according to the *EON*'s Propaganda Office, necessary in every propagandistic activity, were used extensively. ('Slogans of correct wording and psychology delivered at the right moment have a great impact on the masses').[106] Metaxas' inspired phrases like 'Get up Greek Youth; there exists no another reality for you apart from the Greek Nation,'[107] or 'Greece is our Great Mother; when you love Greece you love yourselves,'[108] which were included in his speeches and were chosen and printed on the regime's publications as well as in the daily and periodical press, became the national mottoes of the time.

Metaxas' propaganda also introduced new public holidays such as the anniversary of the 'Fourth of August' regime, as well as the 7 November as *EON* Day, which took the form of national holidays, with the sole objective being the exaltation of the regime.[109] Meanwhile, the existing national holidays were skilfully enriched and adopted by the regime's propaganda to meet the needs of the new political situation and to support the image-building process of Metaxas' charismatic leadership. According to the *EON* leader, after the coming of the 'Fourth of August' all Greek holidays lost 'their past typicality and formality and gained real meaning and significance.'[110] In this respect the celebration of the '25 March' (Greece's Independence Day) was as significant as that of the 'Fourth of August', as both holidays were intrinsically linked with the mission of delivering the Greek Nation from unbearable pain and agony. The following extract from *E Neolea* reflects the effort of the regime's propaganda to propagate such a belief:

> 'If 25 March 1821 was the fateful day of Greek independence from our long enslavement, the 'Fourth of August 1936' constitutes the will of the divine providence to free the Greek people and their conscience from the humiliation which the past hatred had subjected them to, and to wipe out the pettiness of individualism.'[111]

Similarly, other holidays like the ' First of May' became linked with the 'Fourth of August' holiday because, as Metaxas' claimed, 'the well-being of the workers and the people of labour was the supreme objective of

the regime and the motivating force behind the establishment of the
dictatorship.'[112] Even the Chief's name-day on 7 January was used in such
a way as to convey a feeling of continuation and bonding between this
day and the 'Fourth of August' holiday, both dominated by the presence
of Ioannis Metaxas. The following extract from a speech delivered by the
EON leader presents an illustrative account of the propagandists' effort to
link the Chief's name day with his 'sacred' mission.

> 'This celebration today is not just another conventional holiday like all
> the others. The reason for this difference is the fact that our Leader is
> not a conventional Leader but a Leader who has been acknowledged
> by all Greeks as the creator and saviour of the Greek Nation (...) We
> do not celebrate this day only as an ordinary name-day but also as a
> day which symbolises our ideology, our values and our policies, all of
> which are embodied in one person; this person is our Chief. Thus,
> the whole nation as one man, one soul and one spirit celebrates the
> name day of the man whom the whole nation had been expecting
> for such a long time: the man who came and resurrected the nation
> and will lead it to greatness. Indeed the whole nation, the Greek
> Nation, celebrates (...) but for us in *EON*, the rejoicing is much
> greater because we celebrate the name-day of our real father.'[113]

These orchestrated celebrations were dominated by Metaxas' countless
speeches and proclamations, which were all published in the daily press and
the regime's special publications. The propaganda machine relied extensively
on the influential role of those speeches as Metaxas, like Hitler,[114] strongly
believed that the spoken word had a much more effective propagandistic
value than the written one. The following advice, from a speech Metaxas
made to *EON* Officials in May 1940, indicates the value he put on spoken
propaganda:

> 'You must be aware of the fact that the written word has no effect
> on the people; it is the spoken propaganda and indoctrination that
> have the greatest impact. That is how Christianity was propagated
> and this is how *EON* and its ideology will spread'[115]

Thus, the propaganda machine took special care to ensure that the speeches
of the Great Chief dominated the propaganda process and were extensively
used by *EON* officials as an important propaganda instrument.[116] Articles in
the press and the regime's publications underlined their important mission
and urged people to read the 'inspired' speeches:

'The Chief's speeches constitute a unified philosophical, moral and political system. They include and reflect the values and doctrines of the revolutionary change that took place on the 'Fourth of August.' These speeches should become everybody's manual, especially the University students who will understand and master the general theory about the State and the basic principles of our government.'[117]

It must be stressed, however, that Metaxas was a poor orator. He lacked eloquence- a fact that he was aware of: 'I am not an orator; I am unable to delivery a speech with success.. I am not a parliamentarian,' he commented bitterly in his diary on 30 March 1927 long before he established his dictatorship.[118] He spoke at too great a length and he was often repetitive and used long inelegant phrasing and the wrong grammar. Yet, even these poor rhetorical qualities were masterfully presented in his press propaganda as the great qualities of an ethical and caring leader. Kallonas wrote:

'Metaxas is indifferent to phrasal elegance. He speaks the way he dresses; simply, positively, firmly. First, he cares about the substance of his speech and second, about the impact which his rhetorical presentation has on the audience. Most importantly, he has the ability to adapt his speeches according to the level and psychology of his audience. He speaks in a simple *demotic* language, the living language of the people and he never writes his speeches beforehand.'[119]

The extract demonstrates the effort made by the regime's propagandists to conceal the dictator's limited eloquence. However, when Metaxas established his 'Fourth of August' State none of these 'rhetorical' faults seemed to matter. He delivered hundreds of speeches and he seemed to enjoy doing so. All his speeches were published by *EON* in small booklets with titles like *Logoi Pros Tous Ergatas* (Speeches to the Workers), *Logoi Pros tous Agrotas* (Speeches to the Peasants), *Logoi Pros Tous Goneis ke Didaskalous* (Speeches to the Parents and Teachers). By the end of 1939 the regime published a volume of 602 pages containing all the speeches delivered by Metaxas prior to 4 August 1939 to celebrate the third anniversary, and this became a vital propaganda medium for disseminating the themes linked with the regime.

Chapter Two

CHARISMATIC LEADERSHIP

Metaxas - A symbol of the Nation

A recurring theme in the regime's propaganda within the leadership cult concept was that of Metaxas as the Saviour of the Nation, and the Guarantor of national unity. This unity was based on the defeat of past political systems, which had caused a deep political cleavage among the Greek electorate[1] and had driven the country into political chaos, not to mention moral and economic degradation.[2] Metaxas believed that parliamentary politics 'the political application of liberalism'[3] were a hindering factor in any country's progress.[4] He professed an active anti-parliamentarism and a dislike for the whole political world populated by people who he called the 'drones of the political parties and a disgrace.'[5] His antipathy towards the old parties (including traditional conservatism) and what they professed, nourished, according to Sarantis, 'his polemics against parliamentarism, the system on which these parties relied. Metaxas' early attachment to monarchy, and the Crown Prince Constantine in particular, aroused his initial exasperation with parliament during the clash between the King and a number of politicians at the turn of the century.'[6]

The dictator claimed that it was the degradation of the parliamentary system and the forthcoming danger of complete political instability which necessitated the establishment of the 'Fourth of August' State.[7] The old state, being clearly political and party-based, had become, according to Metaxas 'a dead organism with the sole objective of manipulating the Greek people and collecting their votes: a 'rotten' system indifferent to the people's needs which used every unethical means to remain in power.'[8] The need to convince the people of the disastrous effects which the previous political systems had had on their lives and the country at large, and win their support, became one of the main tasks of the regime's propaganda. Government officials, theoreticians of the New State and men of letters were all mobilized to convince the masses of the failure of parliamentarism and the 'saving mission of the 'Fourth of August' State. Naturally, the press predominated in this campaign and Nicoloudis took the lead, analysing the 'curses' of parliamentarism in antithesis to the beneficial role of the New State:

> 'The 'Fourth of August' was initiated by general and local factors(...) The British Parliamentary system, beneficial for its country, has proved to be a great mistake for the rest of the countries in Europe and elsewhere (...) The 'Fourth of August' State is not a parenthesis in the existence of many other political schemes. Nor are we a political dictatorship. 'The Fourth of August' State constitutes a cosmo-theory and a system. Its fundamental principle is its complete predominance: The 'Fourth of August' is a totalitarian State, and it is a non-violent State because it is a powerful State.'[9]

The above speech and its publication in the first issue of the regime's uppermost press propaganda medium *To Neon Kratos* demonstrates the importance that the regime put on the theme of anti-parliamentarism. To underline this importance a great number of articles of a similar nature were published in the 'Fourth of August' publications as well as the *EON* booklets.[10] These publications were intended 'to convince the Greek people of the dangers of parliamentarism, which had failed them from the ancient times to the eve of the 'Fourth of August' State, and would have led to civil war and the complete collapse of Greece, if the 'Saviour of the Nation' Ioannis Metaxas, who believed in the Nation, in himself and in a totalitarian state, had not come alone at the right moment.'[11]

If, however, the 'evils' of parliamentarism were one of the causes that necessitated the establishment of Metaxas' dictatorship, the fundamental reason and motivating force behind Metaxas' political thinking and behaviour was anti-communism. Anti-parliamentarism and anti-Communism were two inter-changeable notions, which according to Metaxas constituted 'the double yoke', which strangled and suppressed every free notion and manifestation of a better life.'[12] It was the inefficiency and failure of parliamentary politics to face up to the Greek reality which threw the Greek people into the embrace of communism.[13]

The theme of anti-communism was very significant and vital for the 'Fourth of August' regime. According to its ideology, *KKE, Komounistiko Komma Ellados* (Greek Communist Party), which during the inter-war period had grown from a small insignificant membership to play a central role within republican Greece,[14] was to be blamed for the degradation of the nation and the loss of all the sacred values that constituted this nation. When Metaxas became Prime Minister in April 1936 he was faced with growing industrial unrest and leftist agitation. The general election held in January 1936 had produced another political crisis. The Liberal alliance won 141 seats while the populist alliance won 143 seats. The balance of power between the two alliances was held by *KKE*, which won 15 seats. While the party leaders struggled to form a coalition government, a series of deaths of leading politicians (Kondylis, Tsaldaris, Demerzis and Venizelos) worsened the political crisis which further deteriorated due to widespread social unease and communist pressure. In April 1936 a parliamentary majority allowed Metaxas to govern by Decree and deal with the communist danger.[15] His effort to suppress the spreading communist influence led to greater communist agitation and a series of strikes, which were promptly and 'efficiently' handled by the Metaxas government.[16]

The establishment of the 'Fourth of August' regime endowed Metaxas with unlimited powers and enabled him, with the help of his competent Deputy Minister for Public Security, Constantinos Maniadakis,[17] to fulfil his historic mission of 'wiping out the danger of communism' and create a new outlook which could reunite and revitalise the Greek people.[18] The police force and the *chorofylaki* (gendarmerie),which had grown in numbers,[19] acquired, through the enactment of Emergency Law 1075 of 11 February 1938 *Peri Metron Asfaleias tou Kinonikou Kathestotos ke Prostasias Ton Politon* (Measures for the safety of the Social Regime and the Protection of the Citizens), extensive powers and responsibility.[20] Article 11 of the above legislation introduced the issuing of *Pistopietiko Kinonikon Fronimaton* (Political Loyalty Certificate), a document which accompanied any kind of application for employment or any other transaction.[21] As soon as Maniadakis took over the sub-Ministry of Public Security he introduced new methods and tactics which were catalytic for the disintegration of the Communist Party.[22] These measures included the seizure of all the communist archives and the arrest and exile of the *KKE* leader Nicos Zachariadis[23] and members of the Central Committee, as well as the introduction of the *Deloseis Metaneias* (Declarations of Repentance) which were declarations signed by the *KKE* members denouncing their party and ideology. These were extracted from them under great psychological and physical pressure which included beatings and interrogations and the notorious ice and 'castor oil' methods.[24]

These *Diloseis Metaneias* had a tremendous psychological effect on the *KKE* members as they undermined the party's morale and smashed internal cohesion.[25] Needless to say, they constituted the most effective propaganda instruments in the regime's effort to convince people of the evils of communism. The daily press published accounts of numerous *Diloseis Metaneias* by 'repentant' communists, who had become aware of the dangerous path they were on, and acknowledged with gratitude the saving intervention of the 'Fourth of August' government, promising to work and live within the lines of the New State.'[26] According to a confidential circular sent by Maniadakis to his officials in February 1939, the publication of these declarations was dictated by two main objectives:

> a. To give those individuals a chance to state publicly their present social ideology and
> b. To shatter any confidence the Communist Party may have in those individuals, making their further association with the Party inadvisable.[27]

According to the regime, from the 47,000 communists who submitted *Diloseis Metaneias* only three were won over by Bolshevik propaganda and returned to the *KKE*.[28] The daily press spoke of the mass arrests of dangerous communists 'who were engaged in anti-regime activities,' supporting these by the names and photographs of the arrested *KKE* members,[29] while the regime tried to deny the 'alleged rumours' about their ill-treatment and their deportation to the islands.[30] At the same time government publications enlightened the people about the evils of communism and the saving mission of Ioannis Metaxas. Similarly, all the theoreticians of the New State and government officials were engaged in a war of words against the Bolshevik danger and its champion, parliamentarism, praising the beneficial intervention of the 'Fourth of August' regime.[31] Nicoloudis delivered several speeches, like the following one, and published many articles severely attacking the *KKE*:

> 'It is not worth mentioning the *KKE* exiles because we know that there were more exiles in the islands during the past parliamentary governments: However we have the right to throw those exiles into the sea, because they are dogs raging with fury and are threatening society with poisoning and death.'[32]

In the same tone, Kotzias, when delivering a speech to *EON* on 7 January 1938 on the occasion of Ioannis Metaxas' name-day warned the young members:

'Look towards the future and close your ears to those who wish to instil doubt in your souls. They are the subversive people who are plotting against this society and this country: towards those people you must be ruthless and cruel; you must crush them; they are the social traitors and communists, and towards them you must be merciless.'[33]

The above extracts, delivered in a most 'inelegant' language, reflected not only the regime's fury but also demonstrated its great concern about a possible resurgence of the communist threat. To emphasise the positive nature of intervention by the regime, the press often quoted the confessions of repentant communists, who exposed the propaganda mechanism of the *KKE*,[34] while Metaxas often undertook the mission of witnessing the 'miserable state that the children of repentant communists were in.'[35] The article published in *E Neolea* with the title 'Oi Parastratimenoi epistrefoun is tas agalas tou Kratous tis 4es Augoustou' (Those that have gone astray are returning to the embrace of the 'Fourth of August' State) provides a vivid picture of the regime's strategy for defeating the communist danger:

'Another communist, and this time an important one, has come forward to declare repentance. Not only does he denounce his old ideas but he feels obliged to fight them. We rejoice when we see people like Manoleas repent and return to our humanitarian family like the prodigal son: because these people were dead and they have been raised from the dead; they were lost and have been found. Yet, the existence of such people should in fact alert us because we must consider that those who repent are few in number while those who are still out there contaminating our social atmosphere are many'[36]

The above extract, written in a harsh, incomprehensible language, which makes it unsuitable and hardly educational material for the young *EON* readers, reflects the regime's hatred of the advocates of communism and its determination to crush them. However, apart from the threats and contempt apparent in the passage there seems to exist a vivid scepticism about the efficiency of these measures and the real strength of communism.

As part of this policy of exposing communism to the people's eyes Metaxas' propaganda published, on a daily basis, accounts with supporting photos of the communist atrocities taking place in Spain, where the communists had caused the most destructive civil war.[37] To emphasise the danger inherent in this, war reports by eyewitnesses and photographs from the battle front adorned most newspapers.[38] All the press forces were mobilised to convey to the people the 'true' picture of the Bolshevik danger and naturally, the Chief's speeches dominated in this anti-communist fever. He warned the people of Greece, especially youth 'to always be alert to the lurking communist danger'[39] and he claimed that 'since 4 August 1936, 98 percent of the Greek population had become anti-communists.'[40]

Within the measures taken to suppress and wipe out communism, the regime, from the very first days of its seizure of power, dealt with what was believed to be a most threatening enemy of the national interest: 'Anti-Greek' literature. Article 3 of Emergency Law 1078 strictly prohibited the publication and circulation of books which contained subversive ideas and harmed the national cohesion. Meanwhile, books found in public libraries or in the houses of the people who had been arrested by the police were confiscated and burned in central squares by the regime's fanatics, in much the same manner as the Nazis had done on 10 May 1933 in Germany.[41] Among the books committed to the flames on 16 August 1936 was a great amount of foreign and Greek literature including books by Goethe, Bernard Shaw, Freud and many others as well as many by Greek authors. The daily press led the way in this spiritual purge by publishing inspired articles calling all the 'patriotically-thinking youth' and their parents to assist in the extermination by fire of all the intellectual communist ammunitions.'[42] The campaign against the printed ideological evidence continued with the issuing of circular order 16/80/151 by Maniadakis on 5 November 1938 which prohibited the circulation of 445 books, while the works of Thucydides, Sophocles and many other ancient and modern writers were strictly censored.[43]

The defiance and elimination of the 'evils' of the past and the danger of communism, especially where youth was concerned, necessitated the reorganisation and centralization of the education system. All the basic and elementary schools of the country, with the enactment of Emergency Laws 2007/39, 2025/39, 2026/39 came under the control of the *ASE Anotaton Symvoulion Ekpedefseos* (Higher Board of Education), while all the higher institutions were supervised by *DAE Diefthinsis Anotatis Ekpedefis* (Higher Education Office); both these offices were under the direct authority of Ioannis Metaxas.[44] Through 'drastic measures,' which included the taking over of the Educational Portfolio by Metaxas himself in 1938, the school system was fully reorganised 'to meet the needs of the new era, imbuing the young members with the everlasting truths and values of the Greek nation and to protect them from the lies that poisoned their minds and souls.'[45] Furthermore the *OSV, Organismos Scholikon Vivlion* (Board of School Texts) was established to supervise the re-writing, publication and circulation of all school books.[46] The schools were thus furnished with books 'written in line with the new spirit, values and ideology of the 'Fourth of August' State,'[47] while EON publications were strongly recommended by the Chief:

'Young people of Greece,
E Neolea is the only magazine which through its valuable articles
of national, historical and encyclopedic nature does not alienate
the school children from their school, but instead, strengthens
their spirit and enriches their knowledge so that they can proceed
with their studies without extra strain (...) Young people at work
will also find in *E Neolea* everything that elevates them ethically
and spiritually, and strengthens their ability to carry on with
their main profession. *E Neolea* is the magazine which is strongly
recommended by our Chief because it constitutes a valuable
companion to all Greek Youth.'[48]

To ensure that the above recommendation was 'heartily' adopted by the
EON members, most schools 'faced with the children's most urgent
demand and need for the magazine' organized reading groups of four or
more people who shared the expense of the magazine and the valuable
knowledge it offered them.[49] Apart, however, from educational measures,
the 'Fourth of August' regime introduced a number of welfare measures
which ensured the well being and correct upbringing of Greek youth,
and their physical along with their spiritual development. These included
measures against the spreading of infectious disease, and the introduction
of a programme of mass school dinners. In charge of these dinners
which were greatly exploited by the regime's propaganda machine, was
Metaxas' wife Mrs. Lela Metaxas.[50] These dinners did not represent an
act of charity but were, according to the regime, 'a voluntary offer from
one society member to another; from a brother to a brother',[51] and were
closely linked with the Chief's vision of a 'regenerating nation;' because as
the propagandists claimed, 'a well fed child was capable of achieving great
things whereas a starving child had no future.'[52]

Having dealt with the two most dangerous and despised enemies,
parliamentarism and communism, Metaxas, assisted by his propaganda
machine, set out to convince the Greek people of his unconditional love and
affection, and to present himself as a leader who looked upon them not
as voters but as individuals. He said to the people of Athens at the Mass
Rally organized by the Propaganda Office and Costantinos Kotzias on 2
October 1936: "The Fourth of August" is a government which belongs to
the whole nation and a Chief who deals with the needs of the nation as a
whole and is concerned with the problems of the people, rich and poor,
strong and weak. Its only duty is to take care of all of you, especially the
weak and the poor'.[53] Papadakis, in an effort to present the dictator as the
'people's leader' wrote:

'Metaxas' love for the poor people is immense. He feels pain and affection for them; and because he is so just, he is extremely lenient towards them.'[54]

Indeed, in many of his speeches he flattered the masses by denouncing the plutocrats and by reaching out for the lower classes which had for so long been exploited and manipulated by the politicians and the elite. 'There is nothing more dangerous for the existence of the State than the governing classes which enjoy all the wealth secured by their position,'[55] he claimed in November 1936.

Apart from the numerous publications which praised Metaxas, regular articles like the following one were written by Ministers and High Officials in an effort to underline his charismatic qualities:

> 'The whole nation, especially the people in the provinces and the people in the countryside, understood and appreciated the efforts of the Government and embraced its work. Never before had this country been more powerful and better governed than now with Metaxas watching over it. This amazing man is obsessed with the reconstruction and the salvation of the nation.'[56]

Similarly, Constadinos Kotzias wrote the following article in November 1936. Entitled *Memories*, it was published in the government's pamphlet *Ellinikon Mellon:*

> 'Metaxas is generous with his friends and ruthless with his enemies. He is a faultless Governor and a gentle human being; an exceptional family man and a caring father. But above all he is a religious man of high principles, values and traditions. One must not forget that he was also a great editor of an astonishing quality. This exceptional man, who has experienced unbelievable hardship in the past, undertook the difficult mission to save the nation and he will do so.'[57]

To reinforce the image of the leader of the people and the 'Saviour of the nation', a number of relevant photos were developed and published in newspapers and the regime's publications. Still 8 depicts Metaxas dominating the picture in front of the Greek map with his right hand raised in a hearty salute. The association of the picture with the image of the Saviour is obvious as Metaxas' figure is depicted on a grander scale than that of the country, implying his ability and determination to embrace and protect the whole nation. The same association is conveyed by the cover page image, which depicts Metaxas on a grand scale dominating the picture while all sections of society are reaching out for him. This recurring theme of Metaxas as a saviour of the nation and a caring leader was often indirectly conveyed by the press through the presentation of similar images from other countries with authoritarian regimes. This was demonstrated when *Estia* ('a paper of Fascist tendencies' according to Waterlow)[58] published its main article on 7 October 1936 with the title 'Ena Politimo Didagma Ethnikis ke Koinonikis Allilegies O Chtesinos Logos tou Hitler epi te Efkairia tis Chimerinis Ergasias'(Hitler's Speech on the Occasion of Winterhilfswerk: A valuable lesson in national and social solidarity). The article stressed at length Hitler's expression of gratitude to the German people for their sacrifices made for the good of the community.[59] The intended association of Metaxas' regime with Hitler's by *Estia* is obvious and the implied urge to the Greek people to support the dictatorship financially is self evident. Almost a year later, in his manifesto on the occasion of the regime's first anniversary, Metaxas thanked the Greek people for their majestic and 'voluntary' contribution towards the Royal Air Force.[60] This contribution, which amounted to 300 million drachmas had been collected within a year.[61] On 5 August 1937 *Estia* published a leading article which praised enthusiastically all authoritarian states, especially those of Mussolini, Salazar and Hitler:

> 'Those states are successful because they have a long duration and can effectively apply their policies. It is this duration that Metaxas wishes for his New State and in this respect he has taken all the necessary measures to ensure this continuity. All opposition and threatening forces have thus been eliminated'[62]

Meanwhile, the projection of Metaxas' image as an exceptional, charismatic leader, a guarantor of unity and a leader of all people, necessitated the organisation of an endless programme of mass parades, rallies, tours and athletic events. National holidays, especially the regime's anniversaries, were given massive coverage by the press and often the written image projected on these occasions was as striking as the visual one, with the press struggling to convey the lively enthusiasm. The spectacular celebration of the regime's first anniversary at the Athens Stadium was the main subject in all the pages of every newspaper. Articles, eulogies, posters and photos of the National Leader[63] ensured that people were reminded of his charisma and achievements. The *Messager d'Athenes* published on 3 August 1937 an article written by Nicoloudis which reflected the determination of the regime's propaganda machine to project a charismatic leadership:

7. 'Fourth of August' celebration

'For the first time in Greek history the provinces are harmoniously linked with the capital. All sections of Greek society will dance and sing tonight at the Athens Stadium to demonstrate the strong links between national traditions and national solidarity.'[64]

Accounts of villagers who arrived dressed in their best clothes, carrying placards bearing the name of their district, happy and proud, parading, dancing and singing with their musical instruments to pay their tribute to the Great Governor, were extensively published. A vivid account of the celebration was given by Waterlow:

'Although the proceedings bore the unmistakable stamp of rejoicing to order, the programme was well chosen to appeal to the taste of the ordinary citizen. More than the military parades, which characterise the 25th March, he enjoys celebrations of a popular and national order such as dances in national dress, open-air feasting and the like. Facilities for the latter were freely provided from public sources, while the display in the Stadium was devoted almost entirely to the former.'[65]

Meanwhile, Metaxas inaugurated several welfare institutions in the capital and the suburbs, in an effort to project a powerful image of a caring leader.[66] A constant psychological mobilisation of the masses was needed through the continual presence of their leader, who would capture their minds and their hearts and create a bond of mutual trust and loyalty. In this respect, the *EON* propagandists in their recommendations 'On Propaganda' in January 1939 emphasised the absolute necessity of an effective propaganda to conquer the masses, and urged their members to follow the example of Germany:

'During the recent *Anschluss* of Austria, Hitler delivered a speech in Berlin which was transmitted by radio all over Germany. Such was the power of his speech that the German people were transformed into a powerless mass. This was achieved because Hitler mastered the psychology of the crowds. If we wish to have the same effect and conquer the masses we must study their psychology and mobilise them through a methodical and effective propaganda. When the masses believe and are convinced about an ideology they can die for it. But the masses cannot act without a leader. The leader through his words and his gestures electrifies the masses and sets an example.'[67]

8. Ioannis Metaxas. 'The Savior of the Nation'

However, apart from the successful projection of the charismatic leader
the mobilisation of the masses served also as a barometer for Metaxas'
popularity, and as such it had to be successful in order to convince him of
the people's growing love and support.

According to Nicoloudis, these manifestations took the form of a
national plebiscite:

> 'Because who will deny it, the celebration of the 'Fourth of August'
> will become an enormous plebiscite; the most natural the most
> joyful, the noblest and the most free plebiscite ever secured by a
> revolution.'[68]

According to Papadakis 'the celebration was for Metaxas a day of joy;
a day of consolation, and the day of his spiritual rest during which the
simple people manifested their joy and gratitude.'[69] These feelings were
acknowledged by Metaxas who said on the occasion of the 'Fourth of
August' regime's first anniversary :

> 'Today, full of gratitude, faith, pride and enthusiasm I shall celebrate
> with you, Greek people, the 'Fourth of August' anniversary. I shall
> participate in your joy and I shall celebrate with you like a simple
> citizen among a large crowd of people.'[70]

Furthermore, articles were published in all papers describing the festive
atmosphere of the celebrations which included the decoration of all central
squares in towns and villages with Greek flags,[71] myrtle garlands, and pictures
of the King and Metaxas. The same articles announced the locations
of the churches where morning services for the well-being of the King and
his Premier were held. The following quotation from *Estia* on 4 August 1937
conveys a fascinating picture of Metaxas' entrance to Athens Stadium on the
celebration of the first anniversary of the 'Fourth of August' dictatorship:

> 'The entrance of the President into the Stadium will be accompanied
> by several parades performed by the Marine Guards, the Town
> band and others. During the festivities bombshells, which contain
> big balloons that depict photos of his Majesty the King and the
> Prime Minister, will be fired every five minutes from a special
> canon located on the hill of Ardytos.'[72]

While the censored press was engaged in an enormous rally to convey the
festive atmosphere and boost Metaxas' personality cult, the clandestine

newspaper *Paligenesia* in her first issue on 5 August 1937 reminded the King of his oath to obey the Greek Constitution and safeguard the freedom of the Greek people.[73] Furthermore the underground *KKE* newspaper *Rizospatistis* published on 12 September 1937 an article which attacked the regime and its 'alleged achievements' and urged people to resist:

> 'A year has passed since the monarcho-Fascist regime sold off our country to German Hitlerism and turned it into a massive concentration camp.'[74]

At this point it must be stressed that one theme that was constantly projected to support the image of the national leader was the close link and relation Metaxas had with the King. Metaxas, who owed his dictatorship to the King and depended greatly on his support in order to remain in power, engaged his propaganda machine to project an image of a charismatic leader who enjoyed the support of the people, but foremost that of his King.[75] This close relation and dependency was made known in every orchestrated manifestation and every speech Metaxas delivered. 'We need the Royal throne as a symbol and guarantee of National unity' he claimed in one of his speeches.[76] This claim was supported by the relevant photographs which depicted Metaxas standing next to the King, (Still 9) while royal events like the marriage of the Crown Prince Paul to the German Princess Frederica on 9 January 1938 and trips by both Metaxas and the King to various parts of the country were used by the propaganda machine to emphasise this harmonious relationship between King and Government. At the same time articles about the Royal House of Greece and its history as well as the announcement of royal events and activities adorned all the government publications, especially *E Neolea*.[77] In addition, booklets with titles such as O *Vasilefs* (The King) constituted educational material for the *EON* members who were taught about the charismatic qualities and the 'sacred mission' of the King.[78] Yet, despite these manifestations and the phenomenal harmony, Metaxas who was aware of the King's faith in democratic values,[79] never overcame his fear of losing the royal support and confidence: a fact often quoted in his diary.[80]

But it was not only the King's attitude towards his dictatorship that troubled Metaxas. Despite the enthusiastic press reports from all over the country, the adulation and the national euphoria which his propaganda made sure was not only produced but conveyed through the media to all the people, the dictator himself was surrounded by deep doubts about his popularity. He often wondered whether these manifestations of love and adulation were genuine. It was only the orchestrated mass parades and mass manifestations that kept Metaxas going: 'I am longing for devotion. My soul is thirsty for love'[81] he admitted in his diary, and his propaganda engaged all the mechanisms to reassure him of such approval and adulation. 'Maniadakis tells me that our popularity is ascending,'[82] he wrote on 20 October 1938 convinced by the confidence and assurance of his effective Chief of Police. This assurance derived from Maniadakis' effective measures to create a climate of fear that helped to neutralise the threat of active opposition, strengthening at the same time the propaganda effort. Indeed, the propaganda of the 'Fourth of August' regime was most effective in times when its existence and permanence were threatened by opposition. Orchestrated grand festivities, tours in the provinces, and exaggerated press reports were well organised to convince the people of the power and stability of the regime. In this respect in 1938 the '25 March' National Holiday was made much of by the regime's propaganda machine in order to operate as a 'safety barrier' and to over-shadow a number of major incidents emanating from the opposition. These expressions of resistance began with the active opposition of the prominent politician Kafandaris who drafted and issued a long proclamation in January 1938, attacking Metaxas and comparing his methods to those of Hitler and Mussolini. This proclamation, distributed in great numbers, created great discomfort among those in power. In an effort to counteract it, Metaxas' close collaborators issued another manifesto which appeared to have been written by Kafandaris, because they had falsified the latter's signature. In this manifesto Kafandaris disclaimed responsibility for the proclamation in question and declared that it was fake. Finally, Kafandaris, along with other politicians who opposed the regime in various ways, was arrested and exiled.[83]

The culmination of the government's distress came, however, with the illness and eventual death of the prominent politician Michalakopoulos,[84] whom Metaxas feared most, for he was a known monarchist and had excellent connections with the British.[85] His death on 27 March 1938 was believed to be the result of his banishment to a remote island while he was seriously ill. This incident initiated open criticism and reactions from both the political world and the public. It is worth noting that none of these reactions, which were effectively dealt with by Maniadakis' *Asfaleia,* saw the light of publication. Instead, the '25 March' National Holiday celebration received a massive coverage, with reports and pictures giving fascinating accounts of the manifestations. The Premier himself commented in his diary:

> 'What a dream that was today and yesterday. This dream took
> place yesterday in Pedion of Areos with my Youth. They are my
> precious creation and work: work which succeeded despite reaction

and opposition. Almost eighteen thousand children from Athens, Piraeus and other regions paraded. Among them the *Phalanx of Ioannis Metaxas* from Patras to whom I spoke. However, I am still concerned about the 'circles' that might try to influence the Crown Prince. With this agony which derives from my uncertainty over the future of my work, I visited the 'Organisation of National Renaissance'. Then I saw the Work Battalions; they are my 'personal guard.' What a ceremony that was; what enthusiasm and apotheosis. The effect on the people was astonishing.'[86]

On the death of Michalakopoulos and the effect that this would have on the public Metaxas wrote in his diary on 31 March 1938:

'On Sunday Michalakopoulos died. People from his entourage are trying to exploit his death. They have no right to do so. Besides, all that has now ended. The only thing that has remained with the people is the great impression made by the majestic celebration of the '25 March.'[87]

The show was repeated on a much grander scale with the celebration of the regime's second anniversary on 4 August 1938,[88] which tried to undermine and conceal the growing feeling of discontent arising from the Cretan Revolt of July 29 1938.[89] The revolt, which was organized by a Central Revolutionary Committee and included ex politicians and military officials, was the most significant one, and, although it was severely suppressed, it created a climate of fear and insecurity for the government. Leading articles in the newspapers spoke of 'the stupid rebels who attempted to abolish the dictatorship only because they wished to established their own', urging people 'to be aware of these dangerous people, and become their ruthless enemies.'[90] The same newspapers, under headlines like 'The whole of Greece condemns the insane rebels,' printed part of what was claimed to be 'a great number' of cables sent to Ioannis Metaxas. These cables conveyed the people's support and congratulated the dictator on the successful suppression of the revolt. At the same time the regime's achievements, especially where the agrarian and the working population was concerned, received front page coverage.[91] The success of the forthcoming celebration of the second anniversary of the 'Fourth of August' became thus an event of great importance. Detailed instructions were issued by the *YTT* to every town and village official to ensure the successful outcome of this most important festivity-plebiscite. The following extract from *Estia* demonstrates the orchestrated efforts to ensure the utmost success of the celebration:

'The celebration will commence with morning services held in
all churches and attended by all authorities, committees and the
people. In the afternoon parades by *EON* members will take place
and large dinners prepared by the municipalities, the committees
and the village communities will be served. Loudspeakers will be
located in the squares of the towns and villages to transmit the
speeches, the songs and the lively enthusiasm from the celebrations
in the Athens Stadium. The houses and shops will be decorated
with myrtle garlands, photos of the Premier and the emblem of the
'Fourth of August' State [92]

The instructions for the successful execution of the celebration in Athens
given by the same newspaper were in the same vein:

'The shopkeepers have been instructed to decorate their shops with
symbolic representation and the 'Fourth of August' emblem, and
the Sign which has been approved by the *YTT*. Similarly, pictures
of his Majesty the King and the Prime Minister will adorn all the
shops(...) The houses will put up both the Greek flag and the
'Fourth of August' emblem. Proper arrangements have been made
by the Minister Theologos Nicoloudis and his colleagues to ensure
shelter and food for the large crowds which are expected to arrive in
Athens for the celebration. For this reason, although a holiday, the
restaurants will remain open.'[93]

Mazarakis Ainian estimated that the cost for this celebration came to 200
million drachmas[94] when the total income of the private sector of the same
year amounted to 73,713 million.[95] The forthcoming celebration was expected
to last three days: 'The sun will set on the horizon and will end this historic
celebration; but we shall continue the festivities until the next day thus declaring
our deep devotion to His Majesty the King and Ioannis Metaxas,'[96] while all
the ideologically committed press, including leaflets, continued to describe the
festive atmosphere in a way designed to attract as many spectators as possible:

'The celebration in Athens will commence with the arrival of the
Prime Minister. On his entrance trumpets and drums will sound
and a chorus of 1500 workers and students will be singing. The
festivities will be marked by the presence of 750 young members of
EON, 400 workers from the Papastratos industry and many athletes.
Furthermore, seventy folk dancers will arrive from the provinces
together with several other teams numbering 2,000 members.'[97]

9. King George II and Ioannis Metaxas

Yet, despite the grand festivities, the impact of the suppressed revolt and the danger inherent in it were an ever-present threat to the regime. In order to undermine its significance and anticipate any future opposition Nicoloudis delivered the following speech, which was transmitted over the radio:

> 'This day the Greek people dance and sing expressing their deep gratitude towards the soldier, the patriot, the politician and the creator. We are the most popular regime in Greek History. The people put aside everything else and loved Ioannis Metaxas with a simple, deep, immense love that only the masses can feel. Unfortunately ten miserable people misunderstood the kindness and generosity of our Leader; Well, these people were punished for they were taken revenge on and buried by the Panhellenic anger and mockery'[98]

Additionally, the newspapers spoke of the celebration's great success underlining the people's 'spontaneous arrival' and their unreserved support for the 'Fourth of August' State, and their *Barba Yiannis* (Uncle Yiannis). The leading article of *Kathimerini* entitled 'E Adolos Psiphos' (The Ingenuous Vote) said on the subject:

> 'Today under the 'Fourth of August' State the citizen is given the opportunity to express in a different, safer and more ethical way, his feelings to the Government. The celebration constitutes a vote of confidence and expresses the people's beliefs and convictions. This is the vote that really matters because, in antithesis to the disgraceful vote of the past, it is an ingenuous vote and cannot be false.'[99]

Furthermore, the regime, in order to efface any signs of weakness and protest, entered what is known as the 'Second Phase' of Metaxas' dictatorship. It involved a number of drastic measures that Metaxas took in order to maintain himself in power. His comments in his diary in September 1938 give a vivid picture of what those measures were:

> 'I returned on 25 September. I took the whip and I dismissed all the unfaithful ones from my 'temple,' Without any hesitation I dismissed most people from the Ministries. Among them the Minister of Education Georgakopoulos who was conspiring against me, and I kept the Ministry under my command. I changed the laws and then I replaced all the ungrateful Ministers and Officials with the ones who were faithful and totally devoted to me.'[100]

By this time his propaganda was becoming more effective, strengthened by the extreme actions of the police. These included conspiracies at home and abroad,[101] imprisonment and exiling, and yet more costly celebrations. These were organised during the regime's third anniversary and were given extensive coverage by the press. The British Ambassador Palairet provided a vivid account of this 'plebiscite' manifestation:

> 'The third anniversary was duly celebrated with what is becoming the customary squandering of public money and with the blare of the propaganda machine working at full blast. The celebrations deviated little from those of the second anniversary. If anything, I think that an even more ludicrous note was struck than has been the case hitherto. Metaxas' busy day included the 'symbolic commencement of the demolition of the old Ministry of Finance Building'. The President of the Council and his suite climbed, under the broiling mid-day sun, up an improvised wooden staircase to the roof of the condemned building. There the little General in his dark blue suit and the tall Minister of Finance exchanged speeches about the 'bad principles and the bad habits' of former regimes, after, General Metaxas received from a member of the Labour Corps a little pick and began with his own hands the symbolic work of destruction'[102]

To add to the reassuring effort, posters[103] and photographs of the Chief were printed everywhere including on the electricity bulbs,[104] while phrases like 'Do not forget that on the 4th August Greece was saved by Ioannis Metaxas,' became postmarks on letters.[105] Additionally, the Chief's phrases that had become national mottoes adorned all leaflets and posters as well as bus tickets. At the same time *EON* launched a propaganda campaign on an unprecedented scale to propagate the charisma of Metaxas, with its members in the streets singing, 'We have but one father and chief: The Leader.'[106]

The projection of this father image was another element of the charismatic leadership process. The *EON* members referred to Metaxas as their father, and photos were produced to emphasize this father and child relationship (still 10). The wider implication of such depiction was the harmonious coexistence of the old and the young that Metaxas' regime accomplished. The 'Fourth of August' anthem spoke of the Great Chief who always guided forth the Greek youth, while the girl Skapanisses sang:

> 'We are full of pride, And our young soul, Is full of the Command Of Our Chief and Father, Like brave Skapanisses, We march always forward, Singing with all our hearts, Long Live our Chief.'[107]

Similarly a plethora of songs sung by *EON* children like the following one, which was dedicated to the Father, played a very significant part in the image - building process of the charismatic leader.

> You came like sweet-smelling air, To lighten up the sky
> You came like a God Chief, Chief and Father of the Truth,
> Father, O FATHER., You showed us a new Life
> And your creation, *EON*, Is your dream that came to life.[108]

All these devices were intended to convey to the people an image of a caring and most devoted *Megas Kyvernitis* (Great Governor) whose only ambition was the interest of his people.

Although the concept of Metaxas as the caring father of the young was part of a larger process which included the dictator's loving attitude towards the workers and the peasants manufactured by his propaganda machine, this process was inextricably bound up with the real behaviour and feelings of the dictator. His repeated entries in his diary written, in a fatherly tone, reveal that he envisaged the young and the poor as his loving children, '*Hara mou Oi ptochoi ke ta paidia* (My joy are the poor and the children),[109] he wrote, and he was filled with joy when he was acknowledged as their father and received their respectful and affectionate adulation. It has been argued that 'this attitude originated from the dictator's attitude towards his family and was expressed in his sentimentality and his constant anxiety over its members, the incessant concern with their welfare, and equally in the rigid hierarchical rules that were strictly observed and did not allow his authority and decisions to be challenged.'[110] Whatever the reason behind this fatherly behaviour, the numerous entries in his diary and the references in many of his speeches suggest that the Metaxas' regime was characterised by a paternalistic attitude towards the people, especially, those less privileged and the children.

O Protos Agrotis (The First Peasant)

The concept of Metaxas as national leader who embraced all sections of community was effectively projected by the propaganda machine through the agrarian sector. Peasants and small farmers formed the majority of the Greek population and given their great degree of illiteracy they provided an easy target for exploitation and manipulation by the dictatorship.[111] In this respect Metaxas' regime from his very first days set out to win over the agrarian population with a very well planned programme of government

10. 'The Father of the Nation' and *EON* member

measures supported by a powerful propaganda machine. In his speech on 2 October 1936 outlining his policy towards the agrarian sector he stated:

> 'Special attention will be given to the peasants, because they constitute the main factor of the nation's wealth-production and form the largest section of the Greek nation.'[112]

Part of this propaganda orchestrated to project the image of Metaxas as a fellow peasant were his journeys and trips to the provinces. These parts of the country had been exploited and forgotten by the politicians in the past. Therefore, the caring presence of a Leader who looked upon them as individual human beings and not as anonymous voters took special significance and enabled his propaganda to be effectively applied. Metaxas' speeches flattered and elevated the peasant population and he was presented as 'an aristocrat who had the soul of a peasant, of a farmer and of the people of the earth, and who was aware that the nation's strength lies in the earth.'[113] When he spoke to them he appealed to their feelings for strong support and requested their hard work for increased productivity. He told the people of Amfiklia on 9 October 1936:

> 'First, I need your unreserved support because without the trust of the people I cannot do anything that is great. Second, I want you to work with all your strength, because in the hands of the peasants lies the fortune and the future of Greece. The agrarian class is proud because out of nothing it extracts wealth while other classes profit by retailing wealth.'[114]

Metaxas claimed to have contributed greatly to the improvement of the conditions of the agrarian population for whom he felt great affection. Indeed, a number of significant measures were taken which increased the amount of land available for cultivation and also the agricultural production.[115] Among those significance measures was the enactment of Emergency Law 677 on 17 May 1937, which aimed to greatly reduce agrarian debts and relieve the peasants from 'the great poverty that the past government had condemned them to,'[116] while on 5 November 1938 Emergency Law 1462 abolished the tax on olive oil. Furthermore, through law 1822 of 1939 the government granted full property titles to the land which had already been allotted to small farmers and the refugees from Asia Minor, while significant welfare measures came into effect.[117] Apart from the beneficial impact these laws had on the peasants they were in themselves masterpieces of propaganda as they were used in Metaxas' speeches as a basis from which to win the peasants' co-operation as well as their moral and financial support; the following extract from a speech delivered by Metaxas to the people of Arta on 16 June 1937 is a sample of this intentional exploitation.

> 'Only the peasants have courage in their hearts and enthusiasm, and only they can achieve the agrarian ideal. Yet, even the peasants have the duty to pay a very small percentage of the debts. This amount you must pay in yearly instalments.. In this respect you will prove that the peasant of Greece is an honourable person.'[118]

The allusion in this speech is quite obvious as Metaxas aimed at the peasants' honour, pride, and dignity (the Greek *filotimo*). By paying their debts the peasants would not only settle their financial matters but above all they would prove themselves trustworthy, a quality which would enable them to transcend the social barriers and become respectable citizens. After all according to the *EON* propagandists, Ioannis Metaxas mastered well the psychology of the Greek masses and 'knew better than anyone their feelings, their beliefs, their dreams and ideals, their anguishes and misfortunes.'[119]

But in order to be successful propaganda required not only a leader who was aware of the people's psychology but also a leader who would share their hardship, their dreams and their expectations. Only then could propaganda build a relationship of solidarity and achieve a strong bond between the leader and the led.

In order to promote this relationship one of the most significant contributions to the projection of charismatic leadership was invented; that of the *Protos Agrotis* (The First Peasant) image. On 1st July 1937 a month before the first anniversary of the 'Fourth of August' regime, the peasants of Argos proclaimed the dictator *O Protos Agrotis* with panegyric manifestations. A striking account of the organised manifestation is given by Kallonas :

> 'Representatives from the Agrarian organisations of the whole country came before the Chief of the Government and after they expressed their gratitude they offered him a silver cap full of grain. On the cap was written in golden letters the phrase: Our National Governor Ioannis Metaxas, with gratitude, we proclaim you the First Peasant; the Agrarian Organisations of Greece.'[120]

The title of the First Peasant expressed Metaxas' complete identification with the agrarian population. On the occasion of his proclamation he addressed the audience with the following speech:

'By proclaiming me the *Protos Agrotis* you have not really separated me
from my inherited status as an agrarian, as my mother and father were
also cultivators of the earth. I thus belong to your family and I deeply
feel your pain and your joy; I deeply feel what the peasants feel.'[121]

In this speech, as in several others, Metaxas identified himself with the
audience. He claimed to be an agrarian by birth, thus creating an emotional
and intimate bond with the peasants.[122] The press, which methodically
emphasised this relationship and took every opportunity to convey it, wrote
on the regime's first anniversary:

'Peasants from Keratea village came close to the Premier and
offered him pies and flowers from their village. The Premier stood
up and received the presents and thanked them shaking hands with
each one.'[123]

The press continued with accounts about the dinner party given by
Nicoloudis for 1,000 peasants 'who danced wearing their colourful local
costumes and who were expressing their deepest devotion to the Minister
in every possible way.'[124] The same dinner party, but for 5,000 peasants, was
repeated on the celebration of the regime's fourth anniversary (an occasion
of unbelievable waste and fanfare)[125] during which the 1st of August was
proclaimed as the 'Day of the Peasant.'

What, however, became the most effective means of projecting
the *Protos Agrotis* image were Metaxas' countless trips to the most remote
regions of the country. Press reports and photos conveyed a fascinating
picture of Metaxas' reception by the agrarian population:

'The appearance of the Premier was met with delirious joy
and enthusiasm by the crowds and cheers like 'Long Live
our Leader, Long Live Barba Yiannis' filled the atmosphere.
The Prime Minister's car covered with flowers thrown from the
balconies was lifted by the crowds and the Prime Minister with tears
in his eyes pleaded with the crowds to allow passage for his car. 'We
shall carry you, you are our saviour, Long Live the King, Long Live
our Leader, the crowds shouted.'[126]

These enthusiastic accounts were directed towards the urban population,
as well as towards the country people. In the case of illiterate peasants
and workers they were properly 'enlightened' as to the contents of the
newspapers as well as of the official directives and propagandistic material

11. Ioannis Metaxas, 'The First Peasant'

by the prefects and other persons vested with the special authority of propagation. A flavour of such a happening is conveyed by the oral account of an elderly man who lived at the time in a village in the Peloponnese:

> 'Illiterate country folks would gather in the *Kafeneion* (coffee shops) to have their coffee when someone whom we knew was a government man would begin to talk about Metaxas' achievements, his charismatic qualities, with emphasis on his trips to the neglected countryside and the enthusiastic receptions. He would display the printed photos of Metaxas' trips, and where necessary, he would often embellish the contents of the newspapers. The role of the propagandist was often taken up by members of the council, the school teacher or even the priest who would include the achievements and charisma of Ioannis Metaxas in his Sunday preaching.'[127]

Most of these 'successful' receptions organised to the last detail by the government officials, were mainly paid for by the agrarian population: 'In front of the Agrarian Bank a grand arch with images of country life was set up and paid for by the Agrarian Committees.'[128] The events were supported by numerous photographs either printed in the papers or distributed by special publications. These presented Metaxas amidst frenzied crowds garlanded with flowers and laurel wreaths, whereas others depicted him ploughing a field (Still 11) to connect him with the agrarian sector. Furthermore, photographs of grateful peasants cultivating the earth and peasant women proud of their caring and supportive leader, adorned most publications.

While the press accounts of the successful tours with the supportive photographs offered a unique picture of the orchestrated propaganda, the same papers devoted other pages to accounts and photographs of Hitler's birthday and the successful German parades thus linking the two regimes.[129]

To support the propaganda effort well selected foreign correspondence spoke of 'the simple man sparing of words, who looks more like a civilian or a military man, more like a teacher and general, but whose voice and gestures are those of a Great Leader';[130] a Leader who kept flattering the masses in his speeches. 'It is I who thank you for your enthusiasm. I am dedicated to you. I have nothing else in my life but you' he claimed in his speech to the peasants of Evros.[131] Furthermore, the *EON* press quoted phrases of the Chief's discussions with the young members: 'I ask from you the young who are children of peasants to cherish your father's occupation, as it is the noblest occupation,'[132] which were intended not only to express the Chief's genuine love for the peasants but to convince also the

EON members coming from peasant families to remain in their rural areas and proudly acknowledge their parents' 'noble' job.[133]

The image of the *Protos Agrotis,* projected by the propaganda machine through mass rallies, speeches and visits to the country, was geared towards the rural population in order to assure them of the Chief's unreserved love and at the same time win their support. To fulfil this twofold purpose the regime made certain that the peasantry was adequately represented in every public manifestation organised by the regime and most importantly that 'its caring leader' played a dominant part in those celebrations.

O Protos Ergatis (First Worker)

Together with the theme of the First Peasant projected by Metaxas' propaganda, another important theme, repeated in the charismatic leadership building process, was that of the Honourable Worker. Workers loosely bracketed with the professions, formed, like the peasants, another target for manipulation. In his speech to the Workers on 8 January 1937 Metaxas said:

> 'A Nation cannot prosper when its foundations upon which the whole national structure is based, suffers; and these foundations are its working class, its agrarian class and the wage-earners(...) You must be aware that the main objectives of the 'Fourth of August' State are the two solid pillars on which Greece stands: The Workers and the Peasants.'[134]

Metaxas set the tone of his programme where the workers were concerned, in his speech at the Mass Rally on 2 October 1936 when he assured the working class that the new regime was there to look after them and protect them by preventing their exploitation by swindlers.[135] Indeed, a number of measures were taken to improve the conditions of the workers whom Metaxas called 'his people.'[136] The eight hour work day was enforced, while a Social Insurance scheme *IKA Idryma Koinonikon Asfaliseon* (Foundation of Social Insurance) came into effect in November 1937.[137] Drastic measures were also taken to improve the health conditions of the workers and to fight and control the endemic disease, while the reduction of unemployment which constituted one of the first priorities had been, according to the regime, successfully accomplished.[138] Other measures included the introduction of a basic wage and entertainment for the workers.

While much legislation was passed to ensure the welfare of the workers, a number of restrictions ensured the complete subordination of the working people to the 'Fourth of August' regime: the trade unions were brought under state control and all decisions concerning the workers were taken by the government in collaboration with the management, while the working organisations were 'purified of the subversive elements,' and the existing class struggle ended.'[139] Strikes and lockouts were considered illegal and collective bargaining and compulsory arbitration were introduced which reduced the workers to passive participants.[140]

No doubt the social reform programme steadily managed to improve the conditions of the workers during the dictatorship, but most importantly, it 'promised sizeable propaganda mileage'[141] for the 'Fourth of August' dictatorship. A wide range of mechanisms and forms of representation were invented by its propaganda machine to project the image of Metaxas as a fellow worker and caring leader. Visits to factories and work-shops,[142] speeches and inaugurations, enthusiastic processions on the First of May Day, as well as the participation of the workers in the regime's celebrations were organised to the last detail. The culmination of such activities was Metaxas' proclamation on 14 August 1937 as the *Protos Ergatis* (The First Worker), a title also claimed by and granted to Hitler.[143] By this proclamation Metaxas was fully identified with the workers. In his speech delivered for the occasion he stated;

> 'Working people of Greece, I am now a colleague of yours; you paid me the greatest honour ever bestowed on a human being: Because for a man, there is no greater honour than the honour of being a worker(...) Now you, the Workers of Greece, come along and attribute this status to me: This is the greatest satisfaction which I have as a human being.'[144]

From that moment manual work took a new perspective and the dignity and the honour of labour became a very noticeable aspect in Metaxas' propaganda. He was presented as a leader whose devotion and respect for work had no boundaries. Work was his joy and his honour; 'there existed for him no other aristocracy than the aristocracy of work'[145] and work had always been the motivating force behind his creativity. The high value he put on work was his life's conviction and he shared this conviction with his fellow workers on 26 November 1939:

> 'I am extremely happy to be with you today and I feel like someone who is among relatives and comrades. And this is not because you proclaimed me the First Worker but because I have been a worker for my whole life; a poor worker(...) If I ever have to choose between the people at the

12. 'Joy Through Work' Poster

top and the people at the bottom I will choose the people at the bottom; the poor people.'[146]

Naturally, the press undertook the predominant role in conveying the First Worker image. Accounts of Metaxas' enthusiastic reception by the workers during his tours in the country and the town enjoyed front page coverage, with the workers acknowledging their gratitude to their comrade and saviour of the nation. *Proia* provided a vivid account of such a manifestation:

> 'Above the streets hung large banners with printed phrases proclaiming the gratitude of the people towards the Prime Minister. Among them many wrote: 'We thank you Great Leader; Saviour of the Nation and First Worker: The Workers and Peasants are grateful.'[147]

Often these expressions of adulation were so exaggerated that they reached a ludicrous point. The following extract from a speech given by the refugee workers and the professionals on Metaxas' name-day reveals the extent of the adulation directed at him and uncontrolled propaganda:

> 'National Chief
> You were and still are a great Engineer. The words of the Engineers and the Architects which have been weighted on a scale of precision and sincerity, are real and mathematical; You are a capable Engineer, who under the wise guidance of our beloved King, is building a concrete structure made of iron with deep and strong foundations: a structure of reinforced concrete, the pillars and beams of which are the whole nation whereas the free professions and the Engineers are the strengthening of this structure. We, the refugee Engineers and Architects are proud because our National Chief is the First Engineer.'[148]

Furthermore the visits to the factories, the face to face conversations and the shaking of hands with the workers organised by his propagandists, all established an image of warmth, solidarity and appreciation for the regime and were well covered by the press. Meanwhile, Metaxas' conversations with the children became significant propaganda material for conveying his devotion towards the labouring classes. An example of such an effort is given by *E Neolea* under the heading 'Ioannis Metaxas O Filos tou Ergatou' ('Ioannis Metaxas: The Friend of the Worker'):

- What is your father's job?
- He is a Worker,
-Well give him my warmest regards.[149]

The above dialogue and a great number of a similar nature were intended to convince the simple working people through their children, who were *EON* members, of the utmost affection Metaxas felt for them, implying at the same time a new status of an elevated and dignified working class. Through associations like the above which reflected their leader's support and acknowledgement, the working masses lost their anonymity and gained their self respect and dignity. A respect which their Great Chief made explicit in several of his speeches:

> 'Although I have respect for the intellectuals I must confess that I come from a practical profession and thus, I communicate better with people with practical professions than with intellectuals.' [150]

To strengthen this projection of a harmonious relation between the leader and the worker and underline the significance of the honour of labour and the joy inherent, a number of *Hara ke Ergasia* (Joy and Work) exhibitions were organised, according to the successful model of Dr. Ley in Hitler's Germany.[151] In the Athens Zapeion, in May 1938, Dr. Ley himself opened the Greek section of the international *Kraft Durch Freude* (Strength Through Joy) exhibition (Still 12) during which Metaxas received the Grand Cross of the German Eagle.[152] Furthermore the social work model 'conceived' by Hitler and 'executed' by Dr. Ley was extensively published and praised by the regime's press.[153]

   No doubt the overall effort made by Metaxas' propaganda machine, to project the Worker image as well as that of the National Leader and the First Peasant was enormous. Through a number of devices adopted by most contemporary authoritarian regimes, the propaganda machine launched a massive, often ludicrous, campaign to meet the objectives of the regime and to create a state worthy of its Governor: A state which according to Metaxas 'on 4 August 1936 became an anti-Communist State; an anti-parliamentarism State, a totalitarian State; a State with a Agrarian and Labour Foundation and thus, anti-plutocratic. Of course it lacked a governing party; but all the Greek people were the governing party; all except the hopeless communists and the reactionary old politicians.'[154]

Chapter Three

FILM PROPAGANDA IN METAXAS' REGIME

The structure of film before Metaxas' regime

Greek film production during and immediately after the First World War amounted to a very small number of unsuccessful feature films and newsreels.[1] The diversion of financial and technical resources to the war effort, followed by the political instability and the disastrous expedition to Asia Minor in 1922, left little room for film-making. However, a number of very efficient and experienced cinematographers like George Prokopiou, The Gaziadis Bros., and Joseph Hepp, among others, produced some excellent examples of political film making of that period in the form of documentary films and newsreels.

The first of these newsreels was the '*Anathema Tou Eleft. Venizelou sto Polygono*' (Elth. Venizelo's Anathema at Polygono) 1916-17, an *Asty-Film* production directed by Joseph Hepp[2] and dealing with the symbolic stoning of Eleftherios Venizelos. Because of its provocative nature the newsreel was confiscated immediately after its release by the District Attorney, and its director Hepp was exiled.[3] The second newsreel was the '*Epanodos Tou Vasileos Kostantinou*' (The Return of King Constantine) 1920, by Constantinos Theodoridis, which provided a record of the exiled King's return to Greece.

These films dealt with issues which concerned the two dominant political figures King Constantine and Prime Minister Eleftherios Venizelos and the National Schism.

However, the finest example of Greek political film making of the time was *The Asia Minor Expedition,* 1920-1921; a 14,000 metres long documentary film shot by George Prokopiou, which dealt with the Asia Minor catastrophe and the evacuation of the refugees who fled to Greece. The film served as a model for future artistic endeavours which drew heavily upon it, and it became an invaluable primary source for modern Greek history.[4] Apart from the very limited number of newsreels and feature films, contemporary filming included *The Greek Miracle*, 1922, commissioned by the Ministry of Foreign Affairs and produced and directed by D.Gaziadis. This film dealt with the Greek Expedition and was expected to end with the liberation of Asia Minor from the Turks and the conquest of Ankara. The 2.000 metres long film was never completed nor was it ever screened.[5] Although these productions are not directly linked to the film propaganda during Metaxas' regime, they are noteworthy because their thematic treatment reflected and projected the political pathos of the time; a pathos which initiated the political upheavals that resulted in the Metaxas' dictatorship. Henceforth, they served as prime examples of film propaganda. Furthermore, those same pioneer cinematographers were the ones who were extensively engaged by Metaxas' dictatorship to produce and direct most of its film propaganda.

The period between 1928 and 1932 was marked by relative political stability and economic improvement as Greece tried to recover from the wounds of the past.[6] This period saw the rise of the cinema industry from a primitive one man enterprise to the establishment of many successful film companies, especially in Thessaloniki.[7] People's growing concerns, and preference for a cheap form of entertainment like the cinema, enriched substantially by the foreign films which offered them escape from everyday problems, encouraged cinema attendance. According to the statistics of the time there were seventy one cinemas operating in Greece during that period: thirteen of them were located in Athens and the rest in the other cities.[8] Unfortunately, just as the Greek cinema, with its limited manpower and equipment, was trying to become a successful enterprise producing a significant number of films for the time (thirty three films were produced during 1928-1933[9] mostly bad imitations of the Hollywood model), several factors hindered its development. The most significant restraint was the coming of the sound film, which necessitated much more advanced film equipment, experienced personnel and substantial funding. This change, supported by the lack of any legislative measures that would encourage indigenous production, once again deterred the development of the Greek film industry and resulted in the disappearance of many small film companies. Meanwhile, the world economic depression had caught up with Greece, aggravating the Greek economy which relied heavily on exports and external borrowing. The social unrest and disorder that followed created once again the political instability which led to the 'Fourth of August' regime in 1936.[10]

The creation of an independent Greek film industry under the Metaxas' dictatorship and its austere censorship became a utopia: the oncoming Second World War, followed by the most destructive Greek Civil War, put a final blow to the Greek film industry (which never really got under-way until after the fifties) and ruled out any possibility of Greece becoming part of a European cinema.

The 'Fourth of August' regime and film legislation

The Metaxas dictatorship found the Greek film industry at a complete stalemate. From the period 1933 until the end 1935 there were only four Greek films produced (two of which were produced in Turkey), while foreign films dominated the Greek cinema. The following statistical table indicates the number of the foreign films imported to Greece during the year 1936.

Eisagogi ke Provoli Ton Kinimatografikon Tenion en Elladi kata to Etos 1936 (Films imported and shown in Greece during the year 1936)

Country of Origin	No	Length in meters
U.S.A.	241	573,894
Germany	71	163,183
U. K.	42	103,732
France	42	81.607
Belgium	12	27,963
Austria	8	18,557
Hungary	1	2,000
Turkey	1	2,202
Palestine	1	1,700
Total	**419** [11]	**974,639**

As we can see from the above table the domination by the American film industry (mostly melodramas of the Hollywood Dream Factory) of the Greek audiences was overwhelming, while for the same period Greek film production was non-existent.[12]

According to a survey published by the film magazine *Kinimatographikos Astir* (Cinema Star)[13] in January 1937, Greek audiences showed a greater preference for the cinema than for any other kind of entertainment. There were twenty six sound cinemas operating in Athens alone, while 80,000 people attended the ten central cinemas in Athens at least once a week: Similar numbers were reported to attend the district ones

ΑΠΟ ΤΟΝ ΕΟΡΤΑΣΜΟΝ ΤΗΣ ΕΡΓΑΤΙΚΗΣ ΠΡΩΤΟΜΑΓΙΑΣ

13. First of May 1938

14. Ioannis Metaxas with Dr. and Mrs. Goebbels,
September 1936

(mainly attended by the working classes). It had been estimated that 25% of the Athenian population were cinemagoers; a figure which remained consistently high in every part of the country. Many new film companies were established to deal with the importing and distribution of foreign films.[14] Contemporary newspapers advertised the new films extensively, urging people to attend the movies and benefit from this new 'seventh' art.[15] A column was dedicated to the cinema activities in Greece and abroad in most daily newspapers and magazines, while extracts like the following were often published and reflected the importance of this means of entertainment and the impact it had not only on the masses but on the elite.

> 'The frequent appearance of the Royal Prince and Princesses at various cinemas is a sign of their liberal convictions and attitudes, a fact which is being appreciated by the people. It also demonstrates their deep love for this 'seventh art.'[16]

Given the population's preference for cinema and the powerful impact that film could have on people,[17] it was inevitable that Metaxas' regime, like all other authoritarian governments of the time, would attempt to exercise full control and regulate this effective means of mass persuasion.[18]

The importance of the cinema as a means of enlightening and indoctrinating Greek people was first discussed at the Convention organised by the Panhellenic Cinema Association in May 1938 in the presence of Constantinos Kotzias, the Director of *YTT* Seferiadis, and Mrs.Koromila, on behalf of the Ministry of Education. Addressing the meeting Mr. Seferiadis conveyed to the participants Nicoloudis's strong conviction that the cinema is a most effective means of entertaining and indoctrinating the masses, and as such it should be well organised and effectively directed. Among the views and propositions expressed by the participants, the ones put forward by Mr. Economou, the editor of *'Kinimatografikos Astir,'* received the committee's special attention as they clearly demonstrated that film, if effectively used by the State, could achieve the following objectives:

1. To build and strengthen the national morale.
2. To elevate people's belief and national feelings.
3. To propagate the cultural development of tourism.
4. To develop the national economy.[19]

Similarly, an account of the government's achievements during its two years (1936-1938) in power published by the *YTT* under the heading *Cinemas,* illustrated the significance of this mass medium:

'The mobile nature of this modern art takes film to the most remote places of the country thus becoming a very popular form of mass entertainment. It is self evident that this mass medium could form, depending on its use, a very useful or destructive instrument. For this reason cinema has attracted the government's attention and significant measures have been taken to protect it.'[20]

It is evident from the above extract that the regime was determined to make use of this vital instrument and benefit from its practical nature and influential power. Indeed, upon its seizure of power the regime put into effect the first 'effective' legislative measures in cinema history.[21] Through the *YTT*, which assumed overall control of all the means of mass communication including film, it ensured the use of the cinema as a means of disseminating the regime's policies and ideologies. The Press Law which specified the duties of the *YTT* offices under paragraph 5 Article 2, stated that the surveillance of the cinema and theatre came under the Domestic Press Control Office. On 25 January 1937, after careful preparation lasting almost six months and a large amount of speculation in the film press regarding the forthcoming measures,[22] the government enacted Emergency Law 445 which replaced Law 4767 of 1930 *Peri tou Kinimatographou* (About the Cinema). This new Law introduced effective measures to ensure the overall control of the film industry. The most important ones concerned the unlimited power endowed upon the sub-Ministry of Public Security which undertook the task of safeguarding the ' proper and correct' operation of the cinema and of intervening when necessary. Article 1(a) of this law stated that the establishment and operation of a cinema within an open or closed space needed the permission of the Police authorities. In case of re-building or technical innovations, the police were to seek the opinion of the *Symvoulion* (Board) which was established under Article 2 of the Cinema Law and consisted of the Director of the Prefecture, the Head of the Police, a qualified Engineer on secondment to the police, a qualified electrician, and the Head of the Health Centre. A member representing the Panhellenic Cinema Union was allowed to be present but without the right to vote. Screening of films in unauthorised places was strictly prohibited under Article 4, unless these had the approval of the Chief of the Police and the Board. Additionally, the police had the power to intervene and prohibit the screening of a film, despite its approval by the Board, if, in their view, its projection endangered public order and safety.

The next important step was the reorganisation of the *Epitropi Kinimatographou* (Censorship Film Committee)[23] as specified by article 5 of the new Cinema Law:

'Prior to any screening and even before a film has been imported to
Greece, an application must be submitted to the *YTT* Home Press
Office, requesting approval for the importing and the screening of
the film, with an attached 'synopsis.' The Domestic Press Office will
forward those documents to the Committee (*Epitropi*) for approval.
This Committee consists of: 1) The Director of the Home Press
Office of the *YTT*; 2) the Head of the Press Surveillance Office;
3) the Head of the Department of Tourist Propaganda; 4) one
Officer from the City Police (*Astinomia),* and one High ranking
Officer from the Gendarmerie (*Chorofilaki),* both appointed by
the Sub-Ministry of Public Security, and 6) of a member of the
Panhellenic Union of Cinema without the right to vote.[24]

If the Committee was not satisfied with the 'synopsis' of the film, or felt
that it contained scenes that threatened the morality and safety of youth, or
it conveyed subversive ideas and communist propaganda, the import and
screening of such film was prohibited. It should also be pointed out that all
the above Committee members were entitled to free entrance to any cinema
they wished. In addition, every cinema company was obliged to grant free
tickets for every film performance to two low-ranking officers from the
local area police or the gendarmerie.[25]

Apart from the above legislation which reflected the regime's
determination to directly control the importation and distribution of film,
Article 8 of the same law demonstrated its will to use this mass medium in
such a way as to manipulate and control public opinion:

'Every cinema enterprise, after the screening of the programmed
film, is obliged to project the regular film material distributed by
the Office of Educational Film of the Ministry of Education, or
the film supplied free of charge by the *YTT.* These films will have
a duration of no more than fifteen minutes. Should the cinema
director fails to comply with these requirements the sub-Ministry
of Public Security will order the closing of the cinema for between
one and fifteen days'[26]

Although the above Article resembles the implementation statutes of the
Reich Cinema Law introduced in February 1934 by which 'every feature film
was to be preceded by the showing of a supporting programme consisting
of newsreels and documentaries,'[27] there is a clear differentiation. The
screening of the German propagandistic material was projected before the
regular programme, while the one provided by the Greek Authorities was

to be screened at the end of the programmed feature film. This difference is very significant as these politically biased visual presentations with the implied propagandistic message and the commentaries projected at the end of the programme ensured that the viewers left with a vivid impression of the last images. If one considers that 25 per cent of the Athenian population and a similar number of the populations of the other towns were regular cinemagoers, this meant that a great number of people shared the regime's beliefs and values as they were demonstrated through the fifteen minute compulsory screening. However, although the new Cinema Law, through the strict censorship, provided the regulations for the establishment and operation of the cinemas and the measures binding imported films, there seemed to be no provision for domestic film production. It was after the Cinema Law had been in effect for ten months that a new Emergency Law (955) of 15 November 1937[28] supplemented the existing regulations by introducing measures which concerned home productions, extending at the same time the power of the Censorship Committee . Through Article 1 of the new legislation the Censorship Committee was strengthen by the presence of two more people. One was a clerk from the management of the *YTT* Home Press Office, and the other a representative from the Educational film Office (*Grafeion Morfotikou Kinimatographou*). The final decision for the formation of the Committee rested, according to Article 2, with the *YTT*.[29] The Ministry of Education was responsible for the appointment of the Educational Office representative, while the sub-Ministry of Public Security controlled the appointments of the police officers. The new appointment of the representative of the Educational Office carried special weight as Metaxas took charge of the Ministry of Education in November 1938 after dismissing the Minister of Education Georgakopolos on the grounds of opposition and conspiracy. He stated on the occasion of the resumption of his duties:

> 'Gentlemen, be aware that my goal is to incorporate the educational issues of the Ministry of Education in to the ideology and values of the 'Fourth of August' State. Let no one have any doubts that this will be so, as my presence in this Ministry has been initiated by this necessity.'[30]

Metaxas' direct intervention through the Educational Office representative indicates the emphasis that the dictator put on this mass medium, especially, as we shall see later in this study, wherever the indoctrination of youth was concerned However, the most significant innovation of the supplementary Law came through Article 5 which introduced for the first time measures concerning domestic film production. According to this Article, prior to any shooting of films by a Greek subject or by a foreigner, permission granted by the Censorship Committee was necessary. The granting of this permission pre-supposed the submission to the *YTT* of an application which included the detailed scenario of the film, its title, the casting, the description of the technical equipment to be used and the location of the shooting. Paragraph 2 of the same Article stated that the Censorship Committee had the right to appoint one or more of its members to supervise the whole film production and the financial cost involved. This representative had the power to intervene and cancel the production. He could ignore all permissions granted by the Censors' Committee, or alternatively, prohibit the exporting of the film and even confiscate its negative if, in his opinion, its content endangered public safety or damaged the prestige of the country.

Yet, surprisingly enough, although all the above measures taken by the 'Fourth of August' regime ensured that film imports as well as home productions were under its complete control, the new Cinema Law lacked any measures that would suggest a state interest in a strategy for building up an effective film propaganda machine similar to that of other states, especially those with a similar regime. In Germany for instance, Goebbels, who believed that cinema was 'one of the most modern means of mass persuasion and therefore could not be left to its own devices,'[31] introduced several measures and forms of protectionism to ensure the dominance of German film. These measures included a system of distinction marks (*Pradikate*) which were in reality a form of negative taxation,[32] and a state-directed film criticism, both employed to boost National Socialist Films. As Welch has observed in his work *Propaganda and the German Cinema 1933-1945,* 'even for a patently bad film a positive review had to be found and politically valuable films were praised on principle.'[33] In addition, Germany's foreign film imports were discouraged by the tendency of the Censorship Office to object to them on ideological and racial grounds, as well as by the negative press reviews. Similarly Mussolini, who claimed that 'the cinema is the strongest weapon,' introduced measures to support Italian films. In 1931 he began to subsidise independent Italian film-making while he took a decisive step in eliminating the American domination of the market by taking direct control of the importation of foreign films. This led to a reduction in the number of licences granted to American films from 163 in 1938, to only 58 in 1939, which was below the Italian output of 79 for the same year.[34] One could thus expect that the 'Fourth of August' regime which adopted most of the fascist and Nazi propaganda devices and tactics, would introduce a system of a similar legislation; a system that could support Greek film productions and provide the conditions for the creation of a National Cinema.[35] This cinema would be bound up with the defence of the national culture and the values and ideologies epitomised by the regime, at the same time restricting foreign imports and the inherent danger of external influences. Furthermore, given the fact that the coming of sound put Greece in an inferior position as far as the foreign language films were concerned (the high percentage of illiteracy prevented a great number of viewers from reading the subtitles), the setting up of a fully controlled Greek film industry seemed more than encouraging for the regime. Yet, the only purely Greek feature films produced between 1937-1940 (alongside which were five artistically poor and unsuccessful films of Greek-Egyptian and Turkish production)[36] were two sound films of 1939: a *Finos-Skuras Film* sound production *To Tragoudi Tou Horismou* (The Parting Song) and an *Athens-Film* production *Nychta Choris Xemeroma* (A Night without a Dawn) which both lacked a political viewpoint and received a negative reception.[37] At the same time, regular surveys conducted by *Kinimatografikos Astir* indicated that cinema attendance was increasing, while new cinemas (among which the *Kalokerinoi* 'summer' cinemas became a revolutionary innovation of the time)[38] and new film companies importing foreign films were established. [39]

We shall at this stage make an attempt to locate the reasons which accounted for both the lack of state interest in home productions, as well as for the regime's indifference to the growing dominance of foreign film imports.

Despite the high percentage of cinema attendance, and although film was highly esteemed in most countries, especially for its influential role, it never gained such a reputation in Greece. In fact, it was considered by contemporary critics to be an inferior form of art and an 'enemy' of the theatre. An article in the pro-Metaxas newspaper *Typos* of 23 September 1937 with the title 'Gargantuas O Exolothreftis tou Ellinikou Theatrou' (Gargantua, The Exterminator of the Greek Theatre) strongly attacked the cinema and reflected the press antipathy towards it.[40] Considering that the press was, at least at the beginning, the most efficient tool of Metaxas' propaganda, one would assume that this article carried special weight, and, to an extent, disseminated the views of the government. Indeed, Metaxas was not very fond of cinema as an art expression,[41] while he strongly believed in the aesthetic and educational value of the theatre as well as in its propagandistic value. In addition, the creation of a national cinema, apart from being time-consuming, involved huge expenditure in the form of advanced technical equipment, experienced personnel and a new strategy which would enable the state-commissioned films to reach the most remote areas of the country, where the illiterate masses lived. After all, Metaxas claimed to be the leader of all people, especially of the working and agrarian class. Thus, the Greek propagandistic films, in order to be effective, had to be designed, distributed and projected in such a way as to entertain the broad masses, while at the same time promoting the government's policy. This objective involved improved artistry, official advertising, close supervision at every stage of production level, and extensive government financial support; conditions which the 'Fourth of August' regime was unable to provide. Furthermore, given the nature of the government and its austere censorship, the screening of state-commissioned feature films risked a poor attendance and a negative reception.

Foreign films on the other hand, carried with them a number of advantages which were of great value to Metaxas' regime. Heavy taxes in the form of import dues and quotas as well as an entertainment tax of 25% on the entrance price, imposed through Emergency Law 505 of 2 March 1937, brought the government great economic gains.[42] In September 1937 it was reported that the Athenian cinemas alone paid the government the sum of 4,500,000[43] in the form of entertainment tax, not to mention the heavy import dues, at a time when theatres, as we shall see in Chapter Four, were not only exempted from such taxes but were substantially subsidised by the regime. Furthermore, because the imported films were completely controlled through the Censors' Committee there was little room left for harmful foreign influences. On the contrary, by offering false promises and Hollywood pleasures to its audiences, those films identified themselves with escapism and emotionalism that prevented political thinking and questioning. In this respect, they offered great service to those regimes which wished to divert the people's attention from specific issues. This was an advantage recognised by most totalitarian regimes. For example, Stalin believed that film played an important role not only as 'a means of comprehensive educational work and communist propaganda' but also as 'a means of educating the masses in the arts and of offering them purposeful relaxation and diversion.'[44] The successful combination of these two contradictictory issues (producing effective and inexpensive domestic films that projected the regime's policies, and at the same time acquiring the financial gains ensured by films imports) came in the form of the production and the fifteen minutes obligatory projection of the state-commissioned film-documentaries and newsreels. With this formula Metaxas' regime managed to retain the great financial gains that the foreign imports ensured, and at the same time, exploited this aesthetic medium to manipulate the cinema going public.

Unlike Goebbels, who believed that 'propaganda was most effective when it was insidious, when the message was concealed within the framework of popular entertainment,'[45] Metaxas encouraged the production of newsreels and film documentaries which proclaimed in a real and direct manner his ideology and beliefs. Thus, when discussing film as a propaganda means during the Metaxas dictatorship, we deal basically with the short-length newsreels produced in great numbers during this period, most of which were compiled to form long-length film documentaries.[46]

Educational and National Youth Film Propaganda

By 1938 Metaxas' regime was well established. His position had been substantially secured and all signs of opposition had been eliminated.[47] His economic and social policies appeared to have the people's consent, or at least their tolerance, and his ideology regarding the 'regeneration of Greece' and the 'Third Greek Civilisation' had been skilfully projected, so that it could appear 'as a coherent system.'[48] Fully aware of his growing dominance, Metaxas wrote in his diary on 30 December 1938:

> 'This year, during which we have suffered conspiracies at the hands of the political parties as well as the Palace, has now ended.[49] Their hatred and envy resulted in their failure. They are the losers, I am the winner. The gains are all mine. The people are with me, and so is the youth.'[50]

In November 1938, after a long and bitter confrontation with Georgako-poulos, the Minister of Education, which ended in Georgakopoulos' dismissal,[51] Metaxas assumed personal control of the Ministry of Education and ensured that the educational system was not only subordinated to the ideology of the regime through *EON*, but often replaced by it: 'The Organisation, he emphatically proclaimed in January 1939, constitutes a primary necessity and a vital supplement to education; and the school should in fact be grateful to the Organisation.'[52] The support and protection of *EON* became Metaxas' imperative aspiration and objective. In his speech at the first congress of *EON* on January 1939 and in the presence of the Crown Prince Paul as well as of both Princess Frederica and Princess Irene, Metaxas referred to the Organisation's sacrifices and struggle to project and safeguard the nation's supreme ideas, and praised its eventual victory against the forces of opposition.[53]

> 'At this moment the opposition has, to a great extent, been eliminated and His Majesty the Crown Prince has become Head of the Organisation and Chief General, while I have assumed control of the Ministry of Education. The time has thus come for the State

to participate in your struggle with all its power and authority and complete what the Organisation with its own means has so far accomplished.[54]

This State intervention took several forms and included the control and exploitation of the cinema. Film propaganda in schools and *EON* Centres became a significant device for the moulding and indoctrination of the Greek Youth. Under a complicated organisational network, similar to that of Nazi Germany,[55] which included the Ministry of Education, *YTT*, the sub-Ministry of Public Security, the Athens Governing Office[56] and *EON*'s III Office, all of which were under the strict surveillance of Ioannis Metaxas, film propaganda ensured that there was no room left for young people wishing to avoid indoctrination.

The use of educational and cultural films in schools had been encouraged prior to the 'Fourth of August' regime with the statutes introduced on 15 September 1935 regarding the formation of the *Grafeion Morfotikou Kinimatographou* (Educational Film Office) under the authority of the Ministry of Education and Religion. The duties of this office were to regulate the production, and mainly, the distribution of educational films and secure the technical means for their projection.[57] On 3 June 1939 through Emergency Law 1779, the Department of Fine Arts responsible for the directorate of Letters took over responsibility for the theatre and the cinema, and the Educational Film Office also came under its control. The director of this Department became Costis Bastias, a faithful supporter and devoted friend of Metaxas.[58] Yet, the problems inherent in the projection of those films in schools due to the lack of projectors (not to mention the lack of schools themselves)[59]and the high cost of purchasing them (the price of each projector came to eight thousand drachmas),[60] restricted the screening of educational films to a very limited number and only in big towns. After a survey made by *EON* officials, it was reported that in May 1939 only three hundred schools in the whole country were equipped with such projectors and the relevant film.[61] It was as late as 14 December 1939 and in the light of the necessity to indoctrinate the young, that by order of the Ministry of Education, a resolution was signed 'for the purchase of new film projectors for the screening of educational and cultural films which would be distributed to every school in the country.'[62]

In this technical and economic vacuum for the effective use of film as a propaganda medium, *EON* was to play a crucial role not only in producing the films, but also in financing their projection in most parts of the country. The following quotation from a recommendation made by the *EON* propaganda officials in 1939 illustrates the above:

'Apart from the general filming activities of *EON*, the Office should pursue the production of educational films as they represent the most crucial means of modern indoctrination. Yet, because the cost of these productions is a deterrent, we suggest the rental of such films. In the most remote places where cinema attendance is non-existent the screening of these films could be undertaken by the *EON* regional offices. In other words, since the technical and financial means needed for a well established state-cinema industry are still unavailable, *EON* will undertake the expense involved for such an enterprise. Furthermore, the Ministry of Education must order the schools which possess such projectors to let the Organisation avail itself of those projectors so that the young *EON* members might be entertained and effectively enlightened.'[63]

With the provision of all schools with the sufficient number of projectors on the one hand, and the financial and technical support of the *EON* officials on the other, the regime hoped to ensure the efficient distribution and projection of the state-controlled films, which, under a direct or skilfully disguised propaganda, disseminated its ideology. Even in the cases where the films lacked direct propagandistic value, the result was always the desired one as the commentator, usually being the teacher or a person entrusted with the special 'job', made sure that the government's cultural and political outlook was successfully conveyed.[64]

The Cinema Law 445 of 20 January 1937 which introduced the first serious regulations on film in Greece, defined the role that film would have on young people, setting out at the same time its limitations. The most significant provisions of this nature were the restrictions controlling the attendance of under-aged cinema-viewers. Article 6 of the Cinema Law clearly stated:

1. 'The City Police with the consent of the Censorship Committee have the right to categorise films as unsuitable for the under aged. Under-aged are considered young people under the age of fourteen.

2. Films suitable for the young are the films that project works of art, cities, landscapes, historical scenes, traditions of various nations, natural history, scientific experiments, agrarian works, the establishment of industries, as well as films that contain material which supports and raises morale, the family, heroic achievements, the safeguarding of public health, as well as films that inspire goodness and courage.'[65]

Paragraph 4 of Article 9 of the same legislation specified that for cities which have more that 10,000 inhabitants the City Police should appoint a clerk (recommended and paid by the Owner of the cinema), for the implementation of the regulations concerning the under-aged. Failure to comply with the regulations resulted in one to six months imprisonment for the person assigned to safeguard those. The same punishment was inflicted on the parents or guardians who permitted their children to enter the cinema and watch a film of an unsuitable nature.[66]

Although the projection of cultural films in schools played a significant role in the education and enlightenment of children, it was the propaganda films produced by *EON* and shown to its members and to the Greek population as a whole, that fulfilled the government's expectations. By August 1939 *EON* had produced sixteen such films and had acquired seventy five new projectors to ensure their effective screening. According to a survey carried out by the *YTT* during the year 1939, 462 screenings of such films, which projected the life and activities of the *EON* members, took place.[67] These productions came in the form of documentary films which disseminated the themes associated with the regime's propaganda, notably charismatic leadership, unity, solidarity and the safeguarding of the monarchy, exemplifying at the same time the values of the Organisation. These values: *Vasilefs, Patris. Thriskeia, Oikogeneia, Anagennisis Tis Ellados* (King, Motherland, Religion, Family, Regeneration of Greece) were set by Metaxas during the first congress of *EON* on 5 January 1939 and were not 'negotiable,' nor even open to discussion. On the contrary, as Maniadakis assured the *EON* members, all the necessary measures had been taken to preserve those ideals at any cost:

> 'We are determined to complete the regeneration of our Country. The decision is final and no force or opposition can prevent this(...) We are the guardians of the nation and we are determined to clear it up from all the 'pests' and 'weeds.' When you are ready, and have realised deep in your hearts the importance of your mission and your historical obligations, this nation will be handed over to you in a well-arranged, disciplined and fertile condition.'[68]

Eventually, the propaganda machine, through the production and projection of educational and enlightening films, was hoping to reach the whole of the young population. The production and promotion of these films was assigned to what was known as the *Tmima E, or Kallitechnikon Tmima* (Section E or Cultural Department), incorporated into the administration of the III Office. This office was entrusted with the national, political and educational youth propaganda through all forms of political, social and cultural expressions.[69]

The task of entertaining the members of the Organisation and the successful projection of all forms of culture in which film played a crucial part, was undertaken, according to article 31 of the Statutes of the Organisation, by the *Diefthinsis Psichagogias* (Directive of Entertainment) to *EON*.[70]

The importance of the cinema as a vital instrument of propaganda was highlighted in the proposals submitted to the Organisation's Committee by the Cultural Department on 20 May 1939 under the heading *Kinimatographos ke EON* (Cinema and *EON*):

> 'As we are all aware, indoctrination by means of film and photographs, wherever those were employed, was extremely successful. Because of the importance of such an outcome *EON* established the *Kallitechnikon Tmima* incorporated within the III Office, which included the Cinema and Photography Department for the overall administration of film and photography.' [71]

This department was responsible for securing finance for the purchase of mobile projectors and for creating the conditions for the production of effective film-documentaries and newsreels.[72] This finance was covered partly from the *EON* central administration by the appropriation of a sum in the yearly budget, and partly, from a small contribution in the form of Phalangite dues *(Phalagosimo)*[73] paid by each *EON* member on special performances. In certain cases a lump-sum of 500 to 1000 drachmas was paid by the periphery offices to the Central Administration for the supply of each film.[74] According to the recommendations of the *EON* officials submitted in 1939, the Organisation was capable, under a carefully planned scheme, of ensuring the supply of a sufficient number of projectors and documentary films for every *EON* recreation centre in the course of three years.[75] These films were distributed in collaboration with the Regional Party Centres, on an exchange basis and special care was taken that they reached the most remote towns and villages.[76] The regime's propaganda ensured, through orders and strict recommendations issued by the III Office, that these films were met with a warm and enthusiastic reception by the viewers.[77] The following extract illustrates the effort put in by the propaganda machine to ensure such a reception:

> 'The performance of an important film took place in the cinemas in recent days. The importance of this film lies within the fact that it was dedicated to *EON* and presented our Chief addressing members of the Organisation in Kilkis. All people who watched the film were moved by the image of a Chief who, despite his

heavy State programme, has time to express his love and affection towards the Greek youth. Therefore, youth of the whole country must not only attend this film in the cities and places where it is being projected, but, most importantly, must express, during the screening, their love, gratitude and faith owed to him, with enthusiastic and delirious manifestations.' [78]

Because most film productions were silent, *EON* members were trained, in the absence of 'suitable' teachers, to enlighten the young viewers and comment on the context of the films which were screened in schools, in the *EON*'s recreation centres, or alternatively in private cinema halls 'rented' for a special performance.[79] It was the objective of the Organisation that propaganda films should be shown to the Greek youth at least once a week.[80] Furthermore, the Cineak cinemas,[81] where most 'educational' films were shown, were extensively advertised in the government controlled press and in posters. One of those depicted a father holding his two small children in front of a Cineak entrance while the caption read: 'It is the obligation of every parent to take their children to an educational programme. Such programmes are always shown in the Cineak cinemas.' [82]

In view of the cinema's great propagandistic significance the regime felt the need to encourage youth to become more frequent cinema-goers, because through the fifteen minutes compulsory state-film projection, this potential audience would be introduced to and convinced of the regime's supreme ideology. To further this goal certain measures were initiated which ensured that young members could attend the cinema as often as they wished. A free entry to the cinemas of the country was granted to all youth, provided they were members of *EON* and produced the Free Pass issued by the III Office and supplied to them by the Administration Office. The objective behind this allowance was twofold: to attract as many children to the cinema as possible, and at the same time ensure their enrolment in the Organisation. The following account from an *EON* member is more than illustrative of the effectiveness of the regime's 'free tickets' strategy:

> 'I was tempted right from the beginning to join the Organisation, when I realised that through *EON* I could not only carry out the most significant hobbies of the time; that is the cinema, football, and out of-school reading practice but most importantly, I would do so free of charge.'[83]

Often, this free ticket allowance caused great problems to the persons concerned. Cinema Owners were constantly faced with aggressive *EON* members demanding a free entry without possessing their free pass. Furthermore, clashes among *EON* members often took place in an attempt to secure more free tickets from the central offices. Teachers on the other hand were not very happy with the situation, as pupils and students often left school to attend the cinema.[84] Besides, free of charge cinema attendance did not necessarily ensure the young viewer's absorption of the regime's ideology projected through the state-commissioned films. There was always the risk of an early departure at the end of the feature film, as the compulsory screening of the documentaries and newsreels shown at the end of the programme did not always consist of samples of artistry but of boring and uninteresting productions.[85] The 'damaging' influence of a feature film was thus ever-present. In an attempt to eliminate this possibility the *EON* officials urged young people to avoid feature films altogether (especially those of a 'romantic' and adventurous nature) and, instead, attend the state-commissioned productions screened in the specially designated areas like the central cinemas chosen for *EON* film performances, and the Organisation's recreation centres:[86]

> 'We believe that the cinema, although we all like it, causes a kind of weariness, confusion and a neurotic emotion. Of course what we mean here is our concern for the usual films of romance and adventure and not for the educational films of history and geography which on the contrary, you should watch regularly.'[87]

A similar piece of advice was given to the girls through *E Neolea* under the heading 'Maskarilikia' (Masquerade) which pointed out the harmful effects of foreign films:

> 'Indeed, it is too ridiculous for a girl of our present heroic days to want to copy the cinema stars who change hair colour and appearances all the time. The Greek woman must remain simple and natural, and must safeguard the pure and true inner and outer self.'[88]

This short extract provides an interesting example of the regime's attitude towards young Greek women but, at the same time, demonstrates the regime's concern about the influence that film might have on young people.

EON Films - Themes and Representation

Most of the state-commissioned films produced to project the ideology of the regime contained at least one sequence devoted to the Metaxas Youth.

However, the first films strictly dealing with *EON* issues were produced by
the Cultural Department between 1938 - 1940 and were a compilation of
a series of very short silent newsreels and documentaries of 34 mm, under
the general title *EON Films*. These films promoted the themes of *EON* and
subsequently those of the regime.

One of those films (a 2.5 minute newsreel) *E Proti Orkomosia ton
Melon tis EON* (*EON*'s First Oath-Taking) which gave the first 'flavour' of
the grandeur of the new Organisation, was shot during the first ceremonial
Oath-Taking of the five hundred *EON* boys and three hundred *EON* girls
on 31 December 1937.[89]

The film opens with an impressive parade of young men and
women dressed in their uniforms, marching in a close, in-line formation in
a proud and self-confident manner. The parade passes in front of Metaxas
who is standing at the top of the stairs in front of the back entrance of
the *Vouli* (Parliament Building). The location chosen for the occasion is
of special significance. Although the ceremony could have taken place
in the Athens Stadium (Metaxas' favourite place for ceremonies and for
most *EON* forthcoming parades), or, alternatively, at the entrance of
Athens University (as these first parading *EON* members were mainly
university students), the regime chose instead the Back Court of the
Parliament Building. The implied message conveyed by this choice and the
intended association, or rather the dissociation, of *EON* with the 'cradle'
of democracy (The Parliament Building) is more than obvious. Metaxas'
regime abolished democracy on 4 August 1936, dissolved Parliament and
launched a ruthless war against parliamentarism.

The location of this official ceremony chosen by the regime and
depicted by the state controlled camera connoted that everything the
Parliament as an institution represented for democracy in the past was now
over. Instead, its place had been taken up by another institution, that of
EON, which represented the present political situation, that of the 'Fourth of
August' State and embodied its objectives and future aspirations. 'You ought
to be aware,' Metaxas stated, 'that *EON* is a State Institution. An Institution
upon which I have entrusted my most supreme hopes and aspirations for
the future.'[90] The sequence of events that follow in the film are dominated
by the oath-taking procedure. The *EON* leader Alexandros Kanellopoulos,
who stands close to Metaxas, addresses the young men and women and
speaks of the importance of that moment and the special significance of the
forthcoming oath to the King, the Chief and the Nation:[91]

> 'From the moment you take this Greek Oath (*par excellence*) you
> will become soldiers of the Greek ideals, and guardians of the

'Fourth of August' State ideals. However, these two ideals are not different, but constitute the same Grand Ideal: thus **Believe, Fight, Win**.' [92]

Yet, an important point should be stressed here; neither the King nor the Crown Prince are depicted in the film. It was a year after this ceremony that Crown Prince Paul was persuaded to enter the Organisation and become 'its most precious and beloved Chief.'[93]

The scene that follows depicts the first *EON* member who steps forward, raises his hand in the fascist manner, salutes Metaxas and receives from him the flag of the Organisation.[94] The rest are lined up waiting for Metaxas' inspection. He walks down with Kanellopoulos at his side, greets the young women first, then the young men and speaks to each one separately. The film ends with the parade leaving, while Metaxas at the top of the stairs raises his hat in a gesture of salutation. Meanwhile, the camera focuses on the young women and men marching triumphantly in a straight upward posture. Then, the camera moves in to close-up, starting from the strong young bodies which radiate health and energy, to the face of a young girl and, as a contrast, to that of a young man; shots of beautiful and determined faces, eyes looking straight up, right into the future with aspiration and anticipation. The strong bodies and the beautiful faces depicted are equally proud and equally significant. After all the concept of a healthy and strong young generation was a most essential component of the 'regeneration of Greece' and Metaxas made sure that the young people were repeatedly reminded of this. 'We want you to grow strong and healthy in your bodies.' he said to them. 'You cannot be part of a family and have children when your bodies are weak and sick;' bear in mind that our Nation's ideal was not only to produce great minds and spirits but beautiful and strong bodies as well.'[95] This harmonious coexistence of Greek Youth within the Organisation presupposed the equality of class and gender which the regime preached, and, to a great extent, accomplished. Metaxas said to them in June 1940: 'You know that within the Organisation we have managed to accomplish the equality of all Greek men and women.'[96] The last scene of the film depicts the hoisted flag being proudly carried away by an *EON* member while Metaxas smiles deeply contented.

The second production celebrating The Metaxas Youth is the documentary film *To Stratopedon EON Ioannis Metaxas* (*EON* Camp *Ioannis Metaxas*).[97] This very short (1.5 minute) film, was shot by *Novak Co.* and gives an insight into the first *EON* Camp, inaugurated by Metaxas on 9 June 1938, and the activities of its inhabitants.

The camp, located at Zouberi, a place outside Athens, was a mixed training camp highly esteemed by Metaxas who visited it very often.[98]

The purpose behind the production of the film *To Stratopedon EON Ioannis Metaxas* was twofold: apart from obviously being conceived as a tribute to the founder of the camp, it also attempted to convince the parents, and society at large, of the ideal conditions under which the *EON* members lived and trained while camping.[99] It also promoted concepts like solidarity, comradeship, discipline and commitment. Metaxas' vision was the creation of a youth force which was physically and mentally fit, disciplined, courageous and committed to the cause of the nation.

The opening sequence of the film introduces us to a well organised march by male *EON* trumpeters. Although the march seems to be a part of an every-day routine activity, it is very well organised and underlines the endeavours of the propaganda machine to present an idealistic picture of a disciplined[100] and efficiently trained force.[101]

The next scene opens with the ceremonial hoisting of the *EON* flag which dominates the screen. The design of the Flag was defined by article 24 of the *Esoterikos Organismos Esoterikis Ypiresias EON* (Internal Regulations of EON).[102] It was the Greek Flag which bore in the middle the emblem of the Organisation. The emblem consisted of the double *Minoan Axe*, circled by a laurel wreath.[103] In the top left hand corner the flag bore the Royal Crown and diagonally opposite the number four which represented the historical date of the 'Fourth of August' State.[104] The film continues with the presentation of one *EON* member who proudly holds up the swinging flag of the Organisation, while Metaxas is depicted walking under it. This mode of representation was intended to bring the three protagonistic elements, that is *Leader-Flag-Youth,* close together and at the same time to reinforce their intrinsic link.[105] As we shall see later in other documentary newsreels, the zooming of the camera on icons like the emblem of the 'Fourth of August' regime,[106] the *EON* uniforms, but above all the flag, forms a constantly repeated sequence. Metaxas, like Hitler and Goebbels,[107] strongly believed in the symbolic attachment to specific images, especially that of the flag; a belief which he conveyed to the school children of Chania on the occasion of the *Imera Tis Simaias* (Flag Day) celebration on 7 November 1936, when he stated:

> 'The Flag that you are now holding is not a piece of cloth attached to a mast. It is the symbol of our Nation; is the Nation itself. In church you received the *Corpus Christi* through the Holy Communion; similarly, through this piece of cloth which has been entrusted to you, you hold in your hands the whole of the Nation; the whole of Greece.'[108]

The importance of the symbols acknowledged by the regime was also reflected in the enactment of Emergency Law 447, passed in January 1937 which determined the tributes and honours that should be paid to symbols like the Flag, the National Anthem and every other national symbol.[109]

In the following sequence the hoisting of the flag comes to an end, while the camera zooms in to reveal a line of well presented children in uniforms. The next scene opens with Metaxas surrounded by a large group of excited young children and looking at a small construction site where he picks up a trowel. He fills it with cement and with the help of children he participates in the building process. This participation is captured by the camera in a prolonged sequence and Metaxas, aware of the importance of this 'casual' and 'spontaneous' projected image, looks at the camera instead of the trowel. This scene is of special significance and conveys a twofold message: the participation of the dictator in the building work has an allegorical meaning and connotes the forthcoming reconstruction of a New Greece. This reconstruction necessitated the participation of Ioannis Metaxas and that of *EON* which constituted a force totally devoted to the regime and the principles of the New State. 'It is of vital importance, he claimed in November 1936, 'that we restrict the boundaries of our individuality to a very limited circle and subject ourselves to the discipline of the State.'[110] The scene was also intended to reveal a sense of familiarity and a special bond between the Chief and the children. The theme of the 'Father of the Nation,' an essential concept of the leadership cult, was thus projected. Metaxas was not a distant leader and a vague unapproachable image for his 'beloved children,'[111] but an active and very human *Megas Kyvernitis* who introduced them to supreme ideals, new experiences and constructive activities. The sequences that follow reveal young children walking and running, and others taking the *EON* Oath or smiling at the camera. Young girls are dancing folk dances while others are posing for a photograph. All these countless activities fed the egos of young people who longed for recognition and action. This was something which had been recognised long before by Adolf Hitler when he wrote: 'In general young people are attracted to anything that is fast-paced, exciting or sensational which reflects the growing need to be active and seek new experiences that is characteristic of this age group.'[112] This action which takes place in a natural, unspoiled environment (clear sky, open space, trees) captured by the camera, is carried out in groups, never individually. The overall impression is that of unity and disciplined 'freedom;'[113] of creative leisure and the sense of belonging to a totality that makes children content and active. In April 1939 the Dictator said to the people of Kalamata: 'I took your girls and your boys and I formed a totality which I incorporated into a State Institution vital for the society and the Nation.'[114] According to Metaxas the 'Fourth of August' ideology was based on the concept of the 'organised national mass.' The New State was considered 'a living organism' which had its own independent will and interests, and because it formed a homogenous whole, it composed the nation. Therefore, he envisaged youth, and the Greek population at large, as a homogenous unit which constituted a living component of the new National State.[115] This unified whole believed in the Greek ideals (captured by the camera in the form of *Oath-Flag-Uniform*) and was effectively trained to preserve and safeguard them. Metaxas emphasised his faith in this in his speech to *EON* on 24 April 1939 when he stated:

> 'You are born and bred a native of the 'Fourth of August' State and you must always cherish deep into your heart the ideals of that State. These ideals are the ideals that make us proud; the Greek Ideals (...) and you must be prepared to die for them.'[116]

This unified totality, a crucial component of the regime's ideology, and a repeated theme in the film propaganda, was accomplished through a number of devices which proved very successful. For the first time in Greek history boys and girls from different social classes were sharing the same food, the same entertainment and the same activities:[117] Rich and poor alike enjoyed the same treatment and any existing class differences were eliminated by the same uniform and the cross-class membership. The great social mission of the uniform was stressed by Metaxas when he spoke to the parents and teachers on 25 October 1939, stating: 'In *EON* there is no room for differences. All children wear the same uniform and are dressed alike: even the material used must be the same.'[118] Thus uniform became a very significant feature in the propaganda machine and served a twofold purpose: it eliminated all social differences and projected the image of a unified youth force harmoniously coexisting, and functioned as a psychological 'bait' for most children deprived of such 'luxuries.' The following memoir from a young *EON* member is more than explicit:

> 'The uniforms had something of the magic of the cinema, starched and magnificent. You can imagine what it is like to watch someone walk with squeaky shoes on when you have no shoes at all, to walk with a starched shirt on in a village full of shacks, because there were only shacks at the time, not houses. Those young men you watched and you envied.'[119]

Additionally, the *EON* uniform provided its young members with an authority and in many cases the same uniform was used to justify a rebellious attitude towards figures of authority such as parents and teachers. It was often claimed that this exceeded a normal rebellious attitude and reached threatening dimensions. In fact it has been argued that the children were asked by the Organisation to spy on their parents. However, this was denied by Metaxas who wrote in his diary on 31 December 1938: 'On top of everything else the King asked Papagos[120] if it was true that the *EON* children are spying on their parents. This information is mere slander.'[121] However, as the memoir of an *EON* member given below illustrates, the Organisation functioned as a form of counter authority:

> '*EON* provided me with a freedom and authority that enabled me to neglect school reading. I had just to inform my teacher that I was an *EON* member and the teacher was deprived of any authority to question my action. On Sundays and Wednesdays we were given special lessons and training.'[122]

The importance of the uniform was greatly appreciated by the *EON* propagandists, who took great care to ensure that all members possessed one. Extravagant amounts of money were squandered for the purchase of uniforms[123] and the people were expected to pay a large part of it.[124]

In the following sequence the camera continues to depict contented children full of energy and creative activity away from the familiar home and school environment. The film ends with the screen filled with the image of a group of smiling uniformed children. Most of these activities presented in the film had the overwhelming support and guidance in the form of the ever-watching presence of the beloved *Father* Ioannis Metaxas. To emphasise the 'Father of all children' theme projected by the film, hundreds of photos were produced by the Organisation which depicted Metaxas being surrounded by young *EON* members.[125]

The documentary-newsreel *To Stratopedon EON Ioannis Metaxas* was one of the first films which projected the ideals of a unified harmonious community and the theme of charismatic leadership. To achieve the successful dissemination and reception of these ideals the propaganda machine ensured that the film was extensively advertised:

> 'The enthusiasm showed by the viewers who watched the performance of *To Stratopedon EON Ioannis Metaxa* film in the cinemas, proves that the *EON* institution has been accepted by everybody. The opening of the film was welcomed by the audience with prolonged applause and became the subject of delirious enthusiasm. The film has proved that *EON* has already begun to

pay back what the Great Chief has invested in and expected from them.' [126]

To facilitate the propagation of the themes projected through *To Stratopedon EON Ioannis Metaxas* the film was shown every afternoon in the Zapeion Pavilion where the first *EON* exhibition was organised. *E Neolea* urged people to visit the exhibition and 'attend with the same admittance ticket the excellent films produced by *EON*, especially *To Stratopedon EON Ioannis Metaxas.*' [127]

Another small documentary film was the *Panellinioi Athletikoi Agones EON* (Panhellenic Athletic Games of *EON*),[128] which featured the athletic games of *EON* in the Athens Stadium in May 1939 and promoted the image of a strong healthy youth, and that of a unified totality.[129] According to *YTT*, 1,380 athletic events were organised all over the country during 1938 involving 200,000 young people.[130] By order of Kanellopoulos every *EON* division was to form an athletic team and the participation of its members became compulsory,[131] while priority was given to physical training and sports activities at the expense of academic education.

Metaxas, a fervent advocate of the athletic spirit, after becoming Chief of the Nation, the First Peasant, and the First Worker, also acquired the title of the First Athlete (*Protos Athlitis*) in December 1938. To underline this new mission and the significant part that athletics was to play in the renaissance of the nation, Constantinos Kotzias (ex Chief of the Athletics), stated on 31 December 1938:

> 'The steering wheel of Greek athletics is now in the hands of our Chief. For the first time in Greek history a Prime Minister will lead athletics, and for the first time athletics will be led by a Prime Minister.'[132]

The nation's future regeneration required strong and healthy young people and athletics was seen as the essential means to achieve this end.[133] As early as September 1936, Metaxas, in a interview with a correspondent of the French newspaper *Paris Echo,* stated:

> 'I want a strong and healthy Youth; an athletic Youth. The blood needs occasional revitalisation. Today athletics remain the only means to revitalise the blood: <u>Athletics for everybody'</u>[134]

To achieve this end and ensure the dissemination of the athletic ideal the regime's propaganda launched a series of athletic events, inaugurated several athletic centres[135] and produced speeches by Metaxas and High Government officials. Additionally, special screenings of the German film *Olympiade*[136] took place in the *EON*'s cultural centres and the Cineak cinema, while visits of the German Minister of Sports underlined the significance of the events.[137]

Panellinioi Athletikoi Agones EON, which can be seen as a hymn to the athletic ideal and a tribute to Greek youth, opens with a panoramic view of a full Stadium. A crowd of men, women and children are awaiting something with anticipation. The scene that follows depicts Metaxas entering the Stadium followed by the Government officials. Kanellopoulos welcomes Metaxas with a fascist salute, bows in a gesture of great admiration and devotion,[138] and walks with him towards the sitting platform. A written account of this grandiose entrance and the atmosphere it generated, found in an article in *E Neolea,* is an example of the propaganda machine's effort to convey an atmosphere of delirious enthusiasm and adulation:

> 'At exactly 4.10 P.M. the Chief arrived. The Head of the Organisation Kanellopoulos rushed to welcome him at the Propylaea. Meanwhile, the young phalangites and spectators of every age and gender stood up, and electrified by the appearance of the *Ethnikos Kyvernitis*, became frenzied with enthusiasm. The short walk of the Chief from the Propylaea towards the platform was a course of triumph as the Stadium was filled throughout by a voice that echoed rhythmically: *Father-Father-Father.* The whole place was practically shaken by the delirious acclamations and the expressions of devotion: From the eyes of the *Father,* who was overcome with emotion, flowed tears of joy: his children had acknowledged and appreciated everything he had done for them, and proved worthy of his aspirations and dreams embodied in their presence.' [139]

The following scene reveals the arrival of the Crown Prince and his wife Princess Frederica walking towards the platform while the camera focuses again on the over-crowded Stadium. The camera pans over large groups of spectators and uniformed *EON* members who are depicted saluting and applauding with great enthusiasm. Hundreds of young men and women in their athletic costumes with the *EON* emblem printed on the front of their white shirts, march proudly in front of Metaxas and take up their position.[140] The screen is filled with slim young men and women in circles and in lines performing their athletic exercises, keeping in step with each other. The concept of a strong healthy body linked with a lofty spirit, which embodied the revival of the ancient athletic model, was the essential component of the supreme ideal and the repeated theme in the regime's propaganda; the 'regeneration of Greece.'[141]

According to Metaxas, a vital precondition was essential for achieving this: that of anti-individualism: 'The ancient athletic ideal, he told the athletes, 'reached the heights of eternal glory because its objective was not to create champions through the athletic events, but to prepare young people to envisage the promotion and defence of the Nation's supreme ideals.'[142] Thus the first duty of each young member was not to pursue prizes for himself, but to merge into the whole.[143] The best way to achieve this was through the participation in the athletic games and the suppression of his own ambition to be a champion, in favour of the promotion of the ideal of a unified harmonious totality, rather than individuality. This issue was highlighted by Metaxas in his speech to the teachers on 14 June 1937:

> 'I was very pleased to have watched the children's performance during the athletic games. Surely, we are individuals but if the individuals do not constitute a totality they are not worthy of anything. The totality must be comprised of individuals who are united by solidarity and comradeship in such a way that they form one part. For this reason the athletic games are of special significance and provide the conditions for such unity.'[144]

The next scene depicts hundreds of young *EON* members receiving the winning prizes from the Crown Prince and Kanellopoulos, who was in charge of the whole operation. The smiling leader had much to feel proud of; after all, it was he who above all embodied the ancient athletic ideal expressed by the song; 'You are a true Spartan in the game; a Champion, a Leader, and a Phivos.'[145] With his living example and his guidance, but above all with the life-giving presence of the First Athlete Ioannis Metaxas, Kanellopoulos inculcated the ancient and sacred Olympian ideals into the *EON* athletes.[146] The film ends with the last scene revealing a panoramic view of a crowded Stadium and looking down at the sports arena where hundreds of healthy young people are demonstrating their athletic games.

These films as well as many others dealing with *EON* issues[147] destined basically for youth consumption were also shown to parental gatherings in an effort to convince them of the advantages of the Organisation and achieve a large scale youth subscription. Yet because of the limited technical and financial means, most of the short length documentaries which depicted the physical education of youth had none of the grandiose artistry of foreign films like *Olympiade* and *Olympia*. They were artistically poor imitations which bored the spectators, especially the

EON members who were often forced to attend films of poor artistic value and with a dubious outcome. In fact *EON* officials from the Cultural Department were very sceptical of the real effect these films had on the children. These doubts, as well as some recommendation for improvements, were submitted by the III Office to the *EON* Central Administration:

'Until today, the Department, due to great financial and technical problems, has been restricted to producing a few promotional films like *To Stratopedo Ioannis Metaxas,* the *Panellinioi Athletkoi Agones EON* and a few others dealing with the activities of the Organisation, as well as the shooting of 1,700 photographs concerning the life of the various *EON* departments. In order to ensure that *EON* 's goals are fulfilled, we suggest that the production of films should not be restricted to those with historical subjects or of an advertising nature but to films with an educational and enlightening context focusing on subjects that can influence the young, and the viewers in general. The topic of those films should be drawn from films with a patriotic or epic contexts and other elevating subjects based on specially written scripts. At least two or three sound films of this kind should be produced every year.'[148]

It can be seen from the above extract that the educational films supplied by the Educational Film Office were to be replaced by the ones produced by *EON*.

Another *EON* film which promoted the image of the Organisation but at the same time projected one of the most essential components in Metaxas' manipulating process, that of monarchy, was the 2 minute newsreel *E Paradosis Ton Simaion Eis tous Phalagitas Tis EON* (The Handing over of the Flags to *EON* Phalangites). The film 'which was commissioned and filmed by the relevant services of the *YTT*'[149] dealt with the royal support granted to the Organisation by members of the Court.[150] On 11 December 1938 Crown Prince Paul, who had been appointed General in Chief, with his wife Princess Frederica, who had been appointed honorary Commander General of the *EON* girls and Princess Irene, who was granted the title of Inspector General,[151] accompanied the Prime Minister to Pedion Tou Areos where a grandiose gathering of 58,000 *EON* members were waiting to greet their new General in Chief and to receive the Organisations' flags.[152]

The opening sequence reveals a large crowd waiting with excitement and anticipation, while a parade of cars is led by the one carrying the Premier. Metaxas with his familiar looks (black suit, his hat and his glasses), is received by Kanellopoulos. He walks through lines of hundreds of young *EON* members who are saluting. The crowds are cheering with enthusiasm while the camera zooms at a billowing *EON* Flag which fills up the whole screen. Thence the camera moves in to capture the arrival of the Crown Prince Paul who is accompanied by his wife Princess Frederica and Princess Irene. Metaxas follows just behind the Crown Prince, while the camera focuses on large groups of people dressed in their best clothes, a presentation which underlines and reinforces the importance of the ceremony. Repeated scenes (the result of skilful editing) of cheering and applauding crowds inter-link with grandiose *EON* parades which culminate in the depiction of Metaxas standing next to the Crown Prince. The scenes projected are intended to convey a sense of familiarity and radiate an atmosphere of national euphoria which will convince the viewer that he is participating in what seems to be a historical event of special significance. According to Welch in his study of the Nazi Cinema: 'the success of the newsreel depends on the skill of the editor in selecting and manipulating an intensive linkage of moving pictures in order to create what was believed to be a 'factual' reportage of reality.'[153] The following sequence presents the actual ceremony of the Flag presentation. The smiling Crown Prince stands up and hands over the Division flags to the first *EON* member,[154] while the camera zooms in to focus on the filmmaker Joseph Hepp in the background whilst he was capturing the important events with his camera. This scene could either be a 'slip' of the camera of no special significance, or alternatively it could imply that what the audience were viewing was simply the result of a good cameraman's work, at the same time reinforcing the importance of the cinema as a propaganda instrument. As observed by Welch, 'the importance of the newsreel was that it offered the propagandist all the advantage of a modern communication medium in that it was topical, periodical and universal. Its success depended on the ability of the cameramen to capture topical and exciting events.'[155]

The following scene presents Princess Frederica smiling and handing the flag over to a young female member of *EON*. [156] This scene also depicts a church representative, possibly the Archbishop, standing next to Princess Frederica. At this point it should be mentioned that religion constituted a very important component of the regime's ideology and it was strongly upheld by Metaxas, who claimed that '*EON* is a Christian Organisation, because our Nation is intrinsically linked with the Greek Orthodoxy.'[157] Religion was one of the regime's goals as these were defined by him in his speech delivered to *EON* members on 5 January 1939 (*King, Fatherland, Religion, Family, Regeneration of Greece*), but it was a goal 'assigned to a subordinate place in the scale of priorities.'[158] and thus not a central and repeated image in the film propaganda process. The next scene depicts Metaxas handing over to Princesses Frederica and Irene one uniform set each, on behalf of *EON*. This scene, apart from presenting a gesture of courtesy, was also intended to connote the complete and irrevocable identification of the princesses with the Organisation. In the final sequences the camera, in repeated shots of the same scene (a montage trick) depicts large *EON* parades, zooming in on their uniforms and their raised hands, while the flags proliferate throughout the ceremony. The cheering crowds, the majestic cars in motion, the grandiose parades and the symbols depicted as well as the open horizon and the trees in the background, all seem to radiate the importance of this special event. This was indeed a grand occasion for the Premier. After two and a half years of haunting doubts[159] concerning the Crown Prince's attitude towards the Organisation, Metaxas finally won his full support and a few months later on 21 June 1939, the Boy Scouts were incorporated into *EON* by the enactment of Emergency Law 1798.[160] This film was intended to demonstrate this 'triumphal victory.' It was the undeniable proof of the inextricable link between the dictatorship and the monarchy, and the propaganda machine had succeeded, with the aid of the camera, in capturing this relation and projecting the same to the viewers. Metaxas wrote in his diary that same day :

> 'Today 11 December a miracle took place. One grand parade in Pedion of Areos in front of a platform. Flags were handed to the children by the Crown Prince and Princess Frederica. The anthem of *EON* and the 'Fourth of August' were heard; Great overwhelming enthusiasm: My Children; my golden children, boys and girls; I guided them to triumph. The domination is now complete.' [161]

A number of other very short sequence films deal with the same or a similar subject. For example in one such film (no title) the opening scene presents a parade of open cars led by one where the Premier sits next to the Crown Prince who is attired in white formal dress. The cars are driven through a crowded street where young *EON* boys and girls are lined up and saluting the passing cars. The sequence that follows presents Metaxas shaking hands with a girl Pioneer. The girl is kissing his hand in a gesture of filial and pious devotion, while the Crown Prince standing at his side seems to greatly enjoy this demonstration of love and affection. The camera focuses on this scene and the screen is filled with the image of a harmonious coexistence. A smiling Crown Prince at the side of an equally happy Premier and right in front of them a small girl in uniform: the embodiment of health, innocence, joy and future regeneration.

The following scenes depict a grandiose parade of proud *EON* members, upright, disciplined in their uniforms. They are saluting while passing in front of the platform on which the high officials are seated. The camera zooms in to reveal the royal crown which dominates the entrance to the platform facade, a tribute to and a grateful acknowledgement of the monarchy. The final scene presents a panoramic view of a large street full of spectators on both sides, trees and a shining sky in the background. This scene is dominated by a procession of hundreds of young people, who are actively marching in the way soldiers always do; a moving sea of uniforms.[162] This was an effective visible display of controlled power aiming to appeal not only to the emotions of the viewers, but to impress the Crown Prince and assure him of his wise choice in offering his royal support: because according to the Third Reich's National Broadcasting Director, 'All the power one has, even more than one has, must be demonstrated. One hundred speeches, five hundred newspapers articles, radio talks, films, and plays are unable to produce the same effect as a procession of huge masses of people taking place with discipline and active participation.'[163]

Another short length newsreel designed to serve the image building process of Metaxas' charismatic leadership was the one which depicted the 'orchestrated manifestations' for the celebration of the '25 of March' National Holiday in 1939. Extreme expressions of adulation, mass rallies and *EON* parades were organised in the presence of the King and the Dictator to demonstrate the children's 'spontaneous' participation. Fifty thousand *EON* members from the Athens district were obliged to participate and project the enthusiasm and patriotic inspiration for this grand National Holiday which would be, according to Kanellopoulos, the starting point for the creation of the 'Third Civilisation:'

> 'The 25 March 1821 was the crowning achievement of a struggle that continued over 3000 years. The objective behind this struggle was the safeguarding of the values and ideas which constitute our civilisation and existence. The 'Fourth of August' State and, our Leader Ioannis Metaxas in person continue this struggle and envisage the creation of the Third Civilisation as well as the spiritual conquest of mankind.'[164]

Unfortunately, the parade was disrupted by heavy rain which lasted many hours and ruined the whole celebration. The young members scattered around Athens looking for shelter, while the parents searched for hours to find their children.[165] Metaxas wrote that day in his diary:

> 'I attended Church and then the Army parade. In the afternoon I watched the *EON* parade. It was pouring with rain. We shall wait and see what will be the outcome of this celebration.'[166]

The short length film opens with a panoramic view of crowded streets and shots of 'Fourth of August' regime flags. The next scene depicts school children and *EON* members parading while the camera zooms in to reveal the *EON* flag flying and Metaxas standing and watching the parade. Yet, no sign of rain or confusion is depicted on the screen. Everything appeared to be quite normal and the celebration was carried out with great success. Through these visual representations the spectators were participating in a grand event and were sharing the enthusiasm of the people who attended the real event. The propaganda machine, through skilful editing, produced a fake authenticity which according to Bela Balazs distracted the viewer from reality. 'The eye of the camera and montage- two devices available to the filmmaker- help the viewer to accept film as reality. Irresistibly, they draw the moviegoer into their version of reality, based on laws established in authoritarian fashion by the director.'[167]

Although these short length and artistically poor newsreels and film-documentaries mentioned represent only a small sample of the many produced by *EON*'s Cultural Department, they reflect the value put on this mass medium by the regime's propaganda. Additionally, the recommendations put forward by the *EON* leadership for their artistic and thematic improvement as well as their efforts to ensure the adequate supply of mobile projectors all over the country, suggest that the indoctrination of Greek Youth through the medium of film was of vital importance to the regime.

EON was a movement which expressed the ideals of the regime. Furthermore, it was formed and destined to promote and safeguard those ideals with the young members' lives if necessary.[168] This task necessitated a physical and spiritual training based on qualities and virtues such as absolute obedience and devotion to the regime, solidarity, hard work and non-individualism. In this respect the *EON* films served a twofold purpose: on one hand, by presenting an ideal picture of *EON* life, they promoted and highlighted the regime's values in such a way as to win the people's consent, especially that of the parents. who feared that the organisation would replace the family 'nest,'[169] and on the other, to embrace and attract the whole of Greek Youth to the movement.

The Principle of Leadership and the People

> 'This Government does not belong to any political parties. This
> Government is a National Government: a Greek Government
> which belongs equally to all the Greeks[170]

The state commissioned film was one of the main instruments used by the
regime's propaganda to project the theme of charismatic leadership. Yet,
this projection posed certain problems for the film propaganda machine. As
mentioned in Chapter One, Metaxas' physical appearance did not constitute the
model of the charismatic leader who, apart from the special powers bestowed
on him, should also possess a dynamic physical appearance. Henceforth,
instead of the production of state commissioned films and documentaries
that featured Metaxas as the main protagonist,[171] the propaganda machine
initiated the production of numerous short length newsreels which depicted
the creative activities and achievements of the regime (Public holidays,
inaugurations, trips, and visits to factories) ensuring at the same time that
Metaxas' presence always played an intrinsic part in the filming procedure:
because according to the propaganda officials, 'the achievements of the
Government apart from being great deeds, could become, if effectively
projected, an invaluable means of political propaganda.'[172] Besides, the lack of
the technical and financial resources restricted the production of expensive
film-documentaries which would deal with the life and 'sacred mission' of
Ioannis Metaxas in a similar manner to the production of *Triumph des Willens.*[173]
The regime was well aware of the power of documentaries and newsreels as a
propaganda medium and many measures were taken to ensure their complete
control and exploitation. The following article published by the *YTT* is an
explicit example of the importance the regime assigned to the newsreels:

> 'Necessary measures have also been taken against the amateur or
> professional cinematographers shooting in Greece, where until
> recently film-production had been out of hand. Since newsreels
> and film-documentaries concerning the people or the natural
> beauty of this country can easily be distorted in order to project a
> false picture at home and abroad, a form of protectionism has been
> imposed through legislation.' [174]

Article 6 of the Cinema Law 955 ensured direct control of the newsreels and
documentaries by controlling the work permits of the cinematographers:

> 1. 'Every cinematographer who wishes to obtain his work permit
> for the shooting of newsreels and film-documentaries must have

15. Ioannis Metaxas. 'The First Athlete'

the approval of the Committee. These licences are always granted within the limits imposed by the present cinema Law. [175]

2. In case harmful intentions and malicious actions are established on the part of the reporter, the Committee has the power to withdraw the professional licence or alternatively forbid the shooting of newsreels and film documentaries for a period up to six months. This period can be extended to one year and in certain cases the Committee can, with the assistance of the police authorities and the district attorney, demand and achieve the criminal prosecution of the cinematographer'[176]

The extract provides an explicit account of the regime's attitude towards the production of newsreels and demonstrates that this mass medium was highly esteemed by the dictatorship. Indeed, newsreels constituted the ideal instrument of the regime's film propaganda as they offered limitless production potentials. They were short, inexpensive, with the ability to capture the immediate events, depicting people who lived in a real world, and offering the audience the impression that what they were viewing was nothing less than reality; a reality, however, which could, according to Hoffman, be 'falsified with the help of sequences that were, as such, authentic.'[177] Therefore, at a time when the preference of the masses for the cinema was overwhelming, the newsreel, through the compulsory screening, became Metaxas' most reliable means of propaganda. Because many districts had no cinemas and people were unable to attend the central ones, the Management Office of Athens (headed by Kotzias) proceeded with the purchase of a mobile cinema which toured most of the Athens districts. This cinema proved so effective in projecting the state commissioned newsreels to an audience that attended the free performances, that Kotzias decided to proceed with the purchase of two more cinema projectors.[178] In this way the regime ensured that its propaganda reached all the people.

The production of short newsreels and the compilation film (a combination of short silent newsreels) occupied a prominent part in the regime's cultural agenda and was assigned to a group of very efficient reporters and state controlled cinematographers.[179]

The first newsreels produced by the propaganda machine were very short shots of Metaxas' first day in power. They depicted people rushing about and titles of the daily newspapers announcing the political change and underlining its necessity. Other newsreels included a few shots of Metaxas' activities including visits to the country, several inaugurations such as the *Ektheseis Zapeiou* (Zapeion Exhibitions), school sports events, and visits of important guests like the arrival of King Edward and Dr.

Goebbels. All these events, which were centred around Metaxas and were skilfully enriched with the presence of people welcoming him with warm manifestations of love, were the result of the cinematic activities of the regime's first year in power. Among these newsreels the only significant one, in terms of duration and artistic endeavour, was the one dealing with the Transportation of the Royal Mortal Remains (*E Epanafora ton Skinomaton ton Vasileon*) from Italy to Greece; a newsreel which was extensively advertised by the regime's propaganda machine and enjoyed a wide projection in Greece and abroad.[180]

In 1938 most of those short newsreels were compiled by Novak Film[181] to form a sound film with the title *E Ellas tou 1938 Omili* (The Voice of Greece in 1938). This compilation film included the following small newsreels and documentaries:

1. *Ta Egenia tis Georgikis Ektheseos sto Zapeio Megaro* (The Inauguration of the Agrarian Exhibition in Zapeion)
2. *Proodos Tis Kapnoviomichanias mas* (The Progress of Our Cigarette Industry)
3. *Lambadiodromia ton Olympiakon Agonon tou Verolinou* (The Torch-Race for the Olympic Games in Berlin)
4. *Ta Scholika Gymnasia Ellados* (School Athletic Games)
5. *Anakyrixis tou Mesologiou eis Iearan Polin* (The Nomination of Messology as a Sacred Town)
6. *Eortai ton Antheon eis Pyrgon Hlias* (The Flower Festival in Pirgos Ilias)
7. *I Niki Tou Lodou is to Stadion* (Lodo's Victory in the Athens Stadium*)*
8. *E Metafora Ton Skinomaton ton Vasileon* (The Transportation of the Royal Remains)

The film was extensively advertised abroad by *YTT* and enjoyed a great reception in the United States where it was screened at the Miami Theatre of New York for eight consecutive days. The Preview leaflet for the screening in the United States with pictures that depicted the marriages of the Crown Prince Paul with the German Princess Frederica (an extra newsreel), and pictures of Metaxas' visits to factories, advertised the compilation film as follows:

> The National Film *E Ellas tou 1938 Omili* is neither an operetta , nor drama or comedy of the kinds that we watch in the cinemas every day. The film *E Ellas tou 1938 Omili* will move you deeply and bring tears to your eyes. This film will make you remember your beloved country, your parents and your brothers and sisters. This is a film which all the Greek Americans are longing to see and must see.'[182]

The success of the *E Ellas tou 1938 Omili* was partly due to the fact that it was one of the first sound films produced in Greece and partly due to the very nature of this film genre. This compilation film together with many similar films produced by Metaxas' film propaganda, represented a reconstructed reality which misled the viewers and played with their emotions. In most cases the compilation filmmakers engaged montage techniques to present a fake authenticity.[183] Almost all the newsreels produced by the regime came in the form of compilation film, and unlike the Nazi newsreels which were highly artistic, impressionist and all conquering,[184] the newsreels concerning the 'Fourth of August' regime were simply informative and descriptive. Their thematic issues mainly dealt with minor events and activities performed and controlled by the government.

Metaxas' film propaganda was a record of the regime's every-day activities, and was geared towards the psychological manipulation of the Greek people with the emphasis on projecting the image of a charismatic leader. The most significant device for such a strategy came mainly from the newsreels which dealt with the 'Fourth of August' anniversaries (*E Epeteios Tis Tetartis Augoustou*) and held a special place in the film propaganda process. These anniversaries, which year after year were becoming better examples of an orchestrated propaganda, initiated the mobilisation of very large parts of the Greek population, involved extravagant spending and were time consuming. On 4 August 1937 the regime, in an effort to convey to the people a sense of unity and solidarity and at the same time to advertise its achievements in a grandiose and impressive manner, organised the celebration of the 'Fourth of August' regime's first anniversary in the Athens Stadium.

The *YTT* in a special edition, produced a written account of a festival that took the form of a social revolution and a grand celebration where all the people, especially the peasants and workers, acquired leading roles. However, this grandiose celebration, which enjoyed a wide and enthusiastic press coverage, did not meet with the same success where film propaganda was concerned. Although the newsreel shot to present the first grand occasion reveals the propaganda mechanism involved in the projection of Metaxas' image as the Chief of the Nation and a Caring Father, it does so in a very poor and limited manner. The whole newsreel consists of a few shots of the crowded Stadium, parading athletes, school girls who danced dressed in traditional country costumes, possibly to convey an atmosphere of rural life, and a limited number of shots of Metaxas himself. It was during the following anniversaries of the 'Fourth of August' regime, in 1938 and 1939, that film propaganda produced a number of newsreels which demonstrate, quite effectively, the devices used for the projection of Metaxas' charismatic leadership and his ideology. The following account given by *Ta Paraskinia* reflects the effort put in by the *YTT* to produce a well organised and successful 'Fourth of August' anniversary film:

> 'The *YTT*, in order to support financially the Greek cinema companies, the majority of which are facing difficulties, has decided to send representatives from each company to the most important Greek towns to screen the second anniversary of our National Regeneration. The screening of the celebration in Athens is assigned to Dag Film, the celebration in Thessaloniki will be covered by Gaziades Bros, the celebration in Patras is assigned to Pr. Meravidis-Kavoukidis and so on. The recordings will be carried out by the Novak workshop. The film will be 3,000 metres long and will be projected in all the cinemas of every Greek town and in the most important capitals of Europe.'[185]

Thus, the whole film producing force was mobilised to shoot the manifestations connected with the grand celebrations of the 'Fourth of August' regime's second anniversary. The newsreel which depicted the 1938 festivities was a compilation of a 2,000 metres film by Dag Co., which used three cameras to film the Stadium festivities. Novak was also assigned to film Nicoloudis' speech delivered for the celebration, as well as several other manifestations taking place in the Athens suburbs. The final newsreel production of 1,500 metres was edited at the Novak Studio under the strict supervision of the *YTT* representatives Messrs. Svolopoulos and Zorbalas. The film was screened at Constitution Square where an open cinema was set up for this purpose. According to *Ta Paraskinia* 'thousands of Athenians gathered at Constitution Square to attend, free of charge, the excellent film dealing with the anniversary celebration while a large number of copies was sent to the Greek provinces and to America to be viewed by the Greek-Americans.'[186] At the same time 600 metres film of various scenes of the manifestations was shot by Hepp to be sent to the American Union for the *Weekly Journal* of Fox Movies, while another small newsreel filmed in 16 mm by Paraskevas Bros., was destined for the Cinema Section of the Ministry of Education. to be forwarded and projected in schools.[187] To emphasise the importance of the film as an effective instrument of propaganda, the regime ensured that on 4 August 1938 all *EON* members had free access to all film screenings. It was reported that during that day the cinemas 'willingly' granted thirty thousand free tickets to *EON* members (in a total of 43 cinemas the average number granted by each cinema was 700-800 tickets) and free entrance for the eight to ten o'clock performances.[188]

The 'Fourth of August' second anniversary celebration film opens with a panoramic view of great parades of groups of *EON* members and the town band. Thence the camera zooms in to depict the Propylea of the Athens Stadium. This place was of special significance and had become the focal point of Metaxas' exhibitions of power and an 'arena' for the people's enthusiasm, adulation and love towards him.[189] These expressions of enthusiasm and adulation (mainly 'manufactured' by the propaganda machine) were perceived by the regime as a plebiscite which reassured the Dictator of people's love and affection. When addressing the people of Heraklion on 8 November 1936, Metaxas stated: 'Your warmest and most enthusiastic welcome constitutes the measure of your trust and confidence in the government's work.'[190] Similarly when addressing the people of Selinuda on 31 October 1937 he said: 'Like you all, I am only human and when I see the people at my side expressing their love with such enthusiasm and faith, I feel extremely happy. For this happiness and for your warm reception I feel grateful'[191]

The scene that follows depicts large crowds in a cheering mood participating in what seems to be a great occasion. Shots of smiling young girls, members of *EON,* are revealed while the camera zooms in to depict the culmination of the great festival: the entrance of Ioannis Metaxas. Dressed in black and followed by members of his cabinet, who are all dressed in white, Metaxas ascends the stairs until he reaches his seat. This visual game of contrasting colours is very effective as the spectator can easily identify the leading figure and respond positively to it.[192] Yet, one cannot really say whether this was a propaganda trick invented to place Ioannis Metaxas in an advanced position, or merely coincidence, bearing in mind that Metaxas has always been depicted dressed in this manner. Whatever the reason behind this mode of representation the result must have been quite striking as the viewers immediately recognised the figure of authority. The camera pans in to reveal a full Stadium with people standing up, cheering and applauding at his presence, while other large groups are moving in with excited haste. Metaxas is depicted taking off his hat, smiling and waving at the people and school children who are sitting in large groups. The whole sequence is intended to convey to the viewer a feeling of euphoria and a sense of sharing this great event with the rest of the participating crowd. In the next scene the screen is full of hundreds of uniformed *EON* members standing up and saluting with their hands raised. In a few seconds the viewer has witnessed a unique and convincing image of the overwhelming approval enjoyed by Metaxas.

To reinforce this image the camera zooms in to depict a large number of cars outside the stadium. As these two scenes form two separate sequences, one can realise that this was the result of skilful editing clearly designed to underline the mass participation of the people. The following shot presents images of many athletes entering the stadium, and moves on to reveal what would be defined as the regime's embodiment of love, purity and unreserved support. Hundreds of country girls dressed in beautiful national and local costumes are forming dancing circles while peasant men with tabors, flutes and other popular instruments are joining in the dances. The viewer is presented with pictures of different people from different places, who form a 'totality' united by their love for their leader. It must be stressed at this point that although Metaxas believed that the individual existed only as an intrinsic part of the whole, a basic concept in most totalitarian states, the propaganda newsreels like this one lacked the symmetrical order seen in the Nazi newsreels, especially those of Leni Riefenstahl where according to Hoffmann, 'the individuality of the people is submerged into symmetry and order; masses tightly unified 'that have been moulded into compact units of movements.'[193] Instead, the Metaxas newsreels depict crowds which represented different segments of society; different social classes, regional backgrounds and gender. The camera, in prolonged shots, zooms in to reveal men with aged faces marked by deep wrinkles, a sign of hard labour and privation.[194] Yet, these faces, which are far from models of beauty, are smiling and applauding with enthusiasm in such a manner that they radiate an air of contentment and happiness. Thus, they demonstrate their utter devotion to the person who brought them here and, for the first time in their lives, gave them a true identity; the identity of their being equally important subjects and dignified members of the Greek community. The camera focuses on the written text which is adapted to their musical instruments and the screen is filled with names like *Ioannina*, (a remote region in the north west of Greece) and then focuses back on the old faces of the peasants. This scene is designed to convince the viewers of the people's unrestricted devotion, and to remind them of the Chief's loving capacity towards the less privileged. The people who are depicted by the camera are the same people that Metaxas had visited a year before in *Ioannina* when he assured them of his genuine interest and support stating:

> 'At this point, I must stress some of the things that this government has done for you. Firstly, it made you feel proud of yourselves and of being Greeks; a fact that you had forgotten for a long time: it established a working class which is on good terms with the state and is highly respected by the nation. This working class is now part of the whole, while before it was treated as an enemy of the State(...) The 'Fourth of August' State has demonstrated its concern for the

peasant and for the worker, and infused you with the feeling of solidarity for others who are less fortunate.'[195]

The camera moves on to capture more figures of old men holding banners with letters on, until a printed image again fills the whole screen and the spectators read the word *Crete*: a place name with a special connotation and of political substance: a part of the country which is synonymous with the threat of opposition. Indeed, the only serious domestic challenge and opposition that Metaxas faced during his four years in power was the Cretan Revolt in July 1938.[196] This visual image was designed to convince the viewers that even *Crete*, the 'symbol' of resistance, was present to acknowledge the important and unifying mission of the 'Fourth of August' regime, and demonstrate its support. Two names, *Ioannina* and *Crete*, two far apart and remote regions and two politically different minded groups, were brought together under the presence and unifying power of Metaxas. The camera then zooms in to reveal smiling and beautifully dressed girls in local costumes carrying products of their native places. Loaves of bread and home made pies fill the screen and are followed by scenes of happy country girls walking towards their Chief to pay their respect and offer him the gifts of their homeland. In a quick shot the camera captures the face of a satisfied and extremely happy Metaxas. The viewer is experiencing a visual ritual which projects the existence of a mystical and unbreakable bond between the leader and the led. After all Metaxas embodied all the dreams and aspirations of the poor and deprived peasants. He was their *Barba Yiannis* and their *Protos Agrotis*; their caring leader who had always addressed them with love and affection. In January 1941 in a speech to farmers, he said: 'My dear friends, representatives of the dear farmers of Greece for whom I always had deep feelings and affection'.[197]

Time and again faces of young girls and old men, farmers and workers dressed in clean working clothes and playing their musical instruments, pass in front of the viewer, while others carrying their working shovels and parading or wandering around the Stadium seem to enjoy this historic moment. The next shot depicts more groups of men; fishermen with their fishing nets, divers with their diving equipment, engineers with their tools, all paying their respect to the man who acknowledged them as 'the Pillars of the Nation.'[198] A group of working girls, presumably from a textile factory, are carrying a tapestry and as the camera focuses on the surface it reveals the emblem of the 'Fourth of August' woven on it. Another sequence presents country girls carrying water pitchers on their heads and walking amidst roughly constructed village huts and trees; a projected image of an idyllic country life.

These visual representations were designed to convey to the spectators the impression that the government enjoyed the overwhelming acceptance and devotion of the whole population, especially that of the workers and the peasants.[199] And the camera moves in to depict more faces of young girls in their national costumes and jewellery, an intentional sign of treasured customs and national wealth. This dignified wealth exhibited by the beautiful country girls was according to the regime 'the outcome of hard labour and part of the national tradition which had nothing in common with the 'flashy' jewellery worn by the foreign models of Hollywood beauty which were projected by the foreign films of the time.'[200] The show continues with more shots of country women carrying their working baskets full of fruits. A game of repetition and skilful editing which ensures the viewers' distraction from reality; a reality which has been misused and distorted by the propaganda machine to serve the regime's ideology and goals. It impressed and mesmerised the viewers, leading them to believe that the participants appeared to be much greater in numbers than they actually were. Furthermore, as the camera zooms in to reveal in close up the beautiful young faces of the country girls and then moves on to depict the smiling old wrinkled faces of the country women, the spectator is presented with a visual representation of contrasting images, which, despite the great differences, form a harmonised totality. This totality has a direct appeal to the viewer's sense and heart; it is a visual image that he recognises and identifies with. It is a technique which Krachauer calls 'the exploitation of physiognomic qualities by contrasting.'[201]

At this point, it must be stressed that unlike most Nazi newsreels where women were usually left out or occupied an insignificant space,[202] the representation of women in Metaxas' propaganda newsreels is quite striking. Peasant women and country girls, working women and *EON* girls in large numbers, were all part of a great mobilisation designed and projected by the film propaganda to emphasise the people's unity, solidarity and devotion to the regime. On the other hand, such a mobilisation sowed the seeds for the acknowledgement of the woman's new role and presence by the Metaxas' dictatorship. Metaxas strongly believed that the place of women in Greek society was within the family sphere where they ought to enjoy the relevant respect and honour.[203] The woman's mission was considered as most important, as she was destined to bring up her children and imbue them with the national values and beliefs epitomised by the 'Fourth of August' regime.

> 'Your mission is of great importance. It is the mission of becoming a mother: and the mother is the pillar of the family. It is she who is responsible for the healthy and correct upbringing of the future

generation. Even if you are not destined to be a mother and you
are engaged in another role, you will always feel like being a mother.
This is the woman's condemnation and glory.'[204]

Yet, the newsreel, through the repeated shots of the great number of women
participating in the celebration, even if it was only a montage trick, explicitly
demonstrated that Metaxas largely approved of the women's presence in
the public sphere. The parading and active participation of women in this
public space during this great festivity elevated their position, especially as
far as peasant and working women were concerned. After all it was Metaxas
himself who urged the working women to claim their right place in society:

> 'Apart from everything else you have a duty towards yourself that
> you must fulfil; none of you must think yourself inferior to any
> other women; just because you are working with your hands this
> does not mean that you are less worthy and important than the
> other women'[205]

The following sequence of the film reveals a panoramic view of the
overcrowded Stadium and the camera moves in to get close ups of the
spectators and the participants, focusing again on old faces of people who
carry banners with written names of places like *Kalamata* and *Chania*, and
then back to the cheering crowds. The finale presents a screen filled by
the fluttering flag of the 'Fourth of August', followed by a prolonged shot
of the nearby ancient columns and the Acropolis. The camera links thus
the enthusiastic crowds with key symbols and icons which epitomise the
regime's values and ensure the 'regeneration of Greece;' images that do
not constitute in themselves a real continuity but, through effective editing,
convey to the viewer a feeling of national pride and patriotic inspiration.

Another documentary film which deals with the same subject
is a colour production and could be considered unique as it presents a
whole series of 'Fourth of August' regime posters in a very descriptive
and effective way. Shot by a Greek-American Professor of Political and
Social Geography at the University of Philadelphia by the name of Michael
Dorizas, this newsreel is an excellent example of colour film making,[206]
and given the nature of the regime and the regulations about film making
in Greece as well as the projected images of the film, we presume that it
must have served as an instrument of propaganda for Metaxas at home
and abroad. The film, a hymn and tribute to the country people and their
struggle, as well as an affirmation in faith to Metaxas' regime, opens with a
panoramic view of a large number of colour posters displayed on the facade

of a four storey central building (most probably the *EON* headquarters). The camera focuses on the emblem of 'Fourth of August' which dominates the centre of the building's facade. Next to it is a poster which depicts a young Phalangite *EON* member saluting in the fascist manner: two visual images intrinsically linked, as the Chief says to the *EON* members: 'You are born and bred a native of the New State: the 'Fourth of August' State.'[207] Then the camera zooms in to present a beautiful poster of a young couple of peasants holding a bundle of wheat. They are both smiling and seem fully content. The written message on the poster revealed by the camera proclaims the benefits of cultivating the earth and of country life: 'Rich are the fruits of the earth: happiness in the village.' A 'Fourth of August' flag is flying and the screen is filled by its image while the next shot reveals a poster of a soldier standing to attention and next to him the camera zooms in to show a poster with Metaxas pointing at something. The focal point of his attention, as the camera reveals, is a poster with the written message:

> 'The battle for grain;
> Bread; Autarky'

Metaxas' agrarian policy aimed at the improvement of agriculture, increased production and autarky and most shots of the opening of this film seem to project that image. 'I ask you to cultivate the land in a variety of ways' he said to the people of Xanthi in March 1939, 'I want the agrarian family to be able to obtain their food through the cultivation of their small garden and their small holdings. This will prove good practice for the difficult times ahead.'[208] Often, several small shots were presented which filled the screen with phrases such as 'The cultivation of land constitutes a National Duty; Every part of Greek land must be cultivated; Every part of the Greek soil must produce something.'

The next sequence zooms in on a poster advertising the Agrarian Bank surrounded by more flags and 'Fourth of August' regime emblems. We then go back to a poster depicting a strong young peasant ploughing the earth and right next to him the produce extracted from that earth. This image reminds us of the early Soviet propaganda films which showed the hero of labour as an individual and portrayed him as the representative of a system that will bring happiness,[209] in antithesis to the Nazi film which, according to Hoffmann, reduced the individual to the status of a purely numerical elements.[210] Time and again posters are shown depicting words *Ethniki Amina* (National Defence) and right next to these two words, in the same poster, a column of figures gives the amounts spent on the defence of the country. Another poster with the written words *Elliniki Viomihania* (Greek Industry) fills the screen.[211]

These very intense and much repeated shots 'bombarding' the viewer were intended to underline the significance of those posters which projected the achievements of the 'Fourth of August' regime. The following scene brings to a climax the whole visual process. The camera pans across to a large round poster, right on top of the small ones we have just seen, which depicts the flag of the 'Fourth of August' regime and right in the middle a burning torch. As this large image of the flag begins to fade away, the camera brings on screen a large group of street spectators looking and pointing at the posters with enthusiasm. The film culminates with the projection of the great poster of Ioannis Metaxas; dark suit, white shirt, blue-grey striped tie, sophisticated and determined face, looking right into the future. A clear and explicit message is thus projected to the viewers: a complete visual representation of the achievements and the ideals of the regime reflecting the contemporary climate as it was intended to be shown. As the camera pans round to more posters of Metaxas, the Greek flag appears and then it is back again to the poster with the burning torch of the 'Fourth of August' regime. The next sequence reveals another flag with the portrait of the King right in the middle. The caption under the flag reads *E Sotiria Tis Ellados* (The Salvation of Greece). The viewer (without a historian's critical eye) is subjected to a chain of visual events which construct reality as the film-maker wishes him to perceive it: images of earthly goods, produce of hard labour, in the hands of happy peasants (an implied 'horn of plenty'): soldiers and industry that ensure a safe future: icons and symbols that embody national inspirations: and overall the loving presence and guidance of Ioannis Metaxas and the King predominate. The following extract taken from an article published in *E Neolea* gives a written account of the propagandistic power of these posters:

> 'The artistic and vivid posters high on the wall talk of and unfold step by step the achievements of the 'Fourth of August' State. They talk about the father who has again found employment and returns home with his shopping: they talk about the young man who does not have to wander about, because the State protects him both in his educational career and in finding him a job: they speak about the mother and her sick child who finds refuge in social security: and they speak about the young boy who from the depths of his heart declares that he will prove himself better than his ancestors. All these colours and captions attract the people because they take the place of a competent speaker who feels the need to talk about a miracle. Thus people believe and hope and rejoice.'[212]

Yet, the picture of national euphoria (so far) projected by the film through the posters is not complete. The camera pans over beautiful country girls dressed in their exquisite local costumes and wearing impressive jewellery; a cinematic game of colours and shapes that impresses the audiences and generates enthusiasm; an image which constitutes an important device in the propaganda process. As Traub put it: 'The first law of all propaganda reads that people must be kept receptive and capable of enthusiasm.'[213] The following sequences reveal *EON* parades, the town band, and more country girls smiling at the camera. This festive atmosphere is disrupted by images that seem to form sequences from another newsreel shot in another place; a village street, men and women on their donkeys, followed by shots which depict flocks of sheep in the fields, ancient ruins and peasants walking in the village streets and playing music with their homespun instruments. These disparate shots either constitute a 'slip' in the compilation procedure, or are designed to present an idyllic portrait of the countryside which is in harmony with the national euphoria of the city. The final scene depicts Metaxas entering the Athens Stadium and accompanied by his officials and *EON* members, while the crowds cheer with enthusiasm.

The last scenes of all these disparate parts which formed the compilation film we have just examined represent different sequences, shot for the occasion and put together by skilful montage to achieve a specific purpose. This purpose was to project an image of a prosperous Greek society which was enjoying the advantages gained thanks to Ioannis Metaxas. The film projected a charismatic leader who had united the whole Greek population with his love and affection; workers and peasants, men and women, young and old alike. The film pays tribute to this great man whom people from all parts of Greece had travelled to see, thereby participating in a grand festival: the second anniversary of the 'Fourth of August' regime.

The third and fourth anniversaries, examples of extravagant spending and manifestations at a time when the Second World War was becoming an inevitability, were projected in a similar way through the regime's film propaganda.

Another newsreel which depicts Metaxas' attitude towards the workers and the effort of his regime film propaganda to convey an image of a charismatic leadership is the *Eortasmos Tis Ergatikis protomagias* (First of May Celebration) in Piraeus in 1938. The film, a black and white sound production lasting two minutes, opens with a panoramic view of what seems to be a festive atmosphere. A large group of girls from the Papastratos Factory[214] parading in their white working uniforms, were followed by uniformed working men holding the flag and marching in a vigorous manner. The camera then zooms in to depict the Work Battalions followed by crowds of people cheering and applauding. Thence, the screen is filled up by what seems to be the culmination of the whole celebration: the coming of Ioannis Metaxas; the *Protos Ergatis*. As the camera zooms in to focus on his majestic entrance the crowds express their love and devotion with warm enthusiasm and adulation gazing at the car with their beloved Chief in it. Shots of old men in their working clothes, old figures and faces, some in national costumes, fill in the screen; faces cheer (it is the first film where one can really hear the loud shouts and applause) and waving hands stretch out to touch the hand of their Great Governor. As the camera moves on, more crowds are revealed and more workers holding their union flag, while individual faces of young men and women, obviously workers, are depicted smiling and saluting with enthusiasm. Then the screen is filled with what should be considered the most significant moment in the regime's history of film propaganda. Metaxas is not only standing on a grand balcony right in front of the spectators and looking at them, but he is actually talking to them. In a loud and firm voice he is delivering one of the longest and most interesting speeches he delivered during his four years in power.[215] Ironically, in this speech Metaxas' policy is completely identified with the goals, hopes and aspirations of the workers as expressed years before when the First of May had been instituted as the day of the working people's right to freedom and better working conditions:

> 'This great gathering of all the workers from Athens and Piraeus to celebrate the First of May gives us the greatest satisfaction and joy, as it demonstrates that Greek Society has now been harmoniously united under the 'Fourth of August' government. A day which only a few years ago was synonymous with severe clashes and bloodshed among the workers. The workers of Greece are intrinsically linked with the 'Fourth of August' State not only because this government brought great social changes that concern them, but most importantly, because it was the need to elevate and improve their position that necessitated this political change.'[216]

As the camera continues to focus on Metaxas while he is delivering his speech, shots of workers applauding and hailing can be seen and their voices and enthusiasm can be heard. More shots of crowds fill the screen; the camera focuses on faces looking up to somebody with a pious gaze, revealed immediately to be Metaxas. More crowds keep waving their union banners as well as the 'Fourth of August' flags, while the camera zooms in to show us a poster with the Royal Crown on it. Banners with messages like

'*O Ethnikos mas Kyvernitis* (Our National Governor) *Zito E 4e Augustu* (Long Live the 4ᵗʰ of August) pass across the screen with the final one reading: *Zito E Adieretos Ellas* (Long Live Undivided Greece) while at the same time Metaxas is heard to repeat this message loudly. Time and again there are faces and flags: repetitions which create a feeling of overwhelming participation. The finale presents Metaxas smiling and waving and the picture fades away with the dictator making his exit through the cheering crowds.

Apart from these newsreels which were intended to boost the morale of the workers and convey to the audience a sense of national euphoria, unity and solidarity, other short sequence shots presented yet more images of the joyful working class at their daily tasks in well organised factories and workshops.

Another newsreel designed to emphasise the dictator's concern for the country and the welfare of his people, underlining at the same time the need for a 'national regeneration', was the newsreel *Ekstrateia Gia to Prasino* (Reforestation Campaign). The film dealt with the first reforestation campaign that took place in December 1938, and was produced to promote the regime's love for Mother Earth which was glorified and cherished because according to Metaxas, 'Earth gives her treasures and wealth to the people' and 'elevates the people's hearts and spirits.' [217] This Earth veneration and the mystical bond of the 'soil and blood' was an essential concept in some totalitarian ideologies, especially in Nazi Germany,[218] where it was considered the source of the pure race, and it was effectively projected through film propaganda. As David Welch observed in his study of the German Cinema, 'film was thought to be a suitable medium for disseminating this type of 'ideological' propaganda, and the doctrine of 'blood and soil' was one of the very few concepts under National Socialism that displayed any sort of consistency.'[219] To demonstrate its love for the Greek soil, especially the forests, Metaxas' regime put into effect a number of measures to prevent the further deforestation of the Greek mountains. The most significant ones were the restriction of pasturage and grassland, and the reduction of the large number of existing goats to a minimum. 'Forest and Goats cannot coexist,' Metaxas claimed in his speech to the people of Egio on 31 October 1937, and on 22 September 1937 he enacted Emergency Law 875 to safeguard the forests and reverse the deforestation process. Additionally the regime launched a vigorous campaign for the reforestation of all the Greek mountains and open spaces.[220] The King, government officials, the Work Battalions, the *EON*,[221] schools, as well as the whole population were mobilised for this important task.

The newsreel *Ekstrateia Gia to Prasino* was designed to convince the audience of the importance of this process and ensure their participation.

At the same time it projected an image of a regime which paid homage to the Greek soil 'the greatest love but also the heaviest cross for every Greek'[222] and was in total harmony with the symbolism inherent in the veneration of the earth. The return to the *Hellenic* ideals and values that were rooted in this soil were the preconditions and precepts for the 'regeneration of Greece,'[223] while the anthem of the 'Fourth of August' State referred to 'the Greek flag which covers the sacred soil that we are now standing on.'[224] It has been argued that Earth was exalted and glorified by Metaxas' regime simply when he was campaigning to boost agriculture.'[225] Although there is truth in this statement,[226] evidence suggests that the land also served as a power base for the projection and reinforcement of Metaxas' nationalistic beliefs. The following extract from a speech delivered to *EON* members by the Minister of Health and Welfare Elias Kribas in the presence of Ioannis Metaxas, illustrates the important role that the land played in the realisation of the national ideals:

> 'The Greek earth has a voice and speaks to the heart of every man who wishes to listen (...) This earth speaks for the Greeks who safeguarded our country and shed their blood for it; it speaks for the enemies who shed blood over this nation when the Greeks were divided by rival parties; it speaks for our Great Governor who united Greece with his love and affection under the Sceptre of our popular King George (…) Our Governor guides us to an end that we must reach at any cost. This end ensures the Salvation of the Nation and the glorious existence of our eternal motherland. The glory of Greece rests on this earth on which Gods, Demigods and great people have lived.' [227]

The opening sequence of the film *Ekstrateia Gia to Prasino* presents a panoramic view of a rural setting and a youth member standing and facing an *EON* official. He salutes and receives from him a large branch of a tree. Then, he is depicted holding the branch carefully, with almost 'pious' care, and running towards more *EON* members. The following scene depicts the King walking among members of the Royal Court, government and army officials as well as civilians and young members of the Boy Scouts.[228] Most of them carry a shovel and smile happily towards the camera. Thence the camera zooms in to reveal Metaxas with a church representative and government officials walking among cheering *EON* members and spectators. The following sequence reveals the King planting a tree among Boy Scouts who are engaged in the same task while, as this image fades away, the screen is filled with the image of Metaxas planting a similar tree, holding it upright and smiling at the camera.[229] The next shot presents the church representative blessing the tree that Metaxas has just planted and is proudly holding. With the projection of these sequences the viewer is participating in a mystical pagan ritual which exemplifies the ideology of the regime. As the planted tree will root and grow to form eternal forests, in the same manner the ideology of the 'Fourth of August' State will be rooted in the minds and hearts of the people and will spread and serve the Greek nation and humanity. The presence of the King and Metaxas, the clergy, the *EON* members and the people, all effectively projected by the film, form the dominant forces for the realisation of the supreme Greek ideals. Although the viewer is under the impression that the events shown represent real moments of a particular occasion during which both the King and Metaxas were present, they are in fact heterogeneous components put together to present a faked reality for propagandistic purposes. A careful viewer will observe that nowhere in the film are the King and Metaxas depicted in the same shot, but form images of successive sequences. Furthermore, the King is surrounded by members of the Royal Court and Boy Scouts without the presence of church representative, while Metaxas, with the clergy at his side, is welcomed and assisted by *EON* members and various crowds. Therefore, the events projected and viewed by the cinema-goer are nothing but the result of a montage trick which constructed a desired reality by bringing together disparate parts that would have an emotional impact on the viewer.[230] By putting together these different visual pieces the propaganda machine, apart from the importance of the reforestation procedure and its symbolism, also projected the image of a regime which enjoyed the support of the King and the love of the whole nation. The following extract from an article with the title 'Symbolismos'(Symbolism) published in *E Neolea* during the reforestation campaign of December 1939 illustrates the propaganda effort to bring those elements together and project them as a unified reality.

> 'The reforestation campaign, apart from having significant national value, embodies also a deep symbolism. The Greek nation led by their King and their Chief are planting the new Greek Tree. They are 'constructing' a new Greece with excellent prospects for 'fruitful trees and good crops'[231]

The next scenes present happy men, women and children all involved in the tree planting process while the image of Metaxas smiling next to a high ranking military official and the church representative fills up the screen. The camera pans over crowds who cheer and applaud the regime to reveal immediately the clergy saluting in the fascist manner. In a quick shot the camera depicts, for the first time in the regime's film history, Metaxas hastily returning the fascist salute. [232] The final scene presents more people cheering and the police corps engaged in the reforestation process, to end with a sign next to a tree with an illegible name on it; presumably the name of the person who planted it.

Apart from the *Ekstrateia Gia to Prasino*, a number of short sequence shots which depicted idealistic images of the Greek countryside with rivers, trees, young people walking, running and enjoying the *Arcadian* scenery were enriched with shots of ancient sites (Cape of Sounion) with girls dressed in archaic manner dancing between the ancient columns. These shots often formed an essential part of compilation films produced by the regime's propaganda. These productions were linked with the return to a 'sacred' earth, which is pure, and in harmony with the ancient Greek ideal, under the guidance of Ioannis Metaxas.

There is no doubt that Metaxas' film propaganda was geared towards the psychological mobilisation of the people and the projection of the regime's ideologies. *Ekstrateia Gia to Prasino,* like most of the films discussed in this section, deals with the central themes of Metaxas' propaganda; the projection of the leadership cult and the need for unity, obedience and work. Metaxas was portrayed in those films as the caring leader who believed in the superiority of ethical values and supreme ideals: a leader who established a close relationship with the whole of the Greek population, especially the less privileged.

In newsreels like those showing the 'Fourth of August' regime's anniversaries, the worker and the peasant were the cultural and the ideological heroes of the film propaganda. Metaxas identified himself with those heroes, whom he freed from the past political antagonisms to help them gain their rightful place in Greek society. Whenever he is shown in the films he is surrounded by people; children, men and women: a unified totality which transcended the social classes and political pathos and looked forward to a New Greece. Furthermore, the achievements of the regime were excessively advertised and eulogised to present a general euphoria intrinsically linked with Metaxas himself. People were depicted at their best; cheering happily, applauding and participating in grand festivities. All negative images that would endanger the national euphoria, such as police surveillance, communist deportations, burning of books, as well as natural disasters,[233] were systematically kept out while the enemy (the communist and the politician) were completely excluded.

Apart from this harmonious link between the leader and the led, another aspect which was projected by film propaganda was the ideal relationship with the monarchy and the support which the Metaxas regime enjoyed from the latter. This projected image had a twofold purpose: to convey to the Greek people an atmosphere of general consensus and support, and to convince their allies abroad, especially the British, that Metaxas' regime was not a fascist regime but one linked to the King ('the King's binding'). [234]

Metaxas film propagandists, through effective editing and the process of 'inclusion', manipulated events and produced films that ensured the propagation of the most significant components of the regime's ideology. The viewer of the time, through the obligatory screening of optimistic images and extracts of reality produced by the propaganda machine, was subjected to a skilful indoctrination which he was unable to detect and oppose.

The films produced by Metaxas' propaganda had little in common with the masterpieces of the German propaganda films nor the artistic values of the earlier Russian productions. The limited technical and financial means left little room for artistic film making. Thus, the Metaxas films were restricted to simple presentations of the regime's achievements, and mass manifestations. On the other hand, one could argue that these films differed from the Nazi films because they represented and reflected a different ideology. Nazi propaganda tried through film to manipulate German opinion, and propagate an aggressive, extreme and ruthless national and racial policy. However, the 'Fourth of August' regime's film propaganda aimed to project a policy which would wipe out the 'evils' of the past and unite the people, ensuring at the same time that Metaxas' remained in power.

Chapter Four

THE 'FOURTH OF AUGUST' REGIME
AND THEATRE PROPAGANDA

The Modern Greek Theatre before Metaxas' regime

Theatre in Greece had always enjoyed a reputation and had been the basic and most popular form of cultural entertainment prior to the arrival of the cinema in the 1930s. At the turn of the nineteenth century Athens was a hub of theatrical activity, with forty five theatres operating within the city at the time.[1] Before the Asia Minor catastrophe in 1922, Greek theatre had been developing rapidly with the creation of theatrical groups and the appearance of new playwrights of great promise.[2] The evolution of the theatre solely rested with two stars, Kyveli Adrianou and Marika Cotopouli, who established their own theatre companies and dominated the Greek theatrical 'arena' for many years.[3] Theatrical life in the whole of Greece was regulated by Athens, and the Athenian theatrical companies toured the rest of Greece and the great Greek communities abroad. The Asia Minor catastrophe created a new reality within modern Greek theatre: it put an end to these tours and the financial gains entailed, and created a new theatrical public made up of the thousands of the refugees who were used to and loved the theatre.[4]

By the time of Metaxas' dictatorship the modern Greek theatre was well established with a plethora of able actors who had graduated from various drama schools, the most important of which was the 'Professional

Theatrical School'.[5] At the same time talented new playwrights and many newly established theatre companies were trying to meet the theatrical demand by introducing new plays to their repertoire.[6] The new repertoire, in an attempt to change direction from the old plays which satisfied the average pre-war spectator, introduced new artistic interpretations of the plays. Yiannis Sideris, the theatre historian, argued that, 'the new repertory succeeded in imposing as a dogma the idea that the times demanded that the public should participate with the new playwrights in their effort to express something deeper: a restlessness, a dramatic uncertainty about human destiny, a certain bitterness left over from the suffering of the First World War. The theatre stopped being a "pleasure" of the senses, and became an intellectual joy.'[7] However, this new tendency towards a better and more artistically 'correct' theatre concerned the 'elite' audiences, while the less educated Athenian masses preferred simpler theatrical plays like the revues, which entertained them and disseminated ideas that were familiar to them. Thus the revue, which played mostly in the summer theatres was, after the cinema, the most popular theatrical genre with the middle classes and for a large proportion of the masses who could afford the admittance ticket. Because of the difficult economic situation and the disturbed political life at the end of the twenties and early thirties the revue offered many subjects for satire and political mockery. People with different political views and ideas were queuing up to attend the performances which best expressed their beliefs. This demand necessitated the establishment of more theatres in the centre of Athens and the suburbs, while yet more people attended those to express their political beliefs indirectly and identify themselves with their political 'heroes.' In 1930, thirty revues were staged in Athens and the suburbs. Some of the titles representative of the majority, which expressed the general political mood, were: *E Lovitoura tou 1930* (The 1930 Corruption), *Treli Athina* (Crazy Athens), *Vavilonia ola* (All is Babylon).[8] The number decreased to twenty four in 1934 but the degree of political and social satire expressed through daring language remained the same, if not more so.[9] Such was the political mood and antagonism of the time, which was reflected and expressed through the revues, that during the municipal elections of 1934 the police issued an order prohibiting the performances of revues which used foul language and satirised political figures.[10]

This was approximately the state of Modern Greek Theatre on 4 August 1936 when Metaxas established his dictatorship and the theatre underwent changes which were dictated by the new political situation and the ideologies and aspirations of the new regime.

Metaxas' Dictatorship and the Theatre

> "I believe that the theatre which is the art of arts, is rooted in the nature of every Greek person. For this reason I myself, and my government place the theatre in the first scale of government priority and interest" [11]

On 25 January 1937 Emergency Law 446 *Peri Theatrou* (About the Theatre) introduced the regulations which would govern the theatre putting it under strict censorship.[12] The regulations that concerned safety measures and the 'correct' operation of the theatre were the same as those applying to the cinema, and were the collective responsibility of the sub-Ministries of *YTT*, Public Security, Transport, and Public Health. Article 2 of the legislation illustrated below, reflects the regime's determination to control theatrical activity and use the theatre as an instrument of propaganda:

> 'We prohibit the performance on the stage of theatrical plays which through their images and the manner in which they are performed, affect public morality, offend the Christian religion and are considered to have unsuitable and damaging effects on the public. Similarly, plays that contain propagandistic elements that originate from communist or other subversive sources are strictly prohibited.'[13]

The formation of the *Epitropi Theatrou* (Theatre Censorship Committee) and its duties were determined by Article 4 of the Theatre Law and comprised the following members:

> a) The director of the Home Press Office, b) the director of the City Police and the Gendarmerie c) the Head of the Surveillance section of the Press Office, d) the Head of the department of Tourist Propaganda, e) one high official of the Chamber of Letters and High Arts, f) one representative of the Greek playwrights and one representative of the theatrical enterprises, without the right to vote. The Committee's secretary would be appointed by and based at the *YTT*.[14]

To ensure the 'proper' operation of the theatre and ascertain the suitable nature and performance of the plays, police or gendarmerie officials attended every theatrical play, and intervened, if necessary, by prohibiting the performance and, in many cases, by closing the theatre. The responsibility for the *Diefthinsis Grammaton ke Theatrou* (Directorate of Letters and the

Theatre) rested, according to Emergency Law 1779 of 1939, with the *Geniki Diefthinsi Grammaton ke Kalon Technon* (Chamber of Letters and Fine Arts), a section of the Ministry of Education, established in November 1937 and headed by Costis Bastias.[15] This legislation supplemented the existing regulations on all cultural expressions and introduced measures which concerned the control of every theatrical expression. The most important innovations came through paragraph one of Article 15, which introduced the establishment of *The Grafeion Elenchou Kallitechnikis Kiniseos* (The Cultural Activity Control Office), and the nomination of a man of 'letters' as its director. Paragraph two defined the functions of this Office which were: a) the control and regulation of all theatrical companies which toured Greece, and the effort to secure suitable places and theatrical halls for the performances; b) the evaluation and assessment of all theatre groups by examining the suitability and virtue of the actors, the musicians, the playwrights and the dancers; c) the formation of a *Mitroon* (Registry) which would include all artists and people of letters; d) the formation of an *Archeio* (File) to contain the contracts of all the people working in the theatre, musical institutions and all the other cultural organisations. Article 16 introduced the establishment of a Permanent Committee to supervise and resolve any dispute concerning the 'correct' operation of cultural activities and the 'proper' behaviour of the people involved. This Committee consisted of : a) the General director of the Directorate of Letters and Theatre, b) the Head of the Control of Cultural Activity Office, c) one representative of the Ministry of Labour, and d) one representative of *Tis Organoseos ton Ergaton tou Pnephmatos* (Organisation of the People of Letters). [16] With these regulations the theatre came under strict censorship and subordinated itself to the dictates of Metaxas' propaganda. Apart from the legislative measures that the 'Fourth of August' regime took to control the theatre, state intervention took several forms which ensured the dissemination of its ideology and the artistic values epitomised by Metaxas.

Metaxas was a man of broad cultural tastes and was fond of displaying his interest in the theatre. He was familiar with the works of the great playwrights and was a regular attendee at theatrical performances in Greece and abroad.[17] His belief in the power of the high arts, a vital part of which was the theatre, and his determination to support them was underlined in his speech during the mass rally in Athens on 2 October 1936 when he stated: 'The government will participate vigorously in the development of arts and science'.[18] At the same time the propaganda machine undertook the task of projecting and promoting the concept of Metaxas' image as ' the great patron of arts' The theatrical press extolled the dictator's beneficial

role in 'uplifting' theatrical art, and the people of the theatre expressed
their deep gratitude to *Megas Kyvernitis*.[19] The theatre, unlike the radio and
the cinema, which have an influential power on the masses, is a form of
art which is mainly directed towards and enjoyed by the elite. Yet, Metaxas,
who adopted and demonstrated a paternalistic attitude towards the Greek
people, believed that, if correctly used, theatre could play a revolutionary
role in educating and elevating the masses, at the same time propagating his
ideology. His belief in the beneficiary role of the theatre for the ordinary
people was expressed during his speech in Thessaloniki on the occasion
of the inauguration of the Royal Theatre: 'I am totally convinced that the
theatre can only survive and achieve great things if and when it becomes a
form of art that involves the broader masses and expresses their spirit. The
theatre must cease to exist as an artistic form enjoyed only by and restricted
to the elite.'[20] Within the strategy of creating a cultural renaissance which
would embrace the whole population the regime undertook a number of
steps intended to bring the theatre closer to the people. However, unlike
the other instruments of propaganda such as press, radio, and to a large
extent film, which supplied the audience with information controlled and
circulated by the regime, theatre was a more complex medium as it involved
a network of different services and cultural expressions. For this reason its
exploitation had to be carefully planned and presented. *To Vasilikon Theatro*
(The Royal Theatre) a much esteemed theatre institution established in
1901 by King George I, became the main instrument of Metaxas' effort
to reinstate the grand spectacles set in the past and to promote his national
ideology.[21] In his interview with Costis Bastias on 15 and 16 September
1936 Metaxas expressed his belief in the reformatory role of the Royal
Theatre and declared his utter support:

> 'The Royal Theatre with its repertoire, direction and play-acting
> has given us theatrical plays which contribute to the service of
> this nation(...) The Royal Theatre constitutes a brilliant example of
> artistic expression and has won my total admiration and support.
> From October I shall attend every staged performance, irrespective
> of the play performed. For this reason I ask that a box is reserved
> for me every Saturday. In conclusion, I declare that every effort
> undertaken by our government to improve and expand the
> theatrical field be based on the performance and the 'know-how'
> of the Royal Theatre.'[22]

The regime's direct interest in the Royal Theatre was demonstrated through
Emergency Law 1504 of 14 December 1938, which imposed special dues

16. Cultural Renaissance

on many forms of entertainment to provide financial support for the Royal Theatre.[23] These included: a) Dues of half a drachma on cinema tickets when the price ranged from five to fifteen drachmas. When the cinema admittance ticket exceeded the amount of fifteen drachmas then the dues paid were one drachma,[24] b) additional special dues of five drachmas were paid on each horse racing ticket; c) five per cent on the entrance price of organised balls and d) additional special dues of twenty five per cent on entertainment hall taxes. These measures represent only a sample of those taken by the Metaxas regime to benefit the Royal Theatre and enhance its enlightening role. The dictator believed that performances of ancient tragedies and comedies would give a new impetus to the revival of ancient heritage and would glorify the past. Soon after he came to power, open performances of Ancient Tragedy were established by the Royal Theatre and *Electra* was the first tragedy to be performed with great success in Herodeum Odeum.[25] This tragedy launched a series of performances of ancient drama which were regularly staged in Herodeum Odeum, and were later followed by performances in the ancient theatre of Epidaurus. These theatrical events, known as *Evdomas Archaiou Dramatos* (Ancient Drama Week), took on special significance for the regime and were met with great support.[26] The interest Metaxas showed in the theatre included the festive inauguration of the Open Royal Theatre in Thessaloniki on 14 May 1938,[27] where regime officials stressed the importance of the theatre and its significant mission in educating and enlightening the masses.[28] Costis Bastias, in an effort to underline the charismatic qualities and artistic inclinations of Metaxas, delivered on that occasion the following speech which reflects the regime's propagandistic efforts to manipulate the masses through the state controlled theatre:

'Our Chief is a man of an exceptional spiritual nature and has indulged in the great classic works of the Italians, the French, the English, and the Germans(...) This encouraged him to declare that every form of art, and culture in general, is not a luxurious way of entertaining the elite, but constitutes a fundamental organic need in the life of a nation. When he watches the enthusiasm of the masses who attend the performances of Shakespearean and other great plays, he smiles and states with delight: 'Those people up there in the upper circles are the true critics of every real poet's work(…)Until yesterday the Greek working masses were squeezed in the galleries of abject revues and were fed on damaging toxins, detestable issues and scenes of repugnant homosexuality.[29] This was the reason that Ioannis Metaxas, like a new Hercules 'mucked out the Augean stables' into which the so-called light musical theatre had plunged. This is why after the imposed censorship on the revues and their deliverance from 'filth', theatrical performances achieved a cultural elevation that ensured their greater popular success.'[30]

The above speech, delivered in harsh language, apart from being a hymn to the Great Patron of Art, also underlined, through the parallel between Metaxas and the mythical Hercules, the intrinsic link between the 'Fourth of August' and the ancient world. Furthermore, it was intended to flatter the masses, stressing at the same time the regime's determination to remove any theatrical 'obstacle' that would jeopardise its elevating mission. In the same vein Metaxas' son-in-law, Georgios Matzufas, a lawyer and theoretician of the New State, claimed that the Board of Directors of the Royal Theatre, of which he was a member, was the instrument which would undertake the indoctrination of public opinion through the theatre. He stressed the great mission of the Thessaloniki Royal Theatre and expressed his conviction that 'the new theatre would flourish in every artistic expression and become an important vehicle for the creation of the *Tritos Ellinikos Politismos* (Third Greek Civilisation): a concept which constituted the supreme ideal and was 'conceived' by the enlightened mind of Ioannis Metaxas.'[31]

To emphasise the significance of the theatre in enlightening the masses and demonstrate his genuine concern for his people, Metaxas announced in May 1938 the construction of an open theatre in Athens. This theatre would be located in the centre of Athens close to the Acropolis (Filoppapou) and would accommodate 10,000 spectators. There the Greek working people would watch the great ancient dramas and comedies, as well as new plays written for their cultural elevation, with a minimum cost admittance ticket.[32] 'Nothing would give me greater pleasure', Metaxas claimed, 'than the realisation that thousands of the working masses would be able to watch the great theatrical plays which could raise their aesthetic standards.'[33] The artistic innovations included the establishment of the Museum of Modern Greek Theatre in Athens which was announced, after much speculation in the press, in June 1938. The announcement became an event for exploitation by the regime's propaganda machine and was given extensive press coverage.[34] Six months later, through Emergency Law 1548, a yearly subsidy of two million drachmas was granted to Cotopouli's theatrical company which, in fact, became semi-governmental.[35] As already mentioned, Cotopouli was one of the two greatest actresses who contributed greatly to the establishment of the National Theatre and promoted the revival of Ancient Drama, and the artistic representation of the great classical works as well as conventional productions.[36]

Apart from being a great actress, Cotopouli was also a devoted royalist, a fact which often caused her great distress.[37] When Metaxas came to power she became one of his most earnest admirers and contributed greatly to the dissemination of his ideas and values. In 1937 Cotopouli was installed in her new theatre in the *Rex* building which became a 'pulpit' for the revival of Ancient Drama and the promotion of good theatrical plays. Her belief in the 'regeneration of Greece' through the theatrical performances of plays which embodied national ideals and were made available to the Greek masses, matched that of Metaxas, and was explicitly demonstrated in her letter to him on 3 November 1939 on the occasion of the celebration of her thirty years theatrical career, an event attended by Metaxas himself:

> "My Chief
> Now that the celebration of the thirtieth anniversary of my theatrical career has come to an end(…)it is the time for me, who is the last but most sincere soldier in your Great Greek Revolution, to come forward and express my gratitude from the depths of my heart. This gratitude originates from the fact that you have always protected me and rewarded my efforts for the last forty years and have made me proud of your congratulations. I feel this deep gratitude because after all these years on stage it is *You* who have given new meaning, new impetus, and new inspiration to my acting(...) It is *You*, who make the thousands of the spectators visit my theatre and share the grief of the ancient heroine *Electra*. It is *You* who, through your words, achievements and enlightened presence, made me re-baptise myself at the eternal springs of *Hellenism* and the everlasting truth. It is *You* who made me sit for a while and think what real Art is(...) it is *You* who guided me in finding a way to come, like a suffering *Electra* of our times, into close contact with the hearts of the masses of our time.. It is from *You* and your words and deeds, which contain true National feelings, that I draw popular new Greek tunes and rhythms. These rhythms constitute the living contemporary Greek human element which speaks directly to the hearts of our people. Now, my dearest *Chief*, that you know my big secret, a secret which I will disclose to the whole of Greece so that it will become a small indication of the role that your great Presence plays in the history of "Greek regeneration," please accept my deepest gratitude and love.'[38]

The above letter vividly illustrates Cotopouli's devotion to Metaxas, and her belief in the power of *Hellenism* and 'national regeneration'.

In addition to the above mentioned measures that Metaxas took to support theatrical activity in Greece, on 8 December 1939 he announced the creation of the Lyric Theatre of Athens as well as the establishment of the state touring theatrical companies (a section of the Royal Theatre) called the '*Arma Thespidos*' (Chariot of Thespis).[39] The mission of those touring theatres was to bring theatrical art to the people in the remote parts of the country. These theatrical companies resembled the Italian touring groups which were established in 1932, during Mussolini's regime, under the same name and met with great success. Theatrical information concerning the *Arma Thespidos* and its artistic activities was published in the daily as well as the theatrical press[40] and special emphasis was given to Metaxas' inspirational participation in setting up these cultural facilities. An article in *Ta Paraskinia* with the title 'Ena Oneiro pou Pragmatopietai - Idriontai to Lyriko Theatro ke Oi Periodevontes Thiasoi' (A Dream Come True - The Establishment of the Lyric Theatre and the Touring Theatres) praised the *Arma Thespidos* and quoted Metaxas' official statement for the occasion. The statement referred to the creation of the Lyric Theatre and the touring theatres which were both born out of the need to enlighten and educate all the Greek people.[41] The formation of touring theatres like the *Arma Thespidos*, expected to reach all the people and contribute to raising cultural standards, and to aid national enlightenment whilst at the same time propagating the regime's beliefs and ideology, was also a practice carried out successfully in Hitler's Germany. Goebbels once stated that 'the theatre is for Germany a matter of the heart and for this matter Germany spends twelve to fifteen million marks a year.'[42] The admiration for the organisation and the operation of the German theatrical touring companies as a means of cultural indoctrination and for the successful completion of their mission to participate in the national spiritual 'uplifting' of the German people was underlined by the theatrical press:

> 'Theatres in Germany are synonymous with the Nation's effort to achieve the reconstruction of German cultural life: Germany believes that in order to reach its destiny, apart from material power, she must also acquire spiritual and cultural supremacy. This great mission was assigned by the *Third Reich* to the theatres, especially the touring ones. Thus we consider to be extremely inspiring, the initial formative action taken to base the creation and operation of the theatrical touring companies on the principles of the 'People's Culture'.[43]

The establishment of a network of cultural activities, controlled by the regime and supported by effective legislation, ensured that the theatre was

used as an instrument of mass indoctrination and dissemination of the
'Fourth of August' ideals and beliefs[44]. One of the most important ideals
was the *Anagennisis Tis Ellados* (regeneration of Greece) and the creation
of the *Tritos Ellinikos Politismos* (Third Greek Civilisation). The projection
and realisation of this ideal could be effected through the theatre, because
according to the regime's propaganda, 'theatre is the means by which to
carry to the most remote places in Greece the 'healthy and strong seeds' of
our spiritual culture and sow them in the fertile national soil' [45]

The 'regeneration of Greece' and the theatre

> 'The word *Hellenism* is a symbol and this symbol is the central point
> around which the civilisations of all the nations on earth will be
> constructed.'[46]

The target of Metaxas' theatre propaganda was the transformation of
the masses in such a way that they could become worthy citizens of a
'regenerating Greece' and participate in the creation of the 'Third Greek
Civilisation'. The 'regeneration of Greece' formed one of the basic
objectives of the new regime and was launched by Metaxas on 10 August
1936 in his radio speech, and was repeated and analysed in Thessaloniki on
6 September 1936:

> 'We were forced to impose a dictatorship(...)in order to be able
> to accomplish our supreme goal which is one and only one:
> the 'regeneration of Greece': a regeneration which is not only
> economic but social. Greece cannot exist socially if its society
> consist of unhappy and miserable people. The Greek people have
> reached such a point of degradation and indifference that they
> have endangered the fate of the Nation and the Country(...) Thus
> I repeat: Regeneration from a National Point of view: because you
> cannot exist but as Greeks; as Greeks who believe in the power
> of *Hellenism*, and through it you can develop and create your own
> civilisation.'[47]

Metaxas envisaged a new state based on the revival of *Hellinismos* (Hellenism-
Greek National Identity), and the supreme Greek ideals. These ideals
and *Hellenism* had been squashed after the Great War and the Asia Minor
catastrophe, together with the *Megali Idea* (The Supreme Idea) of a Greater
Greece, which was the standard-bearer of *Hellenism*.[48] In Metaxas' view
no person, especially a young person, could live without national identity

because he would become disorientated and confused. The neglect of national vision, together with the loss of a large part of the modern Greek state, had led young Greeks to adopt and believe in other peoples ideals, such as Leftism and Fascism. The existing educational system, instead of offering them a cultural education based on national ideals, introduced new theories to instruct and enlighten young people on general matters. This was, according to Metaxas, a fatal mistake: education in Greece should serve no other purpose than to educate Greeks and direct them towards the great national ideals.[49] Spiritually, people could only exist as Greeks, Turks, French, English, Germans and others. Therefore, Greek youth should realise that they could exist and act only through their nationality: *Hellenism*, Metaxas claimed in the 'historical' articles exchanged between him and his political rival Venizelos, (the charismatic protagonist of 'a Greater Greece'), through *Kathimerini* in 1934-1935, had no boundaries and the *Megali Idea* was dead only in its territorial form. By and large, Greek Civilisation and Greek Culture had no boundaries either. Thus, it was imperative that Greek National Culture, the *Hellenic Culture*, should be reconstructed and reinstated in such a way, that it could spread beyond the geographical frontiers of Greece. This was the essence of *Hellenism* and the *Megali Idea* and it became the dream of the 'Fourth of August' State.[50] On 2 October 1936 when Metaxas set out the main objectives and policies of his government, the 'regeneration of Greece' formed a central theme. 'Greece has but one way out,' he strongly emphasised, 'to march ahead determined to achieve her regeneration; this regeneration will be a long and difficult task: but we are determined to accomplish this task completely and thoroughly.'[51] This objective needed the mobilisation of every section of Greek society. Soon after Metaxas came to power the organisation of National Renaissance (*Organosis Ethnikis Anagennisis*) was established by what Metaxas referred to as 'prominent Greeks'[52] with the 'sacred' mission to propagate and support Metaxas' objectives on *Hellenism*. On 14 November 1936 Metaxas attended their official meeting and delivered a speech which underlined the real nature of the objectives of the regime and the Organisation, and the means of their fulfilment:

> 'The routes which must be taken by your Organisation, an Organisation which bears a successful title which signifies your goals, are open to further discussion and meetings. I am sure that you will work very hard so that your ideals will be successfully conveyed to the whole of Greece in such a way that a special class of people, who think alike and are totally devoted to the State, will emerge and form the governing classes of our society.'[53]

The above extract suggests that the regime was determined to use every possible means to ensure the 'regeneration of Greece' and the creation of the 'Third Greek Civilisation.' In his speech to *EON* in Ioannina on 13 June 1937, Metaxas analysed this concept and set out the conditions for its materialisation:

> 'You must be prepared for what is coming because you will live to see the creation of the Third Greek Civilisation, which is the Modern Greek Civilisation. The first civilisation was the ancient civilisation. That civilisation was great in spirit but lacking in religious faith and is gone for ever. Along came the second Greek civilisation (Byzantine) which did not accomplish great spiritual things but had a deep religious faith. Now is your turn to combine the best elements of both these civilisations and with your deep Christian faith(...) and the inspirations drawn from the great accomplishments of your ancestors you must create the 'Third Greek Civilisation.'.[54]

The 'Third Greek Civilisation' demanded a return to national values as they were epitomised by Metaxas's regime. These values would, according to Nicoloudis, urge the 'thirsty' Greek people 'to return to their eternal springs where they would accomplish their spiritual elevation and national regeneration and create a new supreme civilisation: 'The Third Greek Civilisation'.[55]

The first grand manifestations of the new 'cultural nationalism' strategy supported by the regime's theatre propaganda took place in April 1937. The occasion was the celebration of the centenary of the '*Ethnikon ke Kapodistriakon Panepistimion Athinon* (Athens National and Kopodistrian University), 'the most genuine representative of Greek antiquity and education' according to the newspaper *Athinaika Nea.*[56] The celebration, an occasion of extravagant expenditure, became a great opportunity for the regime's propaganda machine to convey its ideology. Well organised by the main Greek University Senate and members of the educational world, this celebration enjoyed the overwhelming support of the government and was attended by the Royal Family, the Government, foreign High Officials, Greek and foreign academics and hundreds of eminent guests.[57] When organising this celebration the regime's propaganda had three recipients in mind: the intellectuals and the men of letters who were to devote their skills and attention to the re-education and reformation of the Greek people, especially the young; the masses who ought to be introduced to the intellectual world and the great national ideals which would ensure their cultural and spiritual elevation; and finally, the foreign governments who were to be impressed by the display of the cultural power and the will of the government to restore the glorious past through educational and cultural enlightenment. This celebration was not intended to be centred around the leader but a festivity to honour and acknowledge this High Institution which glorified and promoted the idea of *Hellenism*, and was intended to become a living testimony of Metaxas' success and the people's genuine support. On the occasion, Metaxas delivered the following speech which reflected the regime's effort to link the centenary of the University with the 'evolution' of the New State':

> 'Now that the Greek Nation upholds again the old and imperishable ideals and, with the support and guidance of a reformed State enters a period of a new life which will enable Greece to rediscover itself the University leaves behind one hundred years of its life and looks forward to another promising hundred years. The University now faces new horizons which are the same horizons that our Greek youth, animated by a new spirit, are longing and searching for. The new reformed State, fully aware of its great mission, is determined to supervise and support the University in order to meet the great and pressing demands of the new regenerating Greek Society.'[58]

The festivities which lasted seven days (18-24 April) were extensively covered by the domestic and foreign press. According to both the daily newspapers and the government publications, the central focal point of the festivities, and an indication of the regime's theatrical propaganda, was the staging on the Acropolis of 'the symbolic representation of an invocation to the goddess *Athena* and by extension to the ancient spirit she represented. The Greek youth would invoke the goddess *Athena* to reach out for the spirit of the contemporary Greece and manifest the unified and everlasting continuity of that one spirit; the Greek Spirit.'[59] The sacred ritual of the Goddess's intervention and sanctioning of the modern Greek spirit, which would take place on the sanctuary of the *Acropolis,* would be manifested by *Athena's* crowning the Greek students. The account of the performance given by the *YTT* is quite striking and expresses the regime's effort to convince the audience of its determination to reinstate the glorious past:

> 'The performance opened with the appearance of forty six maidens coming from the rear of the *Parthenon*. They were dressed in white dresses and veils in an ancient style and were crowned with laurels and flowers. They walked rhythmically(...) until they reached the top

level with the pillars where they lined up: Afterwards, a young maiden impersonating the goddess *Athena* wearing a helmet and holding a spear in one hand , and a wreath of golden laurel in the other, walked slowly, followed by six maidens. On the west side of the *Parthenon*, in front of a small altar, stood the law student *Ph. Mitsopoulos* who recited the invocation to the goddess *Athena* in ancient Greek.'[60] When the invocation came to an end the goddess *Athena* handed over the golden wreath to two of her attendants. They placed it on the *Parthenon* steps, while others threw flowers at *Athena*'s feet. The Goddess re-entered the Temple while the rest of the maidens rhythmically ascended the steps and followed her. The ceremony was brief, simple, and dignified and despite the risk inherent in the Goddess's personification at the noble temple of the *Parthenon*, the revival of the archaic procession proved very successful and was enthusiastically received by the foreign and Greek spectators' [61]

Apart from the effort put in to the above event to convey a festive and 'spiritually elevated' atmosphere, it seems that the organisers were preoccupied by considerable scepticism and concern about the actual outcome of the festivity, as there was great controversy regarding the success of such an undertaking. Before the actual performance took place the daily press, in its entirety, attacked the idea viciously. The newspapers, in front-page articles, spoke of the forthcoming fiasco of the ceremony and advised the people involved in the preparations to avoid this risky attempt of staging the invocation to the goddess *Athena* which was likely to result in ridicule (*maskarilikia*) and debasement of Greek antiquity. Some newspapers went as far as to write that the ceremony at the *Parthenon* and the appearance of the Goddess *Athena* was an act of sacrilege which would discredit not only the theatrical act but the whole of Greece in front of intellectuals from all over the world.[62] Despite the severe criticism, the show took place and strangely enough, the newspapers of the following day extolled the successful attempt undertaken by the government, and praised the people involved. (This change of attitude that the press exhibited could either be the result of a really successful performance, or the dynamic intervention of the regime's censorship).[63]

Other manifestations organised by the regime for the occasion included a concert in the Herodeum Odeum on 21 April 1937, which was attended by King George and other members of the royal family, the Diplomatic Corps, members of the Government and the Academic World. The musical pieces included Byzantine hymns and the *demotic* (folk) songs *Leventia, E Perdika* and *Diamanto.*[64] The use of *demotic* music and songs as a medium of propaganda was of great importance to the regime as 'the *demotic* songs of a nation constitute the mirror of the soul of the nation. Through these songs one meets all the elements which form the social structure of every country(...) The Greek *demotic* songs come straight from the eternal soul of a nation that has existed for four thousand years, and contain an endless vein of artistry, heroism and great achievements.'[65]

The celebration of the centenary of the University, apart from manifesting links with the regime's theme of cultural *Hellenism* and the revival of the ancient ideals, also became an event for promoting relations between Greece and the other countries which took this opportunity to secure economic and political predominance in Greece. Greece in the mid-1930s faced great social and economic problems. The growing foreign or external debts which had been increased by the fall in exports, and the need to secure capital, influenced Greece's foreign relations. In an effort to secure markets for the country's luxury agricultural cash corps, Metaxas' regime turned towards Nazi Germany as the latter was at the time the main importer of Greek exports. Furthermore, as Germany had adopted a new scheme of 'a clearing' system in its foreign trade, Greece was to an extent obliged to accept imports from Germany under the new system.[66] Thus, Greek foreign policy under Metaxas had, at least in the beginning, come under German influence.[67] On the other hand there were a number of outstanding critical British issues which required special treatment and involved the British Government and the 'Fourth of August' regime directly. Those included the issue of the British Bondholders of the Greek Debt, who demanded a substantial increase in payments. Metaxas' initial refusal to comply with this demand was overturned only two weeks after his advent to power, and with the encouragement of King George II, he agreed to pay 40 percent of foreign debt interest for the period 1935-1937. Another urgent matter involved the renewal of several franchises of British monopolies such as Cable and Wireless Ltd. and Eastern Telegraphs, as well as the Electricity Transport Company, all of which Metaxas' regime was willing to take over.[68] However, he failed to assume control and signed new agreements in April 1937 and in July 1937, respectively.[69] Other issues included the operation of the Blackburn air-craft industry in Faliro and the problem which arose when the regime tried to control it by monitoring via the Bodosdakis-Athanassiadis local armament enterprise.[70] British insurance companies also became a problem when Metaxas attempted to nationalise all social insurance in the country. All these issues were difficult matters which the British Foreign Office and the Greek regime were called upon to handle. All the relevant official documentation and letters exchanged between the British and Greek Government, most of which are incidentally dated around April 1937, reveal Britain's growing concern to secure a prominent place in the new economic 'arena' of Greece.[71]

In view of all the above and given the festive climate of the centenary of Athens University, the foreign governments engaged in a display of cultural power, 'tempting offers' and propaganda to win the favour of the 'Fourth of August' regime and protect their economic, political and cultural interests. The account given by the U.S. Ambassador MacVeagh on 20 May 1937 (a few days after the celebration) makes this effort more than explicit:

> 'British and German Propaganda in this country, not to speak of the French and Italian, is now more active than any time since the war days: particularly noticeable is the development of British Propaganda. The British Minister tells me that if he is to go on doing all the propaganda work required of him, his Legation should be doubled. Meanwhile the Germans are not taking all this lying down. Following the visits of Goering, Goebbels and Schacht a whole flock of minor officials visited here and we have seen a big development in German archaeological activity.'[72]

To honour the occasion, which coincided with the celebration of the forty year anniversary of the German School in Athens,[73] and to demonstrate the close friendship with Greece, Berlin named one of its main streets as *Griechische Allee* (Greek Boulevard). The ceremony, which took place with all solemnity on 23 April 1937, was attended by the Mayor of Berlin Dr. Lebbert and all the city officials, as well as representatives of the Ministries of Foreign Affairs and Propaganda. The Greek State was represented by Ambassador A. Rizos-Ragavis and the entire staff of the Greek Embassy. Opening the ceremony Dr. Lebbert stressed the close economic and cultural relations between the two countries and conveyed to the Greek King,[74] through the Greek Ambassador, Germany's good will assuring him of a long lasting friendship. Returning the compliments Ragavis stated:

> 'This Greek Boulevard will constitute a living example of friendship between the two countries, and will prove to us Greeks that Adolf Hitler's Germany not only embraces the words of the poet which read 'seek with your heart and soul the country of the Greeks,'[75] but, through naming the Berlin avenue *Griechische,* conveys those words and their meaning to generations to come. Under this spirit I call upon my compatriots to applaud with me the German Nation and their Chief *Adolf Hitler.*'[76]

Similarly, the British representatives during the ceremony announced the establishment in the University of Athens of the chair of English Institutions and Literature under the name *The Byron Chair*. The announcement was sealed with the reading of state letters sent by the British Foreign Minister Eden which expressed his satisfaction at the new chair at the Greek University and spoke of the unbreakable links and friendship that Greece and Britain had enjoyed so far. France was represented by the Minister of Education, Zean Zay,[77] who, in a long speech, underlined the importance of the Greek spirit and its contribution to the civilisation of the world and referred to the common goals and ideals that connected Greece and France, pleading for a closer political and economic relationship between the two countries. The festivities closed with a grand dinner for 450 foreign and Greek men of letters at Sounion given by Nicoloudis who assured the guests that his government would make sure that a new 'regenerating Greece' would prevail and the ancient and supreme ideals would be reinstated.[78]

The creation of the 'Third Greek Civilisation' was according to Metaxas solely a Greek affair. 'We wish to create a Greek Civilisation,' he said to the people of Komotini on 7 October 1936. 'We do not want the foreign civilisations. What we are aiming at is to create our own civilisation which we shall transform and give such an impetus that it will become superior to any other civilisations.'[79] Any attempt to seek inspiration for this supreme creation in imported models would be in vain. The only place that the Greek people should look for the necessary material to 'build' the 'Third Greek Civilisation' was right in their hearts and spirit, avoiding the 'unbalanced' foreign systems which had nothing in common with the great Greek spirit.[80]

An important vehicle for the national renaissance and people's spiritual enlightenment, and indeed the crucial element in this creation, was culture.

Metaxas envisaged a spiritual revolution which would bring about the noble goals, and the rebirth of the nation. He saw Greek culture as an expression of *Hellenism*, and, although high foreign culture was good,[81] *Hellenic* culture was better. It thus became imperative that this culture be freed from foreign influences and serve the supreme ideals of the nation. The creation of a true national art which would replace the foreign one (so far enjoyed only by the few) and become the property of the ordinary people, constituted a predominant propaganda target for Metaxas' regime. ' Long live our art, long live our Greek art' Metaxas emphatically acclaimed at the end of his speech on 30 December 1938 on the occasion of the dinner given in his honour by the Cultural Organisation. In that speech he likened art to the large and healthy trees of a woodland, the formation of which was the result of the decay and destruction of hundreds of small trees and branches. In a similar way the tree of art needed the sacrifice and the contribution of many small and anonymous artists who were working in insignificant and remote places and contributed their artistic inspirations to the creation of high art. It was those unknown artists whom the 'Fourth of August' regime wished to acknowledge, because they were the 'branches and the small trees' that would form the 'fertiliser' for the creation of Greek art.[82] The ideological 'renewal' and the transformation of the Greek spirit in such a way that it could become worthy of its great historical past, reaching the great standard of ancient times, necessitated the mobilisation not only of the theatre, but the entire range of cultural activities under the wise guidance and strict observation of the Leader (*Archigos*.)[83] All expressions of art which, so far, had caused a national deterioration should rise above the cultural insignificance and glorify the heroic and healthy elements of the Greek nation. A general cultural mobilisation, as Metaxas stated, was needed to fight for the nation. ' It is imperative that all the armed forces of the cultured people of this country begin a cultural struggle against our enemies,[84] this will be a struggle for the same ideals and values which our nation has fought and stood for, for thousands of years now(...); ideals for which our people sacrificed themselves and shed their blood; ideals that have been invested with great glory and fame.'[85] This meant that artists, actors and writers should not only be sympathetic towards the goals and aspirations of the state, but become the pioneers who would extol and disseminate these goals through their intellectual tasks. Art would no longer serve the arrogant and deteriorating elite,[86] but would become the true expression of the Greek people and their 'healthy' spirit. According to the regime's propaganda within this popularly based culture, theatre was to reach out to the broad masses made up of the thousands of Greek working people.[87] In this respect special care was taken to entertain and educate the ordinary people, especially the workers, through the theatre. This task was assigned to *Ergatiki Estia,* (The Workers' Home Organisation) which in 1939 through Emergency Law 1688 expanded its responsibilities to cover all the materialistic and spiritual needs of the workers, and established offices in most of the big cities. According to the regime's sources during the summer of 1937 and 1938 the organisation established and maintained its own theatre in Piraeus, which staged forty performances of moralistic and social plays for a very small admittance fee. When it became well established that the educational and social level of the workers had risen to such a degree that they longed for better spiritual 'food' *Ergatiki Estia* turned for help to the Royal Theatre, the Cotopouli theatre, the Antoniadis theatre and the Argyropoulos theatre These companies, with the help of the *Ergatiki Estia,* which subsidised the fares, staged many performances which were attended

17. 'Fourth of August' Poster

by a great number of working people who paid an entrance fee of only three to eight drachmas. During the spring of 1939 the number of people who attended those plays went up to 23,000.[88] Furthermore, small theatrical groups were encouraged to tour the country and provide entertainment of high standard and quality, with plays of a national and inspiring content. For every member of the touring companies which travelled and performed in places other than Athens, a reduction of 50 per-cent on the rail fare and 25 per-cent on the boat fare was granted by the regime.[89] Care was taken by the regime's propaganda to ensure that these beneficial interventions were made known to the people through its publications as well as by articles written by high officials and men of letters. Costis Bastias, analysing Metaxas' populist 'art for the people' approach in *To Neon Kratos,* wrote:

> 'Culture constitutes an organic need for the people. However, Metaxas never considered people of the rich elite and the upper classes. By people Metaxas means the broad masses who work hard and sweat, some with their hands and others with their mind, to earn their living with dignity and pride. These are the only people that Metaxas has in his mind day and night, and those are the people for whom he works and over whom he loses his sleep. These are the people to whom he wants to offer the theatre, and because he is a genuinely spiritual and cultural man, he believes that without a broader popular footing no theatrical art can prosper and achieve great things. He is aware that the theatre reached glorious moments when it was created and enjoyed by the broad popular masses.' [90]

It is clear from the above passage that the regime's theatre propaganda was directed mainly towards the masses who were to be exploited and manipulated through cultural and spiritual 'elevation.' In the same line Yiannis Sideris underlined the special role played by Ioannis Metaxas in the elevation of Greek Theatre and stated: 'These days, like in ancient times when the State provided and set the rules for Greek theatre, our Chief, more than any other Greek Governor so far, supports the theatre. We only hope that we, the theatre people, can match his dreams and aspirations and contribute to the elevation of our civilisation; a hope which must dominate our thoughts and our actions.'[91]

One of Metaxas' greatest aspirations was the creation of a true national culture which would replace the foreign one enjoyed only by the few, and become the art of the ordinary people. But this culture should be purified because until the coming of the 'Fourth of August' State, the Greek people had been 'fed' with a 'harmful' culture in which light theatre predominated. This artistic degradation had resulted in their deterioration as a nation and the loss of their national pride, dignity and ideals. The *YTT* through its publications underlined the harmful effects which the 'light' theatre had on the Greek people, until Metaxas' 'blessed' intervention put it in its 'proper place' and exploited the beneficial mission of the theatre:

> 'The theatre, which constitutes a vital factor in a country's civilisation with an indisputable power to influence and mould society, had before the coming of the 'Fourth of August' State reached a dangerous and damaging level. Thus our National Government, fully aware of the coming danger which was lurking in the public theatrical performances, turned its attention, (among other pressing issues) towards the cultural sphere. The light theatre had been 'fed' by revues and operettas written by people who had forgotten what their true role and mission as intellectuals was. Those people, who aimed only at serving and satisfying the most vulgar instincts of the audience and were guided by easy profit, had completely diverged from their mission which was the healthy entertainment of the society, especially that of the lower classes. Not only the playwrights, but also the actors contributed greatly to the downfall of the Greek theatre. With their vulgar gestures, dances and alien examples of artistic performance they flattered and provoked the base instincts of the public. To rectify this sad situation the *YTT* enacted Emergency Law 446 which imposed strict control on theatrical plays, laying the foundations for their purification.'[92]

The above extract suggests that the regime was determined to exercise absolute control over the cultural sphere and suppress any reaction that might interfere with its great mission of elevating the Greek masses. Within the context of creating a 'people's culture' which would be pure and reflect the nation's ideals, and in an effort to encourage young writers to create 'healthy' plays, the regime on 7 January 1938 introduced a Royal Decree which established several literary prizes for the best Greek plays produced. Writers, who before the 'Fourth of August' regime had lost their national orientation, were urged to write plays that would elevate the Greek spirit and reinstate the glorious aspirations of the people. Given the scarcity of 'good and proper' Greek theatrical plays in contrast to the foreign ones[93] this seemed a very effective way to ensure a Greek repertoire. On 22 May 1940 during the awards celebration of the cultural and literary prizes for the year 1939, Metaxas delivered the following speech urging the young writers and intellectuals to orientate themselves towards a pure Greek culture:

'If you wish to write plays that will last for ever, you must go directly and draw your inspiration from the supreme and inexhaustible source which is called popular spirit. Your writings must exclude heroes who have no life of their own but imitate the foreign models. Your heroes must be figures that are authentically Greeks. You must go close to the people who work hard and sweat, and you must acknowledge their feelings, their happiness and misfortune, and share their laughter and their tears. Close to those *Piges* (sources) you will be able to find yourselves: because whether you like it or not and, irrespective of any other influence that you might be under, you are Greeks; and you are Greeks because your genetic cells and your sub-conscience are Greek. Therefore, there is no other way left to you but to think in the Greek way. By coming close to the *Hellenic* sources which will provide you with the necessary material, and with your talent, you will discover and express through your writings and performances the Greek lifestyle, honouring at the same time your motherland.'[94]

In a similar fashion Nicoloudis spoke of 'the need to turn to the eternal national sources of inspiration now that the wind of 'national regeneration,' which will inevitably lead to the creation of the 'Third Greek Civilisation,' is blowing in Greece.[95] The national and ideological 'renewal' of the Greek people, promoted by the regime's propaganda, necessitated the creation of a purified Greek art which would glorify the heroic and the great. But most importantly, it demanded that this art be accessible to the masses who would appreciate it, and through their enlightenment, participate in the creation of the 'Third Greek Civilisation'.[96] Thus, Metaxas' policy towards a popularly based culture included the reduction of the ticket price for the Cotopouli, Herodeum Odeum and Epidaurus theatres. This policy formed part of the regime's effort and attempt to bring art to the people, and people to the art. During the 'Week of Ancient Drama' which was greatly advertised in the theatrical press,[97] the theatre tickets were fixed at twenty and fifteen drachmas, instead of the regular prices of a hundred, fifty and thirty drachmas. At the same time articles emphasised the fact that for the first time in the modern history of the theatre, performances of the great ancient dramas came within the reach of ordinary people.[98] In his article 'E Evdomas tou Archaiou Dramatos' Costis Bastias praised the 'sacred mission of these public performances' and emphasised Metaxas' 'effort to link the ordinary people with the great ancient performances which was the only way left to us for our 'national regeneration.'[99] However, an obstacle to the realisation of the people's cultural elevation was language. Indeed, the language issue was a problem that had haunted Greek reality for a long time and had caused great controversies and debates among scholars and politicians. There existed two versions of the Greek language, *katharevousa* (puristic) which was the language spoken and defended by the elite and the conservatives, and *demotic* (populist) the language of the 'progressive.'[100] Metaxas was aware of the language problem and on 15 September 1936 expressed his ideas and beliefs about the language issue in an interview with Costis Bastias in *Vradini*. In this interview Metaxas exhibited a preference for the *demotic* language. He justified this preference by the fact that the 'Fourth of August' State, which claimed to be a national government, could not be an enemy of the language in which the Greek National Anthem was written, and he expressed his belief that the two versions would finally coexist, with the *demotic* one predominating.[101]

When Metaxas took the Education Portfolio in November 1938, in an effort to make progress with his populist educational and cultural policy, and make high art freely available to the ordinary people, he proceeded with the radical language reform of introducing *demotic* language into elementary schools.[102] This reform would also enable new writers to produce plays that would give shape and expression to the great ideals of the nation and enlighten the ordinary people as to their glorious past and their 'sacred' mission to participate in the 'nation's regeneration.' They were urged to write in *demotic,* because this was the language that the people could understand and identify with. Sideris spoke of the great change in the Greek Modern Theatre, which was brought about by the living *demotic* language which replaced the 'dead' *katharevousa,* while others spoke of a cultural regeneration through the *demotic* language and praised the new playwrights for writing plays in the language of the people.[103] The new playwrights, aware of their responsibility towards the New State and the Greek nation, enriched the modern Greek theatre with plays that were destined to arouse feelings of national pride and glory. These plays, which drew their themes mostly from history and paid homage to the simple language, were written and performed in most of the Greek theatres, while the theatrical press, with headlines like 'Ellinika Erga Sta Theatra' (Greek Plays in the Theatres), praised the new trend towards a national orientation.[104] One play representative of this new tendency to produce better works with themes drawn from the past looking with faith towards a promising national and theatrical future was *Papaflessas.* The play, a poetic drama, written in 1937 by Spyros Melas, was based on the heroic figure of the archimandrite *Papaflessas* and the Greek struggle for independence against the Turks in 1821. The play was staged in April 1940 by the Royal Theatre and was enthusiastically received by the press, which spoke of a theatrical masterpiece. They praised its playwright Spyros Melas who had managed 'to present the hero in such a multi-faceted way that he made him an eternal symbol of freedom.'[105] Other significant theatrical plays with a historical content included the *Autokrator Michail* (Emperor Michael) written in 1936, and *Stavros ke Spathi* (Cross and Sword) written in 1939, both by A. Terzakis, *Lambros and Maria* written by M. Scouloudis and performed in 1939 and many others all of which participated in the spiritual elevation and national awareness of the Greek people, especially the working masses.

Ethnikos Organismos Neoleas and Theatre Propaganda

'March ahead to a New Greece, ahead with a Greek spirit, march ahead with pride and bravery, ahead You Children of Greece.'[106]

A large number of theatrical plays which were produced and staged during the Metaxas' dictatorship were those intended for the enlightenment and nationalistic education of Greek youth. All the regime's propaganda, as far as youth was concerned, was geared towards one supreme goal, to inculcate in the minds and hearts of the Greek youth unconditional love, respect and admiration for the *Megas Kyvernitis* and the nation that was Greece. The devotion of Greek youth for their motherland, and their binding duty to work hard for a new Greece was an indisputable fact, and it was stressed by Metaxas at the beginning of his dictatorship when he stated: 'stand up Greek Youth. there exists no other reality for you than the Greek Nation. It is only within this concept and this reality that you will rediscover your true-self.'[107]

The dictator found it necessary to establish the conditions that would facilitate the quick and thorough propagation among the Greek youth of the ideas linked with the 'regeneration of Greece.' Because, according to his propaganda machine 'the youth of every nation is the nation itself and if this healthy youth ceases to exist the nation ceases to exist. Thus youth becomes the effective vehicle for conveying the will of a State.'[108] One effective instrument to instil the regime's cultural and spiritual outlook in the masses of Greek youth was, according to the *EON* propagandists, the theatre: 'The enlightening and educational role of the theatre is so significant that it can become a great school. This is the reason that this medium ought to be given special care by our Organisation. We believe that the establishment of theatres, especially those in the country, will influence and indoctrinate the masses. Because of the special role that the theatre can play for people, and in view of the lack of *EON* theatres and theatrical groups, the *EON* members ought, at least at the beginning, to attend all the great performances given by the good theatrical companies, especially those of the Royal Theatre.'[109] The justification for the preference for this medium, which like the cinema was controlled by the *Diefthinsis Psychagogias Tis EON* (Directive of Entertainment to *EON*) under the III Office,[110] was made explicit by the Propaganda officials during the *EON*'s First Congress when the correct strategy for an effective propaganda was drawn up:

> 'We have an imperative task to indoctrinate our youth with the goals set by our Chief. These goals are nothing else but the supreme idea which constitutes *Hellas*. Our youth must be taught through living images and icons the history of their nation and their motherland. They must learn through our indoctrination why they must be proud of being Greeks. They must be made to believe that because they are Greeks, they are immortal: because Greek Youth is the oldest generation on earth, it never grows old but it remains, forever, young. The young people must also be taught that they must always have one motto and axiom for those who challenge their belief. This motto is: Our Nation is the *Hellenic* Nation: our Motherland is *Hellas* and we constitute *Hellenism*'[111]

Yet, carrying out this strategy was, according to *EON* officials, a time-consuming procedure which necessitated long and demanding work. It should be based on the living example of the ants 'who repeat the same task again and again and collect a grain which is much larger than their body but, because they have patience and work very hard they succeed in their task.'[112] It was imperative that the teachers of the new ideology should teach the young generation the history of the Greek nation with great zeal and enthusiasm, because it was through history that a New Greece would emerge. Most importantly, the teaching of Greek ideals and values should not take the form of a fairy tale but should be based on living examples. History should come out from the dusty libraries and the long forgotten past, and become a guide and a living model of the ideas and values epitomised by the 'Fourth of August:' State because it was those ideals which would create the 'Third Greek Civilisation.'[113] Theatre should form a significant means of indoctrination, and efforts should be made to establish Drama Schools which would teach the young members of *EON* the art of acting.'[114] These actors would then form theatrical groups which would stage Greek plays with nationalist themes. Because the *EON* theatre, apart from being entertaining, also served the goals and ideals of the Organisation and operated in line with those goals, it goes without saying that these groups and the staging of the plays were under the strict control of the *EON* III Office, which supervised every stage of production and performance.

The propagandists believed that for achieving the effective indoctrination of youth, plays which extolled the heroic past and the great achievements of the Greek nation should form compulsory reading in schools. Because of the lack of 'correct plays of national content' competitions were run among the *EON* members for the writing of such plays. The competitions played a significant role in the regime's propaganda, and the *EON* officials, in order to underline the importance of such an event, set the 7 November (*EON*'s anniversary) as the day when the results and the winning plays would be made known[115]. These plays were to be divided into two groups: plays which would be performed by *EON* actors for the members of *EON*, and plays which were to be staged by *EON* actors for the masses of ordinary people.[116] However, 'because in some of the plays there appeared to be elements of negative foreign influences,'[117] great care was taken to avoid such a phenomenon. Through articles such as *E Elleniki techni ke e Gymnotis ton modernon* (Greek art and the spiritual 'nudity of the modern')[118] *EON* writers were strongly advised to produce plays which were free from damaging foreign influences. Instead, they should produce plays which contained all the elements that defined true art and were to be found in Greek tradition, Greek legends and history. To make sure that these recommendations were taken seriously by the readers, in the same issue of *Neolea* the following article with the title 'ATTENTION,' was published:

> 'We strongly recommend to our readers to read carefully the article in this issue about *E Elleniki techni ke e gymnotis ton modernon* (Greek art and the spiritual nudity of the modern). The young generation of the place which gave birth to art is not permitted to deviate from the ideals epitomised by the people who created the world's civilisation, but must follow in their footsteps. By this we do not imply that you must reject the artistic developments of other nations, but you must select only the elements that can elevate Greek art, avoiding the extremities of modern inclinations which will lead to harmful results and ridicule.'[119]

Furthermore, *EON* publications were extensively distributed to 'improve' the cultural education of its young members. The most important one was the *Peri Technis* (About Art) published in 1940 and based on the order issued by Kanellopoulos, which analysed the concept of art within the *EON*, and set the guidelines for the cultural indoctrination of youth. According to the booklet the cultural and spiritual education of the *EON* members was the necessary precondition for the creation of the 'Third Civilisation.' It was through the cultural indoctrination of the young that the enlightenment and cultural elevation of the masses was to be made possible. 'By making the young love the great Greek works of art,' the guidelines read, 'and by creating good theatrical plays which will inspire the young members we shall create the 'public' that our Chief wants to create; a public which will be culturally educated in such a way that, apart from learning to love and appreciate good art and the artists, they will form the revolutionary material out of which will evolve new artists who will glorify our nation.'[120] The strategy for this cultural education was a difficult task and involved a great amount of patience and goodwill. The instructions given through the 'About Art' booklet to the officials entrusted with the mission of cultural indoctrination read as follows:

> 'During our meeting (which incidentally should consist of only a small number of members) we begin by organising a small and easy theatrical performance. We make sure that prior to the performance we prepare the children by briefing them about what they are going to see. We comment on the play and the playwright making sure that everything we say is conditioned by our enthusiasm, love and admiration for the writer and his work. In this way we shall arouse the curiosity of the children who will wish to see and hear more about such plays. By doing so they will begin to love and cherish the 'beautiful' and the 'noble' and they will realise that apart from day-to-day life there exists a life which is enriched by supreme values and ideals. When this realisation has been achieved by our young members, we recommend our plays which have been chosen with great care, hoping that they will study them.'[121]

The above extract suggests that the *EON* officials were well aware of child psychology and had taken all the necessary measures to ensure their exploitation and manipulation. In order to familiarise them with the staging process of a play and ensure their theatrical 'know-how,' the propagandists organised small theatrical workshops during which all steps were taken to ensure the successful completion of their task. The following extract gives an insight into such an undertaking and sets the 'rules' for its successful outcome:

> 'It is well known that children love fairs and festivities because they can amuse themselves: but they love them even more when they can participate in the performances and demonstrate their skills. Organising such a fair thus facilitates our task and contributes to the cultural education of our children: because it is through our

teaching and their reading, as well as the critical process involved in such an undertaking, that they will learn to appreciate art(...) For instance, when we put on a small theatrical performance we shall choose one that contains all the cultural ideas that we wish to convey to our children, provided of course that we have prepared everything with the utmost care(....) These fairs, if prepared carefully, will constitute for us the excuse, but for the children they will constitute a real challenge. In this way we shall create a generation full of national pride and motivation as we shall have evoked from the past all the national virtues and great ideals which will form the necessary base for a new glorious nation.'[122]

By August 1939, 5,000 theatrical shows and fairs were organised by *EON*,[123] while according to the *YTT* during the four years of Metaxas' government 1,450 theatrical performances were organised by *EON* which were attended by 475,000 members of the Organisation and 525,000 other spectators.[124] These performances in which 4,650 *EON* members participated, were given in private theatres, open spaces, schools and the theatres established by the Organisation.[125] In order to imbue the hearts and minds of young *EON* members with national spirit and *Hellenic* values, the playwrights wrote plays where the protagonists were heroes and human stereotypes that the young children, and the Greek public at large, could recognise and identify with. The following extract published in *E Neolea*, demonstrates explicitly the regime's effort to convey and persuade its readers of this vital national necessity:

'Unfortunately in the last years our writers have been enslaved by the works of the foreign authors, who have replaced everything that was Greek. At the beginning of the 'Fourth of August' State, and for a short period after, we were unable to provide our people with a proper performance. Therefore the workers who would attend Ibsen's *Hedda Gabler* would leave the theatre miserable and unsatisfied, while we would have missed the opportunity to entertain them properly, disseminating at the same time our 'disguised' indoctrination. However, during those four years an effort on a gigantic scale has taken place in the field of literature and art in general. Art must remain free; but free art does not necessarily imply a ruined art patched up by foreign manifestations and influences. We have no need for such an art: an art which can not speak to our hearts and tell us about our world, about our pains and our joys. We want to read plays in which we can identify ourselves and our people, and can recognise our friends Helen and

Costas. Thus our Chief, during the meeting on the occasion of presenting the prizes for the best theatrical plays, said to the writers: 'Why do you search in foreign and remote places for material? Turn your faces and look around to find the sources of the everlasting popular spirit. Reach out for the gold of the Greek soul which exists in ancient and recent history.'[126]

Indeed, an 'effort on a gigantic scale' was made by every *EON* official to ensure that sufficient cultural works were produced to meet the Chief's demands and a large number of plays were written by *EON* playwrights.[127] Yet only a minority were of real significance through reference to specific historical events and heroes of Greek History, and because of the time and manner in which they were staged and performed: conditions which were dictated by the needs of the regime's nationalistic propaganda. Parallels between bygone heroic eras and Metaxas' Greece were inserted into most of these 'historical epics' to emphasise the intrinsic link and promote the everlasting ideals of the Greek Nation. Most of these plays were staged during national holidays like the *25 March*, the 'Fourth of August' regime's anniversary, and '*EON* Day', and were extensively advertised by *E Neolea*.

The first performance of a patriotic play entitled *Brosta Sto Thanato* (Facing Death) took place on the 25 March 1939. The play, which was written by the playwright Velisarios Freris was staged at the Olympia Theatre by the phalangites (both boys and girls) and was directed by Moustakis (an *EON* member). The play was centred around the Olokaftoma tou Arkadiou (The Holocaust of the Monastery of Arkadi), and its themes dealt with the idea of self-sacrifice and the depiction of heroes who preferred to die rather than surrender dishonourably to the Turks.[128] The heroic figures in the theatrical plays were of special significance as they set an example for the younger generations, and the masses at large, who identified themselves with those heroes. In order to magnify the dramatisation of the hero figures and imbue the *EON* members with the idea of unconditional and blind devotion to the national ideals, the propaganda officials organised certain events that supported the projected ideology. For instance, the day before the actual plays were staged, *EON* members covered the statues of the heroes of the Greek revolution with wreaths,[129] while on the actual day of the celebration a 'literary memorial' service was organised in Parnassos Hall to pay tribute to their actions.[130] Within the context of promoting the regime's nationalistic ideology the III Office of the *Difthinsis Anotaton Sholon*, Administration of Higher Education, of *EON*, which was known as *DAS*, organised a series of 'Spiritual Competitions' among the student phalangites in which they were asked to write a 3,500 words dissertation concerning the Greek ideals and the 'Fourth of August' State.[131] The themes the young phalangites were asked to work on, which would eventually take the form of a lecture, included:

1. *The Eternal Existence of the Greek Nation*
2. *The Power of Hellenism*
3. *The Hellenic Nature of Science*
4. *Classical Greece-Byzantine Greece-Greece of the 'Fourth Of August'*
5. *Art And the New State, Ethical Values and the 'Fourth of August'*
6. *The Institution of Monarchy in Greece*
7. *Why We Denounce Communism*
8. *The National State*
9. *Youth and The 'Fourth of August State'*
10. *The Personality of Our Chief* [132]

Out of fifteen works, which bore one of the above titles supported by a motto of a the writer's choice, three would be successful. The prizes for the best three works from each unit, which were to form part of the lectures given by *DAS,* were financial. The winner of the first prize received the sum of 2,000 drachmas, the second prize was 1,000 drachmas and the third 500 drachmas.[133]

Another patriotic play intended to mobilise the Greek youth to support the national cause, was *Ta Souliotopoula Den Pethanan* (The Children of *Souli* Did not Die).[134] The play was written by the playwright Nikos Tsekuras, [135] the editor in chief of *E Neolea* magazine. The premiere of this 'Patriotic Drama,' which took place on 26 March 1939 at the Cotopouli theatre and formed part of the '25 March' festivities of that year, was organised by the girls of the Athens *EON* Division.[136] The plot of the play, which was set in 1821, was simple. It was based on the sacrifice made by the people of *Souli* who fought the Turks and died at the end for the supreme ideals of the Greek Nation. The opening act depicted a gathering of young *EON* members surrounding an old man (a grandfather) and ecstatically listening to his stories about the glorious achievements of the Greek heroes who died so that they could live in freedom. As the story unfolded the audience was introduced to the central plot of the play which involved the people who were fighting for their freedom. The hero, *Tousas*, was a young boy of twelve, who in defiance of his captain's objection, took part in the battle. After he was seriously injured by the Turks he died an honourable death with the proud blessing of his mother, who preferred to have her son dead rarather than dishonoured. 'My *Tousas* is not dead since our country lives,'[137] were the mother's last words in the final act when she requested that her son's death should not become an occasion to lament but to be joyful; 'because *Souli* had not been taken.' *Tousas'* death had been associated with the salvation of *Souli* and with the joy that he had brought to the nation with his death.[138] This joy was expressed in the play by the songs and dances performed by the tragic figure of the mother who, just before her life also ended, had been endowed with the supreme honour of being the mother of a hero. In an explicit account of the emotional impact which the last act had on the spectators, a contemporary critic wrote:

> 'The play had reached such a tragic climax that the audience could no longer control their emotions and hold back their tears as the great scenes of the tragic and sacred struggle for freedom unfolded in front of them.'[139]

Strong parallels were drawn between the 'martyr' children of *Souli* and the *EON* members during the plays. For example, the *Souliotopoula* had not died, 'but through their self-sacrifice they had earned their immortality as they lived on in the hearts and minds of *EON* members who were also ready to die for the same supreme ideals.'[140] Because of the young age of the hero one can presume that the play was intended more for the edification of the younger members of *EON* rather than the elder phalangites. To emphasise the intrinsic link between the two generations, during the last act of the play when the *Souliotopoulo* died, the theatre was filled with loud, uplifting music, 'chosen by Mr. Glykofredis to be unadorned and simple, but at the same time grand and majestic like our nation,'[141] while the *EON* anthem was sung by the young actors.[142] The theatre critic Yiannis Sideris, a great supporter of the play, wrote in *Nea Estia* heartily recommending it:

> Before the last phrase of the play we hear the *EON* anthem, a gesture which connotes the real meaning of the title *Ta Souliotopoula Den Pethanan* which is a reference to the young generation of today; this connotation is, in fact, the central and basic theme of the play.'[143]

The play was extensively advertised by the press, and *E Neolea* wrote that it was the best theatrical play for school shows urging people who did not attend the play to ' at least buy the book.'[144]

The third patriotic play intended for the edification of youth was the *Ilthe Mia Mera* (The Day Has Come). This play was performed on 27 March 1939 at the Cotopouli theatre and formed part of the festivities of '25 March'. It was written for the *EON* by M. Anesios and it was staged by the boys of the Athens *EON* Division. It dealt with the theme of the 'regeneration of Greece' and referred to the four great eras of the Greek nation. The first was Ancient Greece: the second the Byzantine era: the third was the time of the struggle for national independence in 1821. The play finished with the phalangites' chorus singing *EON* songs. An act, which together with the implied meaning of the title '*Ilthe Mia Mera*', connoted the last and equally significant period that the Greek nation was going through: the period marked by the 'Fourth of August' State which formed a natural continuity with the glorious past.[145] The intrinsic link between this great glorious past, especially the Independence day of 1821, and the coming of the 'Fourth of August' regime which 'signalled the deliverance' of the Greek nation, was underlined by Kanellopoulos through the order issued on the occasion of the celebration of the 25 March 1939 when he stated:

> 'One hundred and ten years have passed since the sacred struggle for independence. All those years were years dedicated to the national struggle for territorial freedom: a struggle that has successfully ended(…) not however, without mistakes and catastrophic actions(…)until the One and only One came to purify the nation from those mistakes and deliver it from past catastrophes: and thus, the nation's struggle for the creation of the Third Greek Civilisation continues. A struggle for the conquest of the spiritual leadership of mankind which constitutes the greatest expression of our National Glory and justification for our National existence'[146]

Apart from the above plays which 'marked' the celebration of the '25 March' and were intended by the regime's propaganda to awaken the sense of responsibility and national pride of the *EON* members, other plays of a similar nature marked the 'Fourth of August' anniversary celebrations. One of those plays was *To Xanazontanema* (The Revival) written by A.Avdis, an actor with the Cotopouli Theatre company. The play was successfully performed by young boys and girls phalangites at the Cotopouli Theatre on 2 August 1940 and was attended by Ioannis Metaxas, the *EON* Leader, members of the cabinet and a great number of intellectuals.[147] The plot of the play deals with the dull and monotonous everyday lives of the people in a remote village until the coming of a young man, who is studying to become an agronomist, helps to bring life back to the village.[148] The connotation of the young agronomist who revived the forgotten life of the country village, to the Great Chief Ioannis Metaxas, who through his benevolent intervention revived and reinstated the life of the Greek nation which had for so long suffered from the mistakes of previous political life, is more than explicit. According to *E Neolea*, this was a play about 'a new *Pericles* who instead of constructing great marble temples which would inevitably disintegrate over the centuries, created an everlasting 'construction;' *EON*. At this Temple, instead of worshipping the Olympian gods, we worship the Greek Nation.'[149] *To Xanazontanema* was intended to glorify the 'Fourth of August' State and the Great Chief who made the revival of *Hellenism* possible.

Another play intended for the glorification of the 'Fourth of August' regime and the edification of the young generation was *E Ieri Floga* (The Sacred Flame), written by Dimitris Bogris for the celebration of the regime's fourth anniversary. The performance of the play, which was directed by Kotsopoulos of the Royal Theatre and performed by *EON* members, was organised by the manager of the Cultural Section of the III Office, Mrs. Sakellariou. It was staged at the *EON*'s newly established theatre in the quarry of the Lycabetus Hill[150] on 11 August 1940 and took the form of a special performance of great national significance. In the presence of Ioannis Metaxas, Mrs Lela Metaxas, cabinet members and the *EON* leader, thousands of *EON* members and large crowds of people gathered to watch what was advertised as a 'hymn to Greek youth.' The audience was addressed by Dimitris Bogris who placed the play within its historical context, and emphasising its allegorical significance and its importance to the regime and *EON*, he stated: 'Greek Youth, you must be very proud of your country and your nation, because civilisation is a concept which is synonymous with Greece.'[151] According to an article written by Aggelos Metaxas, the play 'which dealt with the projection of the Eternal Greek spirit' was dedicated to Greek youth and its existence over the centuries; 'because youth is the living symbolism and manifestation of the Greek Nation.'[152] The Greek spirit was symbolised within the play by the sacred flame which burned continuously on the Greek Altar and represented the eternal spirit of *Hellenism*. The burning flame also symbolised the Greek nation which had remained united and homogeneous throughout the centuries and had given light to the whole world through its achievements that took place during the *Classical*, the *Alexandrian* and the *Byzantine* eras.[153] The play, which had a cast of over six hundred *EON* members of all ages 'a mass transformed into disciplined and competent actors,'[154] was divided into the following six acts:

1. The Ancient Spartans, 2. The Persian Wars, 3. The Coming of Christ
4. Byzantium, 5. The Turkish Occupation, 6. The Revolution of 1821 and the Coming of the 'Fourth of August' State.'[155]

Each act of the play was dominated by a significant and historical event which represented and outlined the period depicted. For instance, the period of Christianity was outlined by the figure of Christ who preached the significance of love among all people when he said 'Love thy neighbour.'[156] According to contemporary critics the image of Christ and that particular phrase deeply moved the spectators 'because being Greeks they are always touched by the Cross and the Nation. These two concepts which represent Christianity and *Hellas* are intrinsically linked and form a totality.'[157] As cited in Chapter Three religion constituted one of the regime's goals, and (like in other dictatorships) it was often used as an 'alibi' to project and disseminate nationalistic values and beliefs.[158]

The account below given by a journalist who attended the rehearsals of the play the day before the actual performance provides us with an astonishing insight into the last act :

> 'The play unfolds and the Byzantine period is followed by the period of the nation's battle for independence from the Turkish occupation which is marked by the heroism of *Souliotes* (The heroes from *Souli*). What follows is a period of national decline and deterioration of the young generation. A 'flock' of disorganised children who mock the past and wander around without a purpose, appears on the scene. The music is weak, unaccented and lifeless. Suddenly, a loud voice comes out of the speakers: 'Stand Up Greek Youth:' it is the voice of the Chief. Shivers of emotion run through the audience. This was one of the greatest and most dynamic moments of the play: it was the moment that the miracle happened. After a very short while the children, imbued with a new spirit and enthusiasm, gathered together and walked forward holding the Greek flag. The music reached its climax.[159] As the act finished the same voice came through loud and clear, with patriotic words about the Great *Hellenic* spirit it recounted the achievements of the *Hellenic* Nation over the centuries. A great enthusiasm filled the hearts of the spectators. Greece has found itself again and marches at full speed towards the creation of the 'Third Civilisation.'[160]

The content of the above extract and the fact that it was written before the actual show, suggests that it was intended as a 'bait' to attract as many spectators as possible. Furthermore, it demonstrates that the 'regeneration of Greece' and the creation of the 'Third Greek Civilisation' constituted one of the main aims of the regime; a fact demonstrated by the comments in the extract from the beginning of the article:

> 'As you watch the play the whole of Greek history passes before you. Such shows aim to strengthen the faith of the people and

lend wings to their patriotic feelings. When the spectator leaves the theatre, he feels a great respect for his ancestors and becomes aware of the great burden he carries to prove himself worthy of his national heritage.'[161]

These comments on the importance of the Greek spirit, the unity of the nation and the great duty and obligation of the people to prove themselves worthy of their history and national heritage, as stated in the play, served a twofold purpose: to advertise a play which disseminated the regime's ideology and values, and to imbue the people with patriotic inspiration, pride and enthusiasm at a moment when World War II was closing in on Greece.[162] This play was intended to demonstrate the inextricable link between the 'Fourth of August' State and the glorious and heroic moments in Greek history. The final act and the triumphal close of the play, which was dominated by the coming to power of the 'Fourth of August,' was justified by the necessity of preserving this continuity and leading the modern Greek nation to an even more glorious future.

The mission of theatre propaganda, which was to awaken and elicit a positive response from Greek youth that was both heroic and totally devoted to the supreme goals of the regime, especially at moments when those goals were threatened, was strengthened by the propagandists' skilful use of relevant speeches and advice. On the occasion of the regime's fourth anniversary Kanellopoulos issued an order which could be seen as the appropriate ideological platform for the 'correct' appreciation of the patriotic plays which were staged for the occasion:

'We are celebrating today the deliverance, the salvation and the regeneration of our nation. We feel the exaltation and the rejoicing which derives from the awareness of the greatness of this nation. We praise and glorify our Chief and Saviour; our Father, Creator and Warrior; the One and only One. He represents and embodies the national will, the dreams and ideals, and he is the One who will make those dreams come true: Because, we are deeply aware of our commitment, our historical mission and our duty to the national cause, we assure everyone that we shall continue with faith, passion, fanaticism and self-sacrifice (…) our struggle. We are 1,200,000 young men and women and we have taken an oath that we shall for ever dedicate our lives to the Ideals of *Hellenism, Hellas* and the Revolution. It is us that our Great Chief has entrusted with the heavy burden of reinstating the glorious past and creating an equally great future (…) His presence and greatness have created the most heroic army in the world,[163] our national army, which together with *EON* constitutes the best guarantee for our country's freedom. This assurance which is conveyed throughout Greece with pride and confidence, guards our borders and sends this message: 'No one crosses this line.'[164]

The above passage, once more, apart from broadcasting the charismatic qualities of Ioannis Metaxas, leaves no room for scepticism over the mission he had entrusted to the *EON* members, and reflects at the same time the government's anxiety over the forthcoming war.

Another play which was considered a landmark in the regime's theatrical history and constitutes a fine example of its theatre propaganda, was the play *Pentheseleia*[165] chosen for the celebration of the regime's third anniversary. Strangely enough, the play, which brought together more than 30,000 members of *EON* and the Work Battalions, was not a Greek play written by an 'ideologically committed' Greek playwright, but a translation of the German drama *Pentheseleia* written by Heinrich Kleist.[166] Furthermore, unlike the plays discussed above in which the title and the heroic stereotypes suggested male dominance, *Pentheseleia* was a play written about a heroine, or rather about a great number of heroic women, who were not Greek but the mythical Amazons. The staging of the play at the *EON* Theatre newly established in the *Lycabetus* quarry was organised by Lukia Matzufa, secretary of the *EON* and daughter of Ioannis Metaxas. The direction of the play was assigned to a talented new director T. Mouzanidis while the costumes were designed by Antonis Fokas and the choreography was the work of D. Sakellariou and P. Maten.[167] The occasion of the performance became an event of great cultural significance and it was attended by the Crown Prince and his wife Princess Frederica, Ioannis Metaxas, members of the cabinet and academics, alongside both *EON* members and ordinary people. The following extract from an article written by an *EON* member is more than revealing about the effort the propagandists put in to link the play with the themes of charismatic leadership and the 'regeneration of Greece.' Furthermore, the passage conveys the impact which the theatre propaganda had on Greek Youth through the play *Pentheseleia* :

'Once upon a time, in a country where beauty was synonymous with savagery, lived beautiful girls who were called Amazons (…) As the story unfolded the small children dreamed and travelled to this fairy world. But one magical night, at an extraordinary site in Athens where fantasy and reality were intertwined these dreams came true when the *EON* girls were transformed into Amazons.

At Lycabetus the young phalangites and pioneers awaited the appearance of Him with great anticipation: the Man who would sit with them and watch the revival of this fairy tale (…) Suddenly, He, Ioannis Metaxas, appeared; He, who had reinstated the ancient glory and given it back to Greece; and the air was filled throughout with a word which moved the hearts of all the people. It was the word *Patera* (FATHER). Indeed, he is the Father of everything that is beautiful, noble and supreme. He is the Father of Greek Youth.'[168]

The play was set in Ancient Greece when reality was entangled with myth. The opening act presented Pentheseleia and her army of faithful and heroic Amazons lined up along the Trojan Walls ready to fight their enemy. According to the myth the Amazons went to war with the aim of capturing strong men from a chosen race and returning with them to their country. After they had married them and had their children they would send them back to their country. As the play progressed the Amazons got involved in ruthless battles with the Greeks. During the fighting Pentheseleia and Achilles fell in love with each other, before the Greeks won the decisive battle and captured Pentheseleia. She was freed by her army and challenged Achilles to single combat. He, in his efforts to become her prisoner and marry her, went to the duel unarmed. Pentheseleia, blinded by her will to lead her army to victory and thirsty for revenge against Achilles who had captured her, brutally attacked him with her dogs who tore him apart. When she realised what she had done she defied the Amazons' laws and killed herself, next to the dead body of Achilles.[169] The play, and the way it was promoted by the regime's propaganda, especially by theatrical criticism,[170] is particularly interesting, because of the light it sheds on women's role in society within the 'Fourth of August' regime. As cited in Chapter Three, women played a crucial role in Metaxas' dictatorship policy because of their significance within the Greek community as a new work force, as wives, and above all as mothers. [171] However, this role necessitated a new awareness and consciousness. According to the regime's ideology it was imperative that before young women became anything else they should first become worthy *Hellenides* (Greek Women). This necessity and women's supreme mission is reflected in the following passage:

'His great and inspired guidance has shown us the correct route which will lead to the *Elysea* of our civilisation and which through us will create the 'correct and genuine *Hellinides*.
Young girls; whatever route we follow in life, whether within the

family, at work outside the family sphere, or at school, we shall fight
with courage and always follow His ideology and wishes. because
we know that those beliefs come from a Greek heart which wants
only the best for us and the best for our Nation.'[172]

The above extract suggests that the primary target of the regime's policy, as
far as women were concerned, was to create a force of active and vigorous
young women who would be adequately prepared to fulfil their tasks and
'destiny,' always within the boundaries of the 'Fourth of August' ideology.
To define accurately these tasks a lengthy article in *E Neolea* with the title
'E Thesis Tis Gynekas Sto Neon Kratos' (The Position of Women Within
the New State) described clearly the nature and the role of the 'Fourth of
August' women as mothers, working women, students, and Phalangite girls.
At the same time the article stated in detail the beneficial measures taken
by the Great Chief to strengthen and protect women's status. The first role
defined in the article was that of the woman-mother. This order reflects
the importance which this role had for the regime's new policy. Female
emancipation was not a priority issue in the 'Fourth of August' regime, and
the fact that in the past women had been given the right to stand for election
during the municipal and communal elections was, ironically, criticised by
Metaxas,[173] whereas motherhood was considered crucial and served one
supreme purpose, which was to provide the nation with tomorrow's heroes.
The following extract entitled 'E Gyneka Ieria Tis Oikogeneias ke tou
Ethnous'(The Woman: Priestess of the Family and the Nation) published
in *E Neolea* illustrates this belief:

> 'We are not interested in equality only where women's rights and
> votes are concerned. We are not moved by women's suffrage and
> feminism. We are concerned only about our work and whether this
> work is being appreciated on its own merit and terms; because
> although we work next to men, we perform tasks that only women
> can perform for the benefit of our nation.. We are not any longer
> the pale Ophelias, the beautiful but empty vessels, the princesses
> who await their prince to awaken them from their sleep of spiritual
> inaction. Our minds must think hard, our feet must stand firmly
> and our hearts must beat to the ancient tune conveyed to us by a
> Chief, who has given us respect for a true and genuine life.'[174]

The 'Fourth of August' regime placed great emphasis on the role of
women-mothers who believed in the values and ideals epitomised by Ioannis
Metaxas. 'Great is your destiny, women,' Metaxas claimed in 1936, It is the

destiny of becoming a mother; women are the pillars of the home.'[175] A campaign was launched by the regime and measures were taken to promote the institution of the family and support those who were bringing up their children in accordance with the ideals and values of the regime. Between 1937 and 1940 the sum of 8,539,000 drachmas was granted to working women as childbirth allowance and the sum of 5,640,937 as maternity allowance.[176] The campaign included a series of mass weddings of working couples, attended by Ioannis Metaxas who acted as their best-man.[177]

The main theme of *Pentheseleia* was the heroism exhibited by the young and beautiful Amazons, who assumed masculine roles (a successful symbiosis of masculinity and femininity) to serve their national cause which was the preservation of their national existence. Great parallels were drawn between the Amazons and the young *EON* girls who were ready to sacrifice their lives for their national ideals, and the 'regeneration of Greece.' Like new *Spartiatisses* and the women from Souli, these Greek-Amazons would defy all their enemies and bring glory to the nation once again. These parallels could provide the reason why a foreign play was chosen to mark this grand celebration instead of a Greek one. The 'Fourth of August' regime strongly believed in the superiority of the Spartan ideal, ('I believe that from all the ancient Greek models and ideals, the best ones are those found in ancient *Sparta*')[178] rather than the Athenian one: because in his opinion the Spartan ideal, although it lacked cultural expression, was exceptional in terms of heroic achievements and fighting spirit. Similarly, the Spartan women were known for their heroism and willingness to sacrifice not only themselves for the national cause but also their children if necessary (like the women of *Souli* did). In contrast, the Athenian model of women was not as heroic in terms of fighting for the nation, but rather it stressed women's role as 'keepers' of the ethical laws and values of their country and as 'the pillars' of the household. Thus, the aspirations and ideals of the *EON* girls were closer to the Spartan model of women than the Athenian one. For this reason these young *Hellenides* who were expected to 'gradually stop caring about painted nails and perfumes' and become true mothers and priestesses of the Greek nation,'[179] were constantly reminded of those sacred ideals by the anthem of the Phalangite Girl.

> 'In the front line, With our spirit of youth,
> We, the guardians of honour, Stay watchful
> We, the Phalangite girls, March always forward with grace;
> We are the pride and the unsleeping Guards of Greece
> Like New Amazons, With the body of the Souliotisses,
> We, Form the young generation Of our Motherland.' [180]

Thus, the noble values such as heroism which constituted the central theme of the play were linked with the supreme and sacred task of bringing up children and imbuing them with the national values. The Amazons' desire to capture hostages, marry them and have their children preconditioned their fighting skills and heroism. Similarly, the *EON* girls who played the Amazons were encouraged to reject all harmful foreign influences and embrace the supreme national values epitomised by the 'Fourth of August' State which would make them proud Greek mothers. This supreme role, entrusted to them by the Chief, was a task which the young *EON* girls who watched the play would always remember. Therefore, despite *Pentheseleia's* parallels with the ideals of heroism and self-sacrifice the main moral of the play was the value of motherhood. This attitude towards the 'chosen' role endowed upon women, which was deeply ingrained in the regime's policy, is clearly reflected in the following article written by Cotopouli, who watched the performance:

> 'I am not aware whether Kleist's play was deliberately chosen to serve a purpose or if it was a pleasant coincidence. Whatever the reasons behind it, the play spontaneously evoked parallels between the old Amazons and the Amazons of today. These heroic women presented themselves like symbols, and although their goals differed greatly from those of our new Amazons they still project the same pride and grace. Today, the new Amazons are not going to fight and conquer man on the battlefield: they are going to become mothers who will give life and flesh to tomorrow's Greeks. This is the supreme task for which the prime of our Greek youth is prepared today; and for this great task the *EON* girls must grow proud and graceful like the Amazons'[181]

Thus, although *Pentheseleia* departed from the usual male hero stereotype, it did so in order to serve an ideologically important purpose: to imbue young Greek women with an awakened consciousness and to reinstate values which would serve the national ideals. At the same time the play fostered the conditions which Metaxas believed in and which would permit those ideals to become a living reality.

Apart from the plays written for the patriotic enlightenment of the young, the revival of ancient artistic events and their performance by members of *EON* formed part of Greece's cultural education. Such an event was the performance of the *Oi Kallitechnikoi Agones* (The Cultural Games) held in May 1940, which became an occasion for cultural propaganda. During this event, as in ancient Greece young men and women gathered together to participate in *Stefanitis*, a cultural competition which resembled the ancient art contest during which the young people competed in an artistic competition organised by the Muses. The contest, which took place at Herodeum Odeum between *EON* members, included songs from the *Iliad* and the *Odyssey*, folk songs and dances, 'all harmoniously' linked together.[182] A large part of the performance was taken up by the poem *Ellinika Niata* (Greek Youth) which according to *E Neolea* 'constituted a hymn to Greek youth and conveyed the promise that the young will do their duty.'[183] These performances, which were always attended by Metaxas, demonstrating his constant concern for Greek youth and his unshaken belief in the Greek ideals, also illustrated the power which *Hellenism* still possessed even centuries later.

The account given of the performance by *E Neolea* is quite striking:

'Descending the sacred hill that Sunday night in Spring we all felt our hearts full of joy. Our Chief, and through him *EON* realised that neither the Spartan Civilisation nor the Athenian one can alone bring about the 'regeneration of the nation.' The first civilisation took care only of the body, the second one only of the spirit. Thus, neither of these civilisations avoided decline. The combination of the two civilisations constitutes the Greek Ideal: an ideal towards which this generation, under the wise guidance of our Chief, is now headed.'[184]

Metaxas' theatre propaganda produced plays which were intended to manipulate the theatre-going public, especially the young, into grand and noble forms of behaviour such as heroism, and the subordination of their will to that of the nation. The theme of the 'regeneration of Greece' which would lead to the creation of the 'Third Greek Civilisation' was propagated through theatrical representations of glorious visions of the past, self-sacrifice and heroic deaths. In this way the masses would become conscious of their national identity and the importance of *Hellenism*. Once this was achieved, 'Greece would become again the Greek Nation that history had destined it to be : the cradle of true civilisation and the guiding light for the world.'[185]

Chapter Five

RADIO PROPAGANDA IN METAXAS' GREECE

'Radio has become a powerful medium of social and national policy. We hope that Greek Radio will not fall short in the general re-creative spirit of the 'Fourth of August' State.' [1]

Unlike all the instruments of propaganda previously examined which were associated with private interests and conflicting ideologies, radio was a new medium, established by the 'Fourth of August' regime, under direct State organisation, funding and control. Because of this it soon came to be regarded as the regime's most effective propaganda medium.

When Metaxas came to power radio in Europe and the United States, although still a relatively new mass medium, had been elevated to a position of considerable power as an instrument of an informative, entertaining and propagandistic nature.[2] On the contrary, until the late twenties broadcasting activities in Greece were non-existent and the prospects of establishing a wireless system looked 'gloomy.'[3] It has been argued that this ellipsis was mainly due to tight state security as the strict regulations, imposed in order to prevent espionage through the wireless communication antennas, presented great problems for prospective supporters of radio as a source of entertainment or education.[4] The owners of radio sets (in 1926 there were 200 sets in Greece)[5] who picked up foreign stations during the years 1921-1926 were heavily penalised (500 drachmas) and the use of an outdoor antenna, which was a forbidden act, resulted in a fine of 100,000 drachmas.[6] The first serious broadcasts in Greece became possible in 1928, when Christos Tsigiridis[7] established the first wireless transmitter in Thessaloniki, which became the first private Greek Radio Station (*Radio Tsigiridis*) and served as a landmark in Greek Broadcasting history.[8]

During the late twenties and early thirties several attempts to establish a broadcasting network met with indifference from the State and resulted in a few unsuccessful and amateur radio activities.[9] Meanwhile, in July 1934 Italian Radio, within its programme of foreign broadcasts to Europe[10] started transmitting in Greek from Bari. This lasted until July 1937 when the first steps were taken by the Metaxas regime to establish a State-regulated Radio service.[11] The Greek programme transmitted daily, during its three years of operation, programmes 'for women, children, boy scouts and agrarian institutions.'[12] By July 1937 one thousand Greek radio broadcasts had been transmitted from the Bari Station. These included 100 speeches and 250 proclamations delivered by Greek Officials both from the pre-Metaxas governments and the 'Fourth of August' regime.[13]

Metaxas was well aware of the importance of radio as an influential propaganda medium and its great potential to disseminate his ideology and policies over long distances when his physical presence was needed elsewhere. On 10 August 1936 he delivered his first and most important speech on the radio which revealed his future goals and his determination to impose them on the Greek Nation.[14] This important speech was broadcast by *Piraeus Radio*[15] and was heard by those Greeks who were in possession of a radio set. The following table published in 1938 provides an account of radio set ownership in Europe and the Balkans at the end of 1935.

Countries	Numbers of sets end 1935
Britain	7,403,109
Germany	7,192,952
France	2,192,952
Russia	2,800,000
Italy	530,550
Belgium	746,395
Romania	127,041
Yugoslavia	81,385
Bulgaria	17,000
Turkey	15,000
Greece	6,317[16]

The above table demonstrates that the number of people who had the opportunity to listen to Metaxas' speech on the radio must have been relatively small. However, given the newspapers' new role which had been in force since 5 August 1936, this radio communication vacuum was filled by the press on the following day when they undertook the mission to convey the dictator's speech. to the nation. Shortly after, on 25 August, the regime decided to establish and operate one temporary state radio station which would serve the immediate needs of the new government.[17] This decision necessitated a number of 'drastic' measures which would ensure the 'smooth' development of Metaxas' very own propaganda tool. Thus in September 1936 the regime provided a legislative foundation for the formation and operation of an effective Greek wireless system. The enactment of Emergency Law 95 *Peri Systaseos Ypiresias Radiofonikon Ekpobon* (the Formation of a Broadcasting Service) known thereafter as *YPE*, on 7 September 1936[18] supplied the legal base for establishing what in Nicoloudis' words constituted 'a great political and national act,'[19] and one of Metaxas' most significant propaganda vehicles. The objective of the new wireless service was, according to Article 3 of the above legislation, to 'indoctrinate, educate and entertain the public.'[20]

To ensure complete control of this newly established mass medium and obtain its support for the objectives of the 'Fourth of August' State, Recommendation Reports were presented to the King in March 1937 by both Nicolopoulos[21] and Maniadakis. The official recommendation which was submitted to supplement the draft of Emergency Law 541 of 17 March 1937[22] suggested the 'placement of a high ranking officer from the police or the gendamerie entrusted with the supreme task of supervising the safety of the radio station and subsequently that of the Country.'[23] The new legislation backed by the Recommendation Report introduced the following:

> 'The officer, in co-operation with the authorities in charge, will proceed to seek out and discover those illegal radio stations whose operations entail great danger for the nation because these stations transmit information and news which escapes our strict supervision and control. He is also endowed with the power to conduct an official inquiry concerning any act which would constitute unpatriotic propaganda coming from members of staff or anyone else who in his opinion was acting against the safety and security of the Greek Radio Service.'[24]

Alongside these legal measures which ensured the regime's unquestioned dominance of the new medium, a number of activities took place with the aim of establishing a Greek Broadcasting Service. These activities involved endless meetings and negotiations with foreign radio companies and their representatives in Greece, as well as efforts to secure finance and suitable personnel to operate the Station. According to Nicolopoulos, establishing a Greek State Radio was the most pressing and significant issue the sub-Ministry had been faced with since Metaxas came to power.[25] It was clearly not an easy task as there were a number of problems to be solved, especially the difficult financial situation the new state had inherited from the previous governments. The 'Fourth of August' State was presented with two options, either to proceed with the establishment of a powerful wireless service which necessitated great expenditure, or to begin with a relatively small radio station which would serve the immediate needs of the new State with the prospect of future expansion. Given the economic problems of the country the second option was adopted.[26] In November 1936 after much speculation in the press about prospective suppliers, the job of establishing a Greek State Radio was assigned to Ioannis Voulpiotis, a Mechanical Engineer who was the Telefunken Representative in Greece.[27] Two months later the equipment, a 15 KW transmitter of the Telefunken Spez 24260 type No. 42306 arrived in Piraeus where it remained for a year until a suitable site for its installation had been found. Finally in January 1938 the radio equipment was set up in Liosia (a place just outside Athens) where it still transmits the Third programme of *ERT-Elliniki Radiofonia Tileorasi* (Greek Radio and Television) on medium-wave.[28] The operating instructions on the transmitter were given in Spanish, a fact which suggests that its original destination was Franco's Spain. Because of the Spanish Civil War and the problems inherent in this situation, the dispatch met with difficulties, and given the pro-Nazi regime in Greece and Voulpiotis' German connections, the transmitter was instead dispatched to Greece.[29]

With the establishment of the Radio Station in Liosia and its Studios in Zapeion (in the centre of Athens) by the end of 1937 Greece acquired her State Radio Station and Metaxas a powerful weapon with considerable propagandistic value.[30] The official inauguration of the Broadcasting Service took place in 1938 on 25 March, a National Holiday. The day was marked by the King's proclamation speech, which was the first official broadcast on the newly established Radio Service and therefore of great significance.[31] The theme of the close bond between Monarchy and the nation figured prominently in the King's first address to the Greek people, particularly when he stated :

> 'The opening of this first Greek Radio Station which commences broadcasting this evening gives me a pleasant opportunity to communicate orally with my beloved subjects.'[32]

The panegyric opening of the Station actually took place on 21 May 1938[33] during which Nicolopoulos spoke of the importance of the new mass medium and underlined Metaxas' role in its establishment and operation. The King's major contribution to the first successful broadcast marked by his speech in March 1939 was also highly praised.[34] Kyriakakis, the director of *YPE*, delivered the following speech for the occasion which reflected on the important role entrusted to the radio by the regime:

> 'Radio, an instrument of a higher civilisation but also a medium of political indoctrination and guidance, will play a significant role in the realisation of the goals of the New State. The people, thanks to the radio, will gather together, everywhere where the Greek heart beats, and form numerous invisible mass rallies, thus participating in the nation's life. Radio will facilitate and give substance to our Chief's direct communication with the people.'[35]

The next step within the organisational policy of the station was to secure a 'suitable' radio signal which would reflect the ideology of the new regime and demonstrate the 'sacred' mission of this new mass medium. Because radio was endowed with the role of reaching the illiterate masses and conveying the regime's policies and goals to them this sound signal needed to be strongly linked with a significant 'Fourth of August' regime concept: a concept which would appeal to the masses, (especially the peasantry) thus creating uniformity and national awareness. After much speculation in the press the station eventually adopted a 'harmonic' combination of the shepherd's flute and bell, known as the *Tsopanakos* (Little Shepherd) which is still used in some programmes to this day.[36] This 'pastoral' tune was chosen to represent the ever present voice of thousands of country people, and was associated with the regime's most significant theme; that of the charismatic leader and the father of the less privileged.[37] It thus became an effective psychological device intended to convince the distant illiterate listener that he had become the major concern of the regime. Furthermore it reflected Metaxas' love for the Greek 'earth and soil,' which was effectively idealised by his propaganda. However, the choice of the bucolic sound signal gave rise to many objections most of which came from the elite who resented and questioned the validity of such a choice.[38] In addition to the sound signal, a graphic signal was designed which would represent both Metaxas' regime and the new Broadcasting Service: the emblem of the 'Fourth of August' State, with a radio transmitter right in the centre, on top of the torch.[39]

    O Radiofonikos Stathmos Athinon (The Athens Radio Station) as the station was called, continued to broadcast despite great difficulties throughout 1938 until the *YTT,* with Emergency Law 1542[40] P*eri Ypagogis Tis Ypiresias Radiofonikon Ekpobon is ton epi tou Typou kai Tourismou Yfipurgiou*

(Concerning the Subordination of the Broadcasting Services to the sub-Ministry of Press and Tourism) of 30 December 1938, took the *YPE* 'under its wing.' A further Emergency Law (1619) of February 1939[41] made the *YPE* part of the *YTT* under the title *Diefthinsis Radiofonias* (Broadcasting Directorate), and introduced the enlargement of the Censorship Committee and the change of its staff.[42] Additionally it renamed (Article 19) the existing 'Directorate of Home Press;' this became the *Diefthinsis Laikis Diafotiseos* (Directorate of Popular Indoctrination) and the Director of Home Press became the *Diefthintis Laikis Diafotiseos* (Director of Popular Indoctrination)[43] while Article 3 established an advisory board of nine members. Six of these members (the Director of Popular Indoctrination, the Director of Broadcasting and four artists appointed by the *YTT)* formed the *Epitropi Programmatos* (Programming Committee) which was in charge of the radio broadcasts and the selection of the 'ideologically correct' broadcasters. In addition, all radio activities, notably the composition of musical items and the production of gramophone records prior to their broadcast needed the approval of the Censorship Committee. In cases where 'the music or the words offended public moral and corrupted the artistic inclinations of the people or distorted and misrepresented the pure spirit of Greek traditional music,'[44] the Committee had the right to forbid recording and prevent the broadcasting of the whole piece (or whichever part was considered inappropriate). Measures also applied to the proprietors of gramophone records in circulation or in stock, as well as to the owners of gramophone moulds who were obliged to submit to the Directorate of Public Indoctrination Office a complete list of all existing records and moulds. A further Emergency Law (1807) of 22 June 1939 supplemented the previous one and set regulations for the owners and importers of radio sets. The same legislation set the amount required for obtaining a radio license and the yearly running cost.[45]

It can be seen from the above that in the three years following the establishment of the Broadcasting Service, eight Emergency Laws were enacted to define the regulations and the role of Metaxas' new propaganda instrument. The last four bore special weight as they ensured the total submission of the Broadcasting Service to *YTT* and the regime's propaganda authorities.

Organisation of 'Fourth of August' regime radio propaganda

> Let's hope that radio, this crucial propagandistic factor which serves the effort of post 'Fourth of August' Greece will not be neglected. Together with the rest of the propaganda media radio must become a continuous moral power in the form of a steady and

fully organised public service which through its unlimited power will strengthen the nation's beliefs.[46]

One significant change effected on the Broadcasting Service by the *YTT* was the replacement of a large number (40 per cent) of the existing personnel with new employees who according to Nicoloudis 'were committed to and responded to the demands of the reformed Broadcasting Service.'[47] The new staff personnel, under the strict supervision of the under-secretary, organised the programming of the radio station to suit the requirements of the New State. On 5 February 1939 a *Evdomadieon Programma* (weekly Radio Programme) in Greek and French was issued by the Broadcasting Directorate which stated in detail the station's significant features. One of the most crucial parts of the programme was attributed to *To Tmima Omilion* (Speeches Department), because, as the propagandists claimed, 'the implementation of the government's policy on the radio is effected through this department; a section which supervises and approves every written text, in prose or in verse.'[48] The speeches were divided into special categories and their broadcasting time varied according to the concept they presented. Priority was given to the broadcasts which carried a 'heavy thematic weight' and had significant propagandistic value. *E Ora Tou Agroti* (The Hour of the Peasant) for example, figured prominently in the weekly radio programme with three broadcasts a week.[49] According to the *YTT* officials this was due to the fact 'that Greece was basically an agrarian country and four fifths of the population were peasants. Therefore this large section of people needed to be able to be in constant contact with the Centre and keep up with the latest developments. Furthermore through the programme dedicated to them, the agrarian population would be educated and informed about all the things that interested them.'[50] It was extremely important for the regime to reach the millions of peasants far away in all the different parts of the country simultaneously and communicate to them a uniform message assuring them of their First Peasant's' love and affection. Radio made this a reality as it spanned geographical and social distances and provided the dictatorship with a powerful propaganda tool. The following extract from the Panegyric issue of the *Evdomadieon Programma* published on the third anniversary of the 'Fourth of August' is more than indicative of the regime's expectations of this peasant-radio scheme:

> 'In the New State the peasant has taken the place which rightly belongs to him. The Chief Ioannis Metaxas has elevated his status and the *YTT*, which assists the Chief in his work, puts the microphone at the disposal of the peasant to inform him, educate him and become his devoted companion '[51]

Naturally all the information and education was in line with the regime's propagandistic goals and was directed towards creating a national unity and 'winning' the support of the masses. By the end of July 1939, 100 speeches had been delivered during the *E Ora Tou Agroti*. However, although it seemed that the radio could fulfil the regime's expectations in propagating its ideas to a rural population isolated by geography and by illiteracy, economic factors prevented their diffusion. The high cost involved in purchasing the expensive sets[52] together with the running costs[53] inhibited the spread of radio ownership. In March 1939 the regime tried to offset this problem by manufacturing 'popular cheap radios' which people could afford to buy.[54] Furthermore, the government purchased and distributed radio sets to public places and schools in the remote parts of the country to encourage collective listening. In the villages of Macedonia and Thrace alone, the *YTT* distributed 50 radio sets, an act which according to its officials 'reflected the affection of the National State for the less privileged.'[55]

The Workers enjoyed a similar treatment from the Speeches Department. *E Ora Tou Ergatou* (The Hour of The Worker) was broadcast twice a week and enabled the thousands of workers 'to listen to educational programmes and news that would interest them from the radios available in their factories and workshops'.[56] The following speech delivered by a Labour Official on the occasion of the inaugural broadcast of *E Ora tou Ergatou* set the tone for the important mission of this broadcasting time:

> '*E Ora Tou Ergatou* will make a great contribution to the elevation and education of the worker. The workers will have the opportunity to be informed of the beneficial measures of the 'Fourth of August' State, or of any other matter that concerns them. Alongside the press, radio will become another significant medium of enlightenment and indoctrination and will, no doubt, prove to be a vital factor in the country's work progress and productivity. We are convinced that employers and industrialists will assist the government in its work and supply their places of work with radios in the same way as most of the foreign businesses have done.'[57]

Indeed, factories were instructed to acquire radio sets and make them available to the workers enabling them to listen to *E Ora Tou Ergatou*, broadcast at 12.30 noon, their break time. By July 1939, 62 speeches had been delivered, all of which were tokens of the '*Protos Ergatis*' love for the workers.[58]

A significant proportion of the weekly programming (130 speeches until July 1939) was dedicated to *E Ora Tou Pediou* (The Hour of The Child) which reflected the new educational and entertaining spirit of the

New State. *E Ora Tou Pediou* consisted of historical, religious, artistic and literary subjects 'carefully chosen by the Programming Committee to suit the *Hellenic* up-bringing of the nation's youth.'[59] The regime facilitated the supply of radios to schools in the country 'in order to ensure the entertainment of the children and enable them to listen to the inspiring speeches and programmes that were of interest to them.'[60]

E Ora tou Pediou together with the *E Ora Tis Ellinidos* (The Hour of the Greek Woman)and *E Ora Tis Ygeias* (The Hour of Health) was designed to encourage and preserve the concept of the family 'the core of the Greek nation,'[61] which together with the concepts King, Motherland, Religion and 'Regeneration of Greece' constituted the regime's goals as defined by Metaxas in January 1939.[62] In his speech to parents and teachers the dictator highlighted the institution of the Greek family and underlined its importance in constructing a New Greece:

> 'For us Greeks, family is of vital importance and this is an undisputed fact(...) Family is an institution intrinsically linked to our very existence and the survival of the Greek nation. The Greek identity, although it has suffered great catastrophes and enslavement, has managed to retain its civilisation and cultural heritage because this was preserved and transmitted from generation to generation by the family.'[63]

These speeches, which concerned the education and enlightenment of Greek women and the protection of maternity and childhood, were, according to the officials, broadcast 'in a simple and unsophisticated language so that they could be easily understood and appreciated.'[64]

However, according to the *YTT* the most important part of the weekly programme was *To Tmima Eidiseon* (the News Department) which from 22 December 1938, when the Radio Service was taken over by the *YTT*, underwent 'revolutionary' changes which revitalised and updated it. Four News broadcasts (two at noon and two in the evening) informed the listeners of important events. The impact of these news broadcasts was highly praised by the officials.'[65]

The News Department was improved with the addition of 'suitable' personnel and dealt with all the important issues. These included news bulletins already censored, daily official announcements, as well as several speeches written by government officials all of which praised the 'Fourth of August' State.[66] Speeches written by individual commentators with themes relevant to the values of the regime were first submitted to the Indoctrination Office for approval, and very often for rejection, before being read by Greek artists who became professional broadcasters.[67] They were chosen not only for vocal talent but also because the average listener was likely to recognise them and be influenced by the 'enlightened' message they delivered.

The coverage of significant events like the celebration of the 'Fourth of August' regime and *EON* anniversaries, the '25 March', and the trips and speeches of members of the Royal family or Ioannis Metaxas himself were also included in the news programmes. Needless to say, the most prominent place in the news broadcast was kept for the Dictator's speeches. These were read by professional broadcasters who were responsible for the way the speeches were presented. A contemporary news reader Michalis Kofiniotis recalled, 'How would you feel if asked to read on the radio the Chief's political speech consisting of twenty pages when you knew beforehand that the Premier himself was listening. Many times I found myself in this difficult situation.'[68]

Metaxas delivered most of his speeches in front of an audience instead of in the studio.[69] When he spoke in different parts of the country his speeches would immediately be transmitted by a direct connection with the Athens Radio. This was the case when Ioannis Metaxas spoke to the people of Piraeus, Kalamata, Pyrgos and Amfissa, when he delivered speeches of great political significance which were heard all over Greece.[70] During Public Holidays, especially the celebration of the 'Fourth of August' anniversaries, the municipalities and all communities were instructed to equip themselves with radio sets to ensure reception of the dictator's 'ideologically inspired' speeches and to convey the festive atmosphere.[71] The Athenians were obliged to listen to the radio broadcasts from loudspeakers placed in most of the main squares and streets of the capital.[72] Efforts were also made to broadcast the regime's propagandistic material to Greeks living abroad. The connection formed between the Athens Radio and the Radio Station of Geneva made this possible in 1939 and transmitted Nicoloudis' speech and the speech of the U.S Ambassador MacVeagh to the Greek Americans.[73] In addition to the Athens Radio Station the regime could, according to the contract made with the British company Cable and Wireless Ltd., (Emergency Law 705/1937 Article 12) make use of the company's powerful radio-electrical installation in Greece and transmit through the Wireless Station all radio messages of the State, free of charge.[74] A large part of the news bulletin was taken up with foreign news, in particular that of the Spanish Civil War and its consequences as well as with the approaching war in Europe.[75] This news, together with all the significant domestic news, was broadcast prior to its publication in the daily press.[76]

Another significant department which received the officials' special attention was the Music Department. The propaganda machine was well aware of the benefits of music which according to the propagandists 'constituted a significant factor in the formation of the people's feelings.'[77] Musical broadcasts were used by the regime not only as a means of elevating and enlightening the Greek public, but also as a device to attract as many listeners as possible and turn them, via the interspersed political broadcasts, into powerless recipients of the regime's propaganda. The Germans, who first introduced the use of music as a means of attracting listeners, claimed that 'music must first bring the listener to the loudspeaker and relax him'[78] before attempting to win him over by propagandistic broadcasts.[79] Similarly, Metaxas' propaganda machine took special care to ensure that the listener was first attracted to the music which should be 'of the best quality and to everybody's liking,'[80] before he was subjected to any political broadcasting or boring and uninteresting government directives.

Great effort was made by the Broadcasting Service to promote all kinds of music, including serious classic pieces, light music and opera and any other music which would intellectually elevate the Greek public. Special attention was given to the *Hellenic* character of the Athens Radio Station as its power to reinstate the glorious past was greatly appreciated by the propaganda officials:

> 'The Athens Radio Station will become the bright lighthouse of the Third Civilisation which our Governor envisaged. It will constitute the great peaceful expansion of the Eternal Greece and will become a crucial factor in the humanising and assimilating effort of the State'[81]

Within this strategy the regime launched a ruthless persecution campaign against the 'vulgar' music 'which promoted the morbid tendencies and low instincts not only of the Athenians but also of people in the most remote parts of the country where the musical degradation was even worse.'[82] *Rebetiko* and *Amanes* songs were the ones which suffered most under the cultural reforms of the regime as these, it was believed, inflicted the most damaging effects on the lower classes whom Metaxas' dictatorship aimed to elevate and enlighten. *Rebetiko,* which, according to the regime, 'contained obscene and provocative words that could endanger public safety and order and create a climate suitable for the spreading and use of drugs,'[83] was banned from the radio while the police confiscated any such records from the shops. *Amanes* 'the greatest curse, suffered a similar fate since its lamenting and fatalistic nature had, according to the regime, become one of the main reasons behind the degradation of the musical criteria of the Greek nation.'[84] Ordinary Greek people were expected to free themselves from all the harmful foreign influences which had kept them in a state of ignorance and rise to their destiny which was their participation in the creation of the 'Third Greek Civilisation.' Thus, the *YTT* proceeded with the necessary measures to 'cleanse music production from the filth of the past and direct it towards a healthy and inspiring future.'[85] The introduction and broadcasting of serious music was something which, according to the regime, was greatly appreciated by the audience. This appreciation constituted the best guarantee for the future of the Greek nation whose historical mission, as Metaxas had observed, 'was to uphold the lights of education.'[86] The broadcasting time given to music made up 40 per cent of the whole programme. The number of records required for this important mission increased from 1,936 in March 1938, to 3,500 in 1940.[87] Needless to say, a great effort was made by the regime to provide as many Greek musical pieces as possible. A large number of records of Greek music were forwarded by the *YTT* to foreign radio stations 'so that Greek music might be advertised and promulgated abroad.'[88] Special attention was given to *demotic* music which was linked with the aspirations and beliefs of the ordinary Greek people who were expected to proceed with the 'regeneration of Greece.' The transmission of *demotic* songs, together with the reading of historical and heroic plays, formed part of the organised propaganda effort to imbue ordinary people with patriotic feelings and national pride thus creating a popular culture with wide appeal to the masses who could understand these songs and identify with them.[89] The organisation and broadcasting of all these significant programmes as well as any other radio activity took place in the newly established *Thalamoi* (Studios) in Zapeion. These consisted of offices, technical rooms and three studios one of which was substantially larger in order to accommodate and facilitate the transmission of concerts, theatrical plays and choirs.[90]

Despite, however, the numerous measures taken to establish and organise an effective State Radio the results were far from satisfactory. The Athens Radio Station with its 15 kW transmitter was too small to cover what Nicoloudis claimed to be 'the multiple radio needs of a modern State which addresses public opinion at home and abroad.'[91] The *YTT* envisaged a much larger radio station which would facilitate the dissemination of the regime's ideology and compete with the rest of Europe: and 'because the 'Fourth of August' State was a regenerating state with the highest national goals nothing could prevent the acquisition of a more effective broadcasting service which would constitute a national public service of colossal significance.'[92] Soon after the *Athens Radio Station* came into operation, arrangements were under way for the purchase of a 70 kW radio transmitter at the end of 1940. Unfortunately the Italian invasion in October 1940 and the Second World War put an end to the regime's ambitious radio programme.[93]

Taking advantage of being a new 'brand' mass medium and the regime's very own creation, radio acquired a 'pioneer role' in the exploitation and manipulation of Greek youth, the main target of all its propaganda efforts. Thus, included in the weekly programming was *E Ora Tis EON* (The *EON* Hour). This programme was transmitted twice a week and 'consisted of speeches of a nationalistic nature aiming mainly at the young *EON* members, but also at thousands of Greek listeners.'[94] Additionally *EON* acquired a small short-wave transmitter donated by a member of the Organisation, which enabled the daily (from 6 to 8.30) broadcasting of music, enlightening speeches and news bulletins concerning the life and activities of the Organisation. However, broadcasting through this radio transmitter proved inadequate and problematic due to the lack of studios, the deficiencies of the transmitter and the unsuitable personnel.[95]

Given the significance of *EON* and its mission for the realisation of the regime's imperative goals on one hand, and the effectiveness of radio as an instrument of political indoctrination and propaganda on the other, the *EON* officials found it necessary to organise and establish their own powerful radio station. The importance of such an enterprise was summed up by *EON* officials in their recommendations for organising the Radio Broadcasting Department (within the Entertainment Section of the III Office) prior to the establishment of a radio station:

'The mission of *EON* is to indoctrinate and educate Greek youth according to the values set by our Chief on the 4th of August 1936. To achieve this goal *EON* must enjoy the support of every mass medium which would facilitate the achievement of these high national goals. One of the most significant means for their realisation, which enables the Organisation to be in constant and direct contact with all its members, is the radio. With suitable radio broadcasts properly enriched with appropriate music, *EON* will achieve the *Hellenic* education of the Greek youth and will instil in young hearts and minds the healthy values epitomised by our Chief.'[96]

Radio thus, constituted one of the Organisation's most significant propaganda instruments and its acquisition became an imperative objective. *EON*'s new premises in the centre of Athens which provided space for the studios and offices, and the voluntary work of the *EON* members, enabled the establishment of the *Radiofonikos Stathmos EON* (*EON* Radio Station). The cost of installing the radio station equipment, largely borne by the *EON* members, came to 20,000 drachmas., while its yearly running costs amounted to 160,000 drachmas.[97] The radio station transmitted on 37

18. 'Regenerating Greece'

metres or 8,100 kilocycles on a daily basis from 5.30 am to 8.30 pm, while on Sundays and holidays from 10.00 am to 13.00 pm and 5.30 am to 8.30 pm.[98] Its programmes included *EON* news and important speeches, mainly by Metaxas, athletic events, agrarian and workers' hours, historical broadcasts and medical lessons. Ample time was devoted to music (with emphasis on Greek *demotic* music and folk songs), while theatrical plays with nationalistic content and inspiring values were broadcast on a regular basis.[99] The programme also included military marches, battle songs and everything else that might interest, educate and indoctrinate the *EON* members.[100] The inauguration of the *EON* Radio Station took place on Sunday 5 November 1939 and became an eulogistic event of great importance as the day of the opening was carefully chosen to coincide with the celebration of the Organisation's second anniversary. The *EON* Radio Station began broadcasting at 10.30 in the morning, and being a Sunday, the opening ceremony was marked by a religious speech delivered by the bishop of *Talantiou Panteleimon*. The bishop, underlining the importance of the event and expressing his delight at the establishment of the Sunday religious broadcasts on *EON* Radio, stated:

> 'The Chief wants all of you to become real Christians and patriots. He asks and expects this from you because Greek youth is known for its intelligence and virtue and for having faith in religion and in the supreme values of their country. Greek youth indulges in everything that is good, ethical and noble and express its enthusiasm for it. Thus I wish and hope that all of you will become real Christians and real Greeks for your own happiness, for the glory of our country and for the joy of our Church'[101]

As religious speeches continually praised the regime and its great achievements, it was difficult for the young audience to separate the political from the religious broadcasts, making them an easier target for political indoctrination. Thus, the broadcast of a religious speech or sermon served a twofold purpose: to convince the parents (who worried about the freedom their children enjoyed) of the Christian nature of the Organisation, and to manipulate the young members with carefully disguised political propaganda. Furthermore, the Sunday programme, apart from religious preaching and church music, transmitted information concerning the agrarian and working population substantially enriched by material concerning the 'mission to save' of the 'Fourth of August' State. These Sunday broadcasts encouraged group listening and were expected to achieve a wide audience from rural population, both young and old, who, unable to afford a radio set, would gather on Sundays at the coffee shops (*Kafeneia*) to listen to the radio broadcast.

Through its programme *EON* Radio had two main goals: to participate in the elevating reformation of the Greek population, and to attract as many *EON* members as possible. Underlining the important mission of the radio station, Theocharopoulos, the *EON* deputy leader, claimed:

> 'Within our Organisation Greek youth is educated and imbued with the eternal ideals of the nation which strengthen its spirit and its national conscience. They become conscious of their obligations as parts of a national whole and of the values set by the 'Fourth of August' State(...) With the new Radio Station we have the opportunity to be in close contact with our members and communicate with them every day. By listening to the whole programme on our station the members, through the broadcast speeches, will be able to educate themselves and become spiritually and morally better people.[102]

However, the accomplishment of the above tasks presupposed a well organised and entirely competent radio team. The establishment of the following five departments was, according to *EON* officials, necessary for the satisfactory operation of the station.

1. *To Tmima Diafotiseos ke Dialexeon* (The Indoctrination and Speeches Department)
2. *To Tmima Sinennoiseos* (The Communications Department)
3. *To Tmima Musikis* (The Music Department)
4. *To Tmima Dramatologiou* (The Repertoire Department)
5. *To Technikon Tmima* (The Technical Department).

The Indoctrination Department was responsible for the collection of all the propagandistic and educational speeches and lectures, and processing them for broadcasting. The Communications Department was in charge of news broadcasts, official announcements, and the material to be distributed for publications in *E Neolea* and the other *EON* booklets. The Music Department attended to the selection of 'suitable' music, the formation of the *EON* choirs and orchestra, the purchasing of records and the organisation of musical lectures (supported by explanatory material) in co-operation with the Indoctrination Department. The Repertoire department was an important department and was responsible for the appropriate training and indoctrination of *EON* members so that they would become competent speakers and broadcasters. The Technical department was responsible for the satisfactory operation of the radio station. This involved employing good radio technicians and undertaking all the necessary technical work that would ensure the transmission of the Chief's speeches, the mass parades, and the holiday celebrations.[103] The formation of all these departments suggests that the *EON* Radio Station administration was a complex one and involved a large number of employees. Apart from the numerous volunteer members working for the station, the permanent staff of *EON* officials employed by the various departments numbered twenty.[104]

In less than a year the *EON* Radio Station became one of the regime's most important propaganda vehicles. Its significance and its vital mission were summed up by Kanellopoulos in May 1940:

> 'We are all aware of the vital contribution that radio broadcasts can make to the indoctrination work, the analysis of the Organisation's orders and the securing and maintaining of a constant link between the centre, the divisions, and all our members. Radio thus can become a vehicle of vital importance for the promotion of all our work.'[105]

Given the importance that *EON* put on the radio as a means of indoctrinating the young people and imbuing them with a Greek consciousness, Kanellopoulos urged the divisions to supply themselves with cheap radio sets. Furthermore steps were taken for the purchase of a more effective and powerful radio transmitter which would enable the Organisation to 'enter the Greek family and grant the parents of our members the opportunity to follow our important work, and appreciate the effort put in by *EON* to educate and indoctrinate their children.'[106]

Metaxas' radio propaganda was mainly geared towards the illiterate population, aiming to create a public conscious of their Greek heritage, united by the new state's supreme ideals and aspirations. The increase in the number of listeners from 12,000 in 1938 to 62,000 in 1940 enabled Greek listeners to come closer to their 'caring father' and be assured of his love and affection.[107] Besides, through the compulsory installation of radios with loudspeakers in public spaces, factories, schools and *Kafeneia*, the 'Fourth of August' propaganda ensured that the regime's ideology, dominated by Metaxas' inspired speeches, reached the large masses. The regime hoped that if communities in the most distant parts of the country where otherwise communication was difficult could hear the broadcasts, this would create a unified whole. Every individual would identify with the nation and participate in the new national awareness as transmitted through the radio.

Chapter Six

THE IMPACT OF 'FOURTH OF AUGUST' PROPAGANDA

'The purpose of propaganda is not to provide interesting distraction for blasé young gentlemen, but to convince, and what I mean is to convince the masses'[1]

The effective study and analysis of propaganda presupposes a dual and intrinsically linked strategy: the identification and evaluation of the techniques used to disseminate the themes linked with the propagated idea, and the realisation of the aims which necessitated this effort. In other words the effective projection of the themes and their successful acceptance by the masses.

The first task is relatively easy to establish provided the propagandist's objectives are clearly defined. The most difficult aspect of propaganda analysis, especially in a dictatorship, is to evaluate its effectiveness. In Metaxas' Greece public opinion was manufactured by the regime's propaganda. The 'Fourth of August' government denied access to all source of information and it was impossible for people to express their real views in public, unless these were in line with the regime's beliefs. All means of mass communication came under strict censorship and any opinion expressed emanated from the government. There were no public opinion surveys (the available statistics reflected the regime's motives) and any official evidence that could tell us anything about the real psychological impact of the regime's propaganda on the masses has been intentionally or otherwise destroyed. Furthermore, unlike the Nazis who introduced a number of different agencies to assess the state of public opinion,[2] in Metaxas' Greece no such feedback agencies existed.

Clearly the 'Fourth of August' regime was one of very close surveillance, supervision and control and most of the information coming from the Security Police consists of curriculum vitae and surveillance reports on the beliefs and activities of several people, mainly prominent members of Greek society. In contrast to this, ample available evidence suggests that the image of Greek society conveyed by the regime's propaganda was that of a supportive society, full of enthusiasm and consent.

The case study of Metaxas' propaganda presents particular problems as it requires thorough examination and careful evaluation of the evidence presented. Attempts to accurately measure its impact are further weakened by the fact that most of the peasant population who lived in distant and remote rural areas was deprived of the information flow enjoyed by the urban population, due to a number of factors. The illiterate rural masses were unable to read a newspaper, and most villages had no roads,[3] while the lack of electricity[4] prevented the use of radios and cinema projectors. Right from the start, Metaxas' regime tried to remedy these problems and a great effort was made to construct public roads, build schools and create educational facilities for the illiterate population, especially in places like Crete, Macedonia and Thrace where anti-Metaxas feeling was stronger.[5] In many cases each area was supplied with a cinema projector and several 'enlightening films,' while specially trained teachers toured the villages to project them and explain their content.[6] Where the lack of electricity prevented the projection of such films, the projectors despatched were accompanied by generators.[7] It must be stressed, however, that despite the regime's effort to improve conditions (a long and difficult process) and subsequently facilitate the projection of its ideology, its influence among a large number of Greek people was limited. Therefore the evaluation of Greek public opinion concerns mainly the urban population and those country people who could be reached by the government's propaganda.

It was impossible for the ordinary person who lived in Metaxas' Greece and who was able to look at a newspaper or a book, attend a theatrical play, watch a film or listen to a radio broadcast not to come into close contact with the themes linked with the 'Fourth of August' regime, especially that of charismatic leadership. The whole propaganda machine was geared towards conveying such an image and every possible device was engaged for that purpose. Pictures and accounts of mass demonstrations to welcome the Chief in the cities and the provinces were skilfully disseminated through the press, the cinema and the radio and were directed throughout the Greek state. Yet, evidence suggests that many of these popular manifestations were carefully organised by the propaganda machine to present a falsified picture of total devotion and enthusiasm. The following circular, representative of many, was issued on 1 January 1938 by the central committee of the union of agrarian co-operatives of Agrinion (a small town in central Greece) with instructions on welcoming the *Protos Agrotis,* and it effectively illustrates the 'spontaneous' nature of such a manifestation:

> 'Each co-operative and organisation is obliged to send a welcoming delegation of fifty members who will carry appropriate banners and give a dinner in the President's honour. The cost of the welcoming manifestations including that of the dinner will be born equally by all the members of the participant co-operatives.. It must be stressed that the expressions of devotion and love should be demonstrated with loud hailing and applauding and not just clapping of the hands'[8]

The impulsive outburst of national enthusiasm included the previously prepared tokens of the country people's love for their Chief. The British Ambassador Palairet observed in 1939 on such an occasion:

> 'Local worthies throughout Greece were appointed to organise celebrations in their villages (whether they liked it or not) and the local organisation committees were furnished by the *YTT* with the draft telegrams of congratulation which they were to send on the appointed day as spontaneous tokens of their admiration for the great leader'.[9]

The whole propaganda machine was engaged in an effort to convince the people of the necessity to demonstrate their love for the 'blessed presence' of the regime and to express this love with enthusiasm and adulation. Posters and leaflets like the following demanded the participation of the people and their expressions of utter gratitude for the regime's achievements:

> 'We are today celebrating the historic change brought about by the 'Fourth of August': let us manifest our enthusiasm and gratitude for the achievements of national salvation of Ioannis Metaxas'.[10]

Local newspapers were also engaged in a similar effort to persuade the crowds to demonstrate their support for the regime. However, these articles often hinted at opposition and resentment over the regime's propaganda effort. The newspaper *Epirotikos Agon* (Epirus Struggle), reporting on the manifestations which took place on 7 October 1938 on the occasion of the unveiling of king's Constantine's statue stated:

> 'It is certain that many of our fellow-townsmen, due to needless inner reserve, are reluctant to wear their hearts on their sleeves and express their joy: but when they do their enthusiasm has no boundaries. We must admit though that we do not know how to correctly demonstrate our enthusiasm. We ought to learn to do so and express all that is noble and good'[11]

On 13 October of the same year the same newspaper reported that 'unfortunately, despite the government's instructions which demanded that all houses hang out flags many of our fellow-citizens did not comply with the orders. However those who defied the government's instructions will be prosecuted'.[12] Similar actions produced a negative reaction and despite the propaganda machine's efforts to create a climate of national euphoria and support for their *Barba Yiannis*, it was never entirely successful. David Wallace,[13] following a tour of the Peloponnese at the beginning of June 1939 with a visit to a small mountain village of Northern Arcadia, was impressed by the 'amount of discontent with the Metaxas Government and by the people's eagerness to express it.'[14] This discontent was, according to Wallace, mainly the result of over-taxation by an over-centralised administration which prevented any real expression of public opinion and discussion. It could be claimed that these comments which reported dissatisfaction among a minority of the Peloponnesian population do not necessarily portray a general picture of opposition, especially since the report concerned the population of the Southern part of Greece, which had always been considered a 'citadel of Royalist feelings.'[15] However, careful examination of the evidence reveals that there were grounds for dissatisfaction among the Peloponnesian population, especially when the over-taxation was to help finance the efforts of the 'Fourth of August' propaganda to convey the regime's themes. An account of the effort put in by government circles not only to disseminate an image of Metaxas as a charismatic leader but also to organise an enthusiastic reception is given by Waterlow during Metaxas' tour of the Peloponnese in April 1939 (approximately a month before Wallace's visit to the Arcadian village):

> 'Some ten days before the date originally fixed, the Governor of the Agricultural Bank, the Deputy Governor and the Bank's Director of propaganda left for the Peloponnese in order to arrange with the

bank's local branches the preparatory work necessary to ensure an enthusiastic welcome for the Prime Minister and his suite. This was done by regimenting the agricultural population, who can not afford to be in the bank's bad books. Similar preparatory propaganda was organised well in advance by representatives of *EON* in all places of call. Local officials had been instructed in advance to prepare details of any public works in course of execution and to see to it that the populace turned out in force to applaud(...)A visit from a Prime Minister is naturally regarded in the country districts as an occasion for general jollification, but I learn from a good source that the Ministers accompanying him did not receive the impression that the populace was really well disposed towards the regime. No expense appears to have been spared to produce the appearance of success. All transport was free of charge, including fleets of requisitioned motor buses and lorries and the Peloponnesian Railways Company's trains(...) But the population is not likely to swallow with too good a grace the powder, following on the jam of free entertainment, in the shape of measures by the Agricultural Bank to recoup itself for its large expenditure on organisation, placards, banners, triumphal arches, etc., which is estimated at five million drachmas for Messenia alone, and which apparently is to be recovered by a stamp fee of ten drachmas on transactions and a special tax on sulphur imported into the district.'[16]

The above extract efficiently illuminates the economic pressure put on the local populace by government officials in order to secure the financial means required for the organisation of Metaxas' warm and enthusiastic reception.[17] Moreover, it explains the people's discontent at a ruthless propaganda machine which produced the falsified picture of a widely accepted Chief. Similar reports given by the foreign Legations concern other parts of Greece. For example, the U.S. Ambassador MacVeagh, following a tour of the Northern agrarian area of Macedonia in February 1937 noted great dissatisfaction in this rural part of Greece despite the propaganda trips organised by high officials like 'Mr. Kotzias the strutting trumpeter of the regime.'[18] According to MacVeagh considerable resentment was also detected among the numerous veterans of the district who showed neither 'the discipline nor the obedience expected from them.'[19] More general discontent is reported in 1938 and again in 1939.[20] Other reports reveal that in many places the dictatorship inspired mockery[21] and a good deal of grumbling and according to the British Vice-Consul of the island of Samos 'the name of General Metaxas was received with groans whenever mentioned.'[22]

One place where it seems that the regime's propaganda had little or no impact at all it was Crete, the pro-Venizelist stronghold. Like most of the inhabitants of 'New Greece'[23] the majority of Cretans were 'unrepentant' republicans who disliked every form of authoritarianism including Monarchy. The effort made by the propaganda machine to subvert this climate and win the people's support was more intense in Crete than anywhere else, since for Metaxas Cretan public opinion acted as 'a barometer' for national approval and content. In his speech to the people of Crete during his first 'goodwill trip' on 8 November 1936, he stated:

> 'You Cretans possess a youthful enthusiasm and your attitude is entirely patriotic. Your personal interest is put aside if your enthusiasm is aroused and I must admit that I greatly rely on this ability of yours. I believe that if the people of Crete are filled with enthusiasm and begin to express this enthusiasm, we as a nation will move so fast that even if there are a number of people who are still hesitant they will be carried away by your enthusiasm. I came here with this thought in my mind wishing to see for myself if there are grounds for such a possibility. I must say that I am more than thrilled with your enthusiasm which is like a rapid stream and overrides my own. This expression of love has been my best reward.'[24]

It is made explicit in the above extract that public opinion in Crete was of great importance to Metaxas who, through flattery, was trying to win the Cretans' support and eliminate the smouldering discontent. Although the speech presents a picture of overwhelming enthusiasm fostered by the people of Crete, reports by the foreign Legations and government sources contradict this image and reveal that the propaganda machine failed to generate popular consent. The Dictator's first tour of Crete, which according to Metaxas 'proved to be a great success and a token of the Cretans' love for and trust in the 'Fourth of August' government,'[25] was in fact met 'with a very cold public reception, which was overshadowed by the boisterous festivities and pompous formalities organised by the regime. Everywhere Metaxas went the audience turn-out was low and indifferent, despite the impressive preparations for an enthusiastic reception.'[26] The expressions of falsified enthusiasm and adulation, intended to manipulate the Cretan public, were also noted within government circles, who expressed their concern over the ineffectiveness of the propaganda techniques. Confidential reports coming from officials on the island recorded the 'negative' public mood and revealed that 'some of the working and agrarian population were turning to the left and that this turn, which was reaching threatening proportions, was

the result of a systematic and intense effort made by the enemies of the
'Fourth of August' State to undermine its power.'[27] Given the importance
of public opinion in Crete Metaxas attempted to win the support of the
people of Crete for a second time in March 1937 when he toured the
island with the King. Waterlow observed that this time the dictator went
'armed with a large number of laws dealing with improvements which he
had promised at the time of his previous visit,'[28] and with his propaganda
machine 'working at full speed' to organise an effective and 'spontaneous'
reception.[29] While the 'Fourth of August' propaganda used the press to
maintain the illusion that both the King's and Metaxas' visit were met with
overwhelming enthusiasm, the dominant sentiment in Crete appeared to be
one of anger, and discontent:

> 'Outside the Pantheon cinema hall serious anti-Metaxas riots took
> place, with the distribution of anti-government leaflets and slogans
> against Ioannis Metaxas. While the governor-general praised
> Metaxas and the King the lights went off and there was a great
> disturbance. The lights were switched on again. None of these
> incidents was reported in the press.'[30]

Similar reports that reached the British Legation spoke of the difference
between the ovations accorded to the King and to his Prime Minister. The
reports stated that 'in some places, where portraits of both were displayed
side by side, that of General Metaxas was torn down.[31] This discontent
remained constant throughout the Metaxas government (intensified during
the Cretan Revolt) and also had an impact on the growth and success of
EON, which contrary to the rest of the country was somewhat unsuccessful
in Crete. The dictator noted with concern in his diary in May 1939:

> 'Alekos Kanellopoulos returned from Crete. We make no progress
> there-We lack authority. The attitude of the Youth movement is
> everywhere unfavourable.' [32]

It is evident that despite its effort, the regime's propaganda had failed to
convey to the people of Crete an image of a charismatic leader which
would generate their enthusiasm and approval.

That there were signs in the countryside of the people's indifference
towards and in many cases of discontent with the regime's propagandistic
strategy, which gave a false picture of popular support and enthusiasm,
seems clear enough; but evidence also suggests that the same sentiment
was detected in the big cities, especially in the capital where the regime's
propaganda reached its 'peak.' The mass rallies and enthusiastic gatherings

which took place and projected a picture of total support seem to be the product of an orchestrated effort to project such an image. Films depicted large crowds attending the regime's festivals, while the press spoke of the thousands of country people who willingly travelled from their remote homes to pay their respect to the chief and to convey their enthusiasm and gratitude. Yet according to foreign sources most of these mass gatherings were a product of the regime's skilful propaganda efforts to project such an outcome, and in most cases the people's participation was merely for materialistic reasons.[33] An account of the regime's first anniversary given by Waterlow explains the motivation behind the 'spontaneous' enthusiasm and 'impulsive' attendance of the Greek people:

> 'On the present occasion every facility, in the way of cheap fares and so forth, had been given to encourage an influx to Athens from all over the country, and in consequence large numbers poured into town. The Stadium normally holds some 60,000 but on this occasion it was overcrowded and the number of those present may not have fallen far short of 100,000. The majority of these were, however, visitors from outside, and although admittance was free attendance might well have been scanty had it depended on the population of Athens alone(...) The enthusiasm was not overwhelming, and indeed hardly exceeded the ironical applause which had, a few months previously, greeted two sailors who raced from the far end of the Stadium to the entrance.'[34]

The report provides a clear example of the propagandistic techniques used in the manipulation and temptation of the crowds. Furthermore, it demonstrates that neither the 'spontaneous' outburst of national enthusiasm which the celebrations were reported as manifesting nor the Chief's 'inspiring' speeches seem to have made an impact on people's feelings. The general mood, according to Waterlow, remained indifferent: 'The Greek public obstinately refuses to catch fire from the words of a dictator whom it not only dislikes, but does not even respect.'[35] The falsified picture of the 'spontaneous' gatherings and enthusiastic expressions of the crowds that 'poured' into the city to celebrate the regime's anniversaries remained the same throughout the Metaxas dictatorship: but so did the real public sentiment. Ambassador Palairet observed in August 1939 after the third 'Fourth of August' anniversary celebration was over:

> 'The Stadium was packed with a gay throng so much so that the Minister of *YTT* himself could find no seat. The entry of General

Metaxas followed by members of his cabinet and others in a compact phalanx was greeted with applause mingled with cat-calls. I have been unable to ascertain definitely whether this whistling which recurred throughout the proceedings, usually at moments when some indifferent display was taking place, (e.g. when some rather unattractive girls marched along carrying bouquets and garlands), was a sign of disapproval or a new form of applause imported from America). Whatever it was there was no lack of it(…) I still have to receive reports on the festivities in the provinces but the general impression of competent observers is that the occasion fell even flatter than last year. If this is so I should suppose it to be as much due to the gross over-advertisement, the effect of which was only irritating, as to the increase in the unpopularity of the regime'[36]

The above extract suggests that often the efforts of the propaganda machine to present an image of a charismatic leader failed to turn artificial enthusiasm into genuine belief. This is the reason behind the dictator's repeated pleas for more enthusiasm: a word which according to Papadakis is used more than any other in Metaxas' speeches.'[37]

'We need enthusiasm not only as a government but also as a nation. It is imperative that the Greek people realise that great achievements do not become a reality with disappointing attitudes, complaints and slander but only with enthusiasm, optimism and faith in the future(…) I demand that all of you transmit this enthusiasm to your provinces and convey it to your fellow citizens and imbue them with the assurance that this country has now a government which is determined to complete the work for the regeneration of Greece.'[38]

Enthusiasm was thus a vital component in the charismatic leadership process and as such a great effort was made to generate it in all sections of society, especially among the working classes. A strictly confidential surveillance report dated November 1939 and found in Maniadakis's files on Gabriel Alexandros, a factory manager in Piraeus, demonstrates the extent to which the regime's propaganda would go to manipulate public opinion and convey a picture of the First Worker who was loved and respected by his fellow workers:

'He supports and propagates the ideas of the New State with fanaticism. Twice a week he summons the factory workers and speaks to them about the beneficial measures of the New State. On public holidays, especially the First of May and the 'Fourth of August' anniversaries he takes the lead and marches with his workers at the mass rallies, tempting them with various soft drinks and other things. He demands that his workers, on starting work every morning, salute in the *EON* manner.'[39]

However, despite the propaganda machine's efforts to present an image of a widely-loved leader, especially among the lower classes, the dictator himself often doubted these expressions of love, and questioned the workers' participation in the 'spontaneous' gatherings. The entry in his diary on 29 February 1940 reflects these doubts:

'I visited the Woollen Industry. I experienced expressions of love and utter devotion. In the evening I attended a ball given by the Workers Confederation; there were many people present; yet I wonder how many of them were workers? I do not believe many.'[40]

These doubts, which reflect a dichotomy between the manufactured image of the First Worker who enjoyed the unreserved love and support of the working classes, and the 'real one' who felt their resentment, are repeated again and again throughout his diary. It is evident that the gulf between the image manufactured by the 'Fourth of August' propaganda and Metaxas' real public image was striking. Although the propaganda machine saw the cult constructed around Metaxas as an essential and effective device to gain and retain the love and support of the people, evidence suggests that the dictator was not popular, or at least not as popular as his propaganda intended him to be.

The most important evidence supporting this claim comes directly from Metaxas himself and the entries in his diary which demonstrate effectively his insecurities, fears and doubts as to the Greek people's love for him. Even before he came to power in 1936, Metaxas had repeatedly quoted with bitterness the fact that he was a very unpopular person and that he lacked the support of the Greek people 'who recognised his abilities but they did not like him.'[41] This impression is evident throughout Metaxas' rule, despite the efforts of his propagandists to eliminate these feelings through enthusiastic reports and accounts from all over the country which presented a national euphoria. He often wondered whether these manifestations of love and adulation were genuine: 'in spite of all the honours and the applause I have a premonition that something has changed,'[42] while his wife wrote in this respect after his death: 'Very often he had deep doubts about the loyalty and love of the Greek people towards him and their belief in the 'regeneration of Greece.'[43] This self-doubt and failure continued throughout his life despite the reassuring accounts of Maniadakis[44] and his entourage and despite the beneficiary measures introduced by his government. He observed on 28 December 1938 during a dinner party given by the Actors' Society: 'Dinner given by the actors, enthusiasm; I felt that I was someone. Yet is this all true or are they all lying and will they disappear when things turn against me?'[45] Such comments suggest that Metaxas was trapped between his own personal feelings and doubts, which were based on a life-time's experience of personal unpopularity, and the falsified picture manufactured and presented to him by his propaganda machine which flattered and boosted his ego.[46] There were, however, voices within government circles which opposed the extravagant measures and techniques employed by his propaganda officials to convey an atmosphere of total consensus, and attempted to advise Metaxas of the harmful effects of such a process. For example one correspondent, doubtless with great courage, echoed the doubts so often expressed by the dictator, and wrote to him:

'Thessaloniki,

My dear President ,
I consider it a very fortunate fact that the circulation of the leaflets, despite their unfounded claims, prompts you to face the unvarnished truth that the Greek people who are mobilised to participate in the mass rallies and to applaud do not express their own feelings as they are not aware of your true and majestic mission dedicated to their welfare. It is indeed an outrageous and paradoxical phenomenon to have a nation that is not moved by the 'mighty' generosity and 'divine' inspiration of a Giant-Chief who consumes all his energy to ensure a better tomorrow for his people: I am sure that this phenomenon puzzles you(…) Yet Mr. President this is not an unexpected development. On the contrary, it is a normal outcome: You were not told the truth or you were told a truth that would not disappoint and frustrate you. I assure you that there is no popular feeling and substance in those manifestations: yet, I believe that the situation can be amended and you can inspire the nation and imbue the people with your ideals if you will only listen to your real friends and not the people who intentionally harm you with their actions.'[47]

The extract suggests a negative attitude on the part of the people of Thessaloniki who were mobilised to participate in the mass rallies. Moreover, the letter, which according to the writer, 'is a letter of conscience' sent by a 'devoted friend and a great supporter,' is of special significance because apart from shedding light into the ineffectiveness of the regime's propaganda, it also reveals that Ioannis Metaxas was subjected to a falsified picture of national euphoria by his propaganda officials.[48] The following tapped telephone conversation, also found in Metaxas' Private Papers, reveals the people's negative reaction to the efforts of the regime's propaganda to impose a desired outcome:

> '-Polygiorgis: Good morning, have you read today's papers?
> -Mavromihalis : Why? what about them?
> -Polygiorgis :The photos they are publishing
> -Mavromihalis: Yes I saw them
> -Polygiorgis: Everybody is laughing at the state Greece has been reduced to.'[49]

Whether Metaxas himself was convinced that his popularity was improving or he was simply flattered and carried away by the orchestrated efforts of its propaganda officials is difficult to establish. *The Manchester Guardian* which adopted a hostile attitude to Metaxas' dictatorship, wrote on 14 May 1937:

> 'Metaxas did not rise to power on a wave of popular feeling but seized it by means of a trick, and he has not since won the popular support he lacked but has lost what little he had. General Metaxas we feel sure is too clever a stateman not to know that even the most skilful propaganda provides no antidote to truth'[50]

The article is useful as it demonstrates that Metaxas' propaganda failed to establish strong psychological foundations in the wider sections of society and often strengthened the people's feelings against the dictator. Upon resuming his Ambassadorial power in Greece, on 28 June 1939, Palairet observed:

> 'I have not been here long enough to offer a considered opinion on the internal situation in Greece, but I have already formed the impression that the present regime is extremely unpopular' [51]

One of the aims of Metaxas' propaganda was to unite people of all classes into a homogenous society and co-ordinate their will with that of the state. To this end a consensus was manufactured through the means of mass communications and social facilities like communal radio listening in factories and shops, holidays and cheap cinema and theatre tickets.[52]

However, these rewards which were not merely a product of the government's welfare policy to elevate the lower classes, but also a propaganda 'bait', did not have the expected impact on the less privileged. A survey among the lower classes carried out by *Ta Paraskinia* in March 1939 provides a vivid picture of the failure of the regime's propaganda machine to persuade the Athenian working classes of their equality with other sections of society and their potential for advancement. The people asked included typists, factory girls, doormen and office boys. In answer to the question of whether they enjoyed the elevating theatre performances of the Royal Theatre offered to them by the new State, most of them replied that they found the performances boring, difficult to understand, and that they would rather watch the Greek revues or a lighter kind of performance which would make them laugh. Furthermore, they claimed that they could not afford to go to the theatre as they were simple working people.[53]

This survey suggests that there was a difference between the image of a unified, nationally aware working community who enjoyed as equals the rewards of the reformed state, and the social reality of the working people. It seemed that the 'Fourth of August' propaganda failed to achieve true levelling of classes and break down the social and economic barriers. Most importantly, it was unable to destroy class awareness and imbue a national pride and euphoria. The evidence available supports the fact that the regime's efforts to culturally elevate the great masses and transform them into individuals of intellect was often met with elaborate jokes and 'improper' reaction from the public. For instance the circulation of an 'obscene' and 'provocative' *Rebetiko* song with the title *Barbara*[54] provoked a number of reactions and proved an outlet for the true feelings of the public who made an indirect attack on the regime through the mass purchase of recordings of the song. Thousands of gramophone records were sold in the streets and shops while Maniadakis' *Asfaleia* was trying to confiscate them, prosecuting hundreds of shopkeepers, along with the makers of the record. The trial, which took place in Athens in 1937, attracted thousands of people from all segments of society, who queued up to watch the trial, thus expressing their resentment of the government, while the police presence outnumbered the crowds. The public prosecutor, before passing sentence, attacked the immoral and degrading nature of the song and claimed that it should be destroyed because 'it had such an overwhelming effect on the public that every Greek ended up carrying a *Barbara* under its arm'.[55] The point must also be made that, while there were many anthems and songs emanating from the regime's propaganda machine and extolling

Metaxas' regime, there are no popular or *Rebetikco* songs which praise the dictatorship. The incident suggests that negative public opinion was expressed through 'unusual methods' often taking a form of mockery and ridicule- a fact acknowledged by Waterlow who reported in July 1937:

> 'One result of the suppression of public criticism is perhaps worth noting. The disaffected, having no other means of attacking the regime, construct, one after the other, a series of elaborate myths, which, once spread by sensation-mongers, command general belief.'[56]

Extracts such as the above demonstrate that the people were not impressed by the regime's propaganda and often invented their own counter-propaganda tactics to fight the government. All the manipulating techniques used by the regime, especially the ones projecting the charismatic leadership concept, often enough had the opposite effect and provoked people's resentment and opposition. Waterlow observed in July 1937:

> 'Everyone sickens at the adulation of the regime that the press is obliged to feature. In this respect all people of intelligence hold that General Metaxas is making a mistake: he is trying they say, to work on the sub-consciousness of the nation by mass propaganda; which is absurd, because the Greek character is all surface cynicism and scepticism and has no sub-consciousness anyhow; he would be more likely to attain his end by paying writers to criticise him. There is something in this. Self-praise is not likely ever to go down in Greece, much less to generate national enthusiasm'[57]

It seems clear from the evidence so far presented that the regime was unpopular with large sections of the Greek population. A number of factors act as a justification for this negative public opinion, and to some extent, explain why the regime's propaganda failed to win the people's genuine love and enthusiasm: working people were more concerned about everyday problems like unemployment, inflation and the high cost of living, as wages, despite the substantial economic recovery, were not kept in line with rising prices,[58] while most of the national wealth was consumed by the building up of the armed forces. The peasants resented the Law which, as part of the government's reforestation policy, restricted the pasturage of goats in the mountains and on their lands and deprived them of their livelihood.[59] On the other hand the upper classes disapproved of the government's collection of extra taxes for the war effort and were unhappy about the economic 'contributions' they were forced to make to *EON*.[60] Waterlow observed in July 1937:

> 'The Upper classes are the very people whom the dictatorship puts to the greatest personal inconvenience. Their liberty of financial action is restricted in a hundred ways. It is difficult, if not impossible, for them to leave the country on pleasure and even on business and in every detail of their lives they are harassed by police regulations'[61]

Furthermore, their status-conscious superiority prevented a positive response to the populist leadership images projected by the regime's propaganda. However, these factors alone could not justify the unpopular feelings that Metaxas' regime generated and further justification should be searched for in the application of the measures connected with the nature of the regime. The Metaxas dictatorship, through its monopoly of the means of mass communications, the physical and psychological control exercised by the Police, the recruiting of thousands of informers, the extravagant expenditure on indoctrination and propaganda and the financial and political scandals of *EON*, as well as a highly centralised policy, managed to instil hate and fear in the Greek masses who were not deceived by the facade of uniformity and general consensus that the regime was ostensibly projecting. Clearly under these circumstances Metaxas was not popular.

However, the point must be made that although all the evidence examined reveals that Metaxas was an unpopular leader, more evidence coming from the same sources suggests that contrary to his unpopular image, the public reaction was more one of passive tolerance and general apathy.[62] As cited in Chapter One, Metaxas' regime found little or no opposition that would endanger its position. Furthermore the material awards and political stability offered by the government together with the fear of communism and the international crisis of the time provided his government with an alibi and led to many of his measures being welcomed by the people; a fact acknowledged by Waterlow almost a year after Metaxas' coming to power:

> 'General Metaxas may exaggerate when he tells me that the peasants, from whom he has just lifted a millstone of debt, rise up daily and bless him for giving them a freedom to work and make money which they never knew under the tyranny of the politicians. But it is certain that the peasants are quiet and content, and that there is no serious dissatisfaction among the proletariat of the towns'[63]

Similarly MacVeagh reported in June 1937 after a trip to Eastern Macedonia:

> 'The best opinion seemed to be that the present regime and
> particularly the personality of the dictator is not popular but that
> prosperity combined with stability is keeping the favoured country
> of Greece quiet and attentive to business.'[64]

However, apart from the evidence coming mainly from the foreign Legations
which reveal that the masses were indifferent if not, in Vatikiotis' words
'perversely satisfied with the regime's populism,' a large number of personal
letters, postcards, telegrams and poems, many coming from abroad and
found in Metaxas' Private Papers, File 43, demonstrate a genuine love for
and utter devotion to the man they called 'their father and 'Beloved Chief'
and who imbued their hearts with national pride and joy[65]. It is, however,
very difficult to establish if these expressions of love were the result of an
effective propaganda or whether they were true sentiments of a section of
the Greek community who believed in the benevolent intervention of the
Metaxas regime and the ideals and values it epitomised. So, while it remains
difficult to prove a clear connection between the regime's ineffective
propaganda and the lack of enthusiasm of the population at large, it
is important to note that the conditions within the country (economic
improvements, political stability), as well as the impending international
crisis, created a set of circumstances under which propaganda such as that
employed by Metaxas would be able to flourish.

The failure or success of Metaxas' propaganda was not simply the
outcome of the resources and devices used, and its ability or otherwise to
co-ordinate its campaign, but also depended on the contemporary domestic
and international circumstances and the prevailing opinions and prejudices
of the Greek people.

Chapter Seven

CONCLUSION

The 'Fourth of August' regime's propaganda continued its efforts to disseminate its ideology and goals until Metaxas' death on 29 January 1941. However, the objectives and themes had by then considerably changed and were adjusted to serve the new political and military situation that had developed since the summer 1940, and led to the outbreak of the Greco-Italian war in October 1940. Agelos Vlachos described this period as 'the most trying period for the government, the political world and public opinion.'[1] Italian-Greek relations had deteriorated as a result of a sequence of events that had convinced Metaxas of Mussolini's aggressive intentions, culminating on 15th August 1940 with the torpedoing of the cruiser *Elli* in the waters off the island of Tinos.[2] Until this time the regime's propaganda continued to promote its ideology within the framework of the country's supposed neutrality.[3] However, as it became clearer that Greece was going to have to become involved in the war, the public were continually warned of the need for national awareness and alertness, and the regime's propaganda was adjusted to serve the new situation. Metaxas' speech during the regime's fourth anniversary demonstrates this new trend explicitly:

> 'The intensive need of the Greek people to celebrate this 'Fourth of August' anniversary(...) has been totally respected. However, it is my duty to recommend the avoidance of panegyric manifestations like those of previous years, so that we transform this 1940 celebration into a modest and serious celebration dictated by the weight of the circumstances that we are going through'[4]

The prospect of war imposed considerable strain on the structure of the New State as formed by Metaxas' regime, with its propagandists working at full speed to prepare the masses for the oncoming war. For the previous two years the propaganda machine had, amidst all the grand manifestations and the exploitation of the masses, been preparing the people for the possibility of war through appeals and the collections of large amounts of money for rearmament, and the implementation of an extensive programme of autarky.

On 28 October 1940 when Metaxas was served with the Duce's ultimatum and gave his historic *Ochi* (No) as an answer, the following paradox could be detected. Unlike in the Third Reich where according to David Welch in his work *The Third Reich. Politics and Propaganda* 'the difficulties for propaganda were exacerbated by the distinct lack of enthusiasm for the announcement of war,'[5] in Greece the announcement of war had completely the opposite effect, and provided the regime's propaganda with a significant 'alibi' for its previous unpopular conduct of mass manipulation, and gave it a new impetus that served both the 'Fourth of August' themes and the war effort. The testimony given by Agelos Vlachos on the *Ochi* day (the day of the declaration of war) of the following morning, provides a vivid picture of the atmosphere outside the Ministry of Foreign Affairs:

> 'The whole of Athens was out in the streets shouting and cheering(...) Thousands of people rushed to the Ministry's grounds surrounding Metaxas' car. Metaxas appeared at the gate to get into his car. He was holding his walking stick, with his two bodyguards at his side. When the crowds saw Metaxas they went crazy. I was standing behind him and I saw the dictator enjoy the best moments of his life. He ordered his bodyguards aside and gave himself up to the huge crowd which swept him on its shoulders and singing the National Anthem, carried him across to the Army Headquarters (...) One was under the impression that Greece was a tank which had been boiling for months and suddenly, with a noise that could be heard at the end of the world, the lid was off.'[6]

A similar picture is also portrayed in the short newsreel *O Polemos* [7] which presents an image of overwhelming enthusiasm and national pride. And indeed, unlike in most of the regime's film propaganda, one can detect real enthusiasm and national exaltation in this sound newsreel. Children selling newspapers were shouting and cheering and distributed with haste and excitement the news of the declaration of war, while cars and trams are depicted packed with people rushing to offer their services for the good of the country. It seemed that everybody was thrilled with the advent of war.

19. Poster Greco-Italian war

Panagiotis Kanellopoulos, who returned from exile on 2 November 1940 to enlist, wrote of that day:

> 'Returning to Athens on 2 November 1940 I felt, both as an ordinary citizen and as part of a nation, the great national pride and ethical joy felt by all the Greeks.'[8]

The above extracts seem to contradict the image of Metaxas' unpopularity and of his inability to inspire enthusiasm in the hearts of the Greek people despite his propagandists' efforts to make him into a charismatic leader. Could it be that the Dictator's negative image had changed overnight because of his *Ochi* to the Italian invaders, or that his propaganda had not been completely unsuccessful? It has already been demonstrated that no reliable evidence exists which would effectively assess the impact of the 'Fourth of August' regime's propaganda. The situation is further complicated by controversial debates about the historical reality of the *Ochi* and the feelings that it generated. Leftist writers argue that the *Ochi* was not Metaxas' doing, but the outcome of the Greek people's patriotic feelings which forced Metaxas to denounce his beliefs and his fascist ideology and deliver his negative answer, and of the regime's calculated interests.[9] If that was the case, the following day's enthusiasm and support for Metaxas [10] could not be justified, as the people, instead of applauding and embracing Metaxas, could then have taken their chance to strongly express their opposition and possibly overthrow him. The other view, backed by historical evidence, is that it was Metaxas who, with his *Ochi*, stood up to the Italian aggressors. According to the entry in his diary on 4 January 1941 (twenty five days before his death) he would rather 'die' (*Kallitera na apothanomen*) than surrender to the Axis Powers.'[11]

Furthermore, Metaxas continued to receive the people's admiration, love and affection not only for his decision to reject Italy's demands, but also because of his handling of the war. Unlike Hitler, whose charismatic leadership faded away during the war, Metaxas' charismatic qualities became a reality for the fighting Greeks and his death left a great political and military vacuum. His private papers are full of letters and telegrams expressing people's sorrow and in many cases distress at Metaxas' death, while the media of the time reported the great loss.[12] Similarly articles by the majority of the intellectual elite dedicated to Metaxas bearing headlines such as: 'The Great Patriot;' the 'Leader of the all Greek people;' The Governor that Became a Legend,' adorned the daily press and other publications.[13]

It could, of course, be argued that this was all the product of skilful propagandising to project the image of a charismatic leader who had passed away. However, given the seriousness of the circumstances Metaxas' death was, as the events that followed demonstrated, an irreplaceable loss.[14] A short newsreel *O Thanatos tou Ioannou Metaxa,*[15] shot during his funeral, depicts this loss more clearly than anything else. Thousands of people queued up on that rainy winter day to pay their last respect to their *Megas Kyvernitis* and accompany him to his resting place: this did not seem to be the reaction of people who were forced to lament, but rather a spontaneous expression of grief for the loss of their leader, along with a response to the uncertainty that this loss generated. This was a film of the death of a charismatic leader: an unpopular leader who, because of the circumstances, responded to the demands of history and became a Military Chief on 28 October 1940 and managed to do what his propaganda had conspicuously failed to accomplish; to unite the whole Greek nation irrespective of political beliefs[16] and become their beloved Chief. Ambrossios Tzifos, commenting on the funeral of Metaxas, wrote in his unpublished diary:

> 'At that moment Metaxas was the symbol and inspiration of our great national struggle at its most critical moment. The same fear possessed both friend and foe (…) So much talent, determination and glory had gone for ever'[17]

It could be argued that this recognition came about because the Greco-Italian war resulted in victory and no one knows what the people's reaction would have been if Greece had been defeated. It seems likely that the Greek people would have resented Metaxas and blamed their defeat on his Fascist regime: however, the same reaction would most probably be initiated by any defeat, even under a democratic government. Another view, expressed by Metaxas' supporters, is that if Metaxas had been alive when the Germans invaded Greece two months after his death, the Greek people would have resisted much longer and the outcome might have been different.[18] This view might seem rather exaggerated, especially when all the other small countries had been invaded by Hitler. Nevertheless the truth is that after Metaxas' death Greece was left without a leader and since his regime was a personal regime, the country disintegrated.[19] However, the fact remains that at the end of his life Metaxas received more positive recognition than many other leading politicians of his time. Woodhouse remarked on Metaxas' posthumous fame:

> 'Ioannis Metaxas died on 29 January 1941, three months after the Italians attacked Greece.'
> No dictator was more fortunate in the moment of his death. By

his famous 'No' to the Italian ultimatum: by his efficient contact of the Greek mobilisation: by the success won against the Italians: by all these combined with the popularity of the Anglo-Greek alliance he had become endeared not only to the countries which were to form the United Nations, but in an unprecedented degree to his own countrymen(...) But the legacy of his dictatorship was hard. It must be endlessly debated what Metaxas would have done in the circumstances he bequeathed to his successors: but the very fact that the question cannot be answered, argues the difficulty of the problems he had left unsolved and the fortune which saved his reputation from the strain of failure to solve them.'[20]

The above extract indicates that Metaxas had gained a place in Greek history and had, by the end of his life, not only enjoyed the respect of his people but had managed to unite and convince them of the need to safeguard the themes and concepts which his propaganda had extensively disseminated. Ideals like *The King, Country, Religion,* and the *Flag,* again figured prominently in the regime's propaganda (although the 'regeneration of Greece' became 'defending Greece') and had become the dominant influences and decisive forces behind Greece's fighting spirit and her victory over the Italians. Journalists were asked by Metaxas on 30 October 1940 to put aside their major propagandistic role in manipulating the Greek masses and serve their country:

'Gentlemen, I have censorship and I can force you to write only what I wish you to write. But this time I do not need only your pen: I want your souls too(...) I want you to be aware of our national adventure so that you can write not merely according to my instructions but inspired by your personal faith and guided by the facts of the situation(...) Do not lose your courage whatever the outcome; otherwise you will be unable to stand up to the greatness of your people and to your duty, which is to preserve the sacred flame of the *Hellenic* Nation, to help the fighting forces and to co-operate with the government whatever your feelings towards it are.'[21]

The above extract is significant not only because it presents Metaxas' testimony on the use of the press as his propagandistic instrument: 'I do not need only your pen,' but also because it demonstrates that the dictator was still very much concerned about his popularity: 'whatever your feelings are towards me.' This uncertainty seemed to have faded away two months later when he noted in his diary: 'What a love everybody feels for me: how can I describe all these tokens of dedication and love, yet, I remain humble without arrogance because what is great is God, and in Greece what is great are her people.'[22]

It was at this time that Metaxas achieved his life's dream and was able to overcome his past insecurities and become a beloved leader and an accepted politician.[23] The feelings of his people towards him in the final months of his life are reflected in his lament:

> 'They accused me, exiled me, sentenced me to death (in absentia incidentally) but finally even for me there came in my seventieth year the moment of recognition.'[24]

The question still arises whether this recognition, which he undoubtedly received during the last months of his life, was the result of his skilful propaganda or of historical necessity. The answer lies possibly in the reply Metaxas gave to the people (and this included friends and enemies) who praised him on his name-day on 7 January 1941:

> 'All this is not my doing, but that of the Greek people, who always remained true to their tradition, as long as they were united and disciplined, rather than slavishly and blindly following the politicians. Under the factionalism of the past these virtues and attributes disappeared, so that all my efforts from the start - when I assumed power - were directed at the recovery of these virtues, so that the nation would be psychologically ready for the 28th of October.'[25]

Indeed, it could be said that the 'Fourth of August' regime had, through a programme of extensive propaganda to disseminate its themes, awakened the ideals and virtues of the Greek people, giving them a new impetus which led to the '28th of October' and the victories that followed. No doubt some themes, like charismatic leadership and anti-communism, were comprehensible if placed in their political and historical context. Furthermore, Metaxas' anti-parliamentarism could be partially justified given the nature of the regime as well as the failures of the previous political systems to secure stability and win the consent of the Greek people. As far as the concepts King, Religion, Country and Family were concerned, these were ideals propagated and safeguarded by most countries. What distinguished these themes within the 'Fourth of August' regime, and led them to be regarded in a negative light, was the way they were disseminated. It was not only the coarseness with which these themes were propagated and the expense involved, but more importantly, the backing offered by Metaxas' Police State to 'facilitate' the dissemination and realisation of these.

The 'Fourth of August' regime was a regime which lacked popular support and a political base. To remedy the lack of these political 'necessities' the 'Fourth of August' State established the *Ethnikos Organismos Neoleas* which it hoped would take the place of a party mechanism, and applied an extensive programme of propaganda and indoctrination to win over the masses and maintain itself in power. Through a strict censorship of all the mass media and with the establishment of the sub-Ministry of Press and Tourism and the enactment of numerous Emergency Laws, the Metaxas' Dictatorship attempted to disseminate the themes associated with its ideals and policies. Central to those was that of a charismatic leadership which involved extraordinary powers acquired by Metaxas like the 'Saviour of the Nation', the 'First Peasant', the 'First Worker', the 'First Athlete' and the 'Leader of the people', especially the less privileged classes, while his propaganda used these titles to evoke popular enthusiasm and support for the regime: The themes of anti-communism and anti-parliamentarism were skilfully incorporated into the charismatic leadership process to support the image of Metaxas as the 'Saviour of the Nation' and the 'National Governor'.

The main findings of this work support the fact that although Metaxas was a patriot and a man of political vision, broad cultural tastes[26] and a reformer, he was one of the least likeable men. By illustrating the difference between Metaxas' real image and the one manufactured by his propaganda machine it has been demonstrated that the 'Fourth of August' propaganda was not only ineffective but often led to results which were the exact opposite of those desired, and exposed Metaxas in the eyes of the Greek people.

The Dictator remained an unpopular leader until the outbreak of the Greco-Italian war.[27] His decision to resist the invaders, and the course of this war, dramatically altered the masses' perception of him and changed his position from an unpopular dictator to a heroic figure, ensuring him glory after death.

However, the legacy of the 'Fourth of August' regime was hard and the lack of an able successor together with the bitterness of the defeat and the German occupation wiped out Metaxas' posthumous fame and revived the anti-Metaxas feelings and the old political passions, which led Greece into a destructive Civil War.[28]

Notes

INTRODUCTION

1. Taylor, Philip, M., *Munitions of the Mind. A History of Propaganda From The Ancient World To The Present Day.* (Manchester University Press, Manchester, 1995), p. 4.

2. Although Metaxas died in January 1941 the book examines the propaganda as it developed until 28 October 1940 when the Italians invaded Greece. Thereafter propaganda was adjusted to serve the war effort.

3. The most significant works on Metaxas' Dictatorship are those by Spiros Linardatos, Ioannis Koliopoulos, Grigorios Dafnis, Dimitris Kitsikis, Jon Kofas and the collective studies of the International History Conference *'E Ellada 1936-44. Diktatoria, Katochi, Antistasi. Greece 1936-1944,* Athens 1983. Also the work edited by Higham, Robin and Veremis, Thanos in *Aspects of Greece 1936-40. The Metaxas Dictatorship,* and Moschopoulos N., George book *Apo Tin Palinorthosi Sti Vasilo-Metaxiki Diktatoria 1935-1940. Fos Sta Paraskinia.* Valuable information on the ideology of the 'Fourth of August' regime is also found in Sarantis, Constantine, Ph.D Thesis *The Emergency of the Right in Greece, 1922-1936.* All these works have been cited in full in the main section of the bibliography.

4. Vatikiotis in his study on Metaxas, argues that 'Metaxas is 'a prominent feature of the contemporary Greek's political demonology, for he elicits hostility and opprobrium' Vatikiotis, P. J. *Popular Autocracy in Greece 1936-1941. A Political Biography of General Ioannis Metaxas.* (Frank Cass, London, 1999) p. 1.

5. Machera, Eleni, *E Neolea Tis 4es Augoustou. Fotografes* (Istoriko Archeio Ellinikis Neoleas, Geniki Gramateia Neas Genias, Athens, 1987). See also Labrinos Fotis, *ISCHIS MOY E AGAPI TOY FAKOY – Ta Kinimatografika Epikera os tekmiria tis Istorias (1895-1940),* (Kastaniotis, Athens, 2005).

6. On propaganda in those states see: Welch, David., *The Third Reich. Politics and Propaganda,* (Routledge, London, 1995), Hoffmann, Hilmar, *The Triumph of Propaganda, Film and National Socialism 1933-1945* (Berghahm Books, Oxford, 1996) Baird, J.W., *The Mythical World of Nazi Propaganda 1933-1945* (University of Minnesota, Mineapolis, 1974) Taylor, Richard, *Film Propaganda: Soviet Russia and Nazi Germany.* (Croom Helm, London , 1979).

7. The word propaganda was first introduced in 1622 when the Vatican established the 'Sacra Congregatio de Propaganda Fide'(Congregation for the Propagation of the Faith) which was charged with carrying 'the faith' to the New World and with reviving and strengthening it in Europe as a means of countering the Protestant revolution. Jowett, S., Garth, and Victoria O'Donnell, *Propaganda and Persuasion* (SAGE, London, 1992) p.54.

8. From the beginning of the modern period, the British system of government placed persuasion and propaganda at the heart of the working of the state. In 1914 Asquith set up an Office of Propaganda that came directly under the War Cabinet. The basic British approach. known as 'the propaganda facts' set by the Ministry of Information was for official propaganda to present events as accurately as possible, but with an interpretation favourable to British Policy. The United States upon entering the War copied this British policy stressing facts by establishing its own Committee on Public Information (CPI). D.Culbert, N.Cull and D.Welch (eds), *Propaganda and Mass Persuasion. A Historical Encyclopaedia, 1500 to the Present* (ABC-Clio,2003), p. 437- 439.

9. The belief that the war was lost on the home front where the German morale was undermined by skilful British propaganda was widely held in Germany and was extensively analysed in Hitler's *Mein Kampf.* Hitler, Adolf*, Mein Kampf,*, Translation by Ralph Manheim, (Pimlico,London, 1992), pp. 161-185. Hitler believed that it was Germany's failure to recognise the significance of propaganda as a weapon of first order that drove Germany to defeat and humiliating post war peace settlements(Treaty of Versailles (1919). His determination to revise this treaty and recover the lost territories was one of the reasons that facilitated his advent to power. The role of building up a consensus that favoured his policy of revisionism was undertaken in 1933 by the Reichsministerium fur Volksaufklarung und Propaganda (Reich Ministry

for Popular Enlightenment and Propaganda) under his minister Joseph Goebbels. D.Culbert, N.Cull and D.Welch (eds), *Propaganda*, pp. 441-444.

10. Welch, *The Third Reich*, p. 6.

11. Taylor, *Munitions*, p. 10. Taylor defines propaganda as the deliberate attempt to persuade people to think and behave in a desired way'. Ibid., p. 6. Similar is the definition given by Welch in his 'Powers of Persuasion', *History Toady* (August 1999) pp.24-26. He asserts that propaganda is ' consciously designed to serve the interest, either directly or indirectly, of the propagandists and their political masters(..) and its aim is to persuade its subjects that there is only one valid point of view and to eliminate all other options' D.Culbert, N.Cull and D.Welch (eds), *Propaganda*, pp. 318-319.

12. For a brief analysis of propaganda employed in Cold War see, Tory Shaw, Cinematic Propaganda During The Cold War: A Comparison of British and American Movies, in Mark Connely, David Welch(eds), *War and the Media*,(I.B.Tauris, London,2005), p.163.

13. Taylor, *Munitions*, p. 4. Propaganda during the last decades has gained an increasing prominence because of the technological advances in mass communication (explosion of information superhighways and digital data networks).Welch claims that ' Propagandists have been forced to respond to these changes by reassessing their audience and using whatever methods they consider most effective'. D. Culbert, N.Cull and D.Welch (eds), *Propaganda*, p. xix..

14. The inter-war period in Greece was marked by the feud between the Venizelist Camp (republican) and its leader Eleftherios Venizelos, and the anti-Venizelist camp (populist) and its leader King Constantine. This feud which had originated as a dispute between Prime Minister Venizelos and King Constantine over Greece's alignment in the First World War (Venizelos supported a pro-*Entente* policy while Constantine favoured neutrality) brought a deep division in the country known as the *Ethnikos Dichasmos* (National Schism). The situation deteriorated with the defeat of the Greek forces in Asia Minor in 1922 which produced almost one million and half refugees. During the eighteen years that followed the First World War until Metaxas came to power, thirty three governments alternated in power causing greater polarisation. See, Close, David, *The Origins of the Greek Civil War.* (Longman, London, 1995) pp. 32-57. For more about this period see also Dafnis, Grigorios, *E Ellas Metaxy Dyo Polemon.* (Kaktos, Athens, 1997) Vol. 1 - 2., and Woodhouse, C.M., *Modern Greece - A Short History*. (Faber & Faber, London, 1998) pp. 187-237.

An account of the feud between the two protagonists of the National Schism being 'like a disease, which divided their electorate into two camps inflamed by a bitterness of which the quality can only be composed with that which religion hatreds have so often transmitted from generation to generation', is given by Waterlow, Sydney, in *The Decline and Fall of Greek Democracy 1933-1936*, The Political Quarterly Vol. XVIII Nos.2-3 (Turnstile Press Ltd., London 1947) p. 208.

15. The sub-Ministry was established under Emergency Law 45, on 19 August 1936. *FEK (Fyllo Efimeridos Tis Kiverniseos)* - (Government Gazette) 356, pp. 1821-1823.

16. The Archives were donated to the State by Metaxas' wife.

17. *Ioannis Metaxas, To Prosopiko Tou Imerologio* (Ioannis Metaxas, His Personal Diary) (Govosti, Athens, 1950). A unique personal record which he kept for more than forty years and reveals a cultured man full of political vision but also full of ambition insecurities and egoism. Metaxas' diary which consists of eight volumes and covers a period of 45 years (1896-1941), constitutes a significant primary source.

CHAPTER 1

1. The elections of 1932 were to usher in a period of political instability and growing polarisation that was to culminate four years later in the 'Fourth of August' dictatorship. The elections of 1933 secured a comfortable majority for the Populist party headed by Tsaldaris and forced Colonel Plastiras, a devoted Venizelist, to attempt an unsuccessful coup in March 1933, an act which revived the old feud. A further coup in March 1935 by Venizelist officers ended in failure and Venizelos joined Plastiras in

exile. Further elections in June 1935 resulted in the restoration of the monarchy and in April 1936 on the death of Prime Minister Constantinos Demerzis (a caretaker government) the King appointed Metaxas as his successor. Metaxas on the pretext of suppressing the social unrest caused by the communists, suspended the constitution and established his 'Fourth of August' regime. Clogg, *A Concise History*, pp. 112-117; Close, *The Origins*, pp. 32-37.

2. The press has always played a dominant role in the shaping of political attitudes in most countries. According to James Curran and Jean Seaton in their work on the British Press and Broadcasting 'the press was the arena of major political struggle since the nineteenth century' and is still in force despite the 'invasion' of other means of mass media.' Curran James & Seaton Jean, *Power Without Responsibility - The Press and Broadcasting in Britain* (London and New York, Routledge 1997) pp. 2-3.

3. Manolis Paraschos in his study on the Greek media claims that up to the 1980s print was the dominant medium in Greece and had become 'the party followers belief reinforcer, party-activity, bulletin boards and part placards for those wishing to exhibit their feeling'. Manolis Paraschos, 'The Greek Media Face the Twenty-first Century: Will Adam Smith Complex Replace the Oedipus Complex?,' in Constas, Dimitri and Theofanis G. Stavrou, (eds.) *Greece Prepares for the Twenty-first Century* (Washington D.C., The Woodrow Wilson Center Press, 1995) p. 254.

4. From a satirical poem by Soutsos. Quoted by Metaxas in his speech to the editors of the Athenian newspapers, in his effort to underline the damaging political power acquired by the press in the past and justify his imposed censorship. *Ioannis Metaxas, Logoi Ke Skepseis 1936-1941* (Ioannnis Metaxas, Speeches and Thoughts 1936-1941) (Athens, Govosti,, 1969) Vol. 1, p. 42.

5. 'Imerisios ke Periodikos Typos ton Athinon, 1935', in *Statistiki Epetiris Tis Ellados* (Athens, 1936) p. 277. As we note, out of the 49 newspapers 43 were of a political nature. This statistical table was issued before the establishment of Metaxas' dictatorship and demonstrates the large press circulation. Although there are surveys on press circulation carried out by the Metaxas' regime the next official statistics on the press and on most other aspects of Greek life were carried out in 1950.

6. Jowett & O'Donnell assert in *Propaganda and Persuasion* that, 'Propaganda is associated with the control of the information flow. Those who control public opinion and behaviour make maximum and intelligent use of the forms of communication that are available to them.' Jowett & O' Donnell, *Propaganda and Persuasion,* p. 220.

7. Metaxas' speech delivered to the editors of the Athenian newspapers, 13 September 1936. *Logoi ke Skepseis.* Vol, 1, p. 38.

8. Dafnis, *E Ellas Metaxy Dyo Polemon*, p. 423; Linardatos, Spiros, *4e Augoustou* (Athens, Themelio, 1988) pp. 72-77 and FO 371/21147, 9 February 1937.

9. Ibid. See also Kofas, Jon V, *Authoritarianism in Greece, The Metaxas Regime* (New York, East European Monographs, 1983) pp. 98-99.

10. *FEK* 356, 19 August 193 , pp. 1821-1823.

11. Ibid. 379, 31 August 1936 (page unreadable), and *FEK* 380, 31 August 1936, p. 1975. In 1925 Nicoloudis joined the party of *Eleftherofrones* founded by Metaxas in November 1922, and *Politeia* became a great supporter of Metaxas, following a general line of moderate anti-Venizelism. Sarantis, Constantine *The Emergency of the Right in Greece* (1922-1940) Ph.D. Thesis (Oxford, St.Edmund Hall, 1979) p. 491.

12. *FEK.* 379, 31 August 1936, p. 1975.

13. In March 1933 Goebbels had likened the press to a piano, 'on which the Government could plan to influence the public in whatever direction it desired.' David Welch, *The Third Reich.*, p. 35.

14. Metaxas' speech, 13 September 1936. *Logoi ke Skepseis*, Vol. 1., pp. 40-41, and *Eleftheron Vima*, 15 September, 1936.

15. Before coming to power in 1936 Metaxas edited various political newspapers. See *Ioannis Metaxas, To Prosopiko tou Imerologio*, Vol. 5., pp. 129,149,151.

16. Welch, *The Third Reich*, p. 35.

17. Metaxas' speech, 25 October, 1936. .*Logoi ke Skepseis*, Vol. 1, p. 84.

18. *Tessera Chronia Diakiverniseos I.Metaxa 1936-1940* (Four Years of Government by I. Metaxas 1936-1940) (Athens, *YTT*, Ekdoseis *Tetartis Augoustou*, 1940) Vol. 4, p. 167. This publication of four volumes which contained the real and the 'alleged' achievements of the 'Fourth of August' regime was used extensively for propaganda purposes and forms a historical document of great significance.

19. *The Minieon Deltion Typou* was a monthly publication which contained all the regime's achievements, Metaxas' speeches and tours, as well as all the favourable accounts published in the Greek and foreign press. It constitutes a valuable source for the activities and propaganda of the sub-Ministry of Press and Tourism.

20. *FEK.* 93, 12 March 1937, p. 591.

21. Mr. Miller, the *Morning Post* correspondent in Athens, claimed that 'censorship under Mussolini was much less severe than that of Metaxas.' FO 371/21147, 9 February 1937. It must be stressed, however, that Mussolini had also exercised austere censorship on the press as early as 1926 when he suspended many newspapers through Exceptional Decrees and imposed compulsory registration of all journalists with the Fascist Journalist Association. By 1930 this office effectively controlled all kinds of publications. Lee, Stephen J., *The European Dictatorships 1918-1945* (London and New York, Routledge, 1987) p. 104.

22. On the predominance of German news over news from other countries see FO 371/ 21143, 24 July 1937, and Markezinis, Spiros, *Sychroni Politiki Istoria Tis Ellados* (Athens, Papiros, 1994) Vol. 1, p. 92.

23. Sir Sydney Waterlow was the British Ambassador in Greece when Metaxas came to power. He demonstrated an anti-Metaxas attitude and was often critical about the 'Fourth of August' regime. Metaxas resented this attitude and demanded Waterlow's replacement when the British Ambassador informed the Turks in December 1938 that a coup to overthrow Metaxas was imminent. The British, who by that time had decided to support Metaxas' Dictatorship because, according to Vatikiotis, 'Metaxas in British eyes meant stability, and that was best for the British interests,' in 1939 replaced Waterlow with Sir Michael Palairet. Vatikiotis, *Popular Autocracy*, pp. 171-172; *Ioannis Metaxas, To Prosopiko tou Imerologio,* December 1938, and January 1939 Vol. 7, pp. 321-322, 347-350.

24. The information came from the British Consul in Patras. FO 371/21150, 9 April 1937. However, publications of German news must have been gradually reduced, as at the beginning of 1939 Rosner, the representative of the German News Office complained that the Greek press published more news coming from the Reuters News Agency and the French Havas than the German Office. Meissner,Renate 'E Ethnososialistiki Germania ke I Ellada kata ti Diarkeia tis Metaxikis Diktatorias' in Flaicher Ch. & Svoronos N.(eds.) *E Ellada 1936-44-Diktaktoria-Katochi-Antistasi.* (Athens, Morfotiko Instituto *ATE*, 1990) p. 55.

25. *Apologismos Mias Dietias 1936-1938* (Athens, *Tetarti Augoustou*, 1938) p. 214. Great effort was made by the regime's officials abroad to influence the foreign press and have it publish favourable articles on the 'Fourth of August'. On the 'struggle' to influence the French press see, Moschopoulos, N George, *Apo Tin Palinorthosi sti Vasilo-Metaxiki Diktaktoria 1935-1940* (Athens Christakis, 1999) pp. 334-420.

26. *Minieon*, issue 6, 1937, pp. 18-19.

27. *Tessera Chronia,*. Vol. 4, pp. 165-176.

28. Metaxas' speech in Thessaloniki, 25 October 1936, *Logoi ke Skepseis*. Vol. 1, p. 88. About the mission of the journalist and the freedom he enjoyed during the 'Fourth of August' regime see Papalexandrou, Th. K., 'E Eleftheria Tou Typou ke E Eleftheria tou Dimosiografou,' *To Neon Kratos, issue* 10, June 1938, pp. 887-889.

29. Seferis,Georgios *Chirographo Sept.1941* (Athens, Ikaros, 1972), p. 39.

30. Even the liberal newspapers *Athinaika Nea* and *Eleftheron Vima* praised the regime and called all Greeks to support its efforts. Malenos, Milt.I 4e *Augoustou- Pos ke Diati Epevlithi e Diktaktoria tou I.Metaxa* (Athens, 1988) p.165.; Mazarakis-Ainian,Alexandros *Apomnimonefmata* (Athens, 1949), p. 475.

31. Linardatos, 4e *Augoustou,* pp. 74 -77; *Minieon,* issue 3, November 1936, p. 298; and Daphnis, *E Ellas*, Vol. 1., pp. 438-439. Apart from the communist *Rizospastis,* two more daily newspapers the *Anexartitos* and *Eleftheros Anthropos* were also banned. In Thessaloniki the only newspaper which suspended its publication was the *Ellinikos Vorras;* the rest adjusted their publications to the needs of the regime. Athanasiadis, Giorgos, *E Thessaloniki Ton Efimeridon* (Thessaloniki, Ekfrasi, 1994) pp. 71-72.

32. Seferis, *Chirografo.* p.31, *Apologismos*, p. 209, Linardatos, *4e Augoustou*, p. 77.

33. *FEK* 356, 19 August 1936, p. 1823.

34. Over 300 provincial newspapers were issued in 1938. *Apologismos,* p. 122.

35. Ibid, pp..121-122.

36. *Corinthiaki Echo.* Weekly political, social and philological newspaper. Published in Corinth by M. Antoniou. Issue 318, 29 September 1937.

37. *FEK* 68, 22 February 1938, pp. 459-460, and *FEK* 186, 9 May 1938, p. 1138.

38. Fivos Grigoriadis claimed in his work on the Metaxas dictatorship that the only censorship problem, which the regime faced, was with the Armenian newspaper published in Athens, as no Greek could read Armenian. To solve this problem, by order of Ioannis Metaxas the Armenian editor of the newspaper was employed by the censorship office. Grigoriadis, Fivos, N., *Tetarti Augoustou-Albania 1935-1941.* Vol. 4, (Athens, Kedrinos , 1972) p. 191.

39. *Estia*, 20 October 1936. .

40. Ibid, 6 November 1936.

41. Vlachou, Eleni, *Stigmiotypa... Fotographikes Anamnhseis tis Elenis Vlachou.* (Athens, *Kathimerini*, 1986), p. 60.

42. Quoted in Seferis, *Chirographo,* p. 30. No date of the interview is cited

43. Dafnis, *E Ellas,,* pp. 438-439.

44. Ibid., and Linardatos, *4e Augoustou*, pp. 75-77.

45. The *AMN* was a communist youth organisation 'enriched' at the time by the participation of representatives of other democratic youth organisation. Ibid, p. 248.

46. Circular sent in September 1937 to publishers, people of letters, government officials and others announcing the publication of *To Neon Kratos* magazine. *To Neon Kratos,* issue 1, September 1937, pp. 1-5 and issue 25, September 1939, pp. 5-7.

47. The study of the published articles, especially where financial matters were concerned, suggests an admiration and orientation towards the German economic model. Psalidakis, Michalis, 'Morfes Economikis Skepsis stin Ellada 1936-1940' in Flaicher & Svoronos, (eds.) *E Ellada.* pp. 127-131.

48. The magazine professed a pro-Italian propaganda, especially where the Italian economic model of corporatism and autarky was concerned. Ibid., pp.123-126; On Metaxas' economic policy see also Poligenous-Christodoulidis, Ioannis Konst., 'Atomon, Kratos, Syntechneia' in *Nea Politiki,* May 1940, pp. 559-565; Fisher, G. B., 'Economic Autarky', Ibid., March 1940, pp. 316-327.
A magazine with the same name E *Nea Politiki* was first published in 1923 professing the idea of *Hellenism.* Machera, *E Neolea*, p. 24.

49. Tournakis, I., 'Skepseis dia tin Ellinikin Anagennisin,' *Nea Politiki*, issue 9, September 1938, pp. .857-864.

50. *Minieon,* Issue 5, January 1937, pp. 223-247. On the circulation of the Greek press during the inter-war period see Mayer, Costas, *Istoria Tou Elliinikou Typou.* Vol. 2 and , 3 (Athens, Dimakopoulos, 1957).

51. Metaxas' speech, 10 October 1936, *Logoi ke Skepseis*. Vol. 1, p. 65.

52. In November 1921 the Italian *Partito Nationale Fascista* (PNF) was established in Rome and in October 1922 fascism came to power and grew under Mussolini's 'effective' propaganda into a powerful mass party, moving towards a one-party state. Morgan, *Italian Fascism* pp. 43-59 and Lee, *The European*, pp. 88-125. Similarly, the NSDAP (Nationalsozialistische Deutsche Arbeiterpartei) was established in Germany in February 1920. In 1928, 810,127 electors voted for it. In 1932 it became the largest party in the Reichstag preparing Hitler's assumption of the Chancellorship in 1933. Welch, *The Third Reich*, pp. 8-9.

53. Vatikiotis, *Popular Autocracy*. p. 12; Kallonas, D., *Ioannis Metaxas. Mathitis-Stratiotis-Politikos-Agonistis-Kyvernitis* (Athens, 1938) pp. 68-86. This book is a masterpiece on Metaxas' charismatic qualities.

54. The *Eleftherophrones* won 52 seats in the 1926 elections and participated in the *Ekoumeniki* (All Party) government. However, after the 1928 elections the party hardly 'survived' the following elections (in 1936 it won 7 seats) and was dissolved in August 1936. In June 1935 Metaxas had founded, along with few Populists MPs, the *Union of Monarchists* intended to work for the restoration of Monarchy and forced Tsaldaris, the leader of the Populist Party, to promise a referendum which took place in November 1935 and brought King George II back from eleven years of exile. Vatikiotis, *Popular Autocracy*, pp. 121, 153-154 and Sarantis,*The Emergency,* pp. 474,475.

55. Kallonas, *Ioannis Metaxas,*, p. 57.

56. Papadakis, V., *E Chtesini ke E Avriani Ellas* (Cairo, 1945) p. 421.

57. According to Italian official documents Metaxas' favoured the Italian model of Mussolini's Youth, which he fully adopted. Rainero, Romain, H., 'To Praxikopima tou Metaxa ke E apichisi sti Fasistiki Italia', in Fleicher & Svoronos (eds.) *E Ellada* p. 41.On Italian Youth Organization Balilla see Renato Manzolo, *E Orgaboseis Tis Neoleas Eis Tin Italian*, (Rome, Novissima, 1939) However, *EON* adopted many Nazi features as well, and at a point there was a close co-operation between the two youth organisations which included exchange of young members and visits by *EON* officials. FO 371/21147, 3 May 1937 and FO 371/21150, 24 November 1937.

58. *FEK* 499, 10 November 1936, pp. 2666-2667 and Linardatos, *4e Augoustou*, p. 173.

59. Alexandros Kanellopoulos was the son of a large-scale chemicals manufacturer.

60. *Imnos tou Phalangiti* (Phalangite's Anthem) was written by Stilitis-Giannakoudakis, Petros, it consisted of five verses and G Fren composed the music. *Ta Tragoudia Tis Neoleas (EON*, Athens, 1940) p. 11. The *EON* Anthem (four verses) was written by Metaxas P. S., with music by Papadimitriou, Ach. The two verses read:
    > For our sweet Nation, Which is heroic and Great, You Greek Youth Are its everlasting hope, Your dedicated heart Is lightened by a National dawn,And the *Megas Kivernitis* Guides You always forth
    Ta Tragoudia Tis Neoleas, p. 9.

61. In March 1939 the Organisation numbered 1,000,607 members. *Tessera Chronia,* p. 178. In his speech on the third anniversary of the formation of *EON* Metaxas spoke of one million two hundred and fifty thousand members. Metaxas' speech, 7 November 1940. *Logoi ke Skepseis*. Vol. 2., p. 369. The Organisation included two units of young boys and young girls: the *Skapaneis* (Pioneers) between eight and fourteen years old, and the *Phalangites* (Phalangites), between fourteen and twenty five years old. *Organismos Esoterikes Ypiresias EON (Athens, EON*, 1939), p.28.

62. 'Enas Terastios Ethnikos Athlos. Pos Organothi ke ti Apedose E Ethniki Organosis Neoleas'. *Tessera Chronia*. Vol. 2, pp. 172-181. On *EON* see also 'EON. E Megali Dimiourgia Tis 4es Augoustou.' *E Neolea*, issue 44, 3 August 1940, pp. 1396-1397.

63. Sarantis, *The Emergency*, p. 425-427.

64. However, Taylor asserts in his study on propaganda, that youth became a target of propaganda in democratic countries as well. 'It might be added that the youth of democratic systems were also susceptible to all forms of propaganda; in British wartime cinemas, children cheered at newsreels of Churchill, Roosevelt, and Stalin, and booed when Hitler or Mussolini appeared on the screen.' Taylor, *Munitions*, p. 241

65. Sarantis, *The Emergency*, p. 427.

66. *Deftera Diaskepsis EON*. (Athens, *EON*, 1940) p. 278.

67. Metaxas' speech delivered on the occasion of Metaxas' resumption of duties in the Ministry of Education on 29 November 1938. *Logoi ke Skepseis*. Vol.1, p. 426.

68. Emergency Law 1798 of June 1939, which abolished all other youth organisations, was enacted to pursue and safeguard the national and moral enlightenment of Greek youth. According to the propagandists this could only be achieved through 'a national program of enlightenment and education and most importantly, through the proper functioning of *EON.'* *Tessera Chronia*, Vol. 2, pp. 176-177.

69. Metaxas' speech to *EON* officers on 10 January 1939. *Logoi ke Skepseis*. Vol. 2., p. 18. During the Second *EON* Conference in 1940 Kanellopoulos stated that 'although *EON* membership is not compulsory, yet the Organisation cannot endure people who dare say that they do not wish to serve our Organisation and subsequently the State. In this case the State has the right to tell them ' Well I do not recognise you and in this case you can not rely on me.' Quoted in Linardatos, 4e *Augoustou*, p. 163.

70. *Organismos*, p. 8.

71. By a special order the Ministry of Education established Sundays and Wednesdays as days belonging to *EON*. On Wednesdays children did not attend school but were instead obliged to go to *EON* meetings, where an intense programme of indoctrination through lectures, film shows and countless activities took place. On the significance of Wednesdays, see, 'E Tetarti ke E *EON*', *E Neolea*, 16 December 1939, issue 11, p. 322.

72. Linardatos, *4e Augoustou* , pp. 163-167.

73. Metaxas' speech on 2 October 1936. *Logoi ke Skepseis* . Vol.1, p.49

74. The 'Fourth of August' anthem was written in three verses by T. Moraitines and the music was composed by G. Fren. The first verse read:
    'Why are the people merry and smiling father? Why do the sun and the day shine so brightly? Because my child like this golden day that you now, Enjoy the tears dried up and the wounds healed, The crops grew and the mountains around became Flower-fields and land with golden springs'.
    'Ymnos Tis Tetartis Augoustou', *Ta Tragoudia*, p.7

75. *Ioannis Metaxas, To Prosopiko tou Imerologio*, pp. 303, 444.

76. Metaxas' speech on 26 May 1940. *Logoi ke Skepseis*. Vol. 2, p. 305. For a detailed analysis on *EON* devices like uniforms, anthems, fascist salute and their significance see Chapter 3.

77. In May 1940 Kanellopoulos underlining the importance of the III office stated: 'This Office is the most significant one, because its work ensures the ideological indoctrination and the moulding of the character of the Youth. This is its imperative objective and nothing else matters. All other issues constitute the means through which this objective will be accomplished. It is not an office for the dissemination of learning and knowledge but an office for the formation of a conscience and a consciousness.' *Deftera Diaskepsis*, p. 263.

78. *Organismos*, p. 47.

79. *Apospasmata ton Epitelikon Grafeion Dieuthinseos & Ypiresion Kentrikis Dioikiseos Ethnikis Organoseos Neoleas tis Ellados ke ton Periferiion Diekiseos Arrenon ke Thileon .EON. Protevousis Epi tis Prooptiies tis Ergasias Afton* (Athens, *EON*, 1939) p. 134.

80. Ibid., p. 135.

81. *E Neolea* , issues 7, 1938, p.1 and 6, 1939, p. 193.and *Tessera Chronia* , Vol. 2., p. 175.

82. *Circular Order 28 'Peri Genikopn Katefthinseon ke Odgion'* (EON, Athens 1939) p. 75.

83. *Proia, Nea Ellas, Estia,Vradini Athinaika Nea, Ethnos, Eleftheron Vima*, November 1939.Quoted in *E Neolea* , 25 November 1939 p. 257. For the significance of the magazine see .Kaffetzakis, G., 'E Katefthinseis tou Periodikou mas'. *E Neolea*, issue 24, 16 March 1940, pp. 738-739.

84. *Organismos*,, p.10.

85. In 1939 these new publications came to thirty five. *E Neolea*, issue 6, 11 November 1939, p. 193.

86. *Deftera Diaskepsis*, pp. 268-269.

87. Such a book was *Ta Salpismata* written by D.Alibrantis. It contained speeches 'which referred to the most important themes of the 'Fourth of August' State and guided youth to their great mission of regenerating the nation.' *E Neolea*, issue 15, 13 January 1940, p. 459. There is no information whether the cost of those publications was subsidised by the government or if it was individually covered.

88. The *SA* (Storm Troopers-or Brownshirts) was founded in 1921 as a private army of the Nazi Party under Ernest Rohm. Hitler's first bodyguard later eclipsed by the *SS* after the massacre of its leadership in June 1934. On the history of the *SA* and their take over by Himmler's *SS* see Graber, G, S., *History of the SS*. (London, Robert Hale, 1978), pp. 49-64.

89. Vatikiotis, *Popular Autocracy* , p.168
90. Metaxas' speech, 26 December 1937. *Logoi ke Skepseis* Vol. I, pp. 311-312., and *Ioannis Metaxas, To Prosopiko tou Imerologio*. Vol. ,7 p. 290.
91. Metaxas' speech, 24 March 1938, *Logoi ke Skepseis*. Vol.1, p. 347.
92. *E Neolea*, issue 9, 2 December 1939, p. 284.
93. Along with the press Metaxas gradually made full use of the cinema, the theatre and the radio to propagate his ideas and manipulate public opinion.
94. *Ioannis Metaxa. O Anthropos, O Stratiotis, O Politikos. (* Athens. *EON*, 1936) p. 57.
95. Quoted in. Kershaw, I., *Hitler The Myth. Image and Reality in the Third Reich* (Oxford, Oxford University Press, 1987) p. 8.
96. Kallonas, *Ioannis Metaxas*, p. 193. See also FO 371/123770, 7 August 1939.
97. King Constantine and Eleftherios Venizelos, both enjoyed fanatic devotion from their supporters. Mavrokordatos, George, *Stilborn Republic, Social Coalitions and Party Strategies in Greece, 1922-1936* (University of California Press, 1983) pp. 55-65, and Vatikiotis, *Popular Autocracy* , pp. 10- 11- and pp. 155-156.
98. As we shall see later when discussing public opinion Metaxas was an unpopular figure a fact recognised by Metaxas himself as his entries in his diary suggest. *Ioannis Metaxas, To Prosopiko tou Imerologio*. Vol. 5., p. 325 and Vol. 6., pp..590-591.
99. In antithesis to Hitler who refused to be seen wearing spectacles as he was afraid that these would suggest human failings. Kershaw, *The Hitler Myth*, p. 3.
100. The British Ambassador Palairet reported to Halifax on 21 August 1939 commenting on the third anniversary of the 'Fourth of August' regime: 'General Metaxas is far from being endowed with the physical qualities necessary for success as a dictator. His short, corpulent, ill-dressed figure could never evoke popular enthusiasm.' FO 371/23770, 21 August 1939.
101. *Ioannis Metaxas, To Prosopiko tou Imerologio*. Vol. 8., p. 540.
102. According to Metaxas, one of the basic reasons which dictated the establishment of the 'Fourth of August' regime was the failure of the past political schemes, which in a demagogic fashion flattered and deceived the Greek people, to secure a strong political government and offer them a national, political and economic stability. Metaxas' speech, 2 October 1936. *Logoi ke Skepseis*. Vol. 1., pp. 45-46.
103. *Ethnikon Evagelion: Oi Patriotikoi Logoi tou Prothipourgou k. Ioannou Metaxa* (Ekdoseis Tetartis Augoustou, Athens, 1936).
104. Kallonas *Ioannis Metaxas*, pp. 7-8.
105. *Organismos,* pp. 24-25.
106. *Falagitiki Epitheorisis,* issue 2. (Athens, Ekdoseis *EON*, 1940), p. 208. On the significance of slogans see Kallonas, p. 228 and Machera, *E Neolea,,* pp.83-86
107. Metaxas' speech on the Radio, 10 August 1936. *Logoi ke Skepseis*. Vol.1, p. 17.
108. *To Neon Kratos*, issue 29, January 1940, p. 286.
109. *Organismos,* p. 24.
110. *E Neolea,* issue 16, 20 January 1940, p. 482.
111. Karaiskaki, Sitsa, 'Sto Girisma Tis 4es Augoustou, Palia ke Nea Ellada, 25 Martiou ke 4 Augoustou, Epochi Anagenniseos.' *E Neolea,* issue 45, 19 August 1938, p. 1450. See also 'E *EON* ke E 25e Martiou.' *E Neolea,* issue 25, 1 April 1939, p. 813.
112. Metaxas' speech, 1 May 1939. *Logoi ke Skepseis*. Vol. 2, pp. 94-95.
113. Kanellopoulos, Alexandros, 'Sti Giorti sou.' *E Neolea*., issue 16, 20 January 1940, p. 482. See also Nikolaidis, Melis, 'E Giorti.' Ibid., p. 483.
114. According to Bullock in his study *Hitler - A Study in Tyranny* 'speech was the essential medium of Hitler's power, not only over his audience but over his own temperament' Hitler believed that 'words build bridges into unexplored regions.' Bullock Alan, *Hitler - A Study in Tyranny* (London, Penguin Books, 1990) p. 372. On the same issue see also Welch, *The Third Reich,* p. 39.
115. *Deftera Diaskepsis,*. p. 400.
116. During the Second Conference of *EON* Kanellopoulos stressed the significant role of the Chief's speeches,. in indoctrinating youth and urged the officials to make great

use of them. Kanellopoulos Alexandros 'Ideologiki Diafotisis,' in *Deftera Diaskepsis.*, p. 269. On the speeches and their significance see also 'Oi Dyo Epalxeis.' *E Neolea*, issue 4, 28 October 1939, p. 97.

117. Koumaros, Nikolaos, 'Oi Logoi tou Archigou.' *To Neon Kratos*, issue 29, 31 January 1940, pp. 284-289. Metaxas' speeches contain all his beliefs, aspirations and his real or 'alleged' achievements and constitute a significant primary source for research. The revised edition of the speeches in two volumes, which include all his speeches, declarations, statements and thoughts (approximately four hundreds in total), was published in 1969 (during the Colonels' Dictatorship) by Govosti Publications.

118. *Ioannis Metaxas, To Prosopiko tou Imerologio.* Vol. 6, p. 516.

119. Kallonas, *Ioannis Metaxas*, pp. 200-201.

CHAPTER 2

1. Metaxas, who had little respect for the political world, used this political instability as one of his main justification, to impose his dictatorship.

2. Metaxas' speech, 10 August 1936. *Loigoi ke Skepseis*, Vol. 1, p. 16.

3. Sarantis, *The Emergency*, p. 375.

4. 'I am convinced that there is no progress under a parliamentary system,' he noted in his diary, long before he established his dictatorship. *Ioannis Metaxas, to Prosopiko tou Imerologio*, 18 February 1927, Vol. 6, p. 511.

5. Metaxas' speech, 27 October 1936. *Logoi ke Skepseis*, Vol. 1, p. 92. It must be stressed however, that while Metaxas vented his rage against all political parties, he systematically avoided attacking openly any political figures. On the contrary, in his speeches he clarified that what he 'was against was the political system and not the persons involved.' Metaxas' speech, 24 April 1939. Ibid., Vol. 2., p. 56. However, Metaxas' diary contains many entries which refer to several political figures and their role in trying to overthrow him. Ibid., Vol. 8, pp. 285,291,292,305,314, 357, 364.

6. Sarantis, *The Emergency*, p. 373.

7. Metaxas' speech in Patras , 6 November 1937, *Logoi ke Skepseis*, Vol. 1, pp. 259-260. See also his speeches; on the radio, 10 August 1936, p.16; Thessaloniki, 6 September 1936, pp. 29-30; Mass Rally, 2 October 1936, p. 45; Larissa, 9 October 1936, p. 59; Chania, 7 November 1936, p.102; Serres, 27 October 1936, p.92; and Ioannina, 13 June 1937, p. 198. Ibid.

8. Metaxas' speech at the Mass Rally in Athens, 2 October 1936, Ibid., Vol. 1, pp. 45-46.

9. Nicoloudis, Theologos, 'To Neon Kratos.' *To Neon Kratos*, issue 1, September 1937, pp. 1-4. He also delivered a speech on 9 January 1936 in Parnassos Hall in which he compared the failure of the parliamentary systems to the success of the dictatorships. The speech created problems for Metaxas, as Nicoloudis referred to the British parliamentary system- a fact which provoked the reaction of the British Ambassador Waterlow who protested to Metaxas. To *Ethnikon Kratos Os Politikon ke Economikon Systima* (Ekdoseis EON Athens, 1939). On the British reaction see, *Ioannis Metaxas, To Prosopiko tou Imerologio*, entries of 16-17 January 1939, and *Kathimerini* of 10-11 January 1939. On anti-parliamentarism see also Nicoloudis, Theologos *E Elliniki Crisis*, Cairo 1945, p. 26 (No publisher), and his speech to the people of Ioannina during the celebration of the '25 March'. *To Neon Kratos*, issue 5, March 1937, pp. 391-392.

10. As cited in Chapter One, among the strict regulations concerning the press was the one prohibiting any reference to political parties or political persons. This mission was undertaken by the regime's publications *To Neon Kratos, Nea Politiki* and several others including the *EON* pamphlets. On the issue of anti-parliamentarism see; Kabanis, Aristos, 'Afete Tous Nekrous Thaptein tous Eaftous,' *To Neon Kratos*, issue 6, February 1938, pp. 145-152. See also Bamias, G., 'E Chreokopia tou Kinovouleftismou, *To Neon Kratos*, Ibid., pp. 196-199; *Kinovouleftismos ke Kommatismos* lecture delivered by Mallosis, I. (Ekdoseis *EON*, Athens, 1939)

11. Nicoloudis, Thelogos, 'Ena Kyrigma Pisteos,' *To Neon Kratos*, issue 4, December 1937, p. 310.

12. Metaxas' speech on the radio, 10 August 1936, *Logoi ke Skepseis,* Vol. 1., p. 17.

13. Metaxas' Proclamation, on 4 August 1936. *FEK* 323, 4 August 1936, pp. 1655-1657. It has been argued that Metaxas played on the King's fear of communism to reconcile him to the establishment of the 'Fourth of August' dictatorship. Close, D. H., 'The Power-Base of the Metaxas Dictatorship' in Higham & Veremis (eds.) *Aspects of Greece,* p. 15. The threat of communism and its defiance was one of the justifying causes for many European dictatorships during the inter-war period and the fundamental cause behind the bloody civil war in Spain in July 1936. On European Dictatorships see, Lee, and Blinkhorn, Martin, (ed.) *Fascist and Conservatives* (Unwin Hyman, London, 1990).

14. The *KKE* was established in 1920 and joined the Comintern. During Pangalos' dictatorship in 1926 it became an outlawed party and its members were persecuted. In 1929 the Venizelos Government passed the *Idionym* Law which penalised any attempts to propagate dangerous ideas and provoke industrial disputes, while the 'safekeeping' of the social order was assigned to the police who were to be blamed for many arrests and deportations. On the eve of Metaxas' dictatorship the strength of *KKE* grew considerably. From 1,500 in 1931 members rose to 15,000 in 1936. According to Vlavianos this growth in strength was attributed to three factors: First, to the organising skills of its leader Nicos Zachariadis; second, to the adoption by the *KKE* of an 'anti-Fascist' Popular Front policy and third, to the economic depression that hit Greece and 'furnished the *KKE* with fuel for their expansionist drive.' Vlavianos, H., ' The Greek Communist Party under Siege' in Higham & Veremis (eds.) *Aspects.of Greece,* pp. 193-201. Communist agitation was responsible for great industrial unrest during the inter-war period which remained widespread until the coming of the 'Fourth of August' regime and initiated suppression by the police. Koundouros, Roussos, S., E *Asfaleia tou Kathestotos - Politikoi Kratoumeoi, Ektopiseis ke Taxeis stin Ellada 1924-1974* (Kastaniotis, Athens, 1978) pp. 60-73 and pp. 78-92. See also: *KKE Episima Keimena 1931-1940* , Vol. 4 (Athens, 1981) and FO 371/21147, 22 May 1937.

15. Linardatos, Spiros, P*os Efthasame stin 4e Augoustou* (Themelio, Athens, 1986) pp. 163-206 and Close, *The Origins,*, pp. 37-41.

16. Great demonstrations by tobacco workers in Thessaloniki who protested for better tobacco prices, and improved wages on 9 May 1936, led to the most violent confrontations between strikers and police during which twelve demonstrators were killed and many wounded. The announcement of a general strike on 5 August 1936, gave Metaxas the pretext to establish the 'Fourth of August' dictatorship. On 'Bloody May' incidents see Linardatos, *Pos Efthsame,*, pp. 208-225, and *Dokimio Istorias tou KKE 1918-1949,* Vol. 1. (Sychroni Epochi, Athens, 1996) pp. 297-306.

17. Constantinos Maniadakis was an army officer who had been a long and devoted admirer of Ioannis Metaxas and his ideology. A week after the establishment of the 'Fourth of August' regime (14 August 1936) he was appointed by a Royal Decree *(FEK* 344) Deputy-Minister of Public Security and began to reorganise and reinforce the police force in order to achieve his most fearful anti-Communist campaign. His Special Security Force (*Asfaleia*) with the Anti-Communist unit of the General Security Force launched a notorious purge against communists and left-wingers including other politicians who disagreed with the regime's policies. Apart from the regular police force and gendarmerie, Maniadakis' security included the formation of secret police on the German model. Close, D.H., 'The power Base of Metaxas' Dictatorship' in Higham & Veremis (eds.) *Aspects* of *Greece,* pp. 22-28, and Close, D. H., 'E Astynomia Tou Kathestotos Tis 4es Augoustou' in Flaicher & Svoronos (eds.) *E Ellada 1936-1944,* pp. 77-80.

18. A detailed account of the 'National Mission' of the new sub-Ministry can be found in the *Tessera Chronia*. Vol. 2., pp. 211-215.

19. The gendarmerie was increased from 12,200 members in the mid 1936 to 14,600 by the end of 1940 and the City Police Force had also increased by a similar percentage. Although the numbers do not strike us as being exceptionally large one must bear in mind that the Public Security Office mobilised and recruited a great number of civilians who became informers and assisted the police in their duties. Furthermore,

the Anti-Communist Unit of the General Security increased from 15 to 80 selected men, while the Special Security rose from 190 men to 445 officers, 30 political agents and 1,200 privates. All this force including the *Agrofilakes* (Agrarian Constabulary) was ready and waiting to asssist the formal police in mass arrests and other 'difficult tasks.' Close 'The Power-Base.' in Higham & Veremis (eds.) *Aspect of Greece*, pp. 22-28.

20. *FEK* 45, 11 February 1936. Waterlow claimed in February 1937, that 'a decree was enacted, which was not mentioned by the press, under which Maniadakis obtained a credit of 300 millions for recruiting additional gendarmeries, the improvement of the equipment of Force and the creation of a mobile mechanised regiment which would be a praetorian guard for the Dictator.' FO 371/21147, 19 February 1937.

21. *FEK* 45, 11 February 1936, pp. 240 On the issue see also *Tessera Chronia* Vol. 2., p. 215. The introduction of these certificates 'haunted' Greek political life for almost forty years. Their use was terminated in 1974 when the Colonels' Dictatorship was abolished. Koundouros, *E Asfaleia tou Kathestotos* p.106.

22. Within the policy of 'exterminating' the communist danger which had become a 'menace' to the world the regime co-operated closely with Erbach, the German Ambassador in Greece, who assured his government of the efficient measures taken by Maniadakis. Meissner, ' E Ethnososialistiki Germania ke e Ellada' in Flaicher & Svoronos (eds.), *E Ellada 1936 - 1940*, p. 52. In fact Maniadakis co-operated closely with Himmler, the Chief of the German Gestapo, and exchanged information on their operational tactics. In May 1937 Himmler asked Maniadakis to join forces on their common war against communism and share their valuable experience they had so far acquired on the tactics of suppressing this evil. On the subject and the exchanged letters between Maniadakis and Himmler see FO 371/21150, 24 November 1937.

23. Nicos Zachariadis was a leading member of *KKE* since 1923. After his imprisonment by the police he escaped in 1929 and went to the Soviet Union. In 1931 the Comintern appointed him leader of *KKE*. He was imprisoned by Metaxas' regime and in 1942 he was transferred to Dachau concentration camp. After Greece's liberation he resumed the leadership of *KKE*. During the Greek civil war he flew to the Soviet Union where he was expelled from the party and died under inhuman conditions, in Siberia, in 1973. Vlavianos, 'The Greek Communist Party', pp. 218-219.

24. These were tactics invented by Mussolini. The arrested real or 'alleged' *KKE* members were forced to sit naked on a block of ice or drink a considerable amount of castor oil until they confessed and signed the *Diloseis Metaneias*. Linardatos,*4e Augoustou,* pp. 60-6. The Metaxas regime denied allegations about the use of castor oil, ice and other 'ingenious' forms of torture. In fact Maniadakis claimed that the use of castor oil and ice 'was only a myth invented by him to intimidate people, and he had only used it once.' Grigoriades,*'4e Augoustou'* p. 234. However Waterlow claimed in June 1937, that 'the administration of castor oil for minor offences was becoming a regular feature of police practice'. FO 371/21147, 18 June 1937. Similar were the claims made by the American Ambassador MacVeagh. See Iatrides, John, O., (ed.) *Ambassador MacVeagh Reports 1933-1947* (Princeton University Press, Princeton, 1980) p. 111.

25. Vlavianos 'The Greek Communist Party Under Siege' in Higham & Veremis (eds.), *Aspects of Greece,* pp.197-198. Maniadakis extracted information from many arrested members to whom he offered their liberty in return. By 1939 Maniadakis, with the help of members of the real central committee who had been 'won' over and collaborated with the regime, created his own police-controlled *KKE* which issued its own R*izospastis* undermining thus the role of the real clandestine *Rizospastis* and confused the *KKE* members causing an 'irreparable' split within the party. Ibid., p.200. On the same subject see also Close, *The Origins.* p. 48.

26. *Kathimerini*, 5 July 1938 and 19/30 July 1939.

27. Quoted in Vlavianos, 'The Greek Communist Party', pp. 199-200.

28. *Tessera Chronia* Vol. 2., p. 215. This is however, a falsified figure as according to *KKE* official records the total strength of the party in 1936 was 15,000. Kunduros, *'E Asfaleia'*, p. 63 and Vlavianos, The Greek Communist Party', p.195. Thus the regime

either quoted this figure for propaganda consumption to multiply the number of communists in Greece and thus to underline the danger, or the figure included persons who were *KKE* sympathisers, or disagreed with the regime's police and were 'reformed' by the police. It must be noted however, that the publication of these mass declarations by the propaganda machine proved to be a 'boomerang' against the regime as it presented the *KKE* with a wide power base. In 1939 Maniadakis in a confidential memorandum to his officials warned them against obtaining declarations for the sake of appearances. Vlavianos, 'The Greek Communist Part', p. 199.

29. *Kathimerini*, 9 July 1938, 30 July 1938, and in most daily newspapers.

30. *Apologismos,* p. 24. The regime claimed that the *KKE* members exiled in the islands did not exceed 1,000. *Tessera Chronia,* Vol. 2., p..212. Yet, the true figure was much higher. Vlavianos, 'The Greek Communist Party', p. 200. Apart from the communist exiles there were also political exiles. According to Nicoloudis there were only eighteen political exiles and those in 'the most idyllic islands'. *Ta Paraskinia.* Weekly Theatrical and Cinema Review, 9 September 1936, p.6. However, the number must have been much greater as Metaxas claimed in January 1938, that 'the exiles produced positive results.' *Ioannis Metaxas, To Prosopiko tou Imerologio,* Vol. 7., p. 292. On the political exiles in the Cyclades see Marina Petraki '*Oi Kyklades Os Topoi Exorias Sti Metaxiki Periodo'*, 2nd International Sufnian Symposium, 22 June, 2002.

31. Matzufas, Georgios, 'To Ethnikon Symferon Os Gnomon Tis Ermineias ke Tis Efarmogis Tou Nomou', *Neon Kratos*, issue 17, January 1939, , pp. 1449-1455. See also, booklet *To Katantima Tou Bolsevikismou* (Ekdoseis *EON* , Athens, 1939) and Karaiskai , Sitsa, 'To Dilitiro Tis Psichis', *E Neolea*, issue 15, 13 January 1940, p. 450.

32. Nicoloudis' speech in Lamia, *Ta Paraskinia*, 9 September 1938, p. 6.

33. Ibid., 7 January 1938, p. 8.

34. Maniadakis, Constantinos, speech *Kriseis Ke Syberasmata Epi Tis Neoleas Pro Ke Meta Tin 4 Augoustou* published by *EON* officials as a vital piece of propaganda. (Ekdoseis *EON,* Athens, 1939) pp. 1-6. In this speech Maniadakis quoted the 'sad' stories of young communists, who had become 'tangled' in the dangerous circles of communism, but because of the beneficial measures introduced by the 'Fourth of August' State they escaped the forthcoming catastrophe and joined *EON* .

35. Metaxas claimed on 20 December 1948 that he examined fifty *KKE* children whose parents had repented and he 'found them to be in a dramatic state.' *Ioannis Metaxas, To Prosopiko tou Imerologio,* Vol. 7, p. 319.

36. Manoleas was a Communist MP. *E Neolea*, issue 9, December 1938, p. 296.

37. *Estia*, 7 October 1936. The Spanish civil war between the Republican/Communists and the Fascist forces under General Franco began in 1936 and ended in 1939, costing the lives of one million people. Lee, 'The European Dictatorships', pp. 236-241.

38. Ibid. See also *Vradini*, 2 January 1938 and *Kathimerini,* 1 and 17 July 1938.

39. Metaxas' speech, 10 October 1936, *Logoi ke Skepseis* Vol. 1, pp. 65-74.

40. Meissner, ' E Ethnososialistiki Germania. Ke e Ellada.' in Flaicher & Svoronos (eds.) *E Ellada, 1936-44,* p. 52

41. On 10 May 1933 a book burning was staged in Berlin and the public squares of cities and universities towns symbolising the *auto-da-fe* of a century of German and European Literature.' Bracher, Karl Dietrich, *The German Dictatorship-The Origins, Structure and Effects of National Socialism,* (Penguin Middlesex, 1970) p. 325. Parading students and professors mobilised by the Ministry of Propaganda engaged themselves in the barbaric act of eliminating what Goebbels called 'intellectual filth.' Reuth, Ralf, Georg, *Goebbels - The Life of Joseph Goebbels. The Mephistopelean Genius of Nazi Propaganda* (Constable, London, 1993) pp. 182-183. On the same subject see also Kantorowich, Alfred, *Why A Library of the Burned Books* (Paris, 1934) No publisher mentioned.

42. *Kathimerini*, 16 August 1936 and in other daily newspapers. The 'cleansing of the *KKE* publications miasma by fire' took place also in Thessaloniki and other cities. Anastasiadis, Giorgos, *Anexandliti Poli Thessaloniki 1917-91074* (Ekfrasi, Thessaloniki, 1996) p. 140, and Linardatos, *4e Augoustou*, pp. 70-71.

43. Ibid.
44. *Tessera Chronia,* Vol. 3., pp. 188-200.
45. 'Diati to Kratos Prepei na Eleghi Tin Ekpedefsi,' *E Neolea,* issue 23, 18 March 1939, p. 745.
46. *Tessera Chronia* Vol. 3., p. 194. The *OSV* invalidated all existing school books and proceeded with the writing of new ones. Ibid.
47. Ibid., p. 196.
48. *E Neolea,* issue 45, 19 August 1939, p.2.
49. Ibid., issue 7, 18 November 1939, p. 195. A circular sent by the inspector of the elementary schools, after praising the qualities and enlightening mission of the magazine strongly recommended that the same be included in the school teaching material. Ibid., p. 218. Despite, however, the orchestrated efforts *E Neolea* did not meet the wide circulation expected by the regime. In its second year of publication the number of copies sold came up to 40,000, while the expected number was 120,000; a fact which worried immensely the propagandists who urged the *EON* members to work hard for a wider circulation. *Egyklios Diatagi Peri Genikon Tinon Katefthinseon ke Odigion,* (Ekdoseis *EON*, Athens,1939) pp. 74-75.
50. According to the regime's sources from the 424 basic and elementary schools in the Athens district, 346 provided mass school-dinners. In 1939-40 more than 100,000 school children participated in the programme, while the cost involved came up to 16,006,984 drcs. *Tessera Chronia,* Vol. 3., pp. 198-200. It must be stated however, that the success of such a large undertaking to feed the thousands of school children was attributed mostly to the good-will of the Greek people who, according to the regime 'supported the programme heartily.' Ibid. See also *E Neolea,* issue 8, 25 November 1939, p.230.
51. Karaiskaki, Sitsa, 'Chortasmena Pedia, Ikanoi Polites', *E Neolea,* issue 7, 18 February 1939, p. 204.
52. Ibid.
53. Metaxas' speech, 2 October 1936, *Logoi ke Skepseis,* Vol.1, p. 48, and speech, 19 August 1937, Ibid., p. 229.
54. Papadakis," *'E Chthesini',* p. 43.
55. Metaxas' speech to members of the organisation of 'Ethniki Anagennisis' (National Renaissance), 14 November 1936 and his speech in Ioannina, 13 June 1937. *Logoi ke Skepseis,* Vol.1, p. 202 and pp. 124-125. See also article 'Ithynousa Taxis' (The Governing Class) *Estia,* 18 November 1936. Metaxas' sympathies seemed to lie indeed with the less privileged classes for whom he claimed he established his dictatorship. He often attacked the industrialists and threatened to confiscate their industries if they laid off their workers. *Ioannis Metaxas, To Prosopiko tou Imerologio,* 9 September 1939, Vol. 7, p. 393. Similarly, he claimed on 4 March 1938 that 'no sacrifice that the rich made for the poor was enough'. *Logoi ke Skepseis,* Vol. 1, p. 331.
56. Nicoloudis' article in *Vradini,* 14 January 1937.
57. *Ethnikon Evagelion,,* p. 2.
58. FO 371/21147, 22 May 1937, p.193. *Estia* had demonstrated pro-fascists tendencies long before Metaxas'regime. On this see Linardatos, *4e Augoustou,* p. 41.
59. *Estia,*7 October 1936. This was a campaign invented by Goebbels to obtain public money according to which housewives and workers were 'urged to restrict their eating consumption to the *Eintopfgericht* (one pot meal) and save food for the good of the nation. Welch, *The Third Reich,* p. 38.
60. Metaxas' speech, 4 August 1937. *Logoi ke Skepseis,* Vol. 1, p. 225.
61. Metaxas' speech, Xanthi, 4 March 1938. Ibid, p. 331.
    This endless stream of voluntary contributions was according to Waterlow 'spreading over the whole Greek State. The Donors ranged from the widow with her mite to the Bank to the large commercial firms the semi-State institutions and the Holy Synod. These contribution were in fact an unsound method of taxation as the factories, offices and banks were open on a Sunday by Royal Decree and the employees gave up their day's pay to fund the air force'. FO 371/21147, 18 June 1937. There is evidence

however, that many people simultaneously contributed to the aid for the Air Forces. Towards those people Metaxas expressed in writing his sincere thanks and gratitude. Letters exchanged between Metaxas and people on this subject can be found in Arceio Ioannou Metaxas, at the Genika Archeia tou Kratous, File 34.

62. *Estia,* 5 August 1937.
63. Only for the period 13 November 1939 until May 1940 the photos numbered 33,972 and cost 1,698,000 drachmas. Linardatos, *4e Augoustou*, p.193.
64. *Minieon,* issue 12, 1937 (month not readable) p. 468.
65. FO 371/21147, 7 August 1937. In Waterlow's view Metaxas' propaganda encouraged manifestations 'of a Fascist colour among the people, in order that, at the appropriate moment, he can come into the open and claim that the whole country is calling for him to place himself at its head' Ibid.
66. Ibid., and *Estia*, 4 August 1937.
67. *Falagitiki,,* p. 190.
68. *Minieon,* issue 12, 1937, p.468 .
69. Papadakis,' *E Chthesini'*, p. 210.
70. Metaxas' speech, 4 August 1937, *Logoi ke Skepseis*, Vol. 1, p. 226.
71. According to Waterlow 'not a house was allowed to remain without at least one flag' and he cited the case of a modest bank employee who ' because his humble flat lies in the central part of the town was forced to spend a great amount of money to buy a flag of the largest size and he only escaped with difficulty from having to buy two flags because his flat was on a corner'. FO 371/21147, 7 August 1937.
72. *Estia,* 4 August, 1937. The Stadium normally holds 60,000 but on that occasion it was overcrowded with more than 100,000. FO 371/21147, 7 August 1937.
73. Dafnis,' *'E Ellas',* p. 438.
74. *KKE Episima,* Vol. 4., p. 427.
75. On Metaxas' relation with King George II and British involvement in the restoration of monarchy see Kitsikis, Dimitris, *E Ellas Tis 4es Augoustou Ke E Megale Dynameis-To Archeio tou Ellinikou Ypourgeiou Exoterikon 1936-1941* (Ikaros, Athens, 1974) pp. 35-37. On the same subject see also Dafnis, *'E Elllas',* pp. 343-382 and 419-421, and Koliopoulos, *Palinorthosi-Diktatoria-Polemos 1935-1941. O Bretanikos Paragontas Stin Ellada* (Estia, Athens, 1985) .
76. Metaxas' speech in Komotini, 7 October 1936. *Logoi ke Skepseis*, Vol. 1, p. 54.
77. *E Neolea,* issue 36, 17 June 1939 p. 929; issue 11, 16 December 1939, p.324; issue 17, 27 January 1940, p. 517; issue 43, 27 July 1940, p. 1345.
78. O *Vasilefs* (Ekdoseis *EON*, Athens , 1939).
79. On the King's democratic values see Kitsikis, *E Ellas Tis 4es Augoustou*, pp. 30-31.
80. *Ioannis Metaxas, To Prosopiko tou Imerolgio,* Vol.7, pp. 290, 304, 306.
81. Ibid., p. 411.
82. Ibid., p. 312.
83. Ibid., p. 292. On opposition and resistance see also Dafnis., *E Ellas'*, pp. 431-441, Linardatos, *4e Augoustou*, pp.296-304 and Petraki, Marina, 'Tetarti Augoustou'-'Antidrasi ke Dioxeis Antipalon.,' *Kathimerini - Epta Imeres,* 7 November 1999, pp. 14-16.
84. On Michalakopoulos's life and political career see Gatopoulos, A., *Andreas Michalakopoulos 1875-1938* (Eleftheroudakis, Athens, 1947)
85. Kitsikis, *E Ellas Tis 4es Augoustou,* p. 37.
86. *Ioannis Metaxas, To Prosopiko tou Imerologio,* Vol. 7., p. 299.
87. Ibid.
88. Markezinis, *Sychroni Politiki,* p. 87.
89. On the Cretan Revolt see Dafnis, *E Ellas,* , pp.442-444, Kofas, *Authoritarianism* p. 146-167 and Linardatos, *4e Augoustou*, pp. 225-356 .
90. *Kathimerini*, 30 July,1938.
91. Ibid., 30 and 31 July 1938.
92. *Estia* , 25 July 1938.
93. Ibid.

94. Mazarakis-Ainian, *Apomnimonefmata* written in 1949 provides a valuable insight of Metaxas' dictatorship.

95. Kofas, *Authoritarianism.* p. 68.

96. *Eleftheron Vima,* 1 August 1938.

97. *Kathimerini,* August 1938.

98. *Eleftho Vima,* 5 August 1938.

99. *Kathimerini,* 6 August 1938.

100. *Ioannis Metaxas, To Prosopiko tou Imerologio,* Vol. 7, p. 314.

101. Surveillance on political figures and opponents of the 'Fourth of August' regime who lived abroad, especially in France, was extensively carried by Maniadakis' *Asfaleia.* On this and the role played by Spiros Kosmetatos (Metaxas' propagandist in France) see Moschopoulos, *Apo Tin Palinorthosi,* pp. 152-500 .

102. FO 371/23770, 7 August 1939.

103. The British Ambassador Palairet noted in August 1939 just after the third anniversary of the Fourth of August' regime, that during the celebrations 'large buildings were disfigured with huge posters of the Dictator, that other walls were plastered with representations of one of General Metaxas' eyes, enlarged to gigantic size from a photograph, with the legend 'workers have no fear, the eye of John Metaxas is upon you.' Ibid.

104. Pictures of Ioannis Metaxas and the emblem of the 'Fourth of August' were printed on OSRAM electricity bulbs. The connotation of the 'enlightening despot' is self-explanatory. *Kathimerini - Epta Imeres,* 26 October 1997, p. 20.

105. FO 371/21147, 22 March 1937.

106. Rigos, *Ta krisima,* p. 112.

107. *To Tragoudi Ton Skapanisson, Ta Tragoudia,* p. 15.

108. Hymn dedicated to Metaxas. This song and a large collection of poems and hymns written for the Chief and the Organisation from people all over Greece can be found at Metaxas' Personal library in Benaki Library.

109. *Ioannis Metaxas, To Prosopiko tou Imerologio,* Vol. 7, p. 382, and pp. 315-322.

110. Sarandis, *The Emergency,* p.424.

111. According to 1926 statistics in a total of 6,204,634 people the agrarian population was 3,568,253, while the urban was 2,064,696, 571,735 lived in small towns. *Statistiki Epetiris Tis Ellados 1939* (Athens, 1939), p. 50. According to the same statistics (The following statistics were contacted in 1951) the illiterate population over the age of eight years old was 40.91%. Ibid., p. 36.

112. Metaxas' speech, 2 October 1936, *Logoi ke Skepseis,* Vol 1, p. 50.

113. Papadakis, *E Chthesini,* p. 213.

114. Metaxas' speech, 9 October 1936, *Logoi ke Skepseis,* Vol. 1, p. 62.

115. FO 371/21147, 22 March 1937. According to the government sources, grain production doubled in three years, while the cultivated land increased by 484,748 stremmata. *Tessera Chronia* Vol. 4, pp. 75-79. On Metaxas' agrarian policy see his speeches in Thessali, 19 December 1936, *Logoi ke Skepseis* Vol. 1., pp. 140-142, and in Arta , 16 June 1937, Ibid., pp. 209-210. See also speech in Kalamas, 24 April 1939, pp. 63-65 and Pylos, 26 April 1939, Vol. 2., p.70, Ibid.. On the agrarian debts see Metaxas' declarations, 18 May 1937, Ibid., p.188.

116. The effectiveness of this Emergency Law has been confronted by Spiros Linardatos in his work *4e Augoustou* where he argues that it only cancelled a very small percentage of the debts, while it created new ones. Linardatos, *4e Augoustou,* p.120. Similar is the view expressed by Kofas, Authoritarianism, p. 72.

117. For a full account of the 'Fourth of August' regime agrarian policy see *Tessera Chronia,* Vol. 1, pp. 70-118.

118. Metaxas' speech, 16 June 1937. *Logoi ke Skepseis,* Vol.1, p.209.

119. *Ioannis Metaxas* (Ekdoseis *EON,* Athens, 1939) p. 57.

120. Kallonas, *Ioannis Metaxas,* p. 220.

121. Metaxas' speech in Argos, 1 July 1937, *Logoi ke Skepseis,* Vol. 1,p. 211.

122. Papadakis wrote of Metaxas : 'Although a genuine aristocrat, Metaxas is a friend of the people and despises plutocrats. Papadakis, *E Chtesini,,* p. 43.

123. *Minieon,* issue 12, 1937 p. 484 and FO 37121147, 7 August 1937.

124. Ibid.

125. Ambrosios Tzifos, the under-secretary at the Merchant Navy, wrote in his unpublished diary at the time, 'I personally believed that it was a mistake to celebrate the anniversary under those circumstances. The festival of 1940 was indeed, a great failure. The public feels that it is unforgivable to spend time and money for festivities when the enemy is at the doorstep.' Tzifos, Ambrosios, *To Imerologio mou 1939-1945.* Unpublished Diary, Archeio Ioannou Metaxas, Genika Archeia tou Kratous, File 45.

126. *Proia,* 24 April 1939

127. Interview with Dimitrios Farmakis who lived during Metaxas' dictatorship, in a village near Amaliada, Peloponnese.

128. *Proia,* 24 April 1939.

129. Ibid., 26 April 1939.

130. Article written in *Little Paris* and published by *Proia* on 26 April 1939

131. Metaxas' speech, 7 August 1937. *Logoi ke Skepseis,* Vol. 1, p. 226.

132. *E Neolea,* issue 10, 12 December 1938, p. 1.

133. According to a survey carried out in 1939 the urban population was rapidly increasing; a fact which worried Metaxas' regime. *Economiki Epetiris Tis Ellados* 1939 (Athens, 1940) p. 35.

134. Metaxas' speech , 10 January 1937, *Logoi ke Skepseis,* Vol.1, p. 153.

135. Metaxas' speech, 2 October 1936. Ibid., Vol. 1., p 50.

136. FO 371/21143, 16 January 1937.

137. *IKA* was based on the first National Insurance legislation of the 1920s. Vatikiotis, *Popular Autocracy,* p. 167. The regime claimed that by 1938 1,500,000 workers were insured in *IKA. E Neolea,* issue 44, 2 August 1940, p. 1394.

138. For Metaxas' social reforms see *Tessera Chronia,* Vol. 1, p. 240, and FO 371/21147, 31 July 1937.

139. Kalonas, *Ioannis Metaxas,* p. 215.

140. Linardatos, *4e Augoustou,* pp. 112-120.

141. Vatikiotis, *Popular Autocracy,* p. 168.

142. Waterlow reported that, 'The Prime Minister himself will pay a surprise visit to a factory or public utility undertaking, call the working people around him, make a speech assuring them that no employer, and especially no foreign employer, will be allowed to grind their faces, and invite them to submit their grievances. These ill-judged methods ,which recall the methods of the much abused politicians, seem to be on the increase.' FO 371/21147, 22 May 1937.

143. Ludtke, A., 'The Honour of Labour', in Crew, D.F. (ed.), *Nazism and German Society.* (Routledge, London, 1994) pp. 74-75.

144. Metaxas' speech, 17 August 1937. *Logoi ke Skepseis,* Vol.1, p. 227.

145. Papadakis, *E Exoteriki Politiki,* p. 60.

146. Metaxas' speech, 26 November 1939, *Logoi ke Skepseis,* Vol. 2., p. 200.

147. *Proia,* 25 and 24 April 1939.

148. *Enthimion Gefmatos Prosfigikou Kosmou. (* Ekdoseis 'Tetartis Augoustou', Athens, 1939) p. 14.

149. *E Neolea,* issue 7, 26 November 1938, p. 264.

150. Metaxas' speech, 8 August 1939. *Logoi ke Skepseis,* Vol.2., p. 124.

151. Robert Ley was the leader of the German Labour Front from 1933 to 1945. He created the organisation *Kraft durch Freude* (Strength through joy) which undertook the entertainment of workers through sports, recreational activities and mass tourism. The seagoing ships used by 'Strength Through Joy', enabled German workers to travel abroad and propagate the Nazi ideology. Wistrich. S. Robert, *Who's Who in Nazi Germany* (Routledge, London, 1982) p. 155. Such a friendly courtesy visit took place on November 1938, when a ship carrying 680 German members of the *Strength Through Joy* Organisation visited Greece. According to the press of the time the German

workers 'were met with great enthusiasm in Piraeus by Constantinos Kotzias who gave a dinner in their honour. *Vradini,* 12 November 1938.

152. Linardatos, *4e Augustou,* p.102.

153. Stefanides, Demosthenis 'To Koinoniko Zitima Ypo To Fos tou Germanikou Ethnososialismou,' *Neon Kratos,* issue 18, February 1939, pp. 1588-1619.

154. From Metaxas' 'To Tetradio Skepseon' (Book of Thoughts) in. *Logoi ke Skepseis,* Vol. 8., p. 553.

CHAPTER 3

1. Film making was restricted to a few small feature films: *Epi Tis Akropoleos* (On Acropolis) *E Tychi Tis Matoulas* (Maroula's faith) *Kerenia Koukla* (The Wax Doll) produced by individuals who were also the directors and often the actors. Soldatos, Ioannis,, *E Istoria tou Ellinikou Kinimatographou* (Egokeros, Athens, 1988) Vol. 1, pp. 7-29. See also 'O Kinimatografos' in *Encyclopaedia Papyros - Larousse* (Papyros, Athens, 1968) Vol. 2, p. 274.

2. Joseph Hepp was a talented Hungarian cinematographer specialising in the production of newsreels and became one of the creators of Greek Cinema. Soldatos, *E Istoria,* p. 30. On Joseph Hepp and his successful cinematography see *Ta Nea tou ELIA.*(Elliniko Logotechniko ke Istoriko Archeio, Athens, July-September 1998) pp. 16-18. He became one of Metaxas' regime's most effective cinematographers.

3. Soldatos, *E Istoria,* p. 30. In June 1917 after a disastrous clash between Venizelos and King Constantine and the forceful intervention by the foreign powers which brought the country into a state of civil war, the latter was forced to abdicate in favour of his second son Alexandos, and Venizelos became Prime Minister. King Constantine was reinstated in 1920 and again lost his throne in 1922 following the Asia Minor Catastrophe. Dafnis, *E Ellas,* Vol. 1.

4. Soldatos, *E Istoria* , p. 35.

5. Ibid., p. 42.

6. Venizelos won the elections of 1928 by a large majority (61.02%). Sarantis, *The Emergency,* p. 169. The strong government seemed to encourage, at first, a stabilising political and economic situation which offered the country a short respite and laid the foundations for the creation of a Greek Cinema.

7. *Ellinikos Kinimatographos 1906-1960.* Heliadis, F. (ed. Fantasia, Athens, 1960) p. 28.

8. Soldatos, *E Istoria,* pp.57-67. Athens' population of the time was 1.000.000.

9. The film companies included the *Dag Film, Ajax Film,* the *Greek Film,* the *Olympia Film,* the *Ellas Film* , the *Ethniki Film,* the *Nilo Film,* the *Akropol Film,* the *Astro Film,* the *Fivos Film,* the *Hellenic Film,* the *Artistic Film,* the *Dean Dritch Film,* and the *Fizio Film.* However, by 1935 all these companies ceased to exist. 'The Cinema' in *Papyros - Larousse* , Vol. 2, pp. 274-275.

10. Sarantis, *The Emergency,* p.183. On Greek Economy during the inter-war period see Mazower, Mark & Veremis, Thanos, 'The Greek Economy, 1922-1941,' in Higham & Veremis (eds) *Aspects of Greece,* pp. 116-117.

11. 'Eisagogi ke Provoli Ton Kinimatografikon Tenion en Elladi kata to Etos 1936' in *Statistiki Epetiris Tis Ellados 1939* , p. 413.

12. *Papyros-Larousse,* Vol. 2, p. 275. However, Hollywood film hegemony was as much a European phenomenon as a Greek one. Studies on British film history have shown that the inter-war period cinema audiences in Britain were 'infatuated' with Hollywood; by 1926 with around 3.500 cinemas operating in Britain and approximately 40 percent of cinemagoers attending twice a week, only 5 percent of the films were produced in Britain. This phenomenon continued until well into the 1930s, when the coming of the Second World War necessitated the creation of national cinema. Caughie, John, & Rocket Kevin,, *The Companion to British and Irish Cinema* (Cassel and the British Film Institute, London, 1996) p. 2.

13. A fortnightly magazine issued in 1924 by Economou, Heraklis and continued its publication until 1970. The magazine offers a valuable insight into Metaxas' regime and its attitude towards film. Unfortunately only a limited number of issues have survived.

14. *Kinimatografikos Astir,* January 1937, p. 19.
15. *Vradini*, 3 January 1937, 16 March 1937 and 16 January 1938. See also *Nea Estia*, 1 June 1939, p.791, and 22 May 1940, p. 646.
16. *Kinimatografikos Astir*, December 1937, p.18
17. The significance of the cinema as a potential propaganda weapon had been widely recognised by most authoritarian regimes. Lenin remarked that 'of all arts, for us the cinema is the most important. Stalin described it as 'the greatest means of mass agitation, and Trotsky called it 'the best instrument for propaganda.' Goebbels echoed these sentiments when he called the cinema 'one of the most modern and far-reaching media that there is for influencing the masses'. Taylor, Richard, *Film Propaganda. Soviet Russia and Nazi German* (Croom Helm, London , 1979) p. 29.
18. Richard Taylor in his study of *Film Propaganda* argues that the powerful impact film had on people derived from a number of reasons: 'As a visual medium, especially silent film, its appeal was universal, unlimited by consideration of language, culture and literacy. Furthermore, although the high cost of producing and distributing was a negative factor, the number of points at which films could be made was severely limited and thus easier to control. A film, unlike a theatre group, could be despatched from the centre to the periphery and the content of the performance could be determined and guaranteed in advance'. Ibid., p. 31.
19. *Ta Paraskinia*, May 1938, p. 3.
20. *Apologismos,* p. 213.
21. The first measures concerning the safety of the cinemas were imposed in 1925, during the short-lived Pagalos dictatorship, while on May 1930 the law 4767 *Peri Kinimatographou,* introduced the first regulations regarding film. *FEK* 184, 1930 and Soldatos, *E Istoria*, p. 42. However, we can really talk about an extended cinema legislation during Metaxas' regime, as it covered a wide range of filming procedure; its production, its distribution, its screening but above all its complete control by the regime.
22. *Kinimatografikos Astir* in a series of articles pointed out the value of the film as the most effective instrument of mass indoctrination and propaganda, especially where youth was concerned, and implored the regime to introduce measures that would encourage Greek productions. *Kinimatografikos Astir,* January 1937, p. 3, and November 1937, p. 11.
23. *FEK* 22, 25 January 1937, p. 135. A Censorship Committee had already been established in May 1930 with Law 4767 to supervise film projection and the safety of the cinemas; it also introduced restrictions which prohibited young people under the age of sixteen years old to attend films. *FEK* 184, 28 May 1930, p. 1614.
24. *FEK* 22, 25 January 1937, p. 136.
25. Ibid.
26. Ibid., p. 137.
27. Hoffmann, Hilmar, *The Triumph of Propaganda, Film and National Socialism 1933-1945.* (Bergham Books, Providence-Oxford, 1996) p. 193. Similarly, in Mussolini's Italy by 1926 all cinemas were required to show a film produced by LUCE (L'Unione Cinematografa Educativa) the government controlled film institute, producing all Fascist propaganda films, as part of each programme. Warner, Geoffrey, 'Italy 1918-1940, in Golby, John; Waites, Bernard; Warner, Geoffrey; Aldgate, Tony and Lentin, Antony, (eds.) in *War, Peace and Social Change: Europe 1900-1955*, Book III. (Open University Press, London, 1994) p. 129.
28. *FEK* 474, 23 November 1937, pp. 3059-3060
29. In 1939 when *EON* had been powerfully established and produced a great number of propaganda films, there was an intervention by Loukia Manzupha, the daughter of Metaxas, who acted as the Organisation's General Secretary, demanding to participate in the Censorship Committee and determine the suitability of the state commissioned films. Nicoloudis objected to this intervention and complained to Metaxas about this interference which seemed to have the Dictator's consent. On this issue and Nicoloudis' letter to Metaxas see, Genika Archeia tou Kratous, Archeio Ioannou Metaxa. File 41/028.
30. Metaxas' speech, 29 November 1938. *Logoi ke Skepseis*, Vol. 1., p. 426.

31. Hoffmann, *The Triumph*, p. 95.
32. The *Pradikate* was awarded by the Censorship Office and often meant tax benefits for the film studio. Films without a *Pradikate* needed, according to Welch, 'special permission to be shown' Welch, David, *Propaganda and the German Cinema 1933-1945* (Clarendon Press, Oxford, 1983) pp. 20-22.
33. Ibid.
34. Warner, Geoffrey ,'Italy 1918-1940' in John Colby, etal. (eds.) in *War, Peace and Social Change*, p. 129.
35. It is noteworthy that not only in totalitarian countries like Germany and Italy, but also in democratic ones like Britain, measures were taken for the protection of national film. These measures took the form of quotas and finance through Cinematograph Film Acts like the one passed in 1927, and in 1938. Street, *British National Cinema*, p. 9.
36. *Kinimatrografikos Asti,r,* 11 April 1937, p.11.
37. *Nea Estia,* p. 646. On these films and their talented directors see *Ellinikos Kinimatographos,,* pp. 71-72.
38. Fifty summer cinemas were operating in Athens in 1937. *Kinimatografikos Astir,* April 1937, p. 11.
39. Ibid., p. 31.
40. Ibid., September 1937, p. 9.
41. There are very few entries in Metaxas' diary during his dictatorship concerning film. On 15 August 1939 he stated that he attended an *EON* film production with young *EON* members. *Ioannis Metaxas To Prosopiko tou Imerologio* Vol.7., p. 383, while on 19 November 1939 he wrote: 'Film by the Workers Centre. Pleased.' Ibid., p. 406. On the contrary, his diary is full of entries regarding his love and regular attendance at the theatre where he reserved a permanent seat. Ibid., pp. 291,318,321,352 385,396,407-409. See also Vol. 8., pp. 455-459,490 ,507.
42. At the same time the entertainment tax for the Royal theatre came to 1% of the entrance price. *Kinimatografikos Astir,* 28 March 1937, p. 9.
43. *Kinimatografikos Astir,* 23 September 1937, p. 10. In June 1937 it was reported that for two months the entertainment tax paid to the Government by the total of the Greek cinemas amounted to 7.000.000 drachmas, while the theatres paid only 100.000. Ibid., 5 June 1937, p. 7.
44. Hoffmann, *The Triumph* p. 145.
45. Welch, *The Third Reich,* p. 48.
46. Unfortunately a large number of those newsreels has been lost. An account and history of a number of newsreels of that period is given by Fotis Labrinos in his book *ISCHYS MOU E AGAPI TOU FAKOY – Ta kinimatografika epikera os tekmiria tes istorias (1895-1940),* (Kastaniotis, Athens, 2005).
47. All his political opponents had either died (ex-premier Michalakopoulos), or had been eliminated through their imprisonment or deportation to remote islands (Kafandaris, Marcou, Papandreou, Theotokis). Metaxas, aware of the opposition and the 'efficiency' of the measures applied for its suppression, wrote on 11 December 1938: 'The dominance is complete; we shall see what form the reactions will take; Maniadakis has all the information we need; nothing is taking place that we are not aware off.' *Ioannis Metaxas, To Prosopiko tou Imerologio.* Vol. 7., p. 315.
48. Sarantis, *The Emergency,* p. 427.
49. An attempt was made by the Palace in December 1937 to sound out the feasibility of Michalakopoulos replacing the dictatorship. The information was made known to Metaxas who ordered Michalakopoulos' exile. Dafnis, *E Ellas* p. 438.
50. *Ioannis Metaxas, To Prosopiko tou Imerologio,* Vol. 7., p. 322.
51. Georgakopoulos disapproved of and fought against the 'invasion' of schools by the *EON* Linardatos, *4e Augoustou,* p. 157. On this Metaxas wrote in his diary on 19 February 1938: ' I have finished with Georgakopoulos as far as *EON* is concerned; little by little, he submits himself to the idea.' Ibid, Vol. 7, p. 293. On 29 November 1938 a few days after Georgakopoulos was dismissed, the Reich Youth Leader Baldur

von Schirach visited Greece and was met with a warm and enthusiastic welcome by Metaxas. Schirach brought with him gifts and golden medals which he offered to *EON* officials and the Crown Prince. Linardatos, *4e Augoustou*, p. 103.

52. Metaxas' speech , 5 January 1939. *Logoi ke Skepseis* , Vol. 2, p.12.

53. Metaxas named these forces in his speeches to *EON* on 29 December 1938 and on 5 January 1939. In his view, the first opposition came from the teachers of the intermediate school who were reluctant to allow the children's enrolment into the Organisation as this could undermine their authority. The greatest reaction came from the University students and the teachers. The opposition continued from the elite circles who resented the participation of girls and working class children in the Organisation, fearing their children's 'contamination.' Lastly came the family who feared that their children would escape family discipline and control. *Logoi ke Skepseis*, Vol. 1, p 436, and Vol. 2, pp. 10-13, and pp. 172-173.

54. Metaxas' speech to *EON* , 5 January 1939, Ibid., Vol.2, pp. 9-10.

55. On the subject of indoctrination of German Youth through film, see 'Educational Film Propaganda and the Nazi Youth.' in Welch, David, (ed.), *Nazi Propaganda. The Power and The Limitations* (Croom Helm, London, 1983) p. 66.

56. By July 1938 Kotzias had spent the sum of 549,584 drachmas on the educational cinema. *Ta Paraskinia*, 23 July 1938, p. 3.

57. Statute '*Peri Idyiseos Morfotikou Kinimatografou* (About establishing an educational cinema), *FEK* 418, 21 September 1935, p. 2047. This law supplemented statutes 4767 of May 1930 of a similar nature. *FEK* 184, p. 1612.

58. *FEK* 224, 3 June 1939, p. 1481. The Emergency Law which organised the services of the Ministry of Education including culture and fine arts was the 782/1937. Ibid.

59. In 1938, 3.800 villages and districts had no schools, while during the year 1937-1938, 15,311 teachers taught 987,120 pupils. Linardatos, *4e Augoustou*, p 146. In April 1939 the regime claimed that 1,739 schools were established, while 3,288 teachers were appointed to fill the vacant places. Metaxas' speech in Kalamata, 24 April 1939. *Logoi ke Skepseis*, Vol. 2, p. 61.

60. *Apospasmata,* p. 103. This is an extravagant amount if one considers that according to the statistics of 1936 the average income of an agricultural family was 20,000 drachmas per annum, a sum which did not change considerably in the following years. Linardatos, *4e Augoustou*, p. 121 and Vatikiotis, *Popular Autocracy*, p. 167.

61. *Apospasmata.*, p. 103.

62. *Tessera Chronia,,* Vol. 4, p. 23.

63. *Apospasmata,,* p. 59.

64. Ibid., p. 134. The Organisation established the *E Kentriki Scholi Diafotiseos* (The Central School of Indoctrination) which trained specially selected officials entrusted with the mission of propaganda and other activities, which were never disclosed. Linardatos, *4e Augoustou,* p.183. This School was of vital importance to the regime as the 'proper' education and enlightenment of the *EON* members ascertained the successful dissemination of its ideas and policies. *Esoterikos Organismos,* p. 11.

65. *FEK* 22 , 25 January 1937, p. 136.

66. Ibid., pp. 137-138.

67. *Tessera Chronia,* Vol. 2., p. 180. See also *E Neolea*, issue 3, .August 1940, p. 1398.

68. Maniadakis' speech to *EON*, 13 January 1939. *Kriseis kai Siberasmata epi tis Neoleas pro ke meta tin 4en Augoustou (*Ekdoseis *EON*, Athens, 1939) p. 6. The role played by the sub-Ministry of Public Security, and Maniadakis himself in the formation and growth of the Organisation was crucial. According to the Government Order No. 3973/ 21 December 1938, signed by Metaxas and sent to the sub-Ministry of Public Security, *EON* was to enjoy the same privileges as most sections of the Public Services. Another order No. 33 /15/13 issued on 19 November 1939 by the sub-Ministry of Public Security and signed by Maniadakis, emphasised the assistance of the local Police to the *EON* members. This participation, according to the order, contributed greatly to the progress of the Organisation and the fulfilment of its goals. Linardatos, *4e Augoustou*, pp. 162-163.

69. *Esoterikos Organismos,* pp. 47-49.

70. Ibid., p. 29.

71. *Apospasmata,* p. 60.

72. Ibid., p. 61.

73. The *Phalagosima* of one, two, five, ten and twenty drachmas were special dues issued by the *EON* administration office for the financial support of the Organisation. In many cases its purchase by the *EON* members was compulsory. *E Neolea*, issue 22 , 2 March 1940, p. 702.

74. These films dealt mainly with the life and activities of the Organisation's young members. *Apospasmata*, p. 61.

75. Ibid., p. 102.

76. Ibid., pp. 102-103.

77. Hans Traub, an interpreter of Nazi film propaganda, claimed that 'The first law of all propaganda reads that people must be kept receptive and capable of enthusiasm' Quoted in Hoffmann, *The Triumph*, p.193.
   The need for enthusiasm on behalf of the youth was a vital precondition in establishing the necessary psychological ground upon which a new Greece would be built. Metaxas often underlined the importance of this driving force in his speeches. On 29 December 1938 he advised the *EON* members to 'have enthusiasm, fanaticism and passion; because without enthusiasm, without passion and fanaticism for the struggle and the ideals, youth is senility' *Logoi ke Skepseis*, Vol.1, p. 437. On the significance of enthusiasm see also Papadakis, *E Chthesini,*, pp. 206-209

78. *E Neolea*, 11 March 1939, p. 717 and Metaxas' speech in Kilkis, 24 February 1939. *Logoi ke Skepseis*, Vol. 2, p. 31.

79. Where the private cinemas were concerned, the *EON* members were obliged to pay a nominal fee of only one to two drachmas to cover for light and wear and tear expenses. *Apospasmata,* p. 103.

80. Ibid., p. 134.

81. Cineak was a type of state controlled cinema halls established with the mission to screen educational and enlightened films commissioned by the regime. The first Cineak was established in 1936 and proved to be very successful in its mission. The first newsreels produced in 1936 by *Meravidis-Saliveros* and screened there, depicted Metaxas' coming to power. *Ellinikos Kinimatografos,* p. 71.
   The *EON* members enjoyed a free of charge entrance, while the regular entry fee was seven to ten drachmas. The entrance fee for the independent cinemas was 15 to 25 drachmas. *Kinimatografikos Astir,* 14 February 1937,p. 15. See also *Vradini*, 16 March 1937.

82. *Vradini*, 2 January 1938.

83. Quoted in Machera, *E Neolea.* p. 110.

84. Linardatos, *4e Augoustou*, p. 173.

85. Although there was a compulsory screening of the state commissioned newsreels and documentaries there was not, however, a compulsory attendance. Therefore, after the show of the feature film the regime's commissioned newsreels, shown in repeated performances, presented little interest. Furthermore, due to the lack of financial and technical means they were artistically and aesthetically of a poor quality, while the imported feature films offered everything that the Greek productions lacked; a dream world of glamour and wealth.

86. According to *YTT*, two hundred of those centres fully equipped to provide educational and entertaining programmes were established in Athens alone. *Tessera Chronia*, Vol. 2, p.180.

87. *E Neolea* , issue 3, 29 October 1938, p. 89.

88. Ibid.. issue 10, 9 December 1939, p. 301. *E Neolea* included a number of pages *Oi Selides ton Koritsion Mas* (The Pages of Our Girls) devoted to the *EON* girls. These pages contained advice of how the Greek girls would become women and mothers worthy of the New State. ' We want you girls to become Greek mothers who will be able to carry on your shoulders the Nation, and the supreme National values that the State will entrust you with.' Metaxas' speech, in Kalamata, 24 April 1939. *Logoi ke Skepseis* Vol. 2., p. 62.

89. *Tessera Chronia*, Vol. 2., p. 175. This First Oath-taking ceremony took place a year and half after the establishing of the Organisation. The first organised *EON* phalanx named the *Phalanx of Ioannis Metaxas* marched in Patras on 7 November 1937 (thereafter known as the *EON* Day and established as a public holiday) in the presence of Ioannis Metaxas. Linardatos, *4e Augoustou,* p. 154.

90. Metaxas' speech on the occasion of his resumption of duties at the Ministry of Education on 29 November 1938. *Logoi ke Skepseis*, Vol. 1, p. 426. On the significance of *EON* see also his speech to the Workers on 1 May 1939, Ibid., Vol. 2, p. 296.

91. The *EON* Oath : 'I swear in the name of The Father, The Son, and the Holy Spirit, that I shall preserve my faith to my God, my King and my Country: my Chief the Crown Prince, the National Governor and the Inspector General: I shall fully obey every order, and I shall fight everywhere and always for the National Ideals and the ideological, social and moral values of the 'Fourth of August' State: I shall defend the Flags and I shall always obey my Superiors: I will comply with the Laws of the State, and those of the Organisation, and I shall honour my Oath, if necessary with my own life.' Quoted in Machera, *E Neolea*, p. 95.

92. Film's commentary. In fascist Italy the young Fascists motto was: **Believe, Obey, Fight**. Morgan, *Italian Fascism* p. 114.

93. *Ioannis Metaxas, To Prosopiko tou Imerologio*, Vol. 7, p. 315.

94. According to the *EON* officials the *EON* salute originated from the ancient salute and had nothing in common with the Fascist salute. 'The *EON* salute is strictly Greek. It was a manifestation of love and devotion towards the Gods. Later it was taken from the Greeks by the Romans and we have reinstated it, as it belongs to us by right.' *A Panellinios Ekthesis EON* (Ekdoseis *EON*, Athens, 1940) p. 10. The Phalanx's salute (as the 'Fourth of August' regime salute was called) was of vital importance to the regime. In September 1939 the Secretary of the Ministry of Education Spenzas sent a circular to all schools which reflected the significance of the phalanx salute: 'It has come to our attention that some teachers demand that the students salute in several manners. Because all the pupils and students are members of the National Organisation of Youth, we demand that every one of them salutes only in one manner; that is the salute of the Phalangite.' *E Neolea*, November 1939, p.157 (Number of issue unreadable)

95. Metaxas' speech to the University students, 10 October 1936. *Logoi ke Skepseis*, Vol. I., p. 65. The idealisation of body and spirit was a common feature in most of the totalitarian states and it was projected to reinforce themes like regeneration, nationalism and racism. In Germany it was presented through Leni Riefenstahl's Film *Olympia*, 1938. A film in which according to Hoffmann, 'beautiful was seen as the sensual manifestation of an idea and guaranteed the emotionalisation of the viewers through Riefensthal's sure instinct for what is effective in the arts and a sizeable dose of sympathy with nature' Hoffmann, *The Triumph*, p. 158. *Olympia* as well as the *1936 Olympic Games in Berlin* and the *Winter Olympic Games of 1937,* were screened at the *EON* recreation centres and Cineak and received a wide appreciation by the film press. *Kinimatografikos Astr*, 17 October 1937, p. 12, and *Ta Paraskinia* , 11 June 1938, p. 3.

96. Metaxas' speech to *EON*, 2 June 1940. *Logoi ke Skepseis*, Vol. 2, p. 313.
Metaxas very often spoke of his determination to wipe out any remaining social class differences, and he claimed that ' the ' Fourth of August' State acknowledged as equal all Greek children, poor and rich, upper or lower class.' See Metaxas' speech to parents and teachers on 25 October 1939. Ibid., Vol. 2., p. 164. In his view the best way to achieve this equality was to become a member of the National Organisation of Youth and join one of the *EON* camps where all children enjoyed the same privileges and training. Ibid.

97. According to the regime in 1938 seventeen summer camps were established accommodating 17,000 young members, while thirty training camps trained 15,000 *EON* members. *Tessera Chronia*, Vol. 2, p. 178.

98. His diary is full of entries about his visits to the Zuberi and other camps and the pleasure he took from the company of the young members. *Ioannis Metaxas, To Prosopiko tou Imerologio*, Vol. 7, pp. .310,377,389,393. See also Vol. 8, pp. 484,486,490.

99. In his speech on 25 October 1939, he advised the parents to 'take the bus and visit the camp at Zouberi and experience for themselves the morally and physically elevating activities that their children were engaged in.' *Logoi ke Skepseis*, Vol. 7, p. 166.

100. Discipline was, according to Metaxas, one of the preconditions needed for the creation of combatant young people conscious of a struggle that will lead the nation to victory. 'But bear in mind that you cannot set out along this road to victory without absolute and unconditional discipline,' he claimed in his speech to the University students on 10 October 1936. Ibid, Vol. I, p. 73-74. Similarly on 9 June 1938, during the inauguration of the first *EON* Camp, he warned its members: 'In this Camp I demand full and absolute discipline which shall exceed in severity even that of the army.' Ibid., Vol. 2, p. 389.

101. The training of *EON* members in the camps often resembled that of the army. In Vatikiotis' view the Organisation operated as ' an army of Youth which turned its members mentally and physically into patriotic Greeks; it could also be seen as a future combat army.' Vatikiotis, *Popular Autocracy*, p. 187.

102. *Esoterikos Organismos,* p.25

103. The reason that the two Minoan Axes (emblem of the Minoan Civilisation) were chosen over any of the other 'sacred' ancient symbols was according to Papadakis, because the Cretan Axes were a much older and magnificent symbol than any that came later. Because the *EON* symbolised the perpetual national regeneration it was only appropriate that it had as its emblem the oldest and most glorious one available; the Minoan Axe. Papadakis, *E Chthesini*, p. 51

104. *Esoterikos Organismos,* p. 10.

105. This form of representation was, according to Hoffmann, a very effective method: 'psychologists teach us how easy is to fill an emotional vacuum by forming a powerful affective bond with a leadership figure or a fetish (flag).' Hoffmann, *The Triumph*, p. 13.

106. The 'Fourth of August' emblem symbolised: The continuity of national existence; the indomitable spirit and power of the nation; faith in God, the King and the motherland. Politically, the emblem symbolised action against opposition and usurpation. For *EON* it symbolised the objectives and targets of the Organisation, and finally it symbolised the ideology and the values of the 'Fourth of August' State. *A' Panellinios Ekthesis EON*, p. 10.

107. Welch, *Propaganda and the German Cinema*, p. 57.

108. Metaxas' speech, 7 November 1936. *Logoi ke Skepseis*, Vol. 1, p. 104. In a similar way Baldur von Schirach, the Reich Youth Leader, during the dedication of the Hitler Youth's flags in Potsdam on 24 January 1934, had stated: 'Remember whenever you see the flag waving , it isn't some inconsequential piece of cloth. Remember, that behind this flag stands the will of millions of people bound to Germany in loyalty, bravery, and fervent love. You must defend it, and, if need be, cover it with your young bodies.' Quoted in Hoffmann, *The Triumph*, p. 98.

109. *Apologismos,* p .11. See also *FEK* 23, 25 January 1939, p. 142.

110. Metaxas' speech to members of the Organisation 'National Renaissance', 14 November 1936. *Logoi ke Skepseis*, Vol. 1, p. 124.

111. *Ioannis Metaxas, To Prosopiko tou Imerologio*, Vol. 7, p. 315.

112. Quoted in Hoffmann, *The Triumph*, p. 101.

113. The freedom enjoyed by the young members at the *EON* Camps or the *EON* gatherings often worried the parents who lost control of their children and were unable to react. This was a reality acknowledged by Metaxas who admitted that 'The first reaction came from the parents who claim that we took their children and they have no control over them.' *Logoi ke Skepseis*, Vol. 2, p. 170.

114. Metaxas' speech, 24 April 1939. Ibid., p. 64. The 'Fourth of August' ideology, like most ideologies of similar political schemes, included the concept of anti-individualism. The place of the individual was where the interest of the State was. 'The individual should merge with the whole and his own will was to be submitted to that of the Nation.' Sarantis, *The Emergency*, p. 414.

115. Metaxas' speech to the students, 25 October 1936 and 13 May 1937. *Logoi ke Skepseis*, Vol.

1, p. 76 and p. 183 respectively. This concept of a unified whole was a central point in Metaxas' beliefs and he referred to it in several of his speeches. Speech in Thessaloniki, 28 Oct.1936. Ibid., p. 97; to the *EON*, 14 November 1936, Ibid., p. 127; to the students of the Commercial School, Ibid., pp. 290-293; to the Polytechnic students, 25 October 1938, Ibid., p. 420. The same concept was also a dominant subject on the writings and speeches of the regime's theoreticians. Koumaros, Nikolaos, 'E Antilipsis Tou Kratous ke E Tetarth Augoustou', in *To Neon Kratos*, issue 18, 1939.

116. Metaxas' speech , 24 April 1939. *Logoi ke Skepseis*, Vol. 2, p. 65.

117. There were few discriminating incidents but those originated from a few *EON* officials and were strongly criticised by Metaxas. In fact he believed that the rich children could benefit greatly from their association with the children of the working class. Machera, *E Neolea*, p. 108.

118. Metaxas' speech on 25 October 1936. *Logoi ke Skepseis*, Vol. 2., p. 168.

119. Quoted in Machera ,*E Neolea*, p. 110.

120. Alexandros Papagos was A Lieutenant-General and the Commander in Chief during the Greco-Italian War in 1940.

121. *Ioannis Metaxas, To Prosopiko tou Imerologio*, Vol.7., p. 322. See also Linardatos, *4 Augoustou*, p. 183. In Italy the members of the fascist youth organisation *Ballila*, were encouraged to spy upon their families for anti-Fascist sentiment or opinion. Roberts, *The House that Hitler Built*, p. 459 . See also Marzolo Renato, *OE Organoseis Tis Neoleas is Tin Italian*, (Novissima, Rome, 1939)

122. Quoted in Machera, *E Neolea*, p. 109.

123. During the first year *EON* acquired 70,000 uniforms and at the end of 1939 this number reached 400,000. uniforms. *Tessera Chronia*, Vol.. 2., p. 181. According to Linardatos for the purchase of uniforms for the *EON* members of Athens alone, the Government spent 15,000,000, drachmas while for the uniforms of the whole *EON* force, the amount reached the sum of 250,000,000 drachmas (twice the amount of the national budget at a time that the Government claimed to have spent 5,000,000 drachmas to reduce illiteracy) Ibid., Vol. 3., p.189 and Linardatos, *4e Augoustou*, p. 192.

124. A collection was made to finance the purchase of *EON* uniforms. According to Metaxas by 1938 this collection raised in Athens the sum of 8,000,000. Speech to *EON,* 5 January 1939. *Logoi ke Skepseis,* Vol. 2., p. 15. See also *E Neolea,* issue 6, 11 November 1939; issue 62, 16 December 1939 and in most *E Neolea* issues entries under the title 'Doreai Dia Tin EON' (Donations to *EON*).

125. 1,700 photos depicted the life and activities of *EON*. *Apospsmata.,* p.60. Similarly, a plethora of small shots depicting Metaxas among children who kissed his hands, threw flowers at his feet and stood next to him, as well as his visits to children's institutions, was projected as part of compilation films.

126. *E Neolea*, issue 20 , 25 February, 1939, p. 652.

127. The exhibition in Zapeion, which was inaugurated by Ioannis Metaxas and opened to honour the occasion of the Second Panhellenic Conference of *EON* in May 1940, was according to the officials a 'VICTORY of *EON'* and exhibited the life and the achievements of the Organisation. The admittance ticket for the public was five drachmas, while for the uniformed *EON* members the admittance was free. *E Neolea*, 8 June 1940, issue 36, p. 1180, and issue 35, 16 June 1940, p.1117.

128. Another newsreel dealing with Athletic games was the *Athinaiki Agones* (Athenian Games) screened in June 1938 on the occasion of the Athletic Week when there were 10,000 participating athletes. The 1,200 metres film, a Megaloekonomou-Kurbetis-Meravides production recorded by Finos was screened by portable projectors in various places in Athens. Ta *Paraskinia*, 18 June, 1938, p. 3.

129. *Ioannis Metaxas, To Prosopiko tou Imerologio,* Vol. 7, p. 372. The First *EON* Athletic Games lasted seven days and engaged most of the *EON* youth force. *E Neolea*, issue 32, 20 May 1939, pp. 1036-1039.

130. *Tessera Chronia*, Vol. 2, p. 178. Respectively there is a number of very short newsreels, or rather shots from several athletic events and school activities in the Athens Stadium and

elsewhere, which depict young school children engaged in sports and folk dances. Most of those athletic events were attended by Metaxas.

131. *Vradini*, 10 November 1938.

132. *E Neolea*, issue, 12, 1938, p. 397.

133. Physical education was also considered highly important in Nazi German but mainly as the necessary component for maintaining racial purity. Koch asserts in his study on the Hitler Youth that 'Physical education, being of national importance, was no longer a matter for the individual, or even for parents, but directly a matter of state-concern for the protection of the race. Koch,*The Hitler Youth*, p. 163. In fascist Italy athletic activities also constituted a vital training for the fascist youth. Morgan, p. 118. In fact article XXVII of the Royal Decree concerning fascist youth spoke of the necessity of physical training through gymnastics and sports as they strengthened the spiritual education of the young. 'Documents 2: 1925-1959, in Marwick and Simpson (eds.) *War Peace and Social Change - Europe 1900-1955,* p. 18.

134. *Tessera Chronia*, Vol. 2, p. 59.

135. Most of those athletic centres, especially in the country, were the result of hard work by the *EON* members. By order of Metaxas and Kanellopoulos, the young were called to participate 'voluntarily' in the building and reconstruction of the athletic centres. *Vradini*, 17 November 1937.

136. The film was first screened in Greece in June 1938 on the occasion of the First Athletic Week following a special request by Kotzias to the German Authorities in Athens. The film, which 'was sent to Greece by plane,' met with great success and it was extensively advertised by the press. *Ta Paraskinia*, 11 June 1938, p. 3.

137. The Head of the Reich Sport Office, von Tschammer und Osten, visited Greece on 30 November 1939. The *Times* wrote of the visit: 'The Minster of Athletics Tschammer und Osten visited Greece without an invitation, to discuss (it seems) the next Olympics and he was well received by the authorities; but he meant in fact to discuss trade with Germany and the difficulties posed by the sea embargo by the British. *The Times,* 11 December 1939. Archives of the Greek Ministry of Foreign Affairs, File 3, 1940.

138. In another small shot dealing with the celebration of the 'Fourth of August' regime's anniversary Kanellopoulos is depicted kissing the hands of Metaxas with religious piety.

139. *E Neolea*, issue 32, 20 May 1939, p.1037.

140. 250,000 *EON* members participated in this *EON* Athletic Games, while the number of the spectators reached 80,000. Ibid., p. 1037.

141. The German film *Olympiade* filmed in 1936 propagated and reinforced similar ideals. Hitler was impressed by the ancient Greek athletic model and when he saw a photograph of a beautiful woman swimming, he stirred with enthusiasm: 'It is only in our century that young people have once again approached *Hellenistic* ideals through sports'. Quoted in Welch, *Propaganda and the German Cinema*, p.115.

142. Metaxas' speech, 5 June 1938. *Logoi ke Skepseis* Vol.2, p. 388.

143. The notion of the individual being submerged into the whole was also a strong component in the Nazi ideology: 'Though individual effort was rewarded, great care was taken that it was never obtained at the expense of the unit; in the main the competition was between groups and not between individuals, all emphasis centring on obedience, duty to the group, and helping within the group'. Quoted in Koch, *The Hitler Youth*, p.128. See also Welch, *Propaganda and the German Cinema,* p.115. Similarly in Fascist Italy anti-individualism was a vital concept. According to article 8 of Mussolini's *Doctrine of Fascism* 'Outside the State there can be no individuals.' Documents 2: 1925-1959 in Marwick & Simpson (eds.) *War Peace and Social Change - Europe 1900-1955*. p. 18.

144. *Tessera Chronia.*, Vol. 2, p. 75.

145. Extract from the *Phalangite Hymn* dedicated to him from the *EON* members. *Ta Tragoudia*, p.11.

146. *E Neolea*, issue 33, 27 May 1939, p.1075.

147. As already mentioned the number of these newsreels came to sixteen. Unfortunately not all of those have survived. Apart from the films discussed in this chapter, the rest

consisted of small shots depicting the activities of *EON*. These activities included the members' participation in flower festivals, money collection, and several parades. *EON's* participation was a necessary function in every orchestrated manifestation projected by the state-commissioned newsreels. However, their most significant participation was during the celebrations of the anniversaries of the 'Fourth of August' regime in the Athens Stadium.

148. *Apospasmata,* p. 60.

149. *E Neolea*, issue 10, 17 December 1938, p. 336.

150. Metaxas relied heavily on Royal support to maintain himself in Power. This was a fact recognised by the *EON* officials who claimed: 'The King and the Crown Prince are the unbreakable inherited continuation which ensures the existence of the National State. The interest of the throne is intrinsically linked with the interest of the National State. The King ensures the stability of the Government.' O *Vasilefs*, p.4.

151. *Neolea*, issue 10, 17 December 1938, pp. 334-336.

152. *Tessera Chronia*, Vol. 2, p. 176.

153. Welch, *Propaganda and the German Cinema* , p. 196.

154. The Crown Prince delivered a speech for the occasion which reflected the royal support to *EON*. Among other things he said: It is the first time that I have seen you and I present myself to you as your Supreme Chief. We are all Greeks and we are all a family: we will accomplish nothing if we do not have discipline, affection and concord. The future depends on you; I shall do all I can to help you in your work.' *E Neolea*, issue 10, 17 December 1938, p. 335.

155. Welch, *Propaganda and the German Cinema*, p. 196.

156. The regime's propaganda put great emphasis on projecting an image of the young Princess as a caring mother, and a benevolent royal figure. In the booklet *O Vasilefs* this image was projected through the adulation of a very young girl who wrote in her diary. 'I was shaken with 'sacred emotion' and admiration to have seen the Princess looking at me with motherly love and sharing with me a bunch of grapes when she visited our camp *Ioannis Metaxas* at Zouberi.' *O Vasilefs*, p.8.

157. Metaxas' speech on 5 January 1939. *Logoi ke Skepseis*, Vol. 2, p.10.

158. Sarandis, *The Emergency*, p. 429.

159. Metaxas often doubted the genuine support of the Crown Prince who was committed to the Greek Scouts Organisation; He was their Honorary Chief, and originally opposed the formation of *EON*. *Ioannis Metaxas, To Prosopiko tou Imerologio*. Vol. 7, p. 290 and p. 300.

160. Linardatos, *4e Augoustou* , p.16. See also *Tessera Chronia ,* Vol. 2, p. 176.

161. *Ioannis Metaxas, To Prosopiko tou Imerologio*, Vol. 7, p.315.

162. Although Metaxas' propaganda films were full of scenes like this one, they, unlike the Nazi propaganda films, very rarely present soldiers marching. In fact as Sarantis observed 'the Army itself studiously avoided being involved with the regime or any of its manifestations.' Sarantis, *The Emergency*, p. 438. This visual image which puts great emphasis on the *EON* parades but not the soldiers supports the claim that Metaxas considered *EON* as his personal army. During an *EON* parade in the Athens Stadium Metaxas turned to the King and pointing at the parading youth said: 'Here, Your Majesty, this is your army; the only army on which you must depend and rely on.' Quoted in Linardatos, *4e Augoustou*, p. 178. A similar attitude was expressed by Scozza, the head of the young Fascists when he claimed that 'The Duce and Fascism need a Youth organised like an army in closed ranks: huge and imposing, firm and disciplined, masculine, unshakeable in faith.' Quoted in Morgan, *Italian Fascism* p.123.

163. Quoted in Welch, *Propaganda and the German Cinema*, p. 149.

164. *E Neolea,* 7 March, 1939, p.806. Number of issue destroyed.

165. Linardatos, *4e Augoustou*, p. 175. According to Waterlow the celebration which turned out to be a 'a fiasco,' ended in chaos with hundreds of children scattered around Athens completely soaked while a great number of pneumonia cases were reported. FO 371/23770 , 5 April 1939.

166. *Ioannis Metaxas, To Prosopiko tou Imerologio,* Vol. 7, p. 360.

167. Quoted in Hoffmann, *The Triumph* p.71.

168. Metaxas' speech to *EON* : 'Greece is our mother (...) and if you have to you will offer your life for Greece not just out of young enthusiasm but because the nature of things demands.' *E Neolea*, issue 44, 12 August 1940, p. 1422.

169. Metaxas stated on 5 January 1939: 'when *EON* became a reality we heard the parents complain, ' We have lost our children'. *Logoi ke Skepseis*, Vol. 2, p.13.

170. Metaxas' speech in Chania, 7 November 1936, Vol. 1, Ibid, p. 101.

171. Unlike Nazi propaganda which produced the masterpiece *Triumph des Willens* commissioned by Adolf Hitler who had also chosen its title, and featuring him (Welch, *Propaganda and the German Cinema,* p.147) the 'Fourth of August' propaganda did not produce any newsreel featuring Metaxas alone.

172. *Deftera Diaskepsis*, p. 280. Many shots projected the government's work which could be a factory site, a welfare institution or a reforestation campaign. However, his most precious achievements were meant to be the formation of *EON*, the unity and love of the people, and the strengthening of the monarchy. These issues which were the major preconditions for the fulfilment of his expectations were extensively projected through the films. Furthermore, phrases which were included in Metaxas speeches, or formed the central issues of his policies were projected through the cinema. For instance phrases like *Ysichia-Taxis Ke Asfaleia* (Peace-Order-Security or *Patris-Thriskeia-Ecogenia* (Country-Religion-Family) would often fill the screen , forming part of the film.

173. Leni Riefenstahl's film-documentary released in 1935 became a masterpiece of Nazi propaganda which projected the theme of *Fuhrerprinzip*. On the subject see Welch, *Propaganda, and the German Cinema,* pp. 135-159.

174. *Apologismos,* p. 213. The *YTT* commissioned films which dealt with the natural beauties of Greece and facilitated foreign film companies like *TEM* and *Metro-Goldwyn-Mayer* to shoot films of a tourist propagandistic nature. Ibid., p. 234. These films were attended by his Majesty the King, Ioannis Metaxas and members of the cabinet during special performances, before they were forwarded to other countries. *Ta Paraskinia*, July 1938, p.3.

175. In 1934 Goebbels issued an order via the Reich Film Chamber demanding that all cameramen working in the *Reich* had to be members of this institution if they wanted to receive a work permit. Hoffmann, *The Triumph*, p. 197.

176. *FEK* 474, 23 November 1937, p. 3050.

177. Hoffmann, *The Triumph*, p. 193. The potential that the newsreels offered enjoyed a world-wide recognition. A study commissioned by UNESCO about newsreels from all over the world came to the conclusion that the effect the newsreels had on the audience derived from the fact that the viewer 'has to concentrate so much on the fast sequence of pictures that any response that goes beyond simple reception is forced into the subconscious. Even if the viewer is critically disposed, he has no opportunity to check or compare the information that is offered to him.' Quoted in Hoffmann, *The Triumph*, Ibid.

178. *Apologismos,* p. 148.

179. Among those were Joseph Hepp, Dimitris Maravides, Meletopoulos and Gaziades, all very competent and professional cameramen. *Ellinikos Kinimatografos,* pp. 74-75. See also *Ta Paraskinia,* 23 July 1938, p. 3.

180. The remains transported to Greece on 17 November 1936, three months after Metaxas came to power, were those of King Constantine, who died in exile in Italy as well as the remains of his mother Queen Olga, and his wife, Queen Sophia. The ceremony, which lasted six days and cost the extravagant sum of 2,405,765 drachmas, became the subject of considerable exploitation by Metaxas' regime propaganda. *Apologismos*, p. 10. This newsreel was part of the regime's effort to restore the monarchy in the hearts of the people and maintain the King's support. Many newsreels dealing with Royal issues such as the ' The Unveiling of the Equestrian Statue of King Constantine', in October 1938, 'The marriage of Crown Prince Paul and Princess Frederica', in January 1938 and many others of a similar nature, were produced and widely projected by

the regime's film propaganda to reiterate and emphasise the intrinsic link between Metaxas' regime and the monarchy.

181. *Novak Film* had been established in 1921 but it was mainly engaged in the production of advertising shots which resembled the slides of today and continued with the production of small silent newsreels until 1935 when it produced the first sound newsreel dealing with the *Return of King George the Second*. The success of this newsreel encouraged Novak to continue producing a compilation film every fifteen days including the most important events of Metaxas' regime. *E Ellas tou 1938 Omilei* represents the most significant work of film compilation during that period. *Ellinikos Kinimatografos*, p. 72.

182. Ibid.

183. According to Hoffmann, 'The compilation film, with its artificial structure and its violations of aesthetic rules, ignores traditional genre boundaries. The dramaturgy of this parasite genre combines materials that have already been used in other movies that are then put into a thematic and stylistic context different from the original one.' Hoffmann, *The Triumph*, p. 161.

184. Hans Weidemann, the Vice President of the Reich Film Chamber, stated in July 1935: 'The Newsreel shall no longer be a more-or-less interesting and randomly compiled hodge-podge of pictures from all over the world; rather it is to be shaped into an artistic whole that is self-contained. Its optic effect shall be cultural and propagandistic education and construction without the viewer realising it. We intend to use, by means of a newsreel that is artistically rounded, the possibility of spreading state-political, ideological propaganda and popular education.' Quoted in Hoffmann, *The Triumph*, p. 192.

185. *Ta Paraskinia*, 23 July 1938, p. 3.

186. Ibid., 23 July 1938 and 6 August 1938.

187. Ibid.

188. Ibid. The occasion was marked by reports referring to the future joint-venture between the Film Chamber of the Third Reich Ministry of Propaganda and the *EON* management to produce a propaganda film of long length which would be exemplary of its kind. Ibid. No further information exists on the materialisation of such an undertaking.

189. As cited, enthusiasm, along with devotion, faith and joy were the driving forces behind the 'regeneration of Greece' and as such they should be expressed warmly at every popular manifestation. When Metaxas addressed the organising Committee of the second anniversary of 'Fourth of August' he stated: 'I am grateful because you took the heavy burden and responsibility of organising this celebration, and you were able to transform it into a grand demonstration of the people's enthusiasm.' *Logoi ke Skepseis*, Vol.1, p. 408.

190. Ibid., Vol. 1, p. 108.

191. Ibid., p. 254.

192. Goebbels once remarked that if film propaganda was to be successful 'it must make use of painting in black and white since otherwise it cannot be convincing to people.' Welch, *Propaganda and the German Cinema*, , p.254.

193. Hoffmann, *The Triumph*, p.149.

194. Unlike in most of the Nazis newsreels where the camera is directed towards physical beauty and human perfection excluding all phenomena 'that appeared as ugly' (Hoffmann, ibid, p.158) Metaxas' propaganda films often depicted images that were far from models of beauty: old men and women, plain workers and peasants or poor and deprived children. Yet, all these images constituted an intrinsic part of the whole population and were presented in a state of euphoria. This poor physical appearance of the people depicted by the camera served a twofold purpose; it was designed to emphasise the exceptional human qualities of a *Chief* who embraced all members of Greek society, especially the deprived ones, and at the same time convince the audience that such images were going to change under the fatherly concern and welfare of the new regime.
The quest for unity led Metaxas to a number of policies including the promotion of an 'apolitical image.' His effort to unite the nation under his regime was reflected in his social theories and policies. His favourite concept that of *astikon kathestos* (bourgeois

establishment), or *astiki taxis* (bourgeois class) acquired a particular context to serve the guiding cause of national unity. The *astiki taxis* was not determined by the socio-economic position of its members, but by the zest of their nationalism and their loyalty to tradition. Sarantis Constantinos, 'Metaxas Ideology', in Higham & Veremis, (eds.) *Aspects of Greece*, pp. 152-153.

195. Metaxas' speech, 13 June 1937. *Logoi ke Skepseis*, Vol. 1, p. 192.

196. Crete was the birthplace of Eleftherios Venizelos, and the Cretans were known for their loyalty towards him. Two months after Metaxas came to power he visited Crete for the first time, on a goodwill tour, fulfilling as he claimed: 'an old and vital dream,' but in reality hoping to heal the political wounds of the past and gain the Cretans' support and sympathy. ' I have now come to visit you as an Angel of Peace and as a Messenger of National Unity' he stated in his speech in Chania in November 1936. Ibid., Vol. 1, p.100.

197. Metaxas' speech to the representatives of the Agricultural Co-operatives, 7 January 1941, *Logoi ke Skepseis*, Vol. 2, p. 397.
    The peasant was also highly esteemed in Nazi Germany, and was undoubtedly the cultural hero of the National Socialist Movement. The German Minister of Agriculture, underlining the qualities of the peasantry stated: 'First there was the German peasantry in Germany, before what is today served up as German history(..) One can say that the blood of the people digs its roots deep into the homeland earth through its peasant land holdings, from which it continuously receives that life-endowing strength which constitutes its special character.' Quoted in Welch, *Propaganda and the German Cinema,* p.102.

198. Metaxas' speech, 10 January 1937. *Logoi ke Skepseis*, Vol. 1, p. 152.

199. Metaxas envisaged a scheme which would eventually organise all the productive classes into co-operatives that would enable the formation of a 'Corporatist State' which harmonised perfectly with Metaxas' convictions on social and national solidarity as well as his rejection of individualism and class 'struggle.' Despite the government's initial enthusiasm the plan was soon abandoned. Sarantis, *The Emergency,* pp. 422,423.

200. *E Neolea*, issue 11, 16 December 1939, p. 330.

201. Krachauer, Siegfried, *From Caligari to Hitler,A Psychological History of the German Film* (Princeton University Press, 1974) p.279.

202. The woman's mission in the Nazi society was summed up by Goebbels in 1929: 'The mission of women is to be beautiful and to bring children into the world' Quoted in Welch, *The Third Reich*, p.66. Although Metaxas believed that the main task of women was to bring children into the world and undertake their 'healthy' and 'national' upbringing he also claimed that women could play a crucial role in reshaping Greek society through hard work and active participation. This belief was best exemplified in the active participation of girls in *EON*. On the subject see Metaxas' speeches to the Workers, 21 February 1940; p.263; to *EON*, 7 November 1939, p.182; to the Working girls, 24 October 1939, p. 164 and to the Parents and Teachers, p. 174. *Logoi ke Skepseis*, Vol. 2.

203. He stated on 6 December 1937, 'Only if we treat our women with dignity and respect and give them their dominant place in the family, can we claim to be good family men and civilised people.' Ibid., Vol, p. 306.

204. Metaxas' speech to the University Students, 10 October 1936. Ibid., p .65.

205. Metaxas' speech, 24 October 1939. Ibid., Vol. 2, p. 164. For more about women's role within the 'Fourth of August' State see Chapter Four.

206. The information and the film was supplied by the Director of the *Teniothiki Tis Ellados* (Greek Film Institute), Mr. Adamopoulos. Although this newsreel is the first complete colour production of the time, and a fine example of film making, there exists a small sample of colour sequences shot by Maria Bonaparte, the French wife of Prince George. She used a 16mm colour film and given the time and the place (the Greek film industry lacked the technical means to process colour film), she had produced a fine example of colour film making which includes short sequences of *EON* parades. The Maria Bonaparte film was part of the compilation film *Imeres Tis Tetartis Augoustou* (Days of the 'Fourth of August' Dictatorship).

207. Metaxas' speech to *EON* , Kalamata, 24 April 1939. *Logoi ke Skepseis*, Vol. 2, p. 65.

208. Metaxas' speeches in *Xanthi*, 4 March,1938; in Amigdaleo*n*, 5 March 1938; in Drama, 7 March 1938. *Logoi ke Skepseis*, Vol. 2, pp. 328-338-339 respectively. On 9 September 1939 a special order was issued to all the authorities stating that all the Greek people, especially the agrarian population should proceed with the intensive cultivation of all available land to ensure the country's self-sufficiency. The same order was forwarded to all *EON* members who were entrusted with the task of ensuring that no space in school, church, or at home was left uncultivated. Ibid., pp. 139-140. On 13 November 1939 Metaxas noted in his diary: 'If this war goes on for many years all the nations involved will suffer famine. Thus, the only way out for us is autarky.' From ' To Tetradio Ton Skepseon' in *Ioannis Metaxas, To Prosopiko tou Imerologio*, Vol., 7, p. 406.

209. Pudovkin's film, *The End of St.Petesburg*, 1927, was an epic embodied in the life story of an anonymous hero Lad, while in Nikolai Ekkan's film *Road to Life,* 1930, the hero Batalov 'was the social hero: crystal pure, utterly unselfish: a merry man of action.' Zorkaya, *The Illustrated History of Soviet Cinema,* pp. 79-113.

210. Hoffmann, *The Triumph,* p. 142.

211. National defence came first in the list of priorities of the Metaxas regime and it was intrinsically linked with Greek Industry. See his speech, 2 October 1936. *Logoi ke Skepseis*, Vol, p. 50. In March 1937 a newsreel *Ta Egenia tou Obidopieo*u (The Inauguration of the Bombshell Industry) demonstrated this relation and the importance which Metaxas put on building up the defence of the country. The inauguration was a grand celebration attended by the King , the Crown Prince, Metaxas with members of the Government, the Head of the Church and the Supreme Command of the armed forces.

212. Sitsa Karaiskaki 'Enas Laos, Mia Psyhe, Mia Giorte-Ikones Pou Miloun,' *E Neolea*, issue 44, 12 August 1939, p. 1422.

213. Quoted in Hoffmann, *The Triumoh,* p. 193.

214. A tobacco factory. The Greek economy of the time depended heavily on the tobacco exports.

215. This speech is significant because it explicitly demonstrated the regime's policy towards the working class. It also constituted a direct message to the people who were opposing his policy and ideology, and an attack on communism. Metaxas wrote in his diary the same day. 'Celebration in Piraeus; Workers' mass rally; my Speech; great enthusiasm.' *Ioannis Metaxas, To Prosopiko tou Imerologio*, Vol. 7, p. 302.

216. Metaxas' speech to the Workers, 1 May 1938. *Logoi ke Skepseis* , Vol. 1, pp. 354-355.

217. Metaxas' speech in Atalanti,22 August 1938 and Vitina, 16 May 1938. Ibid., p.369.

218. 'No oak tree grows without soil, root, and strength. No man comes out of the unsubstantial. The people are his soil, history his root, blood his strength. Race is the matrix of all creative forces. Reality is only the Volk.(…)'Trees -that is, in their totality a forest. peoples-that is in their totality humanity' A quotation from Goebbels' novel *Michael.* Quoted in Welch, *Propaganda and the German Cinema,* p.104.

219. Welch, Ibid., p.101. This mystical bond between man and earth was projected through the film *Blut und Boden.* Ibid.

220. *Tessera Chronia,* Vol. 4, p. 21. The reforestation campaign was headed by Metaxas and the King, while 3 December was named *E Imera Tou Dasous* (The Day of the Forest). Millions of trees were planted in the regime's effort to improve the Greek natural environment and boost the economy. Ibid., and Metaxas' speech, in Larisa, 5 December 1937. *Logoi ke Skepseis,* Vol. 1, p. 298. The 'Reforestation Campaign' involved great expenditure and the mobilisation of many people, notably civil servants. Agelos Vlahos, a young diplomat at the time, remembers: 'My salary came to 1,700. drcs per month. The first salary was retained 'for the airforce' and the second 'for the green.' Vlachos, Agelos, *Mia Fora Ke Ena Kero Enas Diplomates, (*Estia, Athens, 1985) Vol. 1, p. 23. The reforestation campaign and the restriction of pasturage of goats in mountain forests and grassland caused grievance among the peasants who depended on goats as livestock. .Stevens, M. J., *British Reports on Greece 1943-44.* Baerentzen, Lars, (ed.) (Museum Tusculanum Press, Copenhagen, 1982) p. 28.

221. 1,731,560 trees were planted by *EON* and 17,278 stremmata of waste land were cultivated. *E Neolea*, issue 45, 10 August 1940, p. 1397.

222. Metaxas' speech, 16 February 1939. *Logoi ke Skepseis,* Vol 2, p. 25.

223. An article '*EON* ke to Dentro' underlined the important link between the trees and *Hellenism* and claimed that the decline of ancient Greek civilisation was related to the catastrophe of the forests. *E Neolea*, issue 9, 2 December 1939, p. 257.

224. *Ta Tragoudia,* p. 7.

225. Sarantis, *The Emergency,* p. 438.

226. In 'EON ke to Dentro" special emphasis was given to the significance of the reforestation of the Greek mountains and infertile land with wood and fruit-bearing trees. This effort would ensure autarky and economic gains. *E Neolea,* issue 9, 2 December 1939, p. 257.

227. *To Neon Kratos*, issue 28, 30 December 1939, p. 234. Similarly, Kanellopoulos in his speech to the Students, stated: 'We are intrinsically linked to our earth and are inspired by the Greek spirit. This earth and this Greek spirit, which were the only sources for the creation of all civilisations, will form the base for the creation of the greatest civilisation; the Third Civilisation.' Quoted in Machera *E Neolea*, p. 164.

     In his speech on launching the second reforestation campaign on 3 December 1939 Metaxas traced the history of the Greek peasant back to the ancient times when the mountains were inhabited by the Gods, the nymphs and the fairies and the peasants worshipped the mountains and the Gods and lived in total harmony with the elements of nature and earth. *Logoi ke Skepseis*, Vol. 2, p. 215.

228. Although we have no information on the exact date that this newsreel was produced, the presence of the boy scouts suggests that this reforestation must have taken place at the end of 1938 or the beginning of 1939, given the fact that the boy scouts were incorporated into the *EON* in the summer 1939.

229. The trees planted by Metaxas, the King and the other members of the Royal Court were named after them.

230. Eisenstein observed that ' The essence of a film must not be sought in individual sequences, but in their interactions(…). The expressive impact of a film is the result of combinations.' Quoted in Hoffmann, *The Triumph*, p. 164.

231. *E Neolea*, issue 10, 9 December 1939, p.292.

232. Metaxas, unlike Mussolini and Hitler, avoided saluting in the Fascist manner but always raised his hat or waved to the people. There is, however, a photograph which depicts Metaxas saluting in the fascist manner during the celebration of the First of May 1939. *E Neolea,* issue 30, 6 May 1939. See Still 13.

233. The only natural disaster projected by the regime's propaganda was in a very small newsreel with the title *Sismos Ston Oropo* (Earthquake in Oropos) shot in July 1938 by Gaziadis, Novak, Hepp and Drimaropoulos and which presented the catastrophic earthquake in Oropos. *Ta Paraskinia*, 23 July, 1938, p.3. Although many people were left homeless and injured, the film emphasised more the regime's care and provision for the people than the actual event. The earthquake received a detailed coverage by the daily press where again the effective measures taken by Metaxas' regime were extensively emphasised. *Kathimerini*, 20 July 1938

234. Vatikiotis, *Popular Autocracy,* p.189.

CHAPTER 4

1. Skoumbourdi, Artemis, *Theatra Tis Paleas Athinas.* (Demos Atheneon, Pneumatiko Kentro) (no date) p.77. Apart from European dramas, comedies and *Pantomime* the theatrical activities included the *Comeidyllion (*comic love stories*) (Dramatikon Idyllion* (Dramatic Idyll) the archaic tragedy and the *Epitheorisis* (Revue) the most popular theatrical form until the establishment of the 'Fourth of August' regime. For the history of the Modern Greek Theatre see, Sideris, Yiannis, *The Modern Greek Theatre, A Concise History, (*Hellenic Centre of the International Theatre Institute, Dirfos, Athens, 1957) and Sideris, Yannis, *Istoria tou Neou Ellinikou Theatrou 1784-1944*, Vol.1. (Kastaniotis, Athens, 1990).

2. *The Nea Skeni* (New Stage) and the *Vasilikon Theatro* (Royal Theatre) were the first theatrical groups established in 1901. These two companies set the example and regulated the theatrical life in the whole of Greece for a long time. Sideris, *The Modern Greek Theatre*, pp. 24-28 .

3. Both actresses contributed greatly to the development and flourishing of the Modern Greek Theatre. According to Sideris it was 'only because of the limitations of the period during which they reached their pinnacle that they did not become world famous personalities. Ibid.,p.46

4. The Greek theatrical life in Smyrni and in Constantinopoli was very advanced at the time and included drama schools and young theatrical groups. Ibid., p. 40.

5. The school was established in 1924 and supplied the Modern Greek Theatre with very talented actors. The next school was *The New Dramatic School* established in 1933. Sideris, *The Modern Greek Theatre*, pp. 43-52.

6. Although the popularity of the cinema was increasing, the theatre remained a significant means of entertainment. The Athenians of the early thirties had the opportunity to see all kinds of theatrical plays, such as prose, comedy, revue and drama in the regular and open air theatres. In 1931 there were more than ten open theatres operating in Athens alone. Kerofylas,Yiannis, *E Athina Tou Mesopolemou*, (Filippotis, Athens, 1988) p. 204.

7. Sideris*, The Modern Greek Theatre*, p. 44. This new effort was initiated by three talented theatrical people; Cotopouli, Kyveli and Myrat, who in 1929 established the *Eleftheri Skini* (Free Stage). Ibid., p. 43

8. The theatre critics of the time attacked the contents of the contemporary revue, especially its foul language and vulgarity. 'Athinaiki Epitheorisis' (Athenian Revue*), Kathimerini*, Seven Days, 5 April, 1998, p. 14. However, Hatzipanagis & Maraka claim in their study on the Athenian revue that 'the Athenian revue formed a powerful instrument of propaganda which disseminated the dominant contemporary ideology and shaped values that appealed to the broader masses to a degree that no other theatrical genre could ever accomplish. In fact, it fulfilled needs that only the cinema, gramophone, radio and television (in our days) satisfy.' Hatzipanagis, Theodore, and Maraka, Lila, (eds.) in 'E Thesis tis Epitheorisis sti Neoelliniki Politistiki Exelixi,' *E Athinaiki Epitheorisis,* (Nea Elliniki Vivliothiki, Athens,1977) Vol. 1, p. 215.

9. 'Athinaiki Epitheorisis,' *Kathimerini - Epta Imeres,* 5 April 1998, p. 14.

10. Kerofylas*, E Athina,* p. 232.

11. Metaxas' s interview with Costis Bastias in *Vradini* and *Kathimerini* newspapers on 15, 16 September 1936. On the same issue see also Haris, Petros, 'The Determined Advocate of Demotic', *Nea Estia*, issue 340, February 1941, p.146.

12. The first censorship concerning theatrical performances was imposed in 1895 by the Chief of the Athens Police, Bairaktaris. Skoumbourdi, *Theatra,* p.55.

13. *FEK,* 23, 25 January 1937, p.140.

14. Ibid., p.141.

15. Emergency Law 782/1937, *FEK* 224, 3 June 1939, p. 1481.

16. This representative was appointed by Ministerial Order.

17. His personal library, which he bequeathed to *EON*, contains the works of many great playwrights. During his exile in Corsica, Sardinia and mainland Italy, Metaxas read the works of the Greek philosophers, Greek drama and European classics. Vatikiotis, *Popular Autocracy,* p.204. See also entries in his diary that refer to his love for the theatre and the reading of theatrical plays. *Ioannis Metaxas,* To Prosopiko tou Imerologio, Vol. 4, pp. 499,539,545,581,585,587, 625 and Vol. 5, pp. 451,469,581.

18. Metaxas' speech, 2 October 1936. *Logoi ke Skepseis,* Vol. I, p. 50.

19. *To Elliniko Theatro* (the Greek Theatre), a newspaper issued by the Union of Actors in 1925, in a laborious issue of September 1938, praised the regime's beneficial role in elevating the theatre and its front page was covered by large photos of what the paper referred to as the 'pillars of the Greek Theatre.' These pillars were: C. Kotzias, Governor of Athens, A. Dimitratos, Minister of Labour, A. Plitas, Major of Athens and C. Bastias, Director of Letters. and Art. *Ta Paraskinia* published on the front page

a relevant article with the title 'Constantinos Kotzias - A Patron of Art.' The article referred, vaguely, to a dinner party given in Athens by Kotzias for Dr.Goebbels and his wife, and the presence of Anna Tassopoulou, the distinguished opera Singer (soprano) of the *Greek Odeum* who was specially invited to sing for Dr. Goebbels and his wife. According to the article such was the delight of Dr. Goebbels at Mrs Tassopoulou's singing, that he invited her to Germany to sing at the Berlin Opera House where she made a great career. The propagandistic article was intended to underline the inherent artistic talent of Kotzias, which matched that of Dr Goebbels, and to demonstrate the close relationship of the two men. *Ta Paraskinia,* 2 July 1938. As the date of the event was not stated in the article, it is presumed that it referred to Goebbels' visit to Greece, few weeks after Metaxas' seizure of power. His second visit took place in April 1939, when he was received by Metaxas (Still 14). *Ioannis Metaxas, To Prosopiko tou Imerologio,* Vol .7, p. 362. Kotzias was a strong advocate of Nazi Germany and Dr. Goebbels.

In Metaxas' Private Papers there are a number of confidential despatches from the Greek Embassy in Berlin dated March 1939 which refer to Kotzias' visit to Germany after an official invitation, and his meetings with Dr. Goebbels and other High Officials. According to the correspondence, Kotzias' discussions with Dr. Goebbels exceeded the limits of routine matters and involved issues connected with Greece's foreign policy. This was strongly resented by Metaxas who feared that Kotzias' initiative could jeopardise the harmonious relations that Greece enjoyed with the other great powers, especially those with Britain which Metaxas was at that time trying to strengthen. Metaxas advised Kotzias 'to pay his compliments to Dr. Goebbels and the German Government, but in no circumstances was he allowed to discuss matters concerning foreign policy.' Genika Archeia Tou Kratous, Archeio Ioannou Metaxas, File. 30.

20. Metaxas' speech, 14 May 1938. *Logoi ke Skepseis,* Vol. 1, p.363.
21. King George I, a lover of the theatre and every artistic expression, financed and supervised the construction of the splendid building on St. Constantine Street in Athens. Sideris. *The Modern Greek Theatre,* p.26. According to other sources the money for purchasing the land and the construction of the building came from the Greeks of the *Diaspora* (Greeks living in foreign lands). Skoubourdi, *Theatra,* p.85. During Venizelos's government, the theatre was re-established (Law 4615/1930) as the National Theatre and was restored and reopened in 1932. With the restoration of monarchy in 1935 the theatre was renamed Royal Theatre. Its contribution to the development of Greek Modern Theatre was, and has remained, vital.
22. Metaxas' interview in *Vradini* and *Katrhimerini,* 15-16 September 1936.
23. The first provision for the Royal Theatre was taken on 30 April 1930 and 28 April 1931, through the enactment of decrees which introduced subsidies and dues for the National Theatre. *FEK* 468, 14 December 1938, pp. 3059-3060.
24. Half a drachma might seem an insignificant amount but if one considers that in 1937 there were approximately 150,000 people attending the Athenian cinemas (not to mention the regional ones) every week, one can appreciate the large amount of money raised from the cinema for the benefit of the Royal Theatre.
25. The play was directed by *Rontiris* and the role of *Electra* was played by *Katina Paxinou.* Bastias, Costis 'Ta Grammata ke Oi Technes' (Letters and High Art) *To Neon Kratos,* issue 24, August 1939 p.553. Ancient drama had been performed in the past in the Herodeum Odeum but with no particular success. Sideris, *The Modern Greek Theatre,* p. 49.
26. Metaxas in his interview to Bastias in September 1936, greatly praised the initiative of the Royal Theatre to establish the 'Ancient Drama Week' and stated that the Royal Theatre would be greatly rewarded for this effort. Haris , 'The Determined', p.146.
27. The Royal Theatre of Thessaloniki began its performances on 2 July 1940 and Metaxas, who was unable to attend, issued a statement which contains the essence of his ideology of the 'regeneration of Greece'. *Diloseis Epi ti Enarxei Ton Parastaseon tou Vasilikou Theatrou Eis Thesalonikin, 2 July 1940. Logoi ke Skepseis,* Vol. 2, p. 321.
28. Unfortunately the innovation included the demolition of one the most beautiful and historically significant theatres in Greece, and according to Baron *Rothschild* 'the best

in Europe,' the Athens Municipal Theatre (*To Dimotikon Theatro*). Because the theatre had suffered extensive damages as it had housed 150 refugees families for three years, Kotzias planned to built a better one in its place. Unfortunately, this never materialised and its vacated space became a square named '*Plateia Kotzia* (The Kotzia Square). Skoubourdi, *Theatra,* pp , 49-52.

29. From 1931 onwards, the Athenian revue introduced the issue of homosexuality, and political personalities often became the subject of satire and mockery. Hanzipanages and Maraka (eds.) 'E Thesis Tis Epitheorisis' in *Athinaiki Epitheorisi*, p. 128.

30. Ta *Paraskinia*, 16 July 1938, p. 5.

31. Ibid.

32. Metaxas' speech, 14 May 1938. *Logoi ke Skepseis*, Vol. I, p. 363. Possibly Metaxas envisaged this construction as a lasting memorial to his artistic inclinations. Unfortunately this, like many other ambitious schemes, never materialised.
Constructing grandiose buildings that would become living testimonies for the generations to come was a common practice found in many contemporary dictators, notably Hitler, who with the help of his charismatic architect Albert Speer created majestic buildings like the Third Reich's Chancellery. Speer, Albert, *Inside the Third Reich* (Phoenix, London, 1995) pp.159-195. Metaxas had neither the means and nor it seems the will for such an undertaking. Besides, as he had repeatedly claimed, his everlasting achievement was the formation and 'well being' of the National Organisation of Youth.

33. Ibid.

34. *Athinaika Nea*, 28 February and 19 June 1938, op. cit., also *Ta Paraskinia*, 15 April 1938 and 11 June 1938.

35. *FEK* 5, 4 January 1939, p.19.

36. Marika Cotopouli was an actress of great talent and versatility. Her whole life was a maelstrom of activity, 'a bright light which burned steadily and absolutely for the Modern Greek Theatre.' Sideris, *Istoria*, p. 27. She staged 128 plays (with many of which she toured abroad including America), all great successes, and taught many famous Greek actors the art of acting. Her contribution was acknowledged by the Greek state and she was decorated for her talent and theatrical activity. Metsolis, Georgios, *To Theatro Stin Athina 1936-1967* (New Greek Encyclopaedia, Athens 1968) p. 687.

37. Cotopouli's first theatre was built in 1912 in the place of the *New Skini* (New Stage*)* and it was destroyed by a pro-Venizelist audience in 1920 .Skoumbourdi, *Theatra*, p.78. Her next theatre was demolished in 1936 and the cinema-hall Kronos took its place. Ibid., p. 71.

38. Archeio Ioannou Metaxas, Genika Arceia tou Kratous, File 44/001

39. *Thespis* was an ancient dramatist who introduced theatre touring companies 2,500 years ago. *Ta Paraskinia*, 3 December 1938

40. During Metaxas' dictatorship there was a considerable number of cultural magazines dealing with the theatre. The most significant ones were: the magazine *Theatro* (Theatro) 1938, *Elliniko Theatro* (Greek Theatre) 1920-1936, *Paraskinio* (fortnightly) magazine 1937-1938-1939, *Techne* (Arts) 1938, and *Nea Estia* 1927, until this date. Unfortunately most of the output of the theatrical press has been destroyed and only few issues have survived.

41. *Ta Paraskinia*, 10 December 1938, p.5. The first performance of the *Arma Thespidos* opened with Shakespeare's '*Othello*' in Corinth in September 1939 and Metaxas attended the performance. Ibid., 23 September 1939, p.5.

42. *Ta Paraskinia*, 31 December 1938, p.7. Pelos Katselis, a gifted director, play wright and teacher, was the Director of the *Arma Thespidos*.

43. Ta *Paraskinia,* 7 January 1939, p. 4.
Noakes & Prindham claim in the study of Nazism that 'The Nazis attempted to create a 'people's culture' with new artistic forms designed to express their cultural transformation. They established the 'Thing-Theatre' 'a cross between a pageant and a cult spectacle, held in romantically-situated and specially designed open air theatres

and intended to express the 'national community.' Noakes & Prindham, (eds.), *Nazism*,
p. 409. On the subject of German Popular Culture and its significance see also Reavau,
A., 'To Ergon Tou Laikou Diafotismou Es Tin Germanian, ' *To Neon Kratos*, p. 653.

44. It must be stressed, however, that although theatre was used by the regime as means of
propaganda, it was elevated to a high form of art and did indeed contribute (especially
the Arma Thesppidos) to the cultural enlightenment of the masses under the direction
of gifted persons. The Metaxas' regime actions and effort towards this cause cannot
be underestimated.

45. *E Neolea*, issue 44, 3 August 1940 , p. 1384.

46. Ibid.

47. Metaxas' speech, 6 September 1936. *Logoi ke Skepseis,* Vol.1, pp. 33-34.

48. 'The term *Megali Idea* was first introduced by John Kolettis in the National Assembly in
January 1844 to describe Greece's post-independence irredentist aspirations. Since over
three quarters of Greeks at the time resided outside the realm of the *Hellenic* Kingdom,
it became the conviction and policy of most governments to unite and incorporate all
territories in which the unredeemed Greeks lived. *The Megali Idea,* which was centuries
old and deeply rooted in the Greek's national and religious consciousness, came,
according to Michael Llewellyn Smith in his work *Ionian Vision*, to contain at least three
different strands: The romantic dream of the revival of the Byzantine-Greek Empire:
the aspirations for Greek cultural and economic dominance within the Ottoman
Empire, and thirdly the interpretation of the Idea in terms of the modern nation state
and the incorporation of the Greek *irridenta* in the Greek Kingdom. The realisation of
the *Megali Idea* was achieved during the Balkan Wars 1912-1913 and the World War I
but expired in 1922 after the Asia Minor catastrophe. Llewellyn, Michael, Smith,, *Ioanian
Vision - Greece in Asia Minaor 1919-1922* (Hurst & Company, London 1998) pp. 2-7.

49. 'Education was at the heart of the revival of *Hellenism'* Ibid., p. 24.

50. 'Greek Youth can reinstate the Ideals which were crushed by the calamity caused by
Venizelos.' Article published by Metaxas in *Kathimerini* on 23 January 1935. This article
through which Metaxas offered the youth of Greece a new nation, is the epilogue of a
series of seventy articles exchanged between the two great rivals Metaxas and Venizelos
and published in *Kathimerini* from 11 October 1934 to 23 January 1935. *E Istoria tou
Ethnikou Dichasmou* (Kyromanos, Thessaloniki 1994) pp. 526-526. This historical debate
represented, according to Vatikiotis, an older version of the antagonism between
Republicans and Monarchists and it was the nearest thing then to the televised debates
between politicians today. Vatikiotis*, Popular Autocracy,* pp. 146-148.
Cultural Hellenism, was a widespread movement 'among the literary scholars and
intellectuals of the period from 1880 to 1910 including those among the *Diaspora*
Greeks.' Ibid., p.148. The term *Hellenic Culture* must, however, be distinguished from
the modern term National Heritage, as it was a much wider concept and contained
social, political and national elements.

51. Metaxas' speech , 10 August 1936. *Logoi ke Skepseis*, Vol. 1, p.16 and speech, 2 October
1936 Ibid., pp . 44-51. See also speeches, 4 August 1937, p..219 and 5 June 1938, p. 288,
Ibid., and articles about the New State and the 'regeneration of Greece' by George
Matzufas and Aristos Kabanis in *To Neon Kratos,* issue 11, July 1938, p.751, and issue,
21 May 1939, p. 237, Ibid.

52. Metaxas' reference to prominent Greeks included according to his wording 'prominent
people from all sections of society'.

53. Metaxas' speech, 14 November 1936. *Logoi ke Skepseis*, Vol, p.124. Metaxas often
attacked the elite which he believed was not a social class but the result of a past
'unhealthy' political patronage system which created a network of clientage relations
and ensured them easy wealth and prestige. He believed that a new governing class
should be formed which would contribute to the 'regeneration of Greece.' This
new class the *astiki taxis (*bourgeois class*)* would be determined by the 'zest of their
nationalism and their loyalty to tradition' (which were vital components for the
'regeneration of Greece' and the creation of the 'Third Greek Civilisation') and their

determination to safeguard these supreme ideals. Metaxas' speech, 28 August 1938. *Logoi ke Skepseis*, Vol. 1, p.415. See also Sarantis, *The Emergency*, pp.416-417.

54. Metaxas' speech, 13 June 1937. *Logoi ke Skepseis*, Vol. 1, p.197. See also his speeches, 31 October 1937, Ibid., p. 253 and 20 November 1937, p.285, Ibid..

55. Nicoloudis, Theologos, 'To Neon Kratos' *To Neon Kratos*, issue 1, September 1937, p.1.

56. *Athinaika Nea*, 26 April 1937. See also *O Eortasmos tis Ekatontaetiridos 1837-1937, Ehnikon ke Kapodistrion Panepistimion Athinon* (Athens, April 1937).

57. The celebration was approved by a legislative decree enacted on 30 July 1936. This decree was supplemented by Emergency Law 180/1936 and the manifesto issued by the Celebration Committee on 27 October 1936, as well as by a new Emergency Law of 12 January 1937. *O Eortasmos,* pp.17-20.

58. Metaxas' speech on 22 April 1936. 'E Ekatontaetiris Tou Ethnikou Ke Kapodistriou Panepistimio*u.' Menieon Deltion,* issue 8, April, 1937, p. 619.

59. 'E Ekatontaetiris' pp.595-630. The performance was organised by the *Lykion Ellenidon* (Lyceum of Greek Women) and N.Giokarinis under the strict supervision of the Minister of Education Georgopoulos. *O Eortasmos,* p. 20.

60. The invocation, was written in sixty two verses by Antonios Keramopoulos. 'E Ekatontaeteris,' pp. 612-614.

61. Ibid., pp. 612-516.

62. *Typos*, 22 March 1937.

63. *O Eortasmos,*, pp. 212-231.

64. The songs praised qualities like courage dignity, gallantry and fearlessness (*Leventia*). These qualities, according to Metaxas were to be found in the pure and proud personalities of the simple working people; the same people who would work hard and achieve the nation's regeneration.

65. Siatopoulos, Dim., 'To Kastro Tis Orias' *E Neolea,* issue 44, 12 August 1939, p.1433. The following day *Antigone* was also performed in the Herodeum Odeum to honour the foreign men of letters and intellectuals. 'E Ekantotaentiris', p. 618.

66. Since 1933 Germany carried out a policy of economic and commercial exploitation of the Eastern European countries and the Balkans by using her position as a massive buyer of foodstuffs and raw materials. The Balkan states, unable to find other export markets for their luxury commodities, turned to Germany. Schacht developed a technique whereby Germany built up a large trade deficit with these countries which enabled her to acquire economic power and influence over them. *British Documents on German Foreign Policy 1918-1945. Document 383, Athens June 1936.* (Published by Her Majesty's Stationary Office, London 1966). On Germany's Economic Penetration in the Balkan States see: Noakes & .Pridham, (eds.) *Nazism*, p. 275; Higham, R.,'The Metaxas Years in Perspective' in Higham & Veremis, (eds.) *Aspects of Greece,*., pp. 237-238; Sweet-Escott, Bicham, *Greece-A Political and Economic Survey 1939-1953* (Royal Institute of International Affairs, London, 1954) p.17; Papastratis, Prokopis 'Germaniki Diesdysi Ke Symmachiki Endotikothta' in *Epistimoniko Symposio, E Ellada tou '40* (Etaireia Spoudon Neolellinikou Politismou Ke Genikes Pedias, Athens, 1991)

67. This fact, supported by Metaxas' background and military education in pre-war Germany, won him the reputation of being a Germanophile. However, this accusation was strongly rejected by Metaxas himself. At a cabinet meeting on 28 October 1940, when the Italians attacked Greece and Germany's intentions were made clear to him he stated that 'although he was accused of being a Germanophile, something that he might have been in the past, now he felt like a friend who had been betrayed and for this reason he hated the Germans.' Tzifos, Unpublished Diary, pp. 64-65. See also Metaxas' comments 'Apo To Vivlio Ton Skepseon' in *Logoi ke Skepseis*, Vol. 8, pp. 552-554.

68. On the subject see FO 371/21143, 26 May 1937, and Emergency Law 705/1937. On the Electricity Transport Company see, FO 371/21143, 24 July, 1937.

69. During the first years of Metaxas' dictatorship there was a substantial economic recovery. Mineral exports increased, new industries were established, while Greek shipping and tourism earned record profits. New taxes were collected from the wealthy

and the industrialists for the welfare of the country and the war effort ,and public works and ambitious agricultural programmes were carried out. On these subjects see: *Tessera Chronia,* Vol. 3, Vatikiotis, *Popular Autocrac,* p.159, FO 371/21143, 16 January, 6 April 1937 and FO 371/211476, 31 May 1937. For more information on these issues and a detailed analysis of the Greek Economy during the inter-war period see Mazower, Mark, and Veremis, Thanos, 'The Greek Economy' in Higham & Veremis, (eds.) *Aspects. of Greece,* pp.. 111-128..

70. Metaxas at first seemed unwilling to renew the agreement with the British company as he intended to nationalise the industry and continue to operate it with the assistance of foreign specialists. Given Germany's pre-eminence in Greece's foreign trade and economic transactions the British feared the possibility of Metaxas assigning the management of the Blackburn industry to German experts. Koliopoulos, Ioannis, *E Diktatoria Tou Metaxa Ke O Polemos Tou '40* (Vanias, Thessaloniki, 1994) pp. 98-99. There was also the information that the British industry would be overtaken by the Bodosakis industry which was establishing itself as a major armament industry.

71. FO 371/21143 despatches of January 1937. See also despatches of March, April and July 1937, FO 371/21150. It must be stressed at this point that by 1940 Greek foreign policy, although basically neutral, was essentially pro-British and Metaxas stressed this fact very often. Vatikiotis, *Popular Autocracy,* pp..172-173. See also Papadakis,V.P. ' E Exoteriki Politiki Tou Neou Kratous', *To Neon Kratos,* February 1939, pp.1561-1571. On Greco-British economic relations during the Metaxas' regime see Koliopoulos, Ioannis, S., *Palinorthosi-Diktatoria-Polemos 1935-1941* (Estia, Athens, 1985) pp. 110-116.

72. Iatrides, John O., (ed.), *Ambassador MacVeagh Reports: Greece 1933-1947* (Princeton University Press, Princeton,1980) p.134.

73. To underline the significance of this anniversary and stress the relation of the two countries Bernhard Rust, the Minister of Science, Education and Popular Culture of the Third Reich visited Athens and attended the celebration, while it was announced that the *Fuhrer* took the initiative to order the repetition of the archaeological excavation at *Olympia. O Eortasmos,.* p.205. See also FO 371/21150, 26 March 1937. According to Waterlow the cultural activities between Germany and Greece included the visit of Greek schoolboys to Germany: ' I hear that a hundred schoolboys are shortly to be selected from various Greek schools to be sent to Germany for special training. They will be lodged and taught at the expense of the German Government for a period of six months to one year(…) Also the Professor of Theology Louvaris proceeded to Munich as head of 100-150 Greek men of letters, and was presented to Hitler.' FO 371/21150, 30 July 1937

74. As cited, King George II had lived in England for many years and was known as pro-British despite the fact that his father King Constantine was a strong advocate of Germany (he was married to the Kaiser's sister Sofia who was an admirer of Metaxas). Thus Germany's effort to regain the support of the Greek monarchy and gain superiority against the British became an imperative goal.

75. 'Das Land der Griechen mit der Seele suchend' Taken from Goethe's *Iphigeneia in Tauris.* 'Verolino ke Archaiotita'(Berlin and Antiquity) *Kathimerini, Epta Imeres,* 7 March 1999, p.31.

76. *O Eortasmos,* p.205.

77. Zean Zay's visit to the University as well as his presence at the Parnassos Hall initiated intensive opposition among students and other people towards the Metaxas regime. Linardatos, *4e Augoustou,* pp. 256-259.

78. O *Eortasmos,* p. 99.

79. Metaxas' speech, 7 October 1936. *Logoi ke Skepseis,* Vol. 1, p.53.

80. Metaxas' speech in Selinouda, 31 October 1937. Ibid.,Vol. 1, pp.253-254.

81. Within the regime's policy of promoting good foreign art for the benefit of the people, the English Theatre 'Old Vic' visited Greece in March 1939 and staged very successful performances of the Shakespearean plays. *Ta Paraskinia ,* 25 March 1939,, p.2.

82. Metaxas' speech 30 December 1938. *Logoi ke Skepseis,* Vol. 1, pp. 440-441.

83. On 13 August 1939 Nicoloudis sent Metaxas a letter proposing the establishment of a

separate Ministry of Culture (headed presumably by Nicoloudis). The letter infuriated
Metaxas who replied immediately to Nicoloudis stating that 'culture was the work
of all people led by an inspired leader whom they trusted and who guided them
personally. Popular indoctrination of the people was, according to Metaxas' reply,
the work of many departments of the state co-ordinated by one person who had
the authority by virtue of his position and personality, and that person was the Chief
(*Archigos*)' Archeio Ioannou Metaxas, Genika Archeia tou Kratous, File 34, and *Ioannis
Metaxas, To Prosopiko tou Imerologio,* Vol. 7, p.382.

84. The enemy was everything or everyone who opposed the values and ideals of the regime
    including the foreign forces which 'undermined' the ' regeneration of Greece.'
    It must be stressed however, that Metaxas' struggle was limited to an ideological and
    cultural war. It had nothing in common with the territorial expansion and ambitions of
    Hitler's conquest for *Lebensraum* and Mussolini's perpetual struggle for Mediterranean
    ('the sea of Rome') hegemony. On Nazi Germany's and Fascist Italy's expansion policy
    see MacGregor Knox, 'Conquest,Foreign and Domestic,, in Fascist Italy and Nazi
    Germany', in Emsley, Clive, Marwick Arthur & Simpson Wendy, (eds.) *War Peace.and
    Social Change,* (Open University Press, Milton Keynes,1994), pp. 158-189.

85. *Nea Estia,* issue 340, February 1941, p. 156.

86. In a speech in Patras on 6 November 1937 Metaxas attacked the elite and accused
    them of the deterioration of Greek society, praising at the same time the masses of
    ordinary people. ' I will not mention', he said, 'the ludicrous faces of the socialising
    elite, the 'gentlemen' and the 'ladies,' the young men and women, who dressed in their
    elegant clothes and wearing expensive jewellery, smoking and drinking champagne,
    upset and damaged Greek society in their effort to present themselves as if they were
    worthy people while the great masses struggled desperately for a place in the Greek
    community.' *Logoi ke Skepseis*, Vol. 1, p. 260.

87. One of the basic techniques employed by effective propaganda was, according to
    Hitler, 'that propaganda should be addressed always and exclusively to the masses.'
    Adolf Hitler, *Mein Kampf* (Pimlico, London , 1969) p.163.

88. 'Theatrike Parastaseis ke Synaulie gia Tous Ergatas' (Theatrical Shows and Concerts for
    the Workers) *Tessera Chronia ,* Vol. 1, pp. 185-194.

89. Ibid., Vol. 3, p.209.

90. Bastias, 'Ta Grammata,' *Neon Kratos ,* p.553.

91. Yannis Sideris 'To Neoelleniko Theatro,' *E Neolea'* issue 42, 29 July 1939, p.1363.

92. *Apologismos.,* p. 212.

93. Just before Metaxas' advent to power, from the fifty plays staged in the Greek theatres,
    only five or six were Greek. *Ta Paraskinia,* 9 July 1938.

94. Metaxas' speech , 22 May, 1940. *Logoi ke Skepseis*, Vol. 2, p.304.

95. *Neon Kratos,* September 1937, issue 1, p.5.

96. Similarly, one of Mussolini's fixed ideas was the goal of a new civilisation or more
    specifically 'a revolution by an elite of primitives to inaugurate a 'new civilisation' of
    joyous paganism.' MacGregor, 'Conquest Foreign and Domesttic', p. 159.

97. *Ta Paraskinia,*10 September 1938, p. 2.

98. Ibid., 11 September 1938, p. 6.

99. Ibid., 10 September 1938, p. 6.

100. Sarantis, *The Emergency,* p.421.

101. *Vradini*, 15 September 1936. See also Karagatzis, M. 'O Protos Dimotikistis
     Prothypourgos' and Haris, Petros, O Apofasistikos Dimotikistis' in *Nea Estia* special
     edition dedicated to Ioannis Metraxas,15 February 1941. Metaxas blamed the elite for
     the deterioration of the Greek language. He claimed that *katharevousa* was subjected
     to such a degree of malformation that it resembled a peasant woman who pretended
     to be a lady, while *demotic* resembled a real lady who pretended to be a peasant woman.
     Nea Estia, issue 340, 1941, p. 145.

102. On 5 December 1938 the government issued a circular which defined the changes
     involved and set a committee by Manolis Triandafillidis to compile a new *Demotic*

Grammar. Triandafillidis, Manolis, *Demotikismos ke Andidrasis*, (Athens, 1957), pp. 61-62. Also Karagatsis, M., 'O Protos Dimotikistis Prothepourgos,' (*Nea Estia*, February 1941), pp. 12-13. See also newspapers of 6 December 1938 with the published circular and *Ioannis Metaxa, To Prosopiko tou Imerologio*, Vol. 8, p. 696.

103. *Ta Paraskinia*, 7 January 1939, front page. See also Rumanis, G. I., 'En Ethnos-En Kratos-Mia Glossa', *Nea Politiki*, issue 3, March 1940, p.191.

104. *Nea Estia*, issue 278, 1 May 1938, p. 628.

105. Agelomatis, Chr., 'Ai Theatrikai Parastaseis Tou Etous-Scholeia, Kritiki-Sygrafeis.' *To Neon Kratos*, September 1938, p.75

106. A verse from the *EON* anthem. This verse, which was used as a national motto, was often quoted by Metaxas when he spoke to *EON* members and wished to underline their 'sacred' mission which was the 'regeneration of Greece.' Metaxas' speech to *EON* , 29 December 1938, *Logoi ke Skepseis*, Vol. 1, p. 437. See also his speech to *EON*, 24 April, 1939 p. 65 and 7 November 1939, p.182. Ibid.

107. Metaxas' speech, 10 August 1936. Ibid.,Vol.1, p.16 .

108. Kribas, Elias, 'Ta Kathikonta ke Idanika Tis Neoleas.' Speech delivered at Parnassos Hall on 22 December 1939 at the presence of Metaxas. *To Neon Kratos*, issue 28, 30 December 1939, p. 227.

109. *Apospasmata.*, pp. 56-57.

110. *Organismos Esoterikis*, p.29. This Directive supervised the new theatrical plays written by the *EON* members, which were to be performed during the national holidays of *25 March,* and the 'Fourth of August' anniversary. It also organised a small theatrical group which toured the remote *EON* divisions and performed educational and enlightening plays. *E Neolea*, issue 20, 25 February 1939, p. 676. Regular performances were given by this theatrical group at the *Ioannis Metaxa*s Youth Camp. Ibid., 26 August 1939, p.1509

111. *Falagitiki,* p. 179.

112. Ibid., p. 178.

113. Ibid., pp. 181-182.

114. The responsibility for the organisation and establishment of theatrical schools and the teaching of (theatrical) plays was assigned to the D' Section of the III Office. *Apospasmata,* p. 102.

115. The committee for the competition consisted of Costis Bastias, Pantelis Chorn, theatrical writer, Sotirios Skipis, a poet, St. Kanonidis, a journalist, Takis Mouzenidis, stage director of the Royal Theatre, Melis Nikolaidis and Ioannis Kapsalis, *E Neolea*, issue 45, 19 August 1939, p.1476.

116. Ibid., pp. 56-57-149

117. *E Neolea*, issue 8, 25 November 1939, p. 227.

118. Ibid.

119. Ibid., p. 228 , and Karaiskaki, Sitsa, 'Elliniki Techni-Elliniki Phyli, *E Neolea*, issue 15, 13 January 1940, p.450

120. *Peri Technis* (Ekdoseis *EON* , 1940) pp. 5-15.

121. Ibid., p. 17.

122. Ibid., pp.17-18.

123. *E Neolea*, issue 43, 4 August 1939, p. 1415.

124. *Tessera Chronia* , Vol. 2, p.180.

125. Ibid., p. 1399. The first *EON* theatre was established on 23 December 1938 with the help of the talented actress and theatrical impresario Katerina Andreadi. *Tessera Chronia*, Vol.3, p. 23.

126. Karaiskaki, Sitsa, 'Elliniki Logotechnia,' *E Neolea*, issue, 36, 8 June 1940, p. 1140.

127. These playwrights were either commissioned to write such plays or were simply carrying out a cultural task within the requirements of the Organisation. The performances of these plays in most of the parts of Greece were announced through *E Neolea*. Some of plays were: *E Sklava* (The Enslaved Girl) *Na Zi To Mesologi* (Long Live Mesologi), *Hellas, E 4e Augoustou* ('The 'Fourth of August'*).* *E Neolea,* issue 42, 29 July 1939, pp. 1380-1382 and 1 September 1940, p.1534.

128. *To Olofkaftoma tou Arkadiou* is an event of great significance in Greek history and concerns the heroic death in November 1866 of the Prior of *Arcadi Monastery* in Crete who, together with the men, women and children who had found refuge in the monastery, set fire to a powder-keg killing themselves and a large number of Turks.

129. *E Neolea*, issue 23, 10 March 1939, p.771.

130. The service at Parnassos was attended by Metaxas and cabinet members who listened to a lecture with the title 'Didagmata ek tou Agonos tis Eleftherias dia tas Ellenikas Geneas' (Lessons for the Greek Generation from the Struggle for Freedom) delivered by Apostolos Daskalakis. *E Neolea,* issue 23, 18 March 1940, p.771. The organisation of lectures on the national ideals and the role entrusted to the 'Fourth of August' State and *EON* for the reinstatement and safeguarding of those ideas, was a frequent occurrence which peaked during the national holidays. *EON* officials travelled to towns and remote villages and delivered what the Propaganda Office referred to as *Ekpedeftikes Omilies* (Educational Lectures.) The titles of some of these lectures reflect the propagandists' effort to disseminate the regime's nationalistic propaganda: *To Ethnos* (The Nation*), E Monarchia Dia Meso Ton Aionon (*Monarchy Through the Centuries*), E Anagennisis Tis Ellinikis Filis (*The Regeneration of the Greek Nation) *To Ergon Tis Kiverniseos* (The Work of the Government). *E Neolea*, issue 23, 18 March 1939, p. 775 and issue 33, 27 May 1939, p. 1095.

131. Ibid., 12 August 1939, p.1446.

132. Ibid., p. 1447.

133. Ibid., 19 August 1939, issue 45, p. 1476. Some of the mottoes supporting the titles of the essays submitted were:
   1. *The Eternal Being of the Greek Nation.* Motto*: 'I do not disappear into Hades, but after I have rested for a while, I will come back to reinstate other people's lives also.*
   2. *Youth and the 'Fourth of August' State.* Motto: *'The relationship with one's nation is the same relationship as that between a parent and a child.'*. Another motto for the same essay was:: *' Stand Up Greek Youth: I .Metaxas..'*
   3. *The personality of our Chief.* Motto: *When a nation is determined to fulfil its dreams it will become a powerful nation.'*
   Quoted in Machera *E Neolea*, pp. 140-141.

134. The title refers to event, which took place during Greece's struggle for independence from the Turks in 1821 when the people of the mountainous region, *Souli*, preferred to die in honour rather than submit to a dishonourable surrender.

135. For the play *Ta Souliotopoula Den Pethanan* and its contribution to the 'regeneration of Greece' Tsekuras received a First Prize from the Ministry of Education. *E Neolea*, issue 34, 26 May 1940 , p. 1060.

136. The music of the play was written by T. Glikofridis and the stage designing was done by N. Zografos. *E Neolea* , issue 23, 18 March 1939, p. 771.

137. *Oi* Parastaseis tis *EON* Kata tin 25e Martiou.' Ibid., issue 25, 1 April 1939, p. 839.

138. Ibid.

139. Ibid.

140. Sideris Yannis, 'Ta Souliotopoula Den Pethanan,' *Nea Estia*, issue 315, February 1940, p.197 and *E Neolea*, 1 April 1939, p. 839.

141. Ibid.

142. As cited, the unconditional love and devotion for the motherland constituted the leading theme of the *EON* anthem. *Ta Tragoudia ,* p .9.

143. Sideris, 'Ta Souliotopoula,' p.197. The historic link between the children of *Souli* and the *EON* children is also demonstrated by the title which presents the dying heroes in plural (*Ta Souliotopoula*) when in the play the central martyr figure is one young boy, *Tousas* (To Souliotopoulo).

144. The cost of the book came to twenty drachmas. *E Neolea*, issue 21, February 1940, p. 672. Another play written by Tsekuras was the *Anthropos Eime ke Ego* (I am Human too) performed at the Cotopouli Theatre in May 1940 and according to *E Neolea* 'very well received by the theatrical, literal and general public.' Ibid., issue 34, 26 May 1940, p. 1060. No other information about the play is available.

145. *E Neolea,* issue 23, 18 March 1940, p.771 and issue 25, 1 April 1940, p. 839.

146. Ibid., issue 10, 18 February 1939, p. 806.

147. Ibid., issue 43, 27 July 1940, p. 1372, issue 44, 3 August 1940, p.1405, and issue 45, 10 August 1940, p. 1437.

148. '*E EON* ke E Politistiki Giorti Tis Tetartis Augoustou' (*EON* and The Cultural Celebration of the 'Fourth of August') *Ta Paraskinea,* 27 July 1940, p.2.

149. *E Neolea,* issue 45, 26 August 1939, p. 1508. The effort of the regime's propaganda to compare the *Acropolis* (Perikles' achievement) with *EON* and consider it superior, indicates the great significance which the Organisationhad for Metaxas in terms of disseminating the theme of 'national regeneration'. The *EON* cultural offices organised similar happenings which glorified the 'Fourth of August' regime in other cities. Such was the 'great theatrical representation' *E Apotheosis Tis 4es Augustou*(The Apotheosis of the 'Fourth of August') staged during the regime's third anniversary in *Thessaloniki. E Neolea,*,26 August 1939,p.1485.

150. The *EON* open theatre on Lycabetus was established in the summer 1939 where the first performance to take place was the play '*Pentheseleia*' which will be discussed later in this chapter. The performance of *Ieri Floga* was scheduled for 3 August 1940 but due to heavy rain which damaged the lighting equipment the play was finally staged on 11 August 1940. *E Neolea,* issue 45, 10 August 1940, p.1436. See also *Ioannis Metaxas, To Prosopiko tou Imerologio.* Vol. 8.,pp. 487-490.

151. Ibid.

152. Ibid.

153. Ibid., 24 August 1940, p.1479.

154. Ibid.

155. 'E Neolea Ke O Eortasmos tis 4es Augustou,' *Ta Paraskinia,* 27 July 1940, p. 2.

156 The same phrase was used by Metaxas when he spoke to the Athens University students trying to convince them of the importance of religion and its intrinsic link with *Hellenism.* Metaxas' speech, 10 October 1936. *Logoi ke Skepseis,* Vol.1, p.69. Indeed, the Greek Orthodox Church was a major element in the efforts to preserve the national sentiment.

157. *E Neolea,* 24 August 1940, p.1479. Great effort was put in by the III Office to ensure that this continuity was constantly disseminated to the young members. The director of *EON*'s Political Indoctrination and Propaganda Kyriakos Karamanos instructed his propagandists to 'proceed with the indoctrination of the young members by strengthening their national consciousness through the values and ideals of *Hellenism* that has always united the Greek people; these ideals were: *E Glossa* (The language) *E Thriskia* (Religion), *E Koinonia* (Society) *Ta Ethima* (traditions and *Oi Paradoseis* (customs) as well as the nation's physical and social characteristics.' Karamanos, Kyriakos, M., *Ti Tha Kanoume?* (Ekdoseis *EON,* Athens, 1940) pp., 12-13. On significance of religion and *EON* see also text T*hriskeia* (Religion) (Ekdoseis *EON,* Athens, 1939).

158. The Colonels' Dictatorship of 1967 took as their motto the phrase *Hellas Ellinon Christianon* (Greece of Greek Christians). Metaxas, as his diary suggests, was a pious man and often attended church and appealed to God for help, especially at moments of crisis. *Ioannis Metaxas, To Prosopiko tou Imerologio,* Vol. 8, pp. 464-469-471-479-498-516. However, whenever he referred to Christianity in his speeches, it was always as a supplementary element to *Hellenism* and *EON.* Metaxas' speeches to students, 10 October 1936, *Logoi ke Skepseis,* Vol. 1, p. 69, to teachers, 28 October 1936, Ibid., p. 96, and speech to *EON,* 5 January 1939, Ibid. Vol. 2., p. 9.

159. The music for the play was written by Glikofridis, who was in charge of the *EON* band. *Ta Paraskinia,* 27 July 1940 , p. 6, and *E Neolea,* 25 February 1939, p. 676.

160. Theodosopoulos, T., 'Scholia Gia tis Proves' (Comments on the Rehearsals). *Ta Paraskinia ,* 17 August 1940, p.5.

161. Ibid.

162. On 11 August 1940 Metaxas wrote in his diary ' I have a bad feeling - Tonight *Ieri Floga* (Sacred Flame) at the Lycabetus quarry.' *Ioannis Metaxas, To Prosopiko tou Imerologio,* Vol. 8, p. 490. At that time Mussolini had already begun the preparations for the attack on

Greece. Ciano, Mussolini's son-in-law and Minister of Foreign Affairs wrote in his Diary on 10 August 1940: ' IL Duce plans to attack Greece(...).He says he will attack Greece suddenly sometime in September.' A propaganda campaign against Greece began in the press which culminated on 15 August 1940 when the Greek light cruiser *Elli* was torpedoed by the Italians at the island of Tinos during the traditional annual celebration of *Tis Panagias*. Ibid., p. 490. On the events preceding the *Elli* incident and the following ones that culminated in the Greco-Italian War see *Diplomatika Egrafa E Italiki Epithesis Kata Tis Ellados (Elliniki Leuki Bivlos,)* (Vasilikon Ypourgeio Exoterikon, Athens, 1940).and Petraki Marina O Torpillismos Tis Ellis' in *Kathimerini Epta Hmeres,*5 August 2001,p.13

163. According to Metaxas his government had by 1939 spent more than ten billion drachmas for rearmament. Metaxas' speech, 25 November 1939. *Logoi ke Skepseis*, Vol.2, p. 195.

164. *E Neolea*, issue 44, 3 August 1940, pp. 1406-1407.

165. Pentheseleia was Queen of the Amazons, known for her beauty and courage. She fought in the Trojan war on the side of Priamos against the Greeks and Achilles and she was fatally injured. Her character, beauty and courage inspired many artists. *Papyros Larousse*, Vol. 48, p. 346.

166. Heinrich (Wilhelm) von Kleist was a German dramatist of the 19th century. He wrote *Pentheseleia* in 1808. Ibid., Vol. 34, p.61. The fact that the play chosen was not a Greek play was discussed by the critics, and articles such as the following one were published 'hesitantly.' 'Those who wondered about the choice of a foreign play instead of one of the masterpieces of ancient drama such as *Antigone,* who is the everlasting prototype of the Greek maiden and sister, possibly have a right to feel so. *E Neolea*, issue 44, 12 August 1939, p.1424.

167. Harris, Petros, 'E Parastasi Tis Pentheseleia,' *To Neon Kratos*, 24, August 1939, p. 567.

168. '*Pentheseleia* - Pos eide tin parastasi enas axiomatouxos' (How an *EON* - rank-holder member saw the performance) *E Neolea*, issue 346, 26 August 1939, p. 1509.

169. Ibid., issue 44, 12 August 1939, p. 1424. Kleist's text was altered by the *EON* playwrights to suit the artistic needs and ideology of the regime.

170. The performance of the play was extensively covered by the theatrical press. See Haris, Petros, 'E Parastasis Tis *Pentheseleia*' (The *Pentheseleia* Performance), *To Neon Kratos,* issue 24, August 1939, p. 565.

171. Although the role of the working woman's contribution to the Greek economy, especially in view of the forthcoming war, is widely recognised by the 'Fourth of August' regime and many theoreticians of the New State, her proper place was within the family sphere. See article 'Prepei Na Anagnorisomen Eis Tin Ellinida Pliri Eleftherian Eis Tin Ergasian' (We Must Acknowledge Woman's Right to Work). Avgerinos, Ch., *Nea Politiki*, January 1940, pp.25-29. Women's working capacity was officially acknowledged by the state in 1939 with Emergency Law 2000, which introduced measures to suppress unemployment. A large amount of controversy in the daily press followed the new legislation trying to define women's proper place in society and their contribution to the nation's economy. Avdela, Efi, 'Physikos Proorismos ke O Rolos Tou Kratous' in *Epistimoniko Symbosio, E Ellada Tou'40*, pp. 125-148.

172. *E Neolea,* issue 10, 9 December 1939, p.300.

173. Women won the right to be elected in the municipal and communal elections in 1934. Kerofyla,*E Athina*, p. 235. Metaxas ironically stated in his speech in Ioannina in June 1937: 'In the past the political world was preoccupied with serious matters. They had to think whether women should be elected in the municipal or parliamentary elections. Meanwhile no one had the time to think how you lived and whether there was enough bread to feed you.' Metaxas' speech, 13 June 1937. *Logoi ke Skepseis*, Vol. 1, p.191.

174. *E Neolea,* issue 21, February 1940, p. 971.

175. Metaxas' speech, 10 October 1936. *Logoi ke Skepseis*, Vol.1, p. 72.

176. *Tessera Chronia*, Vol. 3., p. 155. The enactment of Emergency Law 1930/1939, which supplemented the regulations concerning the Patriotic Welfare Institution (*PIKPA*) established a section for the protection of motherhood, and childhood. Ibid.

177. *Tessera Chronia*, Vol. I. The photo at the end of this volume depicts Metaxas among one hundred newly-weds acting as their best man. One bride kisses his hand with religious

piety. The caption reads: 'One working girl bows and kisses with gratitude the hand of the devoted Father who takes care of the well being of his children.' Ibid.

178. Metaxas' speech in Sparta, 20 May 1938. *Logoi ke Skepseis*, Vol. 1, p.382.

179. *E Neolea*, issue 44, 12 August 1939,p.1421.

180. The anthem was written in six verses by P. Menestreas, and the music was written by Ger. Fren. *Ta Tragoudia,* pp. 12-13.

181. Cotopouli, Marika, 'E Pentheseleia Sto Theatro Tou Lycavitou,' *To Neon Kratos*, issue 24, August 1939, p.565.

182. The critics committee consisted of Alexandros Kanellopoulos, Costis Bastias, Marika Cotopouli and the composer Petridis. Karaiskaki, Sitsa, ' Oi Kallitehnikoi Agones.' *E Neolea*, issue 35, June 1940, p.1090.

183. *E Neolea,* issue 34, 26 May 1940, p.1065. During the performance of the Cultural Games the manifestations of love and devotion of the young *EON* members was astonishing as the 'young boys and girls phalangites shouted during the intervals Father- Father'. Ibid.

184. Ibid., p.1090

185. 'The *EON* mottoes.' *E Neole*a, issue 43, 4 August 1930, p. 1415.

CHAPTER 5

1. Nicoloudis' speech in March 1939, on the occasion of reorganising the Radio Services. *Evdomadieon Programma Radiofonikou Stathmou Athinon, 30 Iouliou, 5 Augoustou 1939. Panigiriki Ekdosi 4es Augoustou* (Ekdoseis 4es Augoustou, Athens, 1939), p. 7. On the reorganisation of the radio station *Tessera Chronia*, Vol. 4, p. 150.

2. The first known use of radio for international broadcasting was in 1915 when Germany provided a daily news report on war activities. The Soviets used the radio in 1917 to transmit Lenin's message to the All-Russian Congress and by 1922 it became the most powerful radio in existence .Jowett, & O'Donnell, P*ropaganda* pp. 101-102. By the end of the 1920s almost half of American households owned a radio, while in Britain radio activities began in 1922 with the formation of the first British Broadcasting Company which in 1927 became a state corporation known as the BBC. For a full account on the history of BBC see Briggs, Asa, *The History of Broadcasting in the United Kingdom*. (Oxford University Press, London 1970, revised 1995). In Germany, radio broadcasting had been regulated by the State (Reich Radio Company RRG-Reichsrundfunkgesellschaft) as early as 1925, (Welch, *The Third Reich,* p. 30), while in Italy a national radio network organisation was set up in 1923 and was taken over by the State in 1927. Warner, Geoffrey 'Italy 1918-1940' in John Colby etal. (eds.) in *War, Peace and Social Change,* p.129.

3. The first known radio broadcast in Greece was made in 1923 by the *Diefthinsis Radiofonias Ypourgeiou Naftikon-DRYN* (Broadcasting Administration of the Admiralty) with the use of a Swedish wireless 200 Watt telephone transmitter. In 1925 the first attempts at radio broadcasting were organised by the *Scholi Megareos* (Megareos School*)* and concerned a school celebration. In January 1930 the *Omilos Filon Asyrmatou* (Society of the Friends of the Wireless) broadcast the first lecture from a transmitter of 6 watt in 400 meters length-waves. *Neoteron Egyklopedikon Lexikon Heliou* (Latest Encyclopaedia Helios) ,Vol. IST, (Helios, Athens, 1956), p. 572.

4. Ibid., See also Anastasiadis, *E Thessaloniki,* p.124.

5. Ibid.*,* The first official figures regarding the number of radio sets in Greece concern the year 1938.

6. *Helios,* p. 572.

7. Christos Tsigiridis, an electrical engineer from Stuttgart Polytechnic, was the *Siemens and Halske* representative in Greece. Ibid, p. 125.

8. *Radio Tsigiridis* was located within the grounds of the International Exhibition from which it broadcast until 1941, when the Germans confiscated the equipment. Anastasiadis, *E Thessaloniki,* p.123-127 and Anastasiadis, Giorgos, *Oi Efimerides Sti Thessaloniki ke ta Mesa Mazikis Epikinoniaws* (1912-1974) (Paratiritis, Thessaliniki,) No Date., pp. 310-311

9. In 1929 an unsuccessful attempt was made to purchase a Marconi 12 kW medium-wave radio transmitter. Similar attempts made by the Venizelos Government to gain access

to a Durham-Telefunken transmitter were unsuccessful as the contract was terminated in 1935 by the Kondilis Government through Emergency Law 581/35. From 1932 to 1935 Greek radio activity consisted of a few broadcasts made through the Radio Telegraphic Service of the Ministry of Communication *TTT, Tachidromio-Tilegrafeio-Tilefonia* (Post-Telegram-Telephone) which provided the navigational requirements of the coastal vessels. *Helios,* p. 572. Unfortunately no thorough study is available on the history of the Greek Radio. There is however, a substantial amount of material, mainly obtained from contemporary newspapers, published in the weekly radio magazine *Radiotileorasi,* over a period of three years (1994-1997, by Hatzidakis, Georgios, 'E Proistoria Tis Radiofonias' (The Prehistory of Broadcasting).

10. Italy set up its Foreign Broadcasting Service in 1930. First only Italian domestic programmes were transmitted but they were followed by extensive international broadcasting within Mussolini's propagandistic strategy. Jowett- & O' Donnell, *Propaganda,* p. 104, and Morgan, *Italian Fascism,* p. 115.

11. The inauguration of the Bari Greek Section was celebrated in the presence of members of the Greek Government, people of arts and letters and Italian High Officials. During the celebration the importance of Italian Radio and the personality of Mussolini were highly praised by many speakers, while the leader of the Greek National Socialist Party (Mercouris) spoke of his forthcoming dream of witnessing the 'installation of a transmitter on the Acropolis which would return the Fascist Salute to the Capitol' 'E Elliniki Radiofoniki Metadoseis ke o Stathmos Bari', in *Ente Italiano Audizioni Radiofonich.e Le Tranmissioni Specilli Per La Grecia 1 Luglio 1934 - 1 Luglio 1937* (Stabilmenti Grafici Valechi, Firenze, August 1937) pp. 7-8-9.

12. Ibid.

13. Ibid.

14. Metaxas' speech on the radio, 10 August 1936. *Logoi ke Skepseis* ,Vol. 1, pp.16-18 .

15. In March 1935 through its effective head of Department Stefanos Eleftheriou, the *TTT* established a temporary radio station in Piraeus known as *Piraeus Radio,* or *TTT Radio,* or *Temporary Radio.* The wireless which broadcast over a range of 300 kilometres on a frequency of 200.25, was established on a semi-official basis and its running was at the discretion of the authorities. According to Hatzidakis it was through this station that Ioannis Metaxas delivered his speech of 10 August 1936. The long range broadcast was effected thanks to the contribution of *Tsigiridis Radio.* Hatzidakis, *Radiotileorasi,* issue 1323, 24-30 June, p. 72; issue 1324, 1-7 July, p. 68; issue 1345, 25 November - 1 December 1995, p.68.

16. Karanopoulos, D., 'Kratos ke Radiofono', *To Neon Kratos,* issue 6, February 1938, p. 190. Most of the radio sets belonged to public places like *kafeneia* or to households with extended families. In 1952 in a Greek population of 7,714,680 there existed 285,000 radios, whereas in 1945 there were 5 radios for 1000 persons. *Helios,* p. 573

17. *Apologismos,* p. 9.

18. *FEK* 391, 7 September 1936, pp. 2041-2043.

19. Nicoloudis' speech, March 1939, *Tessera Chronia* , Vol. 4, p.150.

20. *FEK* 391, 7 September 1936. The members who made up the board of the newly *YPE* were Georgios Vlahos, Ph. Economides, Marika Cotopouli and Al. Lalaouni; all people of the arts and letters, supporters of the regime. Hatzidakis 'Epitropes ke Symvoulia (Committes and Boards) *Radiotileorasi,* issue 1347, 9-5 December 1995, p. 47.

21. Nicolopoulos was the under-secretary of the sub-Ministry of Communications. The newly established *YPE* was controlled until the beginning of 1938 by this sub-Ministry.

22. This Emergency Law supplemented Law 404/1936 which was enacted in December 1936 and made a few changes to 95/193. *FEK* 561, 29 December 1936, and *FEK* 96, 17 March 1937.

23. Ibid., 96, 17 March 1937, p. 607.

24. Ibid , pp. 607-608.

25. Broadcast from the Bari Radio Station in 1937. *E.I.A.P.* p. 91.

26. Ibid.

27. Although British Marconi, RGA and the French SFR were also candidates for the post, preference was given to Telefunken and its representative Voulpiotis who was a fervent Germanophile According to Hatzidakis who interviewed Voulpiotis, Ioannis Metaxas personally invited Voulpiotis to accept the job and asked him to supply the necessary equipment for establishing a Radio Station in Greece as soon as possible. Voulpiotis left immediately for Germany and soon the radio equipment arrived in Piraeus. Hatzidakis, *Radiotileorasi*, issue 1348, 16-22 December 1995, p.47 and issue 1352, 13-19 January 1996 p. 47.

28. *Helios,* p. 572, and Hatzidakis, *Radiotileorasi,* issue 1352, 13-19 January 1996, p. 47.

29. Ibid.

30. George Kyriakakis was appointed Director of *YPE. Kathimerini,* 22 May 1938.
    The high costs involved in establishing and running the Radio Station would, according to Emergency Law 95/193 (Article 5) be born by the State with a loan of 10,000,000 drachmas, earnings from advertisements, and yearly contribution from the owners of the radio receivers. *FEK* 391, 7 September 1936, p. 2042.

31. *Tessera Chronia* , Vol. 2, p. 35, and *Kathimerini,* 25 March 1938.

32. Ibid. and *Evdomadieon Programma,* p. 3.

33. *Tessera Chronia,* Vol. 2, p. 45 and *Apologismos,* p. 26.

34. *Kathimerini,* 22 May 1938.

35. Ibid.

36. *Kathimerini*, 30 March 1938. The sound signal, which was followed by the announcer's monumental phrase *Edo Radiofonikos Stathmos Athinon* (This Is the Athens Radio Station) was delivered to the BBC in April 1941 by Mr. Christos Simopoulos, the Greek Ambassador in Britain, to become part of the BBC's newly established Greek Section of International Broadcasting and serve the war effort against the Axis Powers. *Edo Londino: Apo ta Vrachea sta FM kai sto Diadiktio, 60 Chronia BBC sta Ellinika* (This is London. From the Short-waves to FM and Internet-BBC 60 Years of Greek Service). (Conference, Athens, 29 September 1999).

37. According to Professor Agelos Tanagras who suggested the tune, its significance could be attributed to the fact that 'the bucolic theme would remind Greeks abroad, who came mainly from the countryside, of their beloved nation' *Typos,* quoted in Hatzidakis, *Radiotileorasi,* issue 1386, 7-13 December 1996, p. 53

38. Hatzidakis, Giorgos, 'To Sima Tou Stathmou' *Radiotileorasi*, issue 1373, 8-14 June 1996, p.47 and *Kathimerini,* 30 March 1938.

39. The logo adorned most publications concerning radio broadcasts including the weekly radio programme.

40. *FEK* 492, 30 December 1938, p. 3236.

41. *FEK* 61, 16 February 1939, pp. 413-418.

42. Ibid., p. 417.

43. Ibid.

44. Ibid.

45. *FEK* 257, 22 June 1939 and *FEK* 464, 1 November 1939.

46. D.Karanopoulos, 'Kratos ke Radiofono' pp. 191-192.

47. Nicoloudis' speech, March 1939. *Tessera Chronia* Vol. 4, p. 150.

48. Ibid, p. 154.

49. The programme was later reduced to two hours because of the heavy schedule in the Speeches' Department. Ibid.

50. Ibid. The exaggerated percentage indicates the significance the regime placed on the agrarian sector.

51. *Evdomadieon Programma,* p. 66.

52. Indicative of the difficulty in acquiring a radio set is that when Metaxas himself obtained a radio receiver in January 1939, he wrote in his diary; 'We have now a radio in the house' *Ioannis Metaxas, To Prosopiko tou Imerologio,* Vol. 7, p. 347.

53. The cost of the yearly radio licence amounted to 300 drcs. *FEK* 391, 7 September 1936. This amount remained unchanged until 1940 to encourage and facilitate radio ownership. *FEK* 237, 22 June 1939.

54. *Tessera Chronia,* Vol. 3, p. 36. (The feasibility of this scheme was never materialised). In 1933 manufacturers in Germany were persuaded by the Nazis to produce one of the cheapest wireless sets in Europe the VE 3031 *Volksempfanger* (people's receiver) which was subsidised by the State. Welch, *The Third Reich,* p. 32.

55. *Tessera Chronia* Vol.3, p.203 Macedonia and Western Thrace were predominantly Venizelist parts of the country and the regime launched a great propaganda campaign to 'win them over.' Waterlow, Sydney, *The Decline and Fall,* p.209. See also FO 371/21147, 22 March 1937 and Iatrides (ed.) *Ambassador MacVeagh Reports,* pp.. 99-105.

56. *Tessera Chronia,* Vol. 4, p. 155

57. *Evdomadieon Programma,* p. 122.

58. Ibid, p. 67.

59. Ibid,, and *Tessera Chronia,* Vol. 4, pp. 161-162

60. Ibid, pp. 24-34. In 1940 the Ministry of Education forwarded fifty radios to schools in the North. Ibid.

61. Metaxas'speech, 19 October 1939, *Logoi ke Skepseis,* Vol. 2, p. 151.

62. Ibid, 5 January 1939, Vol. 2, p. 10.

63. Ibid, 19 October 1939, Vol. 2, p. 150.
    Among other measures taken by the regime to safeguard the institution of family was the legislation enacted in October 1939 to deal with the subject of *Cohabitation. Tessera Chronia* Vol. 4, p. 11. According to *E Neolea* 'cohabitation, which is a disgrasful and unethical phenomenon, could have endangered and dismantled the foundations of the Greek family, if the 'Fourth of August' did not intervene to put an end to it, thus saving and reinstating the Greek family. 'O Nomos Tis Paranomis Symviosis' in *E Neolea,* issue 7, 7 November 1938, p. 246.

64. *Tessera Chronia,* Vol. 3, p. 143.

65. *Tessera Chronia,* Vol. 4, p. 156.

66. Within the period of twenty months when the Radio Broadcasting Service was under the authority of *YTT* more than two thousand speeches were delivered. Ibid, p. 155.

67. The Broadcasting Service was formed in April 1938 and nine speakers were elected, mainly theatre artists (Veakis, Pratsika), and opera singers (Laoutari). Hatzidakis, *Radiotileorasi,* issue 1372, 1-7 June 1996, p. 47.

68. Michalis Kofiniotis 'Oi Exomologiseis Enos Speaker' (The Confessions of a Speaker) *Evdomadieon Programma,* p. 54.

69. We have no information on how many speeches Metaxas delivered from the Zapeion studios. But he often spoke of his need to communicate in person with his beloved people. Hitler was also a very uncomfortable and ineffective speaker when confined to a studio, a fact which posed certain limitations to the propaganda prospects. Welch, *The Third Reich,* p. 34.

70. The newspapers with titles such as 'Radio: A successful Broadcast,' spoke of the great significance that these broadcasts, which could be heard all over Greece, had for Metaxas and the nation. *Proia* 25 April, 1939.

71. FO 371/21147, 28 July 1937.

72. Rigos, *Ta Krisima,* p. 000160. Mr. Siaskas Ioannis, who was one of the first radio employees recalls that during the regime's festivities loudspeakers were placed in most of the central places of the capital broadcasting the chief's inspiring mottoes, speeches and 'elevating patriotic music'. In that way the regime ensured that its beliefs and objectives reached as many people as possible.

73. *Evdomadieon Programma,* p.15. In January 1939 at the suggestion of the American Ambassador MacVeigh and members of the 'Parnassos' Society, *The Friends of America Society* was founded. The object of the society 'was to achieve a broader connection between the USA and Greece through lectures and exhibitions.' It was during one of these exhibitions that this international speech was made. *Greece Calling, Information Division of the 'Greek Reconstruction Claims Committee* (Athens, 1948) p. 75.

74. *FEK* 202, 26 May 1937, p. 1296.

75. It was the Athens Station which informed the Greeks of the declaration of war on 3 September 1939. *Tessera Chronia,* Vol.4, p.156.

76. Ibid, p.157.
77. *Apologismos,* p. 214.
78. Quoted in Jowett and O'Donnell, *Propaganda*, p. 104.
79. Goebbels believed that music was the best means of sustaining morale and strengthening the resolve of the population at times of crisis. According to Jo Fox contemporary observers noted that one of the most successful means of communicating with the individual and the mass was the careful combination of entertainment and propaganda, stressing that broadcast propaganda if shrewdly interwoven with entertainment will be listened to whether people liked it or not. Fox, Jo, 'The Mediateor':Images of Radio in Wartime Feature Film in Britain and Germany' in M.Connely and D.Welch (eds), *War and The Media,* p101.
80. *Tessera Chronia,* Vol. 4, pp. 157-158.
81. Karanopoulos, '*Kratos Ke radiofono',* p. 192.
82. *Apologismos,* p.214 and *Tessera Chronia,* Vol. 4, p. 160.
83. Ibid.
84. Ibid.
85. Ibid.
86. *Tessera Chronia*, Vol. 4, p. 161.
87. Ibid.
88. *Apologismos,* p. 254
89. An extra fifteen minute of programming was devoted every Sunday to 'Stories of our Land' to remind the listeners of the glorious achievements of their Greek ancestors. *Tessera Chronia*, Vol. 4, p. 155.
90. Ibid, p. 164.
91. *Tessera Chronia,* Vol. 4, p. 151.
92. Ibid.
93. *Tessera Chronia*, Vol. 4, p. 151. Part of the equipment for the new transmitter (assigned to Telefunken) arrived in Greece just before the outbreak of the Greek-Italian War. *Helios,* p. 573.
94. Ibid, Vol. 4, p.155.
95. *Apospasmata,* p.108.
96. Ibid, p.107.
97. *A Panellinios Ekthesis,* p. 13. The radio transmitter was supplied by a Greek from Egypt 'with patriotic feelings.' *E Neolea,* issue 48, October 1939. In view of the time and money involved and the difficulties encountered in the installation of the Athens Radio Station, despite the fact that it was state organised and funded, one becomes aware of how important this medium must have been, for *EON* to be able to establish it in such a short time.
98. *E Neolea ,* issue 6, 11 November 1939, p. 191.
99. Ibid., issue 13, 30 December 1940, p. 413.
100. Ibid., issue 14, 7 January 1940, p. 445
101. Ibid, issue 7, 18 November 1939, p.197.
102. Ibid.
103. *Apospasmata,* pp. 109-110.
104. Linardatos, *4e Augustou,,* p.180. According to Linardatos the permanent personnel employed in the *EON* departments received extravagant wages and enjoyed many privileges such as paid uniforms, free travel and other benefits. Ibid, p.191.
105. *Deftera Diaskepsis,* pp. 338.
106. *Circular Order 28,* p.73. See also *Apospasmata,* p. 97 and *Deftera Diaskepsis,* p. 339. The plans for acquiring a more powerful radio transmitter were interrupted by the war.
107. *Tessera Chronia,* Vol. 4, p. 149.

CHAPTER 6

1. Hitler, *Mein Kampff,* p. 169.
2. Several agencies like the SD, the Gestapo, the Party, local government authorities and

the judiciary employed a great number of officials who were engaged in producing regular reports concerning the mood and morale of the people. Welch, *The Third Reich*, p. 51.

3. Stevens noted in 1944 'the almost complete absence of roads in the mountain districts'. Stevens, 'British Reports' p. 3.

4. According to statistics drawn up on the production of electricity, in 1937 out of total 243 million kwh the Athens region received 181 million kwh and the rest of Greece 62 mkwh. *Synoptiki Statistiki Epetiris. 1954* , p. 101.

5. According to government sources 1,500 night schools were established in Macedonia and Thrace where 86,454 illiterate people from the age of 15 to 50 studied, while more than 21,000,000 drachmas were spent in Crete to improve schooling conditions. *Tria Chronia Ergasias Eis Tin Ellinikin Eparhian 1936-1939 (*Ekdoseis *YTT*, Athens, 1939) pp. 10-16-28-29. However, these schools were established in the big cities to which the villagers had no easy access. Similarly, more than 200,000,000 drachmas were spent for road construction and reconstruction in Macedonia and Thrace. Ibid, pp.5-6-15, while in Crete the sum spent was approx. 150,000,000 drachmas. Ibid, pp. 22-23. It must be noted, however, that the amounts spent for electricity was next to nothing. Ibid.

6. Ibid, p.11.

7. Ibid, p.34

8. Quoted in Linardatos , *4e Augoustou*, p. 122.

9. FO 371/23770, 7 August 1939.

10. Leaflet distributed in Ioannina in 1938, Quoted in Nicolaidis, N., Ioannis *Ta Yannena Tou Mesopolemou ,1936-1940* , Vol. 3., p. 281 (Ioannina, 1970) No publisher mentioned.

11. Ibid, p. 294.

12. Ibid.

13. Press Attaché' at the British Embassy

14. FO 371/23779, 5 June 1939

15. FO 371/21147, 22 March 1937

16. FO 371/23770, 6 May 1939.

17. Similar receptions were 'intensively' organised by Kotzias, during Metaxas' first tour at the Peloponnese in April 1937. FO 371/21147, 22 March 1937.

18. Iatrides (ed.) *Ambassador MacVeagh Reports*, p. 99.

19 Ibid.

20. Ibid, pp. 134-163.

21. A British visitor to Greece in April 1937 wrote: 'Some of the propaganda methods are amusingly silly. An acquaintance of mine reported apropos of the self-laudatory propaganda: 'We have an English proverb, 'Self praise is no recommendation.' The Greek gentleman to whom he made this remark replied at once, 'But if they did not praise themselves nobody else would.' FO 371/21150, 12 April 1937.

22. FO 371/21147, 8 June 1937. In March 1937 Waterlow reported that 'in Chios island Metaxas was regarded as a failure.' FO 371/21147, 22 March 1937.

23. These parts were Macedonia, Western Thrace and the Aegean Islands, with the strongest base in Crete.

24. Metaxas' speech, 8 November 1936. *Logoi ke Skepseis*, Vol. 1, p. 117.

25. Ibid, in Heraklion, 8 November 1936, p. 106.

26. 'E Ellas Choris Dimokratia-Ta Paraskinia Mias krisimis Periodou' (Hellas Without Democracy -The Undisclosed Details of A critical Period) *Acropolis*, 22 January 1972. See also FO 371/21147, March 1937.

27. Archeio Ioannou Metaxas. Genika Archeia Tou Kratous,, File 44.

28. FO 371/21147, 22 March 1937. From 1936 onwards the regime made an extensive number of public improvements and introduced significant welfare measures. For a detailed account of government works in Crete see *Tria Chronia*, pp. 20-31.

29. *Acropolis*, 25 January 1972.

30. Ibid.

31. Ibid. Waterlow maintained that the unpopularity of Metaxas was evident everywhere

he went, in contrast to the King's popularity which grew stronger every day. FO 371/21147, 22 March 1937.

32. *Ioannis Metaxas, To Prosopiko tou Imerologio,* Vol. 7, p. 373.

33. They enjoyed free transportation and free meals.

34. FO 371/21147, 7 August 1937. Mazarakis Ainian claimed that during the regime's second anniversary celebration the government arranged for the transportation of 40,000 people from the provinces to Athens. Mazarakis Ainian, *Apomnimonefmata,* p. 504.

35. FO 371/21147, 22 May 1937.

36. FO 371/23770, 7 August 1939.

37. Papadakis, *E Exoteriki,* p. 111.

38. Metaxas' speech, 21 August 1936. *Logoi ke Skepseis,* Vol. 1, pp. 20.

39. Archeio Ioannou Metaxa. Genika Archeia Tou Kratous, File 43. Maniadakis' comments were those of utmost admiration for the actions and enthusiasm of the industrialist.

40. *Ioannis Metaxas, To Prosopiko tou Imerologio,* Vol. 8, p. 454.

41. Ibid, 10 -26 June 1935, 18 February 1922, 15-19 April 1924, 31 August 1928, and 11 September 1928, when he wrote 'people look at me like the dog looks at the person it has attacked but was unable to tear apart; they despise me.' Ibid., Vol. 6, p.591.

42. Ibid, Vol. 7, p. 411.

43. *To Imerologio Tis Lelas Metaxas* (Lela Metaxas' Diary). The hand written, unpublished diary was kept by the widow of Ioannis Metaxas, after his death. Its entries are from 21 April 1941 to July 1941 and shed light on Metaxas' personality. Archeio Ioannou Metaxas. Genika Archeia tou Kratous, File 45. There is also a hand-written Diary of Mrs Lela Metaxas in File 18 from December 1944 to January 1945.

44. Maniadakis' office was only a few steps away from Metaxas' office in the old Parliament building and it is reported that Maniadakis was always there to assure Metaxas of the people's love when necessary. 'To Aporito Archeio tou Maniadaki'(Maniadakis' Confidential Archives) *Acropolis,* 1 November 1970.

45. *Ioannis Metaxas, To Prosopiko tou Imerologio,* Vol.7, p. 321.

46. Waterlow reported: 'General Metaxas appears, to judge from my recent talks with him, to be increasingly satisfied with himself, in the role of adored leader of his people although the demonstration of flattery continually organised for him hardly seem to be spontaneous' FO 371/21147, 19 February 1937.

47. Arceio Ioannou Metaxas,. Genika Archeia Tou Kratous. File 43/043.

48. Unfortunately the letter is in a very bad state; the name of the sender has been destroyed and there is no evidence as to the date this letter was send. Ibid.

49. Archeio Ioannou Metaxas, Genika Archeia tou Kratous, File 43.

50. FO 371/21150, 19 May 1937. Anti-Metaxas articles in the *Manchester Guardian* initiated strong protest from the Greek regime, and the Foreign Office was asked to intervene to 'use whatever influence they had to induce certain quarters of the press to be less unsympathetic in their reference to the present regime in Greece. Ibid. In February 1939 *The Daily Telegraph* also attacked Metaxas' regime causing tension between the dictatorship and the British Legation. *Ioannis Metaxas, To Prosopiko tou Imerologio,* Vol.7, pp. 354-358. However, in August 1940 the *Manchester Guardian* along with the other British newspapers flattered and praised Metaxas' regime in view of the war crisis. Archeio Ioannou Metaxa. Genika Archeia Tou Kratous, File 69.

51. FO 371/23770, 28 June 1939.

52. Similarly a primary goal of Nazi Germany was the manufacturing of a people's community (*Volksgemeinschaft*). Welch, *The Third Reich,* p. 53.

53. *Ta Paraskinia,* 25 March 1939.

54. It was a song sung by Stellakis Perpiniades and satirised an upper class girl and her improper behaviour. The song, which many people believed satirised the daughter of Ioannis Metaxas, was considered by the regime officials to be immoral and to have damaging effects. Perpiniadis, *Rebetiki Istoria,* pp. 27-29. See also Georgiadis, *Rebetico Ke Politiki,* pp. 84-90

55. Ibid.

56. FO 371/21147, 28 July 1937.

57. Ibid.

58. Ibid, 31 July 1937 and FO 371/23770, 23 March 1939.

59. In fact Malenos claims that 'the only thing the peasants knew about the Metaxas dictatorship was that it was determined to completely destroy their goat-breeding: 'How shall we live without our goats they complained and they were of course right' Malenos, Miltiadis, I., *To Simiomatario Tou Vlasi Roumeli*(I, .Zevra-Vasileiou, Athens, 1959) p. 123.

60. These contributions often reached threatening dimensions. Such was the case with a local manufacturer in Volos who was exiled for failing to contribute 200.000 drachmas to *EON*. According to Waterlow 'his assessment at so high a figure and his punishment for non-compliance were attributed to personal spite.' FO 371/23770, 23 March 1939.

61. FO 371/21147, 26 July 1937.

62. Waterlow and MacVeagh reported that although Metaxas was unpopular, people seemed rather more satisfied with the present situation than with the previous political schemes. FO 371/21147, 19 February 1937, and Iatrides, (ed.) *Ambassador MacVeagh Reports*, p. 105.

63. FO 371/21147, 31 May 1937. In the majority of Waterlow's despatches he makes the point not only of Metaxas' unpopularity but also of people's indifferent reaction, which in many cases was a sign of contentment.

64. Iatrides (ed.) *Ambassador MacVeagh Reports*, p.105.

65. People often sent him icons and lucky charms 'to protect him from negative thoughts and keep him strong for a hundred years'. Archeio Ioannou Metaxas Genika Archeia tou Kratous, File 44

CHAPTER 7

1. Vlachos, *Mia Fora*, p.46. See also *Ioannis Metaxas, To Prosopiko tou Imerologio* , Vol. 8, pp. 471-513.

2. On the events leading to the Greco-Italian war see Petraki Marina 'O Torpillismos tis Ellis(The Torpedoing of *Elli*), *Kathimerini-Epta Imeres*, (Athens, August 2001), p.156-159

3. In 1940 Greek Foreign policy typically professed neutrality. However, it was more and more drawn towards a British alliance working for a common cause which was the war against the Axis powers. Koliopoulos, E *Diktatoria tou Metaxa*, p. 191.

4. Metaxas' speech , 4 August 1940. *Logoi ke Skepseis*, Vol. 2, p. 329.

5. Welch, *The Third Reich*, p. 90

6. Vlachos, *Mia Fora*, p. 67.

7. The short newsreel *O Polemos* is part of the documentary film *Panorama tou Aiona*.

8. Kanellopoulos, Panagiotis, E*nas Apologismos, 1935-1945*, Athens, 1945, p.15

9. *Dokimio Istorias tou KKE*, p.356. Linardatos claims that Metaxas was forced to reject the Italian ultimatum because if he had submitted to the Italian demands his regime would have collapsed with the King's intervention, or worse, Greece would have been occupied by either the Italians or the British forces. Linardatos, O *Ioannis Metaxas ke Oi Megales Dynameis*, p. 179.

10. This enthusiasm, apart from the usual government sources, is well documented through historical evidence from people who criticised the 'Fourth of August' regime. Seferis, *Chirografo*, pp. 44-47, Kanellopoulos, *Pos Efthasame*, p. 15 and Vlachos, *Mia Fora*. p. 46. Malenos argued that 'the truth is that the Dictator's intentions to change Greece were good and sincere. The measures that he took for the working and the agrarian class testify that in his effort to face the great problems he managed to overcome his personal ideologies and preferences and think as a *Ethnikos Kyvernitis* (National Governor). Malenos, *To Simieiomatario,* p.119

11. The Greek Ambassador in Berlin, Ragavis, suggested to Metaxas that Greece should request Hitler's intervention, and surrender to him. Metaxas wrote with contempt of such proposals and claimed 'Kallitera na apothanomen'. *Ioannis Metaxas, To Prosopiko tou Imerologio*, Vol. 8, pp. 549 , 555.

12. *Vradyni , 29 March 1941, Eleftheron Vima,* 30 January, 1941, *O Typos* , 30 January 1941 and in most newspapers.

13. *Tefchos Afieromeno Ston Ioanni Metaxa, Filo ke Prostati ton Grammaton ke Technon, Nea Estia,* issue 340, 15 February 1941.

14. FO 371/29862, 29 January 1941.

15. O *Thanatos tou Ioannou Metaxas* is a short newsreel included in the documentary film *Panorama tou Aiona.*

16. The political exiles on the island returned and fought in the war, while on 31 October 1940, the Communists were asked by their leader Zachariadis who was jailed in the *Geniki Asfaleia Athinon* to fight the Fascist invaders with all their strength. *KKE Episima Keimena,*Vol, 5, 1940-1945, pp. 9-10.

17. Quoted in Vatikiotis, *Popular Autocracy,* p. 203.

18. Nicoloudis in his book *E Elliniki Crisis* written in Cairo in 1945 claims that if it was not for Ioannis Metaxas Greece would have surrendered to the Axis powers without resistance. He further implies that if Metaxas had not died in 1941 the results of the war might have been different. Nicoloudis, Th., *E Elliniki Crisis,* (Cairo, 1948).

19. Although Metaxas had militarily prepared Greece through an extensive and costly rearmament programme (Papagos, *O Polemos*), which enabled Greece to fight and beat the Italian aggressor; he did not politically prepare his country for what was to follow. The political vacuum, the bitterness of the defeat and the harshness of the German occupation stirred up political passions (reviving the anti-Metaxas feelings) and led Greece into its most destructive civil war. This was his great mistake, and given the fact that the members of his cabinet were, in their majority, incompetent, and some of them of a pro-fascist tendency, his great historical responsibility. Seferis, *Chirografo,* pp. 50-52; Stevens, *British Reports,* p. 26, and Mavrogordatos, G. Th., 'To Ochi tou Metaxas (Metaxas' No) *Kathimerini Epta Imeres,* 7 November 1999. See also Nicoloudis, *E Elliniki Crisis.*

20. Woodhouse, C. M., *Apple of Discord - A Survey of Recent Greek Politics in Their International Setting* (Hutchinson & Co. Ltd, London, 1948) p. 9.

21. Metaxas' speech, 30 October 1940. *Logoi ke Skepseis,* Vol. 2, pp. 357-362.

22. *Ioannis Metaxas, To Prosopiko tou Imerologio,* Vol. 8, p. 557.

23. His military competence and patriotic feelings had never been disputed even by his opponents. Malenos wrote: 'He loved his country exceedingly.' Malenos, *To Simiomatario,* p.127, while Theotokis wrote: 'That he was a great Patriot there is no doubt what-so-ever.' Theotokis, Spiros, *Politikai Anamniseis (*Athens, 1986) p. 55.

24. Quoted in Vatikiotis, *Popular Autocracy,* p. 203.

25. Ibid., p.202.

26. 'An enlightened despot' in Vatikiotis view. Vatikiotis, *Polupar Autocracy,* p.201.

27. It must be stressed, however, that foreign accounts praised Metaxas regime before the war for the stability and security it offered to the Greek people. 'Authoritarianism in Greece', *Times,* 5 August 1940: 'Four Years of Stable Government,' *Observer,* 4 August 1940 and *Manchester Guardian,* 6 August 1940. The timing of these articles could very well imply the efforts of British propaganda to persuade Metaxas to end Greece's neutrality and join the allies, which he eventually did, or it is possible that Greece was indeed going through a stable and secure phase.

28. On the subject see Close, *The Origins of the Greek Civil War.*

Bibliography

Primary Sources

Genika Archeia tou Kratous - Archeio Ioannou Metaxa. Athens.
(Greek State Archives - Metaxas' Private Papers)

File 18   *Imerologio Tis Omirias Tis kas Lelas Metaxa December 1944 - January 1945* (Diary of Mrs Lela Metaxas kept during her captivity (December 1944 - January 1945) Unpublished.

File 30   Confidential reports concerning Kotzias and Goebbels from the Greek Embassy in Berlin.

File 31   Various letters - cables 1.2.41

File 33   Various reports on persons, 20.3.1932 - 24.10.1939

File 41   Simopoulos despatches. Nicoloudis' letter to Metaxas and other documents.

File 43   Sub-Ministry of National Security - Reports on citizens. CVs and various letters of extreme adulation 1939.

File 44   Various letters to Metaxas

File 45   *Ambrosios Tzifos. To Imerologio mou 1936-1940* (Amvrosios Tzifos, My Diary 1936-1940 Unpublished). Mrs Lela Metaxa hand - written notes about Ioannis Metaxas.

File 44   Various notes and poems written for Metaxas.

File 53-54 Letters of condolence and poems on Metaxas' death

File 61   Greek Embassy Paris. Articles from the French Press. Praises.

File 62   Newspaper clippings

File 66   Various notes 2.11.40

Files 6-28. Documents on the life and activities of the Youth Organisation

Archeio Ypourgeiou Exoterikon - (Ministry of Foreign Affairs Archives)

Archive 1, *File 4*   *4ᵗʰ August Celebration (Despatches from the Greek Embassy in Berlin)*
4ᵗʰ August Celebrations (Despatches from Consulate General Alexandria)

Archive 2, *File 2*   *Foreign Schools in Greece 1940*

Archive 3, *File 3*   *Foreign Press Publications 1940*

Public Records Office (British Foreign Office). Kew, London.

FO 371/21143   *Affairs of Cable & Wireless Ltd. in Greece, May 1937*

FO 371/21143   *About Electric Transport Company Athens, July 1937*

FO 371/21147   *Press Censorship in Greece, February 1937*

FO 371/21147   *Situation in Greece, February 1937*

FO 371/21150   *German Propaganda in Greece, March 1937*

FO 371/21150   *Manchester Guardian - Articles against the regime, April 1937*

FO 371/21147   *Situation in Greece, March 1937*

FO 371/21147   *Situation in Greece, April 1937*

FO 371/21150   *German Influence in Greece, May 1937*

FO 371/21147   *Situation in Greece, May 1937*

FO 371/21147   *Situation in Greece, June 1937*

FO 371/21147   *Visit to Samos island, June 1937*

FO 371/21147   *Preparations for the 'Fourth of August' anniversary, July 1937*

FO 371/21147   *Celebration/anniversary of the 'Fourth of August', August 1937*

FO 371/21770   *Celebration of 25 March National Holiday, April 1939*

FO 371/21770   *Situation in Greece, May 1939*

FO 371/23770   *Public Opinion in Greece, June 1939*

FO 371/23770   *Situation in Greece, March 1939*

FO 371/23770   *Situation in Greece-Celebration /anniversary, August 1939*

Efimeris Tis Kiverniseos - FEK (Official Greek Gazette)

FEK 184   *28 May 1930*

FEK 418   *21 September 1935*

FEK 323   *4 August 1936*

FEK 325   *4 August 1936*

FEK 326   *4 August 1936*

FEK 328   *5 August 1936*

FEK 344   *14 August 1936*

FEK 358   *19 August 1936*

FEK 367   *24 August 1936*

FEK 379   *31 August 1936*

FEK 380   *31 August 1936*

FEK 391   *7 September 1936*

FEK 499   *10 November 1936*

FEK 561   *29 December 1936*

FEK 23   *25 January 1937*

FEK 93   *12 March 1937*

FEK 96   *17 March 1937*

FEK 33   *2 February 1937*

FEK 202   26 May 1937
FEK 474   23 November 1937
FEK 45   11 February 1938
FEK 68   22 February 1938
FEK 186   9 May 1938
FEK 5   4 January 1939
FEK 61   16 February 1939
FEK 224   3 June 1939
FEK 257   22 June 1939

Periodicals

Kinimatografikos Astir. Fortnightly magazine, Heraklis Economou, Athens 1937)

Nea Estia. Fortnightly Magazine. (Ioannis Kollaros & Co., Athens,1937-1941)

Ta Paraskinia. Weekly Theatre and Cinema Review. (Th. Sinodinos, Athens 1937-1940)

Theatro, Monthly Magazine. (Karantinos, 1938)

To Elliniko Theatro, Monthly Newspaper issued in 1925 by the Union of Artists. 1937-1938

'Fourth of August' and *EON*

E Neolea. Weekly periodical, (*EON* Publications, Athens 1939-1940)

To Neon Kratos. Monthly periodical, (Kabanis, Aristos, Athens, 1937-1940)

Nea Politiki. Monthly periodical. (Tournakis I., Athens, 1940)

Newspapers

Athinaika Nea. (Athens , 1938-1939-1940)

Asyrmatos.. (Athens, 1940-1941)

Elefthero Vima. (Athens, 1939 –1940)

Estia. (Athens, 1938)

Kathimerini. (Athens, 1936-1938)

Proia. (Athens, 1937-1938-1939)

Vradini. (Athens, 1936-1938)

Ethnikos Kyrix (New York, 1939-1940-1945)

Apogevmatini. (Thessaloniki,1937)

Arkadika Nea. (Tripolis, 1939)

Corinthiaki Echo. (Corinth,1937)

Eleftheros Kyrix. (Kavalla,1937)

Ethniki Anagennisi. (Serras, 1938)

Proia, (Drama, 1939)

FILMOGRAPHY 1936 - 1941

EON Newsreels.

1. O Protos Orkos Tis EON, 1938 (The First Taking of the *EON* Oath, 1938)

2. To Stratopedon Ioannis Metaxas, 1938 (The Ioannis Metaxas Youth Camp,1938)

3. Athlitikoi Agones Tis EON, 1938 *(EON* Athletics, 1938)

4. O Eortasmos Tis EON Sto Pedio Tou Areos, 1938. (The Celebration of *EON* in Pedion tou Areos,1938)

'Fourth of August' Newsreels.

1. Proti Epeteios Tis Tetartis Augoustou, 1937 ('Fourth of August' First Anniversary, 1937*)*

2. Deftera Epeteios Tis Tetartis Augustou, 1938 ('Fourth of August' Second Anniversary, 1938)

3. Triti Epeteios Tis Tetartis Augoustou, 1939 ('Fourth of August' Third Anniversary, 1939)

4. 'E 25 Martiou,' 1938 *(*The '25 March,' 1938)

5. Eortasmos Tis Ergatikis Protomagias, 1938 (Celebration of 'The First of May' 1938)

*6. Ekstrateia Gia To Prasino,*1938 (Reforestation Campain, 1938)

7. O Polemos , 1940 (The War, 1940)

8. E Kideia Tou Ioannou Metaxas, 1941 (Ioannis Metaxas' Funeral. 1941)

THEATRIKA ERGA (Theatrical Plays)

1. Papaflessas

*2. Brosta Sto Thanato (*Facing Death*)*

3. Ta Souliotopoula Den Pethanan (The Children of Souli Did Not Die)

4. Elthe Mia Mera (The Day Has Come)

5. E Ieri Floga (The Sacred Flame)

6. Pentheseleia

Contemporary Works

Memoirs and Diaries

Metaxas, Ioannis, *To Prosopiko tou Imerologio* (His Personal Diary) Volumes 1-7, (revised edition., Govosti, Athens. No. Date). Vol. 1-4., Christides, Ch.,(ed.) (August 1950), Vol.5-6., Siphneos P.(ed.) (Athens 1963), Vol.7-8., Vranas Phedon (ed.) (Athens 1960)

Metaxas, Ioannis. *Logoi ke Skepseis 1936- 1941* (Speeches and Thoughts). Two Volumes (Ikaros, Athens, 1969)

Metaxa, Lela, *To Imerologio Tis Omirias Tis kas Lelas Metaxa December 1944 - January 1945* (Unpublished Diary of Mrs Lela Metaxas kept in captivity - December 1944 - January 1945). Archeio Ioannou Metaxa, Genika Arceia tou Kratous. File 18.

Metaxas, Lela, *To Imerologio mou* (My Diary). Unpublished, hand-written diary. Archeio Ioannou Metaxa, Genika Arceia tou Kratous. File 45.

Tzifos, Amvrosios, *To Imerologio mou 1939-1945* (My Diary 1939-1945) Unpublished typewritten diary. Archeio Ioannou Metaxa, Genika Arceia tou Kratous. File 45

Books and Articles

Ae Ideae Tou I.Metaxa Dia Tin Ellada ke Ton Ellinismon (The Beliefs of I.Metaxas for Hellas and Hellenism). (Pyrsos, Athens, undated)

Agelomatis, Christos, 'Ai Theatrikai Parastaseis Tou Etous: Scholeia Kritiki, Syngrafeis' (The Theatrical Performances of this Year: Criticism, Plays, Writers). *To Neon Kratos*, (Kabanis, A., Athens, 1938)

Annuarie Statistige de la Grece 1939. (Athens, 1939)

Apologismos Mias Dietias 1936-1940 (An Account of the Two Years 1936-1940). (Ekdoseis *Tetartis Augoustou*, Athens, 1938)

Athlitiki Istoria Dyo Eton, Tetarti Augoustou 1936-1938 (History of the Athletics Fourth of August 1936-1938). (Ekdoseis *Tetartis Augoustou*, Athens, 1938)

Bamias, G., 'E Chreokopia tou Kinovouleftismou' (The Failure of Parliamentarism). *To Neon Kratos*, issue 6, (Kabanis,A., Athens, 1939)

Bastias, Costis, ' Ta Grammata ke E Technes' (Letters and Art). *To Neon Kratos*, issue 24, (Kabanis, A., Athens, 1939)

Cotopouli, Marika, 'E Penthesileia Sto Theatro Tou Lycavitou'(Penthesileia at the Lycabetous Theatre). *To Neon Kratos*, issue 24, (Kabanis, A., Athens, 1939)

E Istoria tou Ellinikou Dichamsou ke tis Mikrasiatikis Katastrofis (The History of the Greek Schism and the Asia Minor Catastrophe). (*Kathimerini*, Athens, 1935)

E Istoria tou Ethnikou Dichasmou-Kata Tin Arthografia tou Eleftheriou Venizelou ke tou Ioannou Metaxa (History of the National Schism - According to the Articles Exchanged Between Eleftherios Venizelos and Ioannis Metaxas). (Kiromanos, Thessaloniki, 1994)

Evdomadieon Programma Radiofonikou Stathmou Athinon. Panigiriki Ekdosis Tis Tetartis Augoustou (Weekly Programme of the Athens Radio Station. Panegyric issue, of the 'Fourth of August'. (Ekdoseis *Tetartis Augoustou*, 30 July-5 August 1939)

E.I.A.R. Radiofonikos Stathmos Bari - E Idiki Elliniki Metadosis. 1 Iouliou 1934-1 Iouliou 1937. EIAR Ente Italiano Audicione Radiofoniche Le Transussione Speciali Per La Grecia 1 Luglio 1934-1 July 1937 (The Bari Station and Greek Broadcasting 1 July 1934 -1 July 1937). (Stalimenti Grafici Valechi, Firenze, August, 1937)

Economiki Epetiris Tis Ellados (Economic Calendar of Greece). (Athens, 1940)

Enthimion Gefmatos Prosfigikou Kosmou (Token of a Dinner given by the Refugees). (Ekdoseis *Tetartis Augoustou*, Athens, July 1939)

O Eortasmos Tis Ekatontaetiridos tou Ethnikou ke Kapodistriakou Panepistimiou, 1837-1937 (The Centenary of National and Kapodistrian University. (Athens,1937)

Ethnikon Evagelion: Oi Patriotike Logoi tou Prothipourgou k. Ioannou Metaxa (National

Evagelium: The Patriotic Speeches of Prime Minister Ioannis Metaxas). (Ekdoseis *Tetartis Augoustou*, Athens, 1936)

Fisher, G. B. 'Economic Autarky' *Nea Politiki* (Tournakis, I., Athens, 1940)

Freude und Arbeit. Ektheis Hara ke Ergasia Athens-Zapeion 1-15 May 1938 (Ekdoseis *Tetartis Augoustou*, Athens, 1938)

Haris, Petros, 'E Parastasi Tis Penthesileia' (The Penthesileia Performance). *To Neon Kratos*, issue 24, (Kabanis, A., Athens, 1939)

Haris, Petros, 'Ta Laika Theatra' (Popular Theatres). *To Neon Kratos*, issue 11 (Kabanis, A., Athens, 1938)

Haris, Petros, ' O Apofasistikos Dimotikistis' (The Determined Advocate of *Demotic*). *Nea Estia* (Kolllaros, Ioannis, & Co., Athens, 1941)

Kabanis, Aristos, ' Prostagi Synidiseos'(A Command of Conscience). *To Neon Kratos*, issue 10 (Kabanis, A., June, 1938)

Kabanis, Aristos, 'Afete Tous Nekrous Thaptin Tous Eaftous'(Let The Dead Bury Themselves). *To Neon Kratos,* issue 6 (Kabanis, A., February, 1938)

Kabas, A., 'Oi Dianoumenoi ke to Neon Kratos'(The Intellectuals and the New State). *To Neon Kratos* issue 8 (Kabanis, A., Athens, 1938)

Kallonas, D. *Ioannis Metaxas: Mathitis - Stratiotis - Politikos - Agonistis Kyvernitis* (Ioannis Metaxas: Student-Soldier-Politician-Fighter-Governor). (Athens, 1938). No Publisher.

Karagatsis, M., 'O Protos Dimotikistis Prothipourgos' (The First Prime Minister an Advocate of *Demotic*). *Nea Estia* (Kollaros, Ioannis & Co., Athens, 1941)

Karanopoulos, Dimitrios, 'Kratos ke Radiofono' (Radio and the State). *To Neon Kratos*, issue 6 (Kabanis, A., Athens, 1938)

Kofinakis, Michalis, 'E Exomologisis Enos Speaker' (The Confession of a Speaker). *Evdomadieon Programma Radiofonikou Stathmou Athinon, 30 Iouliou, 5 Augoustou 1939-Panigyriki Ekdosi Tetartis Augoustou* (Weekly Radio Programme of Athens Radio Station 30 July, 5 August 1939 - Panegyric issue. (Ekdoseis *Tetartis Augoustou*, Athens, 1939)

Koumaros, N.D. and Matzufas, G.A, 'Ai Themeliodeis Syntagmatike Archai tou Neou Kratous' (The Basic Constitutional Principles of the New State). *To Neon Kratos*, issue 11 (Kabanis, A., Athens, 1938)

Koumaros, Nicolas, D. 'Oi Logoi tou Archigou' (The Chief's Speeches). *To Neon Kratos*, issue 21 (Kabanis, A., Athens, 1940)

Kribas, Elias, 'Kathikoda ke Idanika Tis Neoleas' (The Duties and Ideals of Youth). *To Neon Kratos*, issue 28 (Kabanis, A., Athens, 1939)

Matzufas, Georgios, 'To Ethnikon Symferon Os Gnomon Tis Erminias ke tis Efarmogis Tou Nomou' (The National Interest as a Condition behind the Interpretation and Application of Law). *To Neon Kratos*, issue 17 (Kabanis, A., January 1939)

Menieon Deltion Typou Tou Yfipourgiou Typou ke Tourismou (Monthly Press Review, Sub-Ministry of Press and Tourism), (Ekdoseis *YTT,* Athens,1937, 1938, 1939, 1940)

Nea Estia - Ekdosis Afieromeni ston Ioanni Metaxa, Prostati Ton Grammaton ke Technon (Nea

Estia -Dedicated to Ioannis Metaxas Patron of Letters and Art). (Kollaros, Ioannis, & Co., Athens, 1941)

Nicoloudis, Theologos, 'To Neon Kratos'(The New State). *To Neon Kratos*, issue 1 (Kabanis, A., Athens, 1937)

Nicoloudis, Theologos, *E Elliniki Crisis* (The Greek Crisis). (Cairo ,1945)

Nicoloudis, Theologos, 'O Ioannis Metaxas: 4 Arthra tou Ypourgou Th. Nocoloudi' (Ioannis Metaxas: 4 Articles by the Minister Th.Nicoloudis). *To Neon Kratos*, issue 42 (Kabanis, A., Athens, 1941)

Papadakis, V. P, *E Chthesini ke E Avriani Ellas. Mia Geniki Vasis Politikis Skepseos ke Praxeon* (Greece of Yesterday and of Tomorrow a General analysis of Thought and Action), (Cairo, 1945)

Papalexandrou, H., 'E Eleftheria Tou Typou ke E Eleftheria tou Dimosiografou'(The Freedom of the Press and the Freedom of the Journalist). *To Neon Kratos,* issue 10 (Kabanis,A., Athens, 1938)

Reavau, R., 'To Ergon Tou Laikou Diafotismou es Tin Germanian' (The Popular Enlightement in Germany). *To Neon Kratos*, issue 10 (Kabanis, A., Athens, 1938)

Roumanis, I.G., 'En Ethnos; En Kratos; Mia Glossa' (One Nation; One State; One Language). *Nea Politiki* (Tournakis, I., Athens,1940)

Statistiki Epetirida Tis Ellados (Greek Statistic Calendar). (Athens,1938)

To Neon Kratos, issue 18 (Kabanis, A., Athens, 1939)

Tessera Chronia Diakyverniseos Ioannou Metaxas 1936-1940 (Four Years of Government by Ioannis Metaxas 1936-1940), Four Volumes. (*YTT Tmima Diafotiseos,* Ekdoseis *Tetartis Augoustou,* Athens, 1940)

To Ergon Tis Ethnikis Kyverniseos – E KOINONIKH PRONIA. (The Work of the National Government- Social Welfare).(Ekdoseis *Tetartis Augoustou*, Athens, 1937)

*To Kratos Tis 4es Augoustou kata to 1937 (*The Fourth of August'State During 1937). (Ekdoseis *Tetartis Augoustou*, Athens, 1937)

*To Politefma tou Ioannou Metaxas (*The System of Government according to Ioannis Metaxas). Published by his daughter Loukia Metaxas (Athens, 1945)

Tournakis, I., 'Skepseis dia tin Ellinikin Anagennisin'(Thoughts on the *Hellenic* Regeneration). *Nea Politiki*, issue 9 (Tournakis, I., Athens,1938)

Tria Chronia Ergasias Is Tin Ellinikin Eparhia 4 Augoustou 1936 - 4 Augoustou 1939 (Three Years of Works in the Greek Provinces 4 August 1936 - 4 August 1939) (Ekdoseis *YTT*, Athens, 1939)

Tria Eti Diakiverniseos tou k.Ioannou Metaxa 1936-1939 (Three Years of Goverment by Ioannis Metaxas 1936-1939). (Ekdoseis *Tetartis Augoustou*, Athens, 1939)

Trieris, Leonidas, *Metaxas - O Neos Likourgos. Spoudi* (Metaxas- The New Likourgos. A Study), (Athens, 1940)

Zavitsianos, Evangelos K., *OI Dyo Megaloi Kephalineis Genithentes en Ithaki: Odysseas ke Ioannis Metaxas (*The Two Great Cephalonians born in Ithaka, Ulysses and Ioannis Metaxas). (Athens, 1939)

Ekdoseis *EON* (*EON* Publications)

Apospasmata Ton Epitel. Grafion Dieuthinseos & Ypiresion Kentrikis Dioikhseos Ethnikis Organoseos Neoleas tis Ellados ke ton Periferion. (Extracts from the Recommendations of the *EON* Central and Peripheral Offices). (Ekdoseis *EON*, Athens, 1939)

Diatagi 28, Peri Genikon Katefthinseon ke Odigion (Circular 28 - About General Directions and Instructions). (Ekdoseis *EON*, Athens, 1939)

Deftera Diaskepsis EON (Second Congress of *EON*). (Ekdoseis *EON*, Athens, 1940)

Oi Katefthinseis Tis EON (Guidlines to the *EON*). ((Ekdoseis *EON* , Athens, 1939)

'*EON* ke E 25e Martiou' (*EON* and the 25th of March) *E Neolea*, 25 (Athens, 1939)

E Georgia Stin Ellada (Farming in Greece). (Ekdoseis *EON*, Athens,1939)

Ecogenia (Family). (Ekdoseis *EON* , Athens, 1940)

*Ethnos - Sira Ekdoseon peri Ekpedefseos (*Nation - A Series of educational Publications) (Ekdoseis *EON* , Athens, 1939)

Evreoi ke Kommunismos (Jews and Communism). (Ekdoseis *EON* , Athens, 1939)

Ioannis Metaxas - The Man, The Officer, The Politician (Ekdoseis *EON*, Athens, 1939)

Oikokyrika (Housekeeping). (Ekdoseis *EON*, Athens, 1939)

Kanellopoulos, Alexandros, *Ethniki Kyriarcheia ke Ithiki Anexartisia* (National Supremacy and Moral Independence). (Ekdoseis *EON*, Athens 1939)

Kanellopoulos, Alexandros, 'Sti Giorti Sou' (On Your Name-day) *E Neolea*, issue 16, (Athens, 1940)

Kanellopoulos, Alexandros, *O Kivernitikos Epitropos pros tous Synagonistas tou (* The *EON* Leader to his Comrades*)*. (Ekdoseis *EON* , 1939)

Karamanos, M. Kyriakos, '*Ti Tha Kamoume?*' (What Are We To Do?). (Ekdoseis *EON*, Athens, 1940)

Karaiskaki, Sitsa, 'Oi Kallitechnikoi Agones' (The Cultural Games). *E Neolea*, issue 35 (Athens, 1940)

Karaiskaki, Sitsa, 'Enas Laos, Mia Psyche, Mia Giorti-Ikones Pou Miloun' (One Nation, One Heart, One Celebration-Pictures which Talk). *E Neolea*, issue 44 (Athens, 1939)

Karaiskaki, Sitsa, 'E Thesis Tis Gynekas Sto Neon Kratos'(The Place of Woman in the New State). *E Neolea*, issue 44 (Athens, 1940)

Karaiskaki, Sitsa, 'To Dilitirio Tis Psychis'(The Poisoning of The Soul). *Neolea*, issue 21 (Athens, 1939)

Karaiskaki, Sitsa, 'Hortasmena Pedia, Ikanoi Polites'(Fed Children-Competent Citizens). *E Neolea*, issue 7 (Athens, 1939)

Karaiskaki, Sitsa, 'Elliniki Techni-Elliniki Phyli' (Greek Art-Greek Nation). *E Neolea*, issue 15 (Athens, 1940)

Karaiskaki, Sitsa, 'E Gyneka Ieria Tis Ikogenias ke Tou Etnous'(The Woman-Priestess of the Family and the Nation. *E Neolea*, issue 21 (Athens, 1940)

To Katantima Tou Bolsevikismou (The Misery of Bolshevism). (Ekdoseis *EON*, Athens, 1939)

Kostantinidis, Th., 'E Idea tis 4es Augoustou ke e Techni'(The idea of the '4th of August and Art). *E Neolea*, issue 36 (Athens, 1939)

Mallosis, I., *'Kinovouleftismos ke Kommatismos'* (Parliamentarism and Partisanship). (Ekdoseis *EON*, Athens,1939)

Maniadakis, Costantinos, *'Kriseis Ke Syberasmata Epi Tes Neoleas Pro Ke Meta Tin 4e Augoustou'* (Comments and Conclusions on Youth Before and After the 4th of August). (Ekdoseis *EON*, Athens, 1939)

Milonas, G., 'E Epanastasis Tis 4es Augoustou' (The 4th of August Revolution). *E Neolea,* issue 44 (Athens, 1940)

Nicoloudis, Theologos, *'Ena Kyrigma Pisteos'* (A Sermon of Faith). (Ekdoseis *EON*, Athens, 1937)

Nicoloudis, Theologos, *'To Ethnikon Kratos Os Politikon ke Economicon Systima'* (The National State as a Political and Economic System). (Ekdoseis *EON*, Athens, 1939)

Nicolaidis Melis, 'E Giorti' (The Name-Day). *E Neolea*, issue 16 (Athens, 1940)

Organismos Esoterikis Ipiresias EON (Regulations of *EON* Internal Services). (Ekdoseis *EON*, Athens, 1939)

Odigos Pros Hrisin Ton Fallagiton ke Falaggitisson ton Metehonton is ton en Athines Eortasmon tis 4es Augoustou (A Guide for the Phallangite Boys and Girls participating in the celebration of 4th August) (Ekdoseis *EON*, Athens 1938.)

*Peri Technis (*About Art). (Ekdoseis *EON*, Athens, 1940)

*Peri Genikon Katefthinseon ke Odigion (*About General Instructions and Orders). (Ekdoseis *EON*, Athens, 1939)

Phalagites ke Skapaneis Grigorite Kapios Karadoki (Phalangites and Pioneers Be Aware Some-one is Lurking). (Ekdoseis *EON*, Athens, 1939)

Phalagitiki Epitheorisis (Phalangite Review). (Ekdoseis *EON*, Athens, 1940)

A' Panellinios Ekthesis EON 26 Maiou-30 Iouniou 1940 (A Panhellenic *EON* Exhibition 26 May-30 June 1940). (Ekdoseis *EON*, Athens, 1940)

B Panellinioi Athlitikoi Agones Ethnikis Organoseos Neoleas Ellados (B Panhellenic Athletic Games of the National Organisation of Youth). (Ekdoseis *EON*, Athens, 1940)

Panellinios Ekthesis EON (Panhellenic *EON* Exhibition). (Ekdoseis *EON*, Athens, 1939)

Sideris, Yannis, 'To Neoelliniko Theatro' (The Modern Greek Theatre). *E Neolea*, issue 42 (Athens, 1939)

Thriskia (Religion). (Ekdoseis *EON*, Athens, 1939)

To Katantima Tou Bolsevikismou (The Misery of Bolshevism). (Ekdoseis *EON*, Athens, 1939)

Ta Tragoudia tis Neoleas (The *EON* Songs). (Ekdoseis *EON*, Athens, 1940)

Ta Ideodi Tis Filis Os Gnomon Tis Ellinikis Neotitos (The Ideals of the Nation as the decisive factor for Youth). (Ekdoseis *EON*, Athens,1939)

Ypothike tou Archigou (Moral Injunction by the Chief). (Ekdoseis *EON*, Athens, 1939

O Vasilefs (The King). (Ekdoseis *EON*, Athens, 1939)

Secondary Sources

Anastasiadis, Giorgos, *Anexandliti Polis-Thessaloniki 1917-1974* (Inexhaustable City-Thessaloniki 1917-1974). (Ekfrasi, Thessaloniki 1996)

Anastasiadis, Giorgos, *E Thessaloniki Ton Efimeridon* (Thessaloniki of The Newspapers). (Ekfrasi, Thessaloniki, 1994)

Anastasiadis, Giorgos, *Thessaloniki-Istoria Ke Politismos. Oi Efimerides Sti Thessaloniki ke ta Mesa Mazikis Epikinonias* (Thessaloniki History and Civilisation-Newspapers in Thessaloniki and the Means of Mass Communication). (Paratiritis, Thessaloniki) No Date.

Andrikopoulos, Yannis, *Oi Rizes Tou Ellinikou Fasismou-Stratos Politiki* (The Roots of Greek Fascism - Army and Politics). (Digenis , Athens, 1977)

Bastias, Yiannis C., *O Costis Bastias Sta Chronia tou Mesopolemou* (Costis Bastias in the Inter-war Period). (Ekdotiki, Athens, 1997)

Blinkhorn, Martin (ed), *Fascist and Conservatives* (Unwin Hyman, London, 1990)

Borejsza,W. Jerry, 'E Ellada ke E Valkaniki Politiki Tis Fasistikis Italias, 1936-1940' (Greece and Italy's Policy on the Balkans 1936-1940) in Fleicher & Svoronos,(eds.) *E Ellada 1936-1944. Diktaktoria, Katochi, Antistasi* (Greece 1936-1944. Dictatorship Occupation, Resistance). (Morfotiko Instituto *ATE*, Athens, 1985)

Bracher, Dietrich Karl, *The German Dictatorship - The Origins, structure and consequences of National Socialism* (Penguin, Suffolk, 1973)

Bullock, Alan, *Hitler and Stalin-Parallel Lives* (Fontana, London, 1991)

Bullock, Alan, *Hitler - A Study in Tyranny* (Penguin, London, 1990)

Caughie, John and Rocket, Kevin, *The Companion to British and Irish Cinema* (Cassell, London, 1996)

Clogg, Richard, *A Concise History of GREECE* (Cambridge University Press, London, 1992)

Close, H. David, *The Origins of the Greek Civil War* (Longman, London and New York, 1995)

Close, H. David, 'E Astynomia sto kathestos tis 4es Avgoustou' (Police under the 4th of August Regime) in Fleicher & Svoronos(eds..) *E Ellada 1936-1944. Diktaktoria, Katochi, Antistasi,* (Greece 1936-1944. Dictatorship, Occupation, Resistance). (Morfotiko Instituto *ATE*, Athens, 1985)

Close, H. David. 'The Power Base of the Metaxas' Dictatorship' in *Aspects of Greece 1936-1940, The Metaxas Dictatorship*, Robin Higham and Thanos Veremis (eds.) (ELIAMEP-Vryonis Center, Athens,1993)

Cocket, Richard, *Twilight of Truth - Chamberlain, Appeasement and the Manipulation of the Press.* (Weidenfeld & Nicolson, London, 1989)

Crew, David, F., (ed.) *Nazism and German Society 1933-1945* (Routledge, London, 1994)

Curan, James and Seaton, Jean, *Power Without Responsibility - The Press and Broadcasting in Britain* (Routledge, London and New York, 1997)

Dafnis, Grigorios, *E Ellas Metaxy Dio Polemon* (Greece Between Two Wars), Two Volumes (Kaktos, Athens,1997)

Damaskos, Dimitris, (ed), Verolino ke Archeotira (Berlin and Antiquity) *Kathimerini-Epta Imeres* (7 March, 1999)

Demethas, Zacharias, 'E Exelixi Vasikon Megethon Tis Ellinikis Oikonomias, 1935-1939' (The Development of the Basic Aspects of the Greek Economy 1935-1939) in Fleicher & Svoronos (eds.) *E Ellada 1936-1944. Diktaktoria, Katochi, Antistasi,* (Greece 1936-1944. Dictatorship, Occupation, Resistance). (Morfotiko Instituto *ATE,* Athens,1985)

Dokimio Istorias tou KKE A Tomos 1918-1949 Second Edition. Treatise of trhe History of the *KKE* Vol. 1, second edition (Sychroni Epochi, Athens 1996)

*Egiklopedia Papyros-Larousse Britanica (*Encyclopaedia Papyros-Larousse-Britanica), Volumes 31,33,35,40,43,45,51,61 (Papyros, Athens, 1989)

Egiklopedikon Lexikon Helios, (Encyclopedian Dictionary Helios)Vol. IST (Helios Athens,1965)

Escott-Sweet, Bickham, *A Political & Economic Survey 1939-1953* (Royal Institute of International Affairs, London & N.Y.,1954)

Gavriilidis, Costas, *To Imerologio Tis Anafis Sti Diktatoria Tou Metaxa* (The Anafi Diary During Metaxas Diktatorship). (Entos, Athens, 1997)

Gatopoulos, A., *Andreas Michalakopoulos 1875-1938 - E Viographia ke to Ergo tou* (Andreas Michalakopoulos 1875-1938 - His Biography and his Work). (Eleftheroudakis, Athens,1947)

Connely, Mark., Welch, David (eds), *WAR AND THE MEDIA* – *Reportage and Propaganda 1900-2003.* (I.B.Tauris, London, 2005)

Genitsaris, Michalis, 'Autoviografia'(Autobiography) in Hatzidoulis Costas(ed) *Rebetiki Istoria*(Rebetic Story). (Nefeli, Athens,) No Date.

Graber, G. S., *History of the SS* (Robert Hale, London ,1978)

Georgiadis, Nearchos, *Rebetico ke Politiki* (Rebetico and Politics). (Sychroni Epochi, Athens, 1993)

Grigoriades, Phivos, *4e Augoustou - Albania 1935-1941* (Kedrinos, Athens,1972)

Gulbert, D., Cull, N.,Welch, D. (eds*), Propaganda and Mass Persuasion, A Historical Encyclopedia, 1500 to the Present* (ABC-Clio,2003)

Hatzidakis, Giorgos, 'E Radifoniki Protoporia (Radio Advances)' *Kathimerini-Epta Imeres,* (31 December, 1996)

Hatzidakis, Giorgos, *To Tragoudi sto Radiofono* (The Songs on the Radio) *Kathimerini Epta Imeres,* (26 April, 1998)

Hatzidakis,Giorgos, 'E Proistoria Tis Radiofonias' (The Prehistory of Radio Broadcasting). *Radiotileoras,* issues 1322-1342, June to November 1995

Hatzidakis, Giorgos, 'E Istoria Tis Radiofonias (The History of Radio Broadcasting) *Radiotileorasi,* issues 1343-1380, November 1995 - July 1996

Hatzipanagis, Th. and Maraka, Lila (eds.), *E Athinaiki Epitheorisis* (The Athenian Revue) Vol.1. (Nea Elliniki Vivliothiki, Athens, 1977)

Heliadis, (ed), *Ellinikos Kinimatografos 1906-1960* (Greek Cinema 1906-1960). (Fantasia, Athens, 1960)

Hitler, Adolf, *Mein Kampf,* translated by Ralph Manheim (Pimlico, London 1992).

Hoffmann, Hilmar, *The Triumph of Propaganda, Film and National Socialism 1933-1945* (Bergham Books, Providence-Oxford, 1996)

Iatrides, John O., (ed.) *Ambassador MacVeagh Reports, Greece 1933-1947* (Princeton University Press, Princeton, 1980)

Iatrides. John O, (ed.) *GREECE IN THE 1940s - A Nation in Crisis* (University Press of New England Hanover and London, 1981)

Irmscher, Johannes, ' Oi Epistimonikes Scheseis tou Panepistimiou tou Verolinou me ti Fasistikh Ellada' (The Scientific Relations between the Berlin University and Fascist Greece' in Fleichr & Svoronos (eds.) *E Ellada 1936-1944. Diktaktoria, Katochi, Antistasi,* (Greece 1936-1944, Dictatorship, Occupation, Resistance).

Jelavich, Barbara, *History of The Balkans - Twentieth Century*, Vol. II. (Cambridge University Press, Cambridge ,1983)

Jowett, S.Garth and Victoria, O'Donnell, *Propaganda and Persuasion* (Sage Publications, London,1992)

Kanellopoulos, Panagiotis, *Pos Efthasame stin 21e Apriliou 1967.* (How We came to 21st April 1967). (Estia Athens, 1997)

Kanellopoulos, Panagiotis, *1935-1945 Enas Apologismos* (1935-1945 A Recollection). (Athens, 1945) No.Publisher.

Kantorowich, Alfred, *Why A Library of the Burned Books?* (Paris,1934)

Kapogiannopoulos, A., *O I. Metaxas Autopsychoanalyete* (I. Metaxas - A Self-analysis), (Athens, 1986)

Karras, Nikolaos, *O Ioannis Metaxas, Istoriki - Politiki Prosegisi* (Ioannis Metaxas. A Historical and Political Approach). (Pelasgos, Athens, 1994)

Katsoulis, Georgios D., *To Katestimeno Stin Neoelliniki Istoria* (The Establishment in Modern Greek History). (Nea Sinora, Athens,1975)

Kerophylas, Yiannis, *E Athina Tou Mesopolemou* (Inter-war Athens). (Filippoti, Athens, 1988)

Kershaw, Ian, *The Hitler Myth* (Oxford University Press, Oxford, 1987)

Kershaw, Ian, *Hitler* (Longman, London ,1991)

'Kinimatografos' (Cinema), *Encyclopedia Papyros-Larousse,* (Papyros-Larousse, Athens, 1968)

Kiskilas, Panagiotis, *Simioseis Gia Tin Istoria Tou Radiofonou* (Brief Notes For the History of The Radio) (Athens, undated)

Kitsikis, Dimitris, *E Ellas Tis 4es Augoustou ke e Megale Dynameis-To Archeio tou Ellinkou Ypourgiou Exoterikon 1936-1941* (Greece of the 4th of August and the Great Powers-Greek Foreign Office Archives 1936-1941). (Ikaros, Athens,1974)

Kofas, Jon, V., *Authoritarianism in Greece - The Metaxas Regime* (East European Monographs, New York, 1983)

Koliopoulos, John, S., 'Metaxas and Greek Foreign Relations, 1936-1941', in *Aspects of Greece 1936-1940, The Metaxas Dictatorship*, Robin Higham and Thanos Veremis (eds.). (ELIAMEP-Vryonis Center, Athens,1993)

Koliopoulos, Ioannis, S., *E Diktatoria tou Metaxas ke O Polemos tou 40* (Metaxas' Dictatorship and the 1940 War). (Vanias, Thessaloniki,1994)

Koliopoulos, Ioannis, S., *Palinorthosi Diktatoria Polemos 1935-1941-O Bretanikos Paragontas Stin Ellada* (Restoration Dictatorship War 1935-1941- The British Factor in Greece). (Estia, Athens,1985)

Koch, H.W., *The Hitler Youth, Origins & Developments 1922-1945* (MacDonald & Jane's, London,1983)

KKE Episima Keimena 1931-1940 (*KKE* Official Documents) 1931-1940, Vol. 4 (Athens, 1981)

Kracauer, Siegfried, *From Caligari to Hitler, A Psychological Histroy of the German Film* (Princeton University Press, United states of America,1974)

Kunduros, S.Roussos, *E Asfaleia tou Kathestotos - Politikoi Kratumenoi - Ektopiseis ke Taxeis Stin Ellada 1924-74* (The Security of the Regime's Political Prisoners, Deportations and Classes in Greece 1924-74). (Kastaniotis, Athens,1978)

Lee, Arthur S. Gould, *The Royal House of Greece* (Ward Lock & Co. Limited, London & Melbourne, 1948)

Lee, J. Stephen, *The European Dictatorships 1918-1945* (Routledge, London,1987)

Linardatos, Spiros, *E 4e Augoustou* (The 4th of August). (Dialogos, Athens, 1974)

Linardatos, Spiros, *Pos Efthasame Stin 4e Avgoustou* (How we reached the 4th August). (Themelio, Athens, 1975)

Linardatos, Spiros, *O Ioannis Metaxas ke E Megales Dynameis, 1936-1940* (Ioannis Metaxas and the Great Powers, 1936-1940). (Proskinio, Athens, 1993)

MacGregor, Knox, 'Conquest Foreign and Domestic in Fascist Italy and Nazi Germany' in Emsley Clive, Marwick Arthur, and Simpson Wendy, (eds..) *War Peace and Social Change in Twentieth Century Europe* (Open University Press, Milton Keynes, 1994)

Machera, Eleni, *E Neolea Tis 4es Augoustou* (The 4th of August Youth). (Istoriko Archeio Ellinikis Neoleas,Geniki Gramatia Neas Genias, Athens, 1987)

Malenos, Miltiadis, I., *4e Augoustou Pos ke Diati Epevlithi E Diktaktoria tou Metaxa* (4th of August. How and Why the Metaxas Dictatorship was Imposed). (Athens, 1947)

Malenos, Miltiadis, I., *To Simiomatario Tou Vlassi Roumeli* (The Diary of Vlassis Roumelis). (Zabra-Vasileiou Bros., Athens, 1959)

Markezinis, Spiros, *Synhroni Politiki Istoria Tis Ellados* (Modern Political History of Greece), Vol. I. (Papyros, Athens, 1994)

Mayer, Costas, *Istoria tou Ellinikou Typou* (The History of the Greek Press). Three Volumes. (Dimopoulos, Athens,1957)

Mavrokordatos, George, Th., *Stillborn Republic. Social Coalitions and Party Strategies in Greece, 1922-1936* (University of California Press , L.A., London , 1983)

Mazarakis Ainian Alexandros, *Apomnimonefmata* (Memoirs). (Ikaros, Athens, 1949)

Mazower, Mark and Veremins, Thanos, 'The Greek Economy 1922-1941', in Higham & Verremis (eds.) *Aspects of Greece 1936-1940, The Metaxas Dictatorship*. (Eliamep-Vryonis Center, Athens 1993)

Meissner, Renate, 'E Ethnososialistiki Germania ke e Ellada kata tin Diarkia tis Metaxikis Diktaktorias' (National-Socialist Germany and Greece during the Metaxas' Dictatorship) in Fleicher & Svoronos (eds.) *E Ellada 1936-1944. Diktaktoria, Katochi, Antistasi*. (Greece 1936-1944. Dictatorship, Occupation, Resistance). (Morfotiko Instituto *ATE*, Athens,1985

Metsolis, Georgios, 'To Theatro Stin Athina 1936-1967'(Theatre in Athens 1936-1967) (Nea Elliniki Encyclopedia, Athens, 1968)

Morgan, Philip, *Italian Fascism 1919-1945* (MacMillan Press Ltd., London , 1995)

Moschopoulos,Georgios N., *Apo Tin Palinorthosi Sti Vasilo-Metaxiki Diktatoria 1935-1940* (From Restoration to Monarcho-Metaxic Dictatorship 1935-1940) (Ath.Christaki, Athens, 1999)

Nicolas, Sian, *The Echo of War, Home Front Propaganda and the Wartime BBC, 1939-1945* (Manchester University Press, Manchester 1996)

Nicolaidis, Ioannis N., *Ta Gianenna tou Mesopolemou* (Yannena in the Interwar Years) Vol. 3 (Ioannina, 1970)

Noakes. J., & Pridham, G. (eds.) *Nazism 1919-1945. State, Economy and Society 1933-1939* (Exeter Press, Exeter, 1984)

Papagos, Alexandros, *O Polemos Tis Ellados 1940-1941* (The War of Greece 1940-1941) New Edition. (Idryma Goulandri Horn, Athens, 1995)

Papastratis, Prokopis, Germaniki 'Diesdysi ke Symachiki Endotikotita'(German Penetration and Allied Compliance) *in E Ellada tou '40* (Greece of the 40s) Scientific Symposium, (Eteria Spoudon Neoellinikou Politismou ke Genikis Pedias, Athens, 1991)

Paraschos, Manolis, 'The Greek Media Face the Twenty-first Century:Will Adam Smith Complex Replace the Oedipus Complex?' in Dimitris Constas and Theofanis G. Stavrou (eds.) *Greece Prepares for the Twenty- First Century*. (The Woodrow, Wilson Centre Press, Washington DC, 1995)

Paulopoulos, Dimitris, 'Christika ke Diakosmitika Antikimena tou 1940' (Usage and Decorative Items of 1940). *Kathimerin-Epta Imeres* (26 October, 1940).

Pavlovich, K. Stevan, *A History of the Balkans 1804-1945* (Longman, London, 1999)

Peukert, J. K. Detlev, *Inside Nazi Germany - Conformity, Opposition and Racism in Everyday Life* (Penguin, London, 1993)

Petraki, Marina, 'Tetarti Augoustou-Antidrasi ke Dioxeis Antipalon' ('Fourth of August'-Opposition and Persecutions). *Kathimerini-Epta Imeres* (Athens, 7 November, 1999)

Petraki, Marina, 'O Torpillismos tis Ellis (The Torpedoing of *Elli*), *Kathimerini-Epta Imeres*, (Athens, August 2001)

Pipinelis, P., *George II* (Athens, 1951)

Plevris, Kostantinos, *Ioannis Metaxas - Viografia* (Ioannis Metaxas -Biography). (Nea Thesis, Athens, 1996)

Pratkanis, Antony-Aronson, Eliot, *Age of Propaganda - The Everyday Use and Abuse of Persuasion* (W.H.Freeman & Company, New York,1991)

Psalidakis, Michalis 'Morfes Economikis Skepsis stin Ellada 1936-1940' (Aspects of Economic Thought in Greece 1936-1940) in Fleicher & Svoronos (eds.) E *Ellada 1936-44. Diktaktoria, Katochi, Antistasi,* (Greece 1936-1944. Dictatorship, Occupation, Resistance) (Morfotiko Instituto *ATE,* Athens,1985)

Rainero, H. Romain, 'To Praxikopima tou Metaxa ke e apichisi sti Fasistiki Italia'(Metaxas' *coup d'etat* and its impact on Fascist Italy), in Fleicher & Svorons eds.) E *Ellada 1936-1944. Diktaktoria, Katochi, Antistasi,* (Greece 1936-1944. Dictatorship, Occupation, Resistance). (Morfotiko Instituto *ATE,* Athens,1985)

Reuth, Georg. Ralf, *Goebbels - The Life of Joseph Goebbels, The Mephistophelean Genius of Nazi Propaganda* (Constable, London, 1993)

Richter, Heinz, *Griechenland, Zwischen: Revolution und Konterrevolution (1936-1946)* (Two Revolutions and counter-revolutions in Greece 1936-1946). Vol. 2. (Exantas, Athens, 1975)

Rigos, Alkis, *Ta Krisima Chronia 1935-1941* (The Critical Years), Vol.2 (Papazisi, Athens, 1995)

Rigos, Alkis, *E B' Elliniki Dimokratia 1924-1935 - Koinonikes Diastaseis Tis Politikis Skinis* (Second Greek Democracy 1924-1935 - Social Dimensions of the Political Scenery). (Themelio, Athens, 1992)

Roberts, J. M., *Europe 1880-1945 - A General History of Europe* (Longman, London and New York, 1989)

Roberts, Stephen, H., *The House that Hitler Built* (Metbuen Publishers, London, 1938)

Sarantis, Constantine, *The Emergency of the Right in Greece, 1922-1940* (PhD Thesis, St.Edmund Hall, Oxford, 1979)

Sarantis, Constantine, 'Metaxas Ideology & Character', in Higham & Veremis (eds..) *Aspects of Greece 1936-1940, The Metaxas Dictatorship* (*EΛAMEP*-Vryonis Center, Athens,1993)

Schoenbaum, David, *Hitler's Social Revolution - Class and Status in Nazi Germany 1933-1939* (W. W. Norton & Company, New York, 1997)

Seferis, Giorgos, *Chirografo Septembrios 1941* (Manuscript September 1941). (Ikaros, Athens, 1972)

Sideris, Yiannis, *The Modern Greek Theatre - A Conscise History* (Hellenic Centre of International Theatre Institute, Dirfos, Athens, 1957)

Sideris, Yiannis, *Istoria Tou Ellinikou Theatrou 1794-1944* (History of the Modern Greek Theatre 1794-1944, Vol. 1. (Kastaniotis, Athens, 1990)

Skoubourdi, Artemis, *Theatra Tis Paleas Athinas* (The Old Athenian Theatres). (Ekdoseis Dimou Athinaion, Athens) No Date.

Smith, Michael, Llewellyn, *Ioanian Vision - Greece in Asia Minor 1919-1922* (Hurst & Company, London,1998)

Soldatos, Yiannis, *Istoria Tou Ellinikou Kinimatografou* (The History of the Greek Cinema*)* Vol. 1. (Egokeros, Athens, 1988)

Speer, Albert, *Inside the Third Reich* (Phoenix, London, 1995)

Spencer, Floyd. A.,(ed.), *War and Post-war Greece - An Analysis based on Greek Writings* (The Library of Congress European Affairs, Washington, 1952)

Spiliotopoulos, Stathis, *To Theatro Opos to Ezisa* (The Theatre as I have lived it). (Estia, Athens, 1995)

Stevens, C.M, Woodhouse, C. M., Wallace, D. J., *British Reports on Greece* 1943-44. Edited by Baerentzen, Lars (Museum Tusculanum Press, Copenhagen, 1982)

Street, Sarah, *British National Cinema* (Routledge, London and New York,1997)

Statistical Summary of Greece. (Athens, 1954)

Svolopoulos, D.K, *Ai Idee Tou I. Metaxa dia tin Ellada ke Ton Ellinismo* (The Ideas of I. Metaxas for Hellas and Hellenism). (Pirsos, 1955)

Ta Agnosta Paraskinia Mias Periodou (Unknown Events Behind the Scenes). *Acropolis*, (January 1972)

Taylor, Philip,M., *Munitions of the Mind. A History of Propaganda From the Ancient World To the Present Day* (Manchester University Press, Manchester and New York, 1995)

Taylor, Richard, *Film Propaganda, Soviet Russia and Nazi Germany* (Croom Helm, London, 1979)

Taylor, Richard and Spring, Derek, *Stalinism and Soviet Cinema* (Routledge, London, 1993)

Theofilopoulos, Ntinos, *Anamniseis apo tin Radiofonia ke tin Tileorasi (1937-1968)* (Memoirs from the Radio broadcast and Television). (Athens, 1989)

Theotokis, Spiros I., *Politike Anamniseis* (Political Memories). (Athens, 1986)

'To Aporito Archio tou Maniadaki' (Maniadakis' Secret Archives) *Akropolis,* (November 1970)

Triantafillidis, Manolis, *Demotikismos ke Antidrasis* (Demoticism and Opposition), (Athens, 1957)

Vatikiotis, Panagiotis, J., *Popular Autocracy in Greece 1936-1941, A Political Biography of General Ioannis Metaxas* (Frank Cass, London - Portland, Or., 1998)

Vatikiotis, Panagiotis, J., 'Metaxas-The Man', in Higham & Veremis (eds.) *Aspects of Greece 1936-1940, The Metaxas Dictatorship* (EllAMEP-Vryonis Center, Athens, 1993)

Veremis, M. Thanos, 'Introduction' in Higham & Veremis (eds.) *Aspects of Greece 1936-1940, The Metaxas Dictatorship (EΠAMEP*-Vryonis Center, Athens, 1993)

Veremis, M. Thanos, and Dragoumis Mark, *Historical Dictionary of Greece* (The Scarecrow Press, Inc., Lanham, Md., & London, 1995)

Vlachos, Agelos, *Mia Fora ke Enan Kero Enas Diplomatis* (Once Upon A Time There was A Diplomat) Vol.1 (Estia, Athens, 1985)

Vlachou, Eleni, *Stigmiotipa Fotografikes Anamniseis tis Elenis Vlachou* (Snapshots, Photographic Memmoirs of Eleni Vlachou). (Kath*i*merini, Athens, 1986)

Vlavianos, H., 'The Greek Communist Party Under Siege' in Higham & Veremis (eds.) *Aspects of Greece 1936-1940, The Metaxas Dictatorship* (EllAMEP-Vryonis Center, Athens, 1993)

Warner, Geoffrey, 'Italy 1918-1940' in John Golby, Bernard Waites, Geoffrey Warner, Tony Algate and Antony Lentin (eds.), *War Peace and Social Change: Europe 1900-1955* (Open University Press, Buckingham, 1994)

Waterlow, Sydney, *The Decline and Fall of Greek Democracy,* Political Quarterly, Vol. XVIII, No. 2-3 (Turnstile Press Ltd., London, 1947)

Watts, Duncan, *Political Communication Today* (Manchester University Press, Manchester, 1997)

Welch, David, *The Third Reich. Politics and Propaganda* (Routledge, London and New York, 1993)

Welch, David, *Propaganda and the German Cinema 1933-1945* (Clarendon Press, Oxford, 1983)

Welch, David, 'Educational Film Propaganda and the Nazi Youth' in Welch, David, (ed.) *Nazi Propaganda The Power and the Limitations* (Croom Helm, London, 1983)

Welch, David, *Modern European History 1971-2000 - A Documentary Reader* (Routledge, London and New York, 1999)

Welch, David, *Germany, Propaganda and Total War 1914-1918: The Sins of Omission* (Athlone/Rutgers University Press, London,2000)

Wistrich, S.Robert , *Who's Who in Nazi Germany.* (Routledge, London, 1995)

Woodhouse, C.M., *Modern Greece - A Short History* (Faber and Faber, London, 1998)

Woodhouse, C.M., *Apple of Discord. A Survey of Recent Greek Politics in Their International Setting* (Hutchinson & Co. Ltd., London, 1948)

Wolfson, Robert, *Years of Change. European History 1890-1945* (Hodder & Stoughton, London, 1998)

Zaousis, Alexandros, L., *Anamniseis Enos Antiiroa 1933-1940* (Recollections of an anti-hero). (Estia, Athens, 1980)

Zaousis, Alexandros, L., *Oi Dyo Oxthes 1939-1945. Mia Prospatheia Ethnikis Symfiliosis* (The Two Banks 1930-1040. An effort at National Reconciliation). (Papazisi, Athens, 1987)

Zorkaya, Neya, *The Illustrated History of Soviet Cinema* (Hippocrene Books, New York, 1991)

Newspapers

Acropolis 1970-1971

Kathimerini 1996-1998-1999

Tetarti Augoustou. Weekly National Revue (Kabis, T., Athens, 1967-1974)

Index